DISCARD

AMERICAN LITERATURE IN THE WORLD

AMERICAN LITERATURE IN THE WORLD

AN ANTHOLOGY FROM ANNE BRADSTREET TO OCTAVIA BUTLER

WAI CHEE DIMOCK,

WITH JORDAN BROWER, EDGAR GARCIA,

KYLE HUTZLER, AND NICHOLAS RINEHART, EDITORS

COLUMBIA

UNIVERSITY

PRESS

NEW YORK

Columbia University Press
Publishers Since 1893
New York   Chichester, West Sussex
cup.columbia.edu

Published with assistance from the Frederick W. Hilles Publication
Fund of Yale University

Library of Congress Cataloging-in-Publication Data
Names: Dimock, Wai Chee, 1953– editor.
Title: American literature in the world: an anthology from Anne Bradstreet to Octavia
    Butler / [edited by] Wai Chee Dimock.
Description: New York : Columbia University Press, 2016. | Includes
    bibliographical references and index.
Identifiers: LCCN 2016014671| ISBN 9780231157360 (cloth : acid-free paper) |
    ISBN 9780231157377 (pbk. : acid-free paper) | ISBN 9780231543040 (e-book)
Subjects: LCSH: American literature. | Geography and literature. | Literature
    and globalization. | American literature—Foreign influences.
Classification: LCC PS507 .A59 2016 | DDC 810.8—dc23
LC record available at https://lccn.loc.gov/2016014671

Columbia University Press books are printed on permanent
and durable acid-free paper.

Printed in the United States of America

Cover and book design: Lisa Hamm

CONTENTS

II. Food 139

III. Work, Play, Travel 243

VERNACULAR DEVOTIONS

MANY ISLAMS

V. Human and Nonhuman Interfaces 405

ANTS

AMERICAN LITERATURE IN THE WORLD

INTRODUCTION

A Twenty-First-Century Platform

T his anthology is an attempt to broaden the scope of American literature, opening it to a more complex sense of geography and to a variety of genres and media. It is impossible to read the work of Junot Díaz and Edwidge Danticat, Robert Hass and Jorie Graham, Dave Eggers and Jhumpa Lahiri without seeing that—for all these authors—the frames of reference are not just the United States, but a larger, looser set of coordinates, populated by laboring bodies, migrating faiths, generational sagas, memories of war, and accompanied by the accents of unforgotten tongues, the tastes and smells of beloved foods and spices. Tracing these planet-wide arcs through the microhistories of individual lives, they distill broad swaths of the world into intimate settings, into the heat and furor of local conflicts, giving us both the amplitude of space and the jaggedness of embodied passions.

The twenty-first century is a good one in which to think about American literature in the world. But this anthology is by no means a showcase only of recent works. As evidenced by Anne Bradstreet, Olaudah Equiano, Thomas Jefferson, Frederick Douglass, Mark Twain, Gertrude Stein, Richard Wright, Ezra Pound, and Elizabeth Bishop, other centuries also bear witness to the commingling of near and far, with words and worlds continually in motion, fueled by large-scale forces such as colonialism, the transatlantic slave trade, the movement of capital, the movement of troops, the attendant diplomacies, and reproducing these within the contours of day-to-day living. To study these and countless other authors is to see that the United States and the world are neither separate nor antithetical, but part of the same analytic fabric. American literature has always been energized by input from the rest of the world; it has played host to large disputes and wide cross-currents; its versions of the local have been sharpened and intensified by nonlocal events. These broad horizons, evolving over the course of several hundred years, make such works a durable prism to what lies beyond the nation, and an important counterpoint to the more recent examples of globalization in the twentieth and twenty-first centuries. They remind us that this latest development is only one in a long line, one that must be seen in perspective against other, prior instances, suggesting more than one way to connect.

This anthology does not aspire to be a full-dressed alternative history. It does hope, however, to add complexity as well as clarity to the story, looking at American literature not as a self-contained archive underwritten by the jurisdictional map of a single nation, but as a multi-variable and tangent-producing network, with many layers of narrative, pulled in different directions by different contributing players. This large force field cautions us against any vainglorious or exceptionalist view of the United States. It invites us to see the nation not as a closed chapter but as one endlessly in flux, endlessly in relation. This body of material remains fresh and vibrant precisely because its geographical boundaries are not fixed, because its centers and peripheries can so easily trade places. This fluid landscape injects a corresponding fluidity into self-evident concepts such as the "United States" and indeed "American literature" itself, making each less a foregone conclusion than a heuristic occasion. Readers are invited to think further, to raise new questions, some coming from left field perhaps, and to be taken seriously for just that reason, not settling for a standard definition or explanation.

How exactly is *American Literature in the World* different from other anthologies? The simplest answer is also the most obvious: this is a web and print anthology, part of an online teaching initiative, http://amlitintheworld.yale.edu, the only anthology we know edited by a team of students and faculty. We will have more to say about this. Focusing for now on the print content, we would like to point to some experimental features that mark not so much a sharp break from existing practices as the beginning of a different roadmap, set forth by a different organizational structure. The three headings familiar to us—race, gender, and class—have done much to reshape the field in the past fifty years, with far-reaching consequences both for the curriculum and for scholarly research. At this point, though, they run the danger of being automatic reflexes. To try something different, we have come up with an alternative playlist, with these five headings: "War;" "Food;" "Work, Play, Travel;" "Religions;" and "Human and Nonhuman Interfaces." These five organizational nodes lend themselves to macro- as well as micro-analysis; they speak to systemic forces on the one hand, and minute local embodiments on the other. They highlight the dual focus of the anthology, our emphasis on the reciprocal constitution of the global and the local. Flexible and inter- connected, they are meant to be remixed and recombined, used in differ- ent ways by different readers. Bringing together the large and the small, they bring into relief a networked field anchored by five elemental processes: the ruptures occasioned by armed conflict; the physical need for nourishment; the rhythms of everyday life; forms of spirituality; and the coevolution of the human and nonhuman worlds. Both the quirkiness of American literature and the planet-wide processes of which it partakes come into play through these networks. Giving equal attention to both, we trace the tangled genesis of the intimate and the systemic across five centuries, shaped both by the dictates of large force fields and the minute confluences of local particulars.

MACRO AND MICRO

Interconnectedness is a key feature of American literature, with a long his- tory across various scales and realms of experience. "War," our first and most extensive section, highlights this phenomenon, focusing on the injurability and perishability of the human body as the most tangible, and most ironic, instance of global causation and local expression, at once non- negotiable and unavoidable. The literature on this subject is staggering; we have picked texts both for their individual salience and for the breadth of horizon they open up. Since what is required here is a working knowledge of several hundred years of armed conflict and the accompanying civilian life, involving the rest of the world as much as the United States, we have tried to provide basic orientation by listing each war individually, using the dates and the participants as signposts to create a relatively straightforward and easily graspable chronology. At the same time, the multilateral nature of war and the variety of ways they filter into noncombat zones make it clear that each war would need to be contextualized: studied from opposing perspectives, with an eye to accompanying effects such as food shortages, ruptures in the daily routine, intensified religious conflict, and breakdowns in human and nonhuman ecologies.

Many classics are included here, but there are also some pieces that will be new to most readers. The entries for World War II, for instance, include not only Kurt Vonnegut's account of the firebombing of Dresden and John Hersey's classic reporting from postwar Hiroshima, but also "Two Soldiers" (1942), a short story by Faulkner about the attack on Pearl Harbor as heard on the radio in Mississippi; followed by Norman Mailer's account of the maiming of a single insect against the massive suffering of human beings in the South Pacific. This is in turn followed by a hallucinatory sequence by Leslie Marmon Silko, recounting a traumatic encounter between a Native American and a dead Japanese soldier. The cluster ends with one other unusual perspective on the Pacific theater by Chang-Rae Lee, with an elderly doctor recalling his time as a medic among the Korean comfort women serving the Japanese army.

This abundance of material makes it easy for us to tell any story from several points of view, highlighting the fact that World War II was indeed a "world" war, a cataclysm affecting the entire planet, seen differently among different populations. For that reason alone, war needs to be studied as it is fought, which is to say, from opposing sides, across the divides among nations—a position at once immersive and contextualizing, asking the reader to zoom in to see how it feels to be personally touched by war, to be in the thick of it, and then to zoom out again to recognize, at the same time, that the very emotional and visceral intensity of being "in" makes that perspective unavoidably limiting. Ernest Hemingway seemed to have this dynamic in mind when, speaking of *In Our Time* (1925), he said that the interweaving of war in Europe with civilian life in America comes from his need to "give the picture of the whole between examining it in detail. Like looking with your eyes at something, say a passing coastline, and then looking at it with 15× binoculars. Or rather, maybe, looking at it and then going in and living in it—and then coming out and looking at it again."[1]

NONSTANDARD HISTORIES

Nothing offers this dual perspective—the telescoping of large-scale events coupled with close-ups of sensory experience—better than works of literature.

They are not history textbooks for just that reason. Rather than giving us agreed-upon accounts of the past, they extend the resources of fiction to dimensions of the world too messy and uncertain to count as history: parallel universes, where not implausible events that never made it across the finish line can have a limited second hearing. Could things have been otherwise? Given the simultaneously arbitrary and terminal logic of war, with winning or losing often resting on accidental turns of events, alternative outcomes are hard to banish from our imagination. We are proud to have here an entire subgenre dedicated to these counterfactual exercises. Here we find various degrees of deviation from the historical record: some thoroughgoing, others less so, but with enough irregularities to trouble the thin line separating the realm of actualized facts from the vast penumbra of the possible, giving "what if?" a momentary place in the world.

Philip K. Dick's science fiction account of World War II in *The Man in the High Castle* (1962)—with the Japanese and the Germans as victors—is a striking example of this subgenre, giving us an upside-down though oddly not unrecognizable landscape. This is probably one of the few occasions when World War II is experienced not as concluded, but as an open book, still in progress. Counterfactual histories resequence time, making the past not past, but an unconcluded force field extending into the present. Ursula Le Guin says that speculative fiction—her name for science fiction—is not a prediction of the future, but parallel descriptions of the present projected forward.[2] These parallel descriptions can be projected backward as well, which is why science fiction doubles so handily as alternative history. *The Man in the High Castle* works in just these dual capacities: its futuristic universe is also a rescripting of the past, reaching back to not unlikely scenarios and holding them up for our consideration. One such scenario is the "indigenization" of newly defeated groups: white Californians, for instance, are now the Native Americans of the PSA—the Pacific States of America—treated courteously enough by their Japanese rulers, but nonetheless treated as indigenous populations tend to be treated. Counterfactual fabrications of this sort serve as a prelude to the Mary Rowlandson/Louise Erdrich duo from the "Food" section: a rewriting of the past done with gusto, with a vengeance, and perhaps with a method as well. Together, they point to the heuristic value of thinking of literary works as "speculative fiction" in various shapes and forms, departures from the official record at once distorting and instructive, making us take a second look at the world by turning it first into undisguised fiction.

We are happy to include another text in this vein, one that wears its counterfactual credentials on its sleeve: Michael Chabon's *The Yiddish Policemen's Union* (2007). Detective fiction doubling as alternative history, this novel is set in a Yiddish-speaking refugee settlement established in Sitka, Alaska, in 1941 for a period of sixty years and now faced with imminent "reversion" to the State of Alaska. Apprehensive about this, and trying at the same time to solve a murder case, detective Meyer Landsman and his partner, the half-Tlingit, half-Jewish Berko Shemets, uncover a vast conspiracy, which gives Chabon a chance to spin out an entire fabricated history: with the Soviet Union crushed by Germany in 1942, and World War II coming to an end only in 1946, when Berlin is destroyed by nuclear weapons. Meanwhile, the new state of Israel, lasting only three years, is destroyed in 1948, and Jerusalem (as we learn in the excerpt) is now "a city of blood and slogan painted on the wall, severed heads on telephone poles." Against that distant nightmare, the unquestionably local, unquestionably funny, but also strangely haunting run-in between Landsman and the "prophet" Elijah (an echo of *Moby-Dick* as well as the Old Testament) gives a whole new meaning to detective fiction.

Popular genres are important to this anthology. Poetry is important as well. We see the two as complementary rather than antithetical, and have made a special effort to build around their partnership, hoping our colleagues might do likewise, integrating into their syllabi material at different levels of cultural elevation, poetry as well as prose. Alternative history shows just how easily this could be done, for poetry turns out to be entirely at home on this platform, comfortable next to science fiction and crime novels. We include here Jorie Graham's "Soldatenfriedhof" (2004), set in the computer terminal of the German cemetery in La Combe, Normandy. The poem is not science fiction, although by juxtaposing two time frames—1945 of Normandy and 2003 of the user-friendly computer screen—it is relying on the same backward-and-forward projections that give science fiction its special effects. "To find a fallen person, it says, 'push green key.' / Fill in name, last name, first name, I put in / Klein. 210 Kleins in the Soldatenfriedhof." World War II mediated by the computer screen is quantitative, matter-of-fact, but, in this context, also eerie, almost surreal:

I scroll. Klein stays the same.
The first name changes, rank, row, plot.

No. The graveyard changes too. At 88 Klein's in
Colleville (US graveyard). At 93 he's in the British one (Bayeux).
Have you found your fallen person says the program
when I go back to the home page. No slot for
nationality. None for religion. Just date of birth,
then rank, row, plot, and field come forth . . .

It is that numbers-crunching computer program—with built-in limits, true even of new technology—that frees Graham up for a brief foray
into the counterfactual. This program turns out to have no algorithm for
either nationality or religion; Graham accordingly brackets both, paying
her respects instead to a nation-less and religion-less "possible person," a
conjectural being who could be German, French, British, or American,
Christian or Jew, as indeed the name "Klein" is. Distributed on both sides
of the Allied/Axis divide, the name points to a forlorn hope that this stark
dividing line would not inscribe itself in an equally stark military solution.
History, of course, squelched that hope, resulting, among other things,
in those 210 Kleins being found in the Soldatenfriedhof at Normandy. It
is not till six decades later, with the help of the computer program, that
the prematurely interred is able to show faint signs of life. Klein is by no
means resurrected—he is in the cemetery and will always stay there—but
the unactualized hope that he embodied is, at least within the space of this
poem, real enough to be given a hearing.

INTERCONNECTED WORLD

What counts as the "reality" of World War II will be answered differently
by different authors. Philip K. Dick, Michael Chabon, and Jorie Graham
are unusually forthright about where their imaginations have taken them.
Together, they outline alternate routes that are intriguing to contemplate,
played out in a variety of genres and media. We celebrate this elasticity both
in the range of our selections and sometimes in the multitasking of a single
work. *Moby-Dick,* for instance, is part tragedy, part comedy, part metaphys-
ics, part whaling yarn, part marine biology, a floating encyclopedia cir-
cumnavigating the globe. It is included in four of our five sections, which
says something about the multitude of genres in that novel, and something

about the interconnections running throughout the entire anthology, a key feature of the world we present.

Nothing demonstrates those interconnections more vividly than the next section, "Food," designed with just this in mind, meant as an index both to world markets and to everyday life, and in the negative form of hunger, as a shared lack known to much of the world's population. This section opens with a cluster of three texts: Cabeza de Vaca's 1542 *La Relación,* giving pride of place to the prickly pear, crucial to the survival of the native populations of Florida. This is followed by Mary Rowlandson's likewise starvation-driven and food-obsessed *Sovereignty and Goodness of God* (1682); this is in turn followed by Louise Erdrich's poem "Captivity" (1984), an upfront rewriting of Rowlandson. The conflict generated by these three seems to us an ideal moment to discuss the changing conventions of literature, bringing into focus a key genre of the sixteenth and seventeenth centuries—the captivity narrative—written in Spanish as well as English, with Native Americans alternately demonized and humanized. These early generic conventions are then contrasted with the vastly different ones of the late twentieth century. A Native American author now takes over, also dwelling on the scarcity of food and the wild urges of hunger, but otherwise telling a new story in every way.

Not all the selections are clustered to such good effect, but we have tried hard to make juxtaposition a spur to thinking. "Work, Play, Travel," which comes after "Food," also features many texts meant to be discussed together. This section explores the increasingly globalized organization of labor, with leisure-time activities sometimes reflecting that development, and sometimes running counter to it, giving a different meaning to globalization itself. One of the highlights of this section is a textual cluster beginning with Walt Whitman's "Proud Music of the Storm" (1900), a tribute to the sounds of nature as a mysterious repository and mixture of the sounds of "all the world's musicians"—French and German, Irish and Italian, Persian, Arabic, Egyptian, Hindu, and Chinese. An excerpt from Claude McKay's *Banjo* (1929) then takes us to one particular place, the waterfront of Marseilles, France, to witness another sonic fusion, bringing together black seamen from Martinique, Senegal, Cameroon, Algeria, Madagascar, and the United States. Sonic fusion is, of course, not limited to adults, nor to one ethnic group, a point underscored by the next selection from Toni Morrison's *Song of Solomon* (1977), an origins story claiming joint descent from

Native Americans and "flying" Africans, immortalized through a song sung by children. Finally, this cluster ends with Robert Pinsky's "Ginza Samba" (1996), a poem that, in its very title, names jazz as a music at once Asian, European, African, and American, with cross-currents from every corner of the planet.

As with music, so too with spirituality. In "Religions," the fourth section of the anthology, we follow authors from the seventeenth century on as they chart the trajectories of their faiths across continents and oceans—sometimes staying mainstream, but also straying when they go native, which is indeed more often the case. The "vernacularization" of devotional practices is one of our highlights. Olaudah Equiano's folk belief in the kinship of Africans and Jews; Zora Neale Hurston's Haitian Moses, renamed Damballa Ouedo Ouedo Tocan Freda Dahomey; Denise Levertov's tribute to Buddhist altars on the streets of Saigon during the Vietnam War; Gloria Anzaldúa's bold equation of the Virgin of Guadalupe with the Aztec Coatlalopeuh—these and much more bear witness to the global footprints of religions and the crucial input from the ground up, making the reciprocity between these two a long-running saga, a testimony to the shared ecologies of the far and the near.

Shared ecologies become the explicit and explosive focus in the last section, "Human and Nonhuman Interfaces." How should our species dwell among other life forms? What sort of classifying mechanisms enable us to make sharp distinctions among those living in close proximity, extending group membership to some but not to others? The instability of these mechanisms has always been a fault line in American life, exploding with traumatic force when some subgroups—African Americans, for instance—hitherto not granted full membership, suddenly show troubling signs of full-throated humanity. In the twenty-first century, these unstable boundaries have exploded yet again—prompted, on the one hand, by the growing co-dependency of humans and intelligent machines, and on the other hand, by the growing co-vulnerability of humans and other species as we jointly face the effects of climate change: rising sea levels, more extreme weather, greater frequency of floods and droughts.

As with the other sections, we have made a special effort to suggest clusters of texts that could be read together. One of the highlights here is a six-text sequence beginning with Henry David Thoreau's humorous account of a battle of ants in *Walden* (1854): "as important and memorable to those whom it concerns as those of the battle of Bunker Hill, at least." This musing is followed by Marianne Moore's "fastidious ant carrying a stick," and then six lines from Ezra Pound's Canto LXXXI, a lyrical interlude occasioned by an ant, in a situation otherwise not in the least lyrical. Robert Lowell comes next, with an explicit reference back to *Walden*. From there we move on to a breathtaking passage from *Tar Baby* (1981), with Jadine, Toni Morrison's protagonist, ensconced in her first-class seat on a flight to Paris, momentarily conjuring up a queen ant, somewhere between "the thirtieth and fortieth generation" of her reproductive labor, allowing herself briefly to see herself as she once was: "airborne, suspended, open, trusting, frightened, determined, vulnerable, girlish, even." This melancholy but relatively nonlethal scene of cross-species identification then gives way to Barbara Kingsolver's horrendous account of the attack of the *nsongonya* (driver ant)—nature up in arms, perhaps a parable for a newly independent Congo, erupting with violence on multiple fronts as it tries to cast off its colonial yoke. For Kingsolver, the African setting, both historical and metaphoric, offers insights into the relation between human and nonhuman ecologies as few other places can. We honor that perspective, adding as a further reference Elizabeth Alexander's terse lyric about rebellious slaves on the *Amistad*, and Dave Eggers's and Valentino Achak Deng's searing account of the politics of oil in the Sudanese Civil War. As we move on to other nonhuman ecologies—from the debris field defined by bullets and bombs, to a computer capable of taking a PhD qualifying exam, to extraterrestrial aliens who need humans to reproduce—the long shadows of Africa remain of undiminished importance in our present moment.

Though the authors who show up here are, for the most part, familiar names, some of the selections that represent them might be new to many of us. What the anthology offers is not so much a brand-new canon of American literature as a different kind of field guide, reorienting the pieces we have grown used to, pairing them with ones less well known, calling attention to parallels and overlaps, and pedagogic possibilities newly arisen. The global networks that we now take for granted have long been an animating force in American literature. This volume brings their linked ecologies to the foreground.

While poems, short stories, letters, pamphlets, field reports, and other compact prose pieces are included in their entirety, novels necessarily have to be excerpted, often featured here as cliffhangers. We see this as a heuristic spur. Students are invited to read further on their own, and teachers to use these excerpts as handy material to update their existing syllabi or design new ones. Our five interconnected nodes, and the clustering of texts throughout, are meant to be suggestive rather than prescriptive, outlining possible combinations, and encouraging readers to come up with others. The selections can certainly be read in their current order, but just as easily they can be separated and re-sequenced, used in classes with other objectives in mind. A course on the environment, for instance, could use material not only from "Human and Nonhuman Interfaces," but also from "War" (to highlight the environmental impact of armed conflict), as well as from "Food" (to explore the ways dietary habits can affect the health of the planet no less than the health of individual consumers). The entire anthology is meant to be cross-cut and cross-referenced in this way, assembled for particular effects and calling for other arrangements to serve other purposes.

HEMINGWAY, FITZGERALD, HUGHES

The Great Gatsby (1925), that quintessential American story about a self-made man, speaks directly to such complex networks, trailing a tangled web from a European past that shapes the here and now of its two protagonists. It is this that comes into play when Nick meets Gatsby for the first time, before he even realizes that it is Gatsby:

> "Your face is familiar," he said, politely. "Weren't you in the Third Division during the war?"
> "Why yes. I was in the ninth machine-gun battalion."
> "I was in the Seventh Infantry until June nineteen-eighteen. I knew I'd seen you somewhere before."[3]

For F. Scott Fitzgerald, World War I combat isn't just background information, it is a still-vital and still-pertinent part of the story, framing the action now unfolding in New York. The prior enlistment in the war, the fact that these two had dutifully fought and gone through what most would agree was a new and unprecedented kind of hell, goes a long way toward explaining why there should be an instant bond of friendship, the only one either

Nick or Gatsby is privileged to have. The fact that Tom Buchanan has not fought also goes a long way toward explaining why, in the end, he has no place in the affections of someone who, ever since his return "from the East last autumn, [has] wanted the world to be in uniform and at a sort of moral attention forever."[4]

World War I stands as a kind of ethical road map to both Nick and Gatsby in at least two senses: marking the linked locales that have seen action, and anchoring the moral compass issuing from that fact. Gatsby later says to Nick: "In the Argonne Forest I took two machine-gun detachments so far forward that there was a half mile gap on either side of us where the infantry couldn't advance. We stayed there two days and two nights, a hundred and thirty men with sixteen Lewis guns, and when the infantry came up at last they found the insignia of three German divisions among the piles of dead. I was promoted to be a major, and every Allied government gave me a decoration—even Montenegro, little Montenegro down on the Adriatic Sea!"[5] Gatsby's moral biography is a biography of place names. Beyond these, there are also the numbers: the Third Division, the ninth machine-gun battalion, the Seventh Infantry, not to say the year 1918. It is Fitzgerald who is writing here, not Hemingway, although it is Hemingway who said that "abstract words such as glory, honor, courage, or hallow were obscene beside the concrete names of villages, the numbers of roads, the names of rivers, the numbers of regiments and the dates."[6] For both, these names and numbers are the only reliable cues to the twentieth century. Without these geographical and numerical markers, American literature would have been lost indeed, would have been ungrounded, unmoored.

Hemingway and Fitzgerald, most canonical of authors, are not in this anthology for a simple reason: high permissions fees. *A Farewell to Arms* (1929) would of course have been splendid for this volume, although when it comes to the organic interweaving of action overseas and action back home, *For Whom the Bell Tolls* (1940) is still more impressive. Hemingway probably had a deeper connection to the Spanish Civil War than to any other war he covered. He had been working as a correspondent in Europe since 1922, initially for the *Toronto Star*;[7] his dispatches from Spain then went to the North American Newspapers Alliance.[8] With the defeat of the Republicans in 1939, he left Spain for Cuba, eventually settling down with Martha Gellhorn in Finca Vigía, a one-story villa fifteen miles from Havana, his home for the next twenty-one years. Three of his best-known works—*For Whom the Bell Tolls, The Old Man and the Sea* (1952), and *A Moveable Feast* (1964)—were written there. The archives from that period, thanks to a collaboration with the Cuban Council of National Heritage, are now housed in the John F. Kennedy Presidential Library.[9]

A Cuban Hemingway writing about the Spanish Civil War makes it clear just how unwise it is to separate the United States from the rest of the world, or to imagine that its territorial borders could govern the associative webs generated by its literature. This anthology would certainly have benefited from his presence, and from Fitzgerald's, although, since the works of these two are regularly taught in their entirety, we feel that the inclusion of a few pages here is less crucial. Indeed there is much to be said for ceding their places to figures somewhat less canonical and more likely to spark fresh responses. Langston Hughes strikes us as an especially vital alternative here, rich in interpretive possibilities. Working in a nonfictional genre, working in haste, under the pressures of siege and bombardment, he experienced the Spanish Civil War as civilians did, with a sense of unreality alternating with a shock of recognition that gives his writings a visceral rhythm, grounded as much in physiology as in geopolitics.

Hughes had gone to Spain with the Cuban poet Nicolás Guillén to write a column for the *Baltimore Afro-American*. We are able to include two of those essays, "Harlem Swing and Spanish Shells" and "General Franco's Moors." The former, about the lack of food in shell-racked Madrid and the jazz-flavored exquisiteness of the little that was available, seems to us as much a feast as any in Hemingway, suggesting that the physical needs of the body remain the anchoring coordinates even in the most unhinged of contexts, linking Harlem and Madrid both on the macro scale of political allegiances and on the micro scale of taste, smell, and sound. The other essay, recounting Hughes's disconcerting encounter with one of the Moorish troops brought over by General Franco and fighting on the Fascist side, shows just how unfamiliar race can look when it is mapped onto a new setting. Prejudices in Spain, equally entrenched but differently aligned, and inflamed by centuries of religious conflict and now the bitter passions of the civil war, can make race every bit as toxic as it is in the United States. In such a country, supposedly without color prejudices—"Color? *No le hace nada en España*"—it is not only the Moors that are the Negroes, but Hughes himself is in danger of being racialized anew, projected back to North Africa rather than North America.

Transnational race opens up issues that continue to vex us today. At the same time, the replacement of Hemingway by Hughes also raises questions about the impact of copyright, weighing as much as literary merit. We call attention to both to reflect on the task of anthology-making against the challenges posed by intellectual property and by the daunting vastness of the field. Why Hemingway—or for that matter, why Hughes? The over-abundance of material that is more than acceptable, more than selection-worthy, points to a virtually unlimited pool of resources; it also points to the need for the anthology to be continually added to, if only to keep up with the new works continually appearing.

DIGITAL PLATFORM

It is beyond the capability of the printed book to update itself in this way. We use this intractable problem to argue for the crucial importance of the accompanying digital platform, turning the medium-specific limits of print into an occasion for online experimentation. And indeed, even as it now stands, the anthology is very much the outgrowth of its many online itera-tions. Part of a digital initiative at Yale, http://amlitintheworld.yale.edu, it was a Facebook page, a conference site for an annual graduate conference, and an open-source teaching platform before it became a printed book. The world-linking properties of the Internet are as important here as the world-traversing properties of the material that appears in these pages. Online connectivity offers a new environment for the literature gathered here; it has also been a catalyst for many of the questions we ask, highlight-ing the layers of mediation that create reciprocal play between the local and the global, between site-specific efforts and system-wide developments. The defining coordinates of American literature, the force fields animating it and threaded through it, also look very different as a result.

These force fields, in turn, ask of us a new kind of literacy, a new set of navigational skills made necessary by the continual emergence of new digital forms and the increasingly frequent movement of material across media. Jay David Bolter and Richard Grusin refer to this phenomenon as "remediation"—a process of transposing and remixing, by which the new media absorb, extend, and update their predecessors.[10] What results is a field-wide synthesis, a revamping on multiple fronts, making the old media as freshly equipped as the new. Literature is no exception to this development: it too is part of this networked field—which is to say, experienced not as purely text-based but as transmedia extensions into the visual, auditory, and digital realms. Literary scholars need to follow suit. As instructors facing changing demographics, we can go forward only by keeping pace with practices outside the classroom, taking advantage of the technology-enabled mediascape to better connect with our students, and with our objects of study.

In this context, we are especially proud of the open-source platform that accompanies the print anthology. Syllabi from several classes, paper topics and outlines, peer comments, sample papers, and class highlights are all featured on this platform, along with annotations that try to do digitally what we cannot do in print. As a crowdsourced mechanism, an unsupervised but reliably incremental aggregate of background information, audio and visual material, and often inspired readings, these annotations try to give some sense of the literary ecologies revolving around any given text. Through the force of example they show just how much could be brought to bear on this material. And, by doing so from one particular vantage point, through a determined marshalling of evidence, and using sound recordings as well as visual images to make their case, the annotations collectively point to the multiple and often conflicting possibilities within any piece of writing, infinitely more complex than any single interpretation. The totality of literature can never be fully grasped, yet we can surmise that its baseline at the moment is already quite different from what it was just a couple of decades ago. The literary field is being reconstituted from the ground up. Our project both exemplifies that process and hopes to contribute to it.

"From the ground up" is not a mere turn of phrase: horizontality is an important feature of our digital platform, just as it is of the Internet as a whole. Though hierarchies are never entirely absent online (in fact, search engines such as Google have for years been customizing our information to stream hierarchically—which is to say, according to our preferential search histories),[11] web-based input networks and participatory forums nonetheless remain significantly more egalitarian than those organized by more traditional means. Facebook is a case in point. This social network is often criticized for violating privacy and promoting faux friendships, yet its effectiveness as a grassroots instrument in many parts of the world suggests that its low-bar flatness nonetheless serves an important function, providing a communicative forum at once non-governmental, and to some extent, unpoliceable.[12] Facebook is "democratic" in this sense: the excellence or not of the postings, the depth or shallowness of the affections, the rightness or wrongness of the politics—these qualitative distinctions are beyond its call. This content-neutrality has made it a valuable resource to activists and a perceived threat to some governments, banned in Syria, Iran, and China for just that reason.[13]

Even in the United States, Facebook has untried potential, especially when it comes to dissemination and participation. As of March 2016, Facebook has more than 1.65 billion monthly active users, 84.2 percent of whom live outside the United States. Most who join are young (the median age is twenty-two), with the largest numbers coming from India, Indonesia, Brazil, and Mexico.[14] So from the first, we had thought of a Facebook page as a demographic statement of sorts, highlighting the youthfulness even of works with venerable dates. These works are "news that stays news," as Ezra Pound said. To capture that newsworthiness, we post photos of authors; announcements from libraries about newly acquired manuscripts and digitalized collections; and updates about film adaptations, musical renditions, and art exhibits associated with these works. In doing so, we rub shoulders with countless other Facebook users, claiming this broad-based venue as a rallying cry for the project as a whole.

What kind of pedagogy might be gleaned from Facebook as an index to the strengths and limits of online experience? Taking a page from its playbook, we make a virtue of its low-bar flatness, reasoning that while there is learning to be done here and information to change hands, who should be doing the instructing and who should be instructed are not foregone conclusions. Pedagogic bi-directionality is worth considering, especially when knowledge is removed from its customary setting and configured anew in the freewheeling arena that is Facebook, where work and play are not so easily distinguishable, and where expertise is not only less well defined but also more likely to be in need of renewal. Professors who received their PhDs years ago have much to gain by conceding that there is, once again, a learning curve ahead, while those still in training could perhaps take on tasks they are preparing for sooner rather than later, and in being responsible for the knowledge they gather and disseminate, developing a close, lifelong commitment to it. With these two goals in mind, we have tried to make this project philosophically as well as pragmatically multi-generational, channeling the creative energies of those at different stages of their careers. From decisions large and small regarding the graduate conference to the free-for-all annotations, this digital platform is an attempt to create a half-work, half-play environment, premised on equal participation and ease of input as the key to innovation, and creating structural guarantees that separate this project as much as possible from asymmetries in past accomplishment and academic rank.

The coeditorship of the print anthology by students and faculty is very much in that spirit. One of us has been teaching since 1982; two are in the graduate program; one has just received his PhD and is now a tenure-track assistant professor at the University of Chicago. The youngest—Kyle Hutzler, an economics major—meanwhile knows more about the globalized world than the rest of us, having worked for the U.S. International Trade Commission as well as McKinsey & Co, where he is now employed full time. We see these generational differences as generative. Kyle brings the perspective of a non-English major who has taken an American literature course, and who chooses to stay with the project because of his love of the material. Jordan Brower, Edgar Garcia, and Nick Rinehart come with the energy and enthusiasm of young teachers. Since this is a Yale teaching initiative, most of us are from that school, but we are especially proud that our collaboration with Nick has developed through the annual graduate conference. Nick, a graduate student at Harvard, brings with him a different institutional culture while enlisting the help of his family in the final stages of the editing. This has grown to be a project unlike anything we have seen. We are thrilled to experience firsthand all the benefits and surprises of online connectivity.

Beyond this immediate collaboration among the five of us, the online platform points to a coeditorship in another sense: a long-term partnership with any reader interested enough to spend time with the anthology. One advantage of our five flexible nodes is that they are meant to be interactive, meant to yield to those who engage them. Readers are encouraged to experiment with different clusters, different connecting threads, and indeed different pedagogic goals altogether. User-generated input of this sort is the lifeblood of this undertaking. While the print format is fixed, online input will produce as many variants as there is need for them. To facilitate these input streams, we will be adding new features to our website, offering possible syllabi, and inviting readers to share information wherever relevant.

This is the best way for the anthology to stay networked. In his essay "Fate," Emerson says: "But to see how fate slides into freedom and freedom into fate, observe how far the roots of every creature run, or find if you can a point where there is no thread of connection. Our life is consentaneous and far-related." There are no better words to sum up this project. The proceeds from the anthology, to be donated to Doctors Without Borders, offer our final token and commitment to being in the world and of it.

I. War

Section I, "War," the most extensive part of the anthology, serves several pragmatic purposes. The selections here, clustered around major episodes of military conflict and arranged chronologically, provide basic orientation and easily recognizable signposts: World War I, War World II, the Korean War, Vietnam. These wars, fought on foreign soil, against the added terror of alien environments, produce psychic landscapes far more tortuous than any straightforward combat history. Highlighting literature's ability to give voice to experiential distortions, to bear witness to both the magnitude of unknowable forces and the intense concentration of personal trauma, they are important and instructive for just that reason.

The American Revolution would have been a natural place to begin. We made the decision, however, to go further back, to pay tribute to what came before the founding of the nation, before even the arrival of Columbus in the New World, in recognition of the long afterlives that wars have tended to enjoy. Some from antiquity—the Trojan War, say—continue to haunt our collective imagination as echoes and emblems. Recovering these is not as difficult as it might seem; the task has already been given a head start by many authors. Here we feature five, to our surprise mostly poets. Anne Bradstreet, Louise Glück, William Carlos Williams, Elizabeth Bishop, and William Apess wrote in different times and in different genres, and invoked memories of past wars for different reasons. They all seem to agree, however, that something is gained by not allowing the bygone to be bygone.

Together they give the anthology scope and depth, time frames as complexly recursive as their geographical horizons are richly varied.

We begin with Bradstreet's portrait of the magnificence of Babylon, the capital of the Assyrian queen, Semiramis. "This wonder of the world" came to naught, however, when this warrior queen sent an army of four million against King Stratobatis of India, an expedition from which "but twenty" came back. Does this disastrous final battle undo her reign of forty-two years? Anne Bradstreet is surprisingly restrained in her judgment. Why go back at all to this particular bit of ancient history, and what exactly is the appeal of the pagan queen for the Puritan poet? Is this tribute an anomaly, the sole instance in Bradstreet, or will there be others, to other queens also better known for their military prowess than their religious piety? We invite speculation, argument, as well as further research, as we do throughout the "War" section, since the pieces here, condensed nodes of much larger debates, are meant as spurs for students to read and think on their own, to discover for themselves a past perhaps a bit different from what they might have imagined, delving into the material as thoroughly as they wish.

Our next selection, Louise Glück's "Parable of the Hostages," continues in this vein, giving us a teasing view of Greek soldiers sunning themselves on the beach, feeling no particular urgency to go home. The war here is the Trojan War, but Glück's deliberately chatty accents bring it up to our own time, highlighting its continued ability to make "hostages" of all of us, ensnaring us in an addictive cycle of pleasure, resignation, and dependency. Hernan Cortés, the Spanish conquistador (or Cortez, as William Carlos Williams calls him), might be said to be "hostage" to war in just this sense, entirely matter-of-fact in the destruction of Tenochtitlán. "Cortez was neither malicious, stupid nor blind, but a conqueror like other conquerors," Williams writes in *In the American Grain*. Faced with the magnificence of the Aztec civilization, and treated with extravagant hospitality by King Montezuma, "Cortez could reply nothing save to demand that the man declare himself a subject to the Spanish king." The blinkered narrowness of that response is stunning, but perhaps only to be expected. Once conquest is set into motion, it sets into motion as well a script independent of human volition and perceptions, a script that binds us to its inevitable course as surely as if we were physical hostages.

How far does that hostage-taking extend? Are we still in its thrall, an eternal fixture in its field of operation? Our next text, Elizabeth Bishop's "Brazil,

January 1, 1502," takes on that question but (as we might expect with Bishop) obliquely, with a harmless-seeming focus on the "tapestried landscape" of Brazil that "greets our eyes / exactly as she must have greeted theirs." The syntactical parallel between the two possessive pronouns—*ours* and *theirs*—points to two lines of sight more or less parallel, making Bishop herself (not to say her readers) the unwitting descendants of the Portuguese conquistadors, with the same predatory eyes, each "ripping away" at the landscape, "each out to catch an Indian." Conquest is reproductive across time, it seems, a script of domination and subjection that continues to claim us.

Is that really true? Are we still hostage to an event that happened back in 1502? Not everyone would be persuaded by that exceptionally long genealogy. Once again, debate and disagreement, rather than ready consensus, is what we are aiming for. Our next selection, early American history from the standpoint of a Native American author, is chosen for much the same reason. In 1836 William Apess decided to go back two hundred years to pay a tribute to King Philip, or Metacomet, the Wampanoag chief who in 1675 led a coalition of Native American tribes against white settlements. King Philip's War has since become a byword for indigenous resistance. Apess invokes it not to applaud the use of force, but to remind us of an authentic American hero whose "virtues remain untold" in the official story about the founding of the nation, a story so celebratory that most of us tend to overlook the "deeds and depredations committed by whites upon Indians." Should past wrongs be insisted upon in this way? Isn't there something to be said for strategic oblivion as the ground for reconciliation? Addressing that question from the other side, and not always with a great deal of optimism, the selections here invite each of us to revisit that fraught terrain and come to our own judgment. In their misgivings no less than their provocations, they set the tone for the anthology as a whole.

ANNE BRADSTREET

Semiramis

Anne Bradstreet (1612–1672) arrived in North America 1630 in the company of her father and husband, both of whom would later serve as governors of the Massachusetts Bay Colony. She had grown up in an aristocratic household in England, learning Hebrew, Greek, Latin, and French from her father, Thomas Dudley, steward to the Earl of Lincoln. Somehow finding the time despite bouts of illness and the rearing of her eight children, Bradstreet completed a volume of poetry, *The Tenth Muse Lately Spring Up in America*, printed in England in 1650 to wide acclaim, making her the first female poet to be published on both sides of the Atlantic. Many of the poems were love poems to her husband ("If ever two were one, then surely we") or elegies mourning the death of her grandchildren and daughter-in-law. Her best-known poem is probably "Upon the Burning of Our House, July 10, 1666," a traumatic event that occurred just six years before her death. The selection below shows an earlier poet unexpectedly paying tribute to the military exploits and eventual defeat of a pagan Assyrian queen, Semiramis.

This gallant dame unto the Bactrian war
Accompanying her husband Menon far,
Taking a town such valor she did show
That Ninus amorous of her soon did grow,
And thought her fit to make a monarch's wife,
Which was the cause poor Menon lost his life.
She flourishing with Ninus long did reign,
Till her ambition caused him to be slain
That, having no compeer, she might rule all,
Or else she sought revenge for Menon's fall.
Some think the Greeks this slander on her cast,
As on her life licentious and unchaste;
That, undeserved, they blurred her name and fame
By their aspersions cast upon the same.

But were her virtues more or less or none,
She for her potency must go alone.
Her wealth she showed in building Babylon,
Admired of all, but equalized of none;
The wall so strong and curiously was wrought,
That after ages skill by it was taught.
With towers and bulwarks made of costly stone,
Quadrangle was the form it stood upon.
Each square was fifteen thousand paces long.
An hundred gates it had of metal strong.
Three hundred sixty feet the wall in height,
Almost incredible it was in breadth
Some writers say six chariots might a-front
With great facility march safe upon 't.
About the wall a ditch so deep and wide
That like a river long it did abide;
Three hundred thousand men here day by day
Bestowed their labor and received their pay.
And that which did all cost and art excel
The wondrous temple was she reared to Bel,
Which in the midst of this brave town was placed,
Continuing till Xerxes it defaced;
Whose stately top above the clouds did rise,
From whence astrologers oft viewed the skies.
This to describe in each particular,
A structure rare I should but rudely mar.
Her gardens, bridges, arches, mounts, and spires
Each eye that saw or ear that heard admires.
In Shinar plain, on the Euphratean flood,
This wonder of the world, this Babel, stood.
An expedition to the east she made
Stratobatis his country to invade.
Her army of four millions did consist
(Each may believe it as his fancy list);
Her camels, chariots, galleys, in such number
As puzzles best historians to remember.
But this is wonderful of all those men

They say but twenty e'er came back again;
The river Indus swept them half away,
The rest Stratobatis in fight did slay.
This was last progress of this mighty queen,
Who in her country never more was seen.
The poets feigned her turned into a dove,
Leaving the world to Venus, soared above;
Which made the Assyrians many a day
A dove within their ensigns to display.
Forty-two years she reigned, and then she died,
But by what means we are not certified.

LOUISE GLÜCK

Parable of the Hostages

Louise Glück (born 1943) has published more than a dozen books of poetry distinctive in their use of idiomatic speech to invoke a damaged world. She has won numerous awards, including a National Book Critics Award for *The Triumph of Achilles* (1985); the Pulitzer Prize for *The Wild Iris* (1993); the Bollingen Prize (2001), given biennially for lifetime achievement; and most recently, another National Book Award for *Faithful and Virtuous Night* (2014). In 2003 she was named poet laureate of the United States. Though Glück's poem cycles have always used multiple voices to tell interconnected stories—the gardener, the flowers, and an omniscient god in *The Wild Iris;* Aeneas, Dido, Eurydice, and Orpheus in *Vita Nova* (1999); Persephone and Demeter in *Averno* (2006); Telemachus, Penelope, Odysseus, and Circe in *Meadowlands* (1996)—this novelistic quality is especially pronounced in *A Village Life* (2009). Glück has also published a collection of essays, *Proofs and Theories* (1994). The following selection from *Meadowlands* meditates on the mental state of those who are "hostages" to war, from Troy on.

The Greeks are sitting on the beach
wondering what to do when the war ends. No one
wants to go home, back
to that bony island; everyone wants a little more
of what there is in Troy, more
life on the edge, that sense of every day as being
packed with surprises. But how to explain this
to the ones at home to whom
fighting a war is a plausible
excuse for absence, whereas
exploring one's capacity for diversion
is not. Well, this can be faced
later; these
are men of action, ready to leave
insight to the women and children.
Thinking things over in the hot sun, pleased
by a new strength in their forearms, which seem
more golden than they did at home, some
begin to miss their families a little,
to miss their wives, to want to see
if the war has aged them. And a few grow
slightly uneasy: what if war
is just a male version of dressing up,
a game devised to avoid
profound spiritual questions? Ah,
but it wasn't only the war. The world had begun
calling them, an opera beginning with the war's
loud chords and ending with the floating aria of the sirens.
There on the beach, discussing the various
timetables for getting home, no one believed
it could take ten years to get back to Ithaca;
no one foresaw that decade of insoluble dilemmas—oh unanswerable
affliction of the human heart: how to divide
the world's beauty into acceptable
and unacceptable loves! On the shores of Troy,
how could the Greeks know
they were hostages already: who once

delays the journey is
already enthralled; how could they know
that of their small number
some would be held forever by the dreams of pleasure,
some by sleep, some by music?

WILLIAM CARLOS WILLIAMS

The Destruction of Tenochtitlán

William Carlos Williams (1883–1963), poet, novelist, essayist, and playwright, was also a medical doctor all his life, practicing in Rutherford, New Jersey. Born and raised in a multiethnic family (his father was English; his mother a Puerto Rican of Dutch, Spanish, and Jewish descent), he studied medicine at the University of Pennsylvania, where he met Ezra Pound and Hilda Doolittle. Williams was initially associated with Pound's Imagist movement, but took off on his own with a poetic language based on ordinary speech that would later become the rallying cry for poets such as Allen Ginsberg, Charles Olson, and Robert Creeley. His best-known works include *Kora in Hell* (1920), *Spring and All* (1923), *Pictures from Brueghel and Other Poems* (1962), and the five-volume epic *Paterson* (1963, 1992). His genre-bending book *In the American Grain* (1925) takes a long view of American history, beginning with the destruction of Tenochtitlán by the conquistadors, excerpted here.

Cortez was neither malicious, stupid nor blind but a conqueror like other conquerors. Courageous almost beyond precedent, tactful, resourceful in misfortune, he was a man of genius superbly suited to his task. What his hand touched went down in spite of him. He was one among the rest. Velasquez, the Cuban Governor who sent him out, traitorously attacked him from the rear a week afterward. His own captains would have deserted him, so hard was he to follow. But the entire enterprise lived for many years on the verge of being allowed to languish, ruin to succeed destruction, because of the fortuitous anger which blossomed so naively, so mysteriously in Fonseca, Bishop of Burgos, President of the Council of the Indies. This the man, Cortez' most powerful enemy, already so notorious for the spiteful malevolence with which he thwarted the views of Columbus—a logic clearer had there been two Fonsecas instead of the one. After a rough voyage from Cuba, across the gulf, Cortez landed his small force safely before what is now Vera Cruz, near the native city of Cempoal. There lest his men should desert him in view of the hardships which lay ahead, he had his vessels beached, under pretext of their being no longer seaworthy, and destroyed them. Montezuma immediately sent gifts, at the same time begging the Spaniard not to risk coming up into the back country: a gold necklace of seven pieces, set with many gems like small rubies, a hundred and eighty-three emeralds and ten fine pearls, and hung with twenty seven little bells of gold.—Two wheels, one of gold like the sun and the other of silver with the image of the moon upon it, made of plates of those metals, twenty-eight hands in circumference, with figures of animals and other things in bas relief, finished with great skill and ingenuity.—A headpiece of wood and gold, adorned with gems, from which hung twenty five little bells of gold and on it, instead of plume, a green bird with eyes, beak and feet of gold.—Several shoes of the skin of deer, sewed with gold thread, the soles of which were made of blue and white stones of a brilliant appearance.—A shield of wood and leather, with little bells hanging to it and covered with plates of gold, in the middle of which was cut the image of the god of war between four heads of a lion, a tiger, an eagle and an owl represented alive with their hair and feathers.—Twenty four curious and beautiful shields of gold, of feathers and very small pearls, and four of feathers and silver only.—Four fishes, two ducks and some other birds of molten gold.—A large mirror adorned with gold and many small.—Mitres and crowns of feathers and gold ornamented with pearls and gems.—Several large plumes of beautiful feathers, fretted with gold and small pearls.—Several fans of gold and silver mixed together; others of feathers only, of different forms and sizes.—A variety of cotton mantles, some all white, others chequered with white and black, or red, green, yellow and blue; on the outside rough like shaggy cloth and within destitute of color and nap.—A number of underwaistcoats, handkerchiefs, counterpanes, tapestries and carpets of cotton, the workmanship superior to the materials of which they were composed.—And books made of tablets with a smooth surface for writing which being joined might be folded together or stretched out to a considerable length, "the characters inscribed thereon resembling nothing so much as Egyptian hieroglyphics."—But Cortez was unwilling to turn back; rather these things whetted his appetite for the adventure. Without more ado he sent letters to his king advising him that having come to these lands to conquer them, in the royal name and that of the true church, he would forthwith proceed to take Montezuma, dead or alive, unless he should accept the faith and acknowledge himself a subject to the Spanish throne. The advance was like any similar military enterprise: it accomplished its purpose. Surmounting every difficulty Cortez went his way into the country past the quiet cempoalan maizefields, past the smoking summit of Popocatepetl until, after weeks of labor, he arrived upon the great lakes and the small cities in them adjoining Tenochtitlan itself. Montezuma seeing that there was nothing else for it, sent envoys accompanied by three hundred warriors, who met the Spaniard advancing on the lake road and there welcomed him to the district with great ceremony and show of friendliness. Noticeable among them was one young man of magnificent appearance who descended from his litter and walked to meet the Conqueror while his followers ran before him, picking up stones and other small obstructions which lay in his path. Cortez now passed over his first causeway into one of the lesser lake cities, built of well-hewn stone sheer from the water. He was overcome with wonder. The houses were so excellently put together, so well decorated with cloths and carven wood, so embellished with metalwork and other marks of a beautiful civilization; the people were so gracious; there were such gardens, such trees, such conservatories of flowers that nothing like it had ever been seen or imagined. At the house where the Conqueror was entertained that day and night he especially noted a pool built of stone into the clear waters of which stone steps descended while round it were paven paths lined with sweet-smelling shrubs and plants and trees of all sorts. Also he noted the well stocked kitchen garden. The following day at noon he arrived at the end of his journey. There it lay! a city as large as Cordova or Seville, entirely within the lake two miles from the mainland: Tenochtitlan. Four avenues or entrances led to it all formed of artificial causeways. Along the most easterly of these, constructed of great beams perfectly hewn and fitted together, and measuring two spears-lengths in width, the Christian advanced. Running in at one side of the city and out at the other this avenue constituted at the same time its principal street. As Cortez drew nearer he saw, right and left, magnificent houses and temples, close to the walls of which, each side, moved parallel rows of priests in black robes and between them, supported by two attendants, Montezuma, on foot, down the center of the roadway. Cortez stepped forward but the attendants interceded. The Emperor then advanced alone and with great simpleness of manner placed a golden chain about the Christian's neck. Then taking him by the hand, and the whole procession following, he conducted him to the quarters which had been chosen for the visitors, a great building close to the royal palaces in the center of the city. Everything had been prepared in advance: all the material needs together with rich gifts, as before: precious metals, gems, male and female apparel of remarkable elegance, ornamental hangings for bed-chambers, tapestries for halls and temples, counterpanes composed of feathers interwoven with cotton and many beautiful and curious artifices of so costly and unusual workmanship that considering their novelty and wonderful beauty no price could be set on them. Here in this large building whose great hall was to serve the Spaniards for barracks from that time until the end, Montezuma and Cortez found themselves seated at last face to face. Montezuma spoke: They have told you that I possess houses with walls of gold and many other such things and that I am a god or make myself one. The houses you see are of stone and lime and earth.—Then opening his robe: You see that I am composed of flesh and bone like yourselves and that I am mortal and palpable to the touch.—To this smiling sally, so full of gentleness and amused irony, Cortez could reply nothing save to demand that the man declare himself a subject of the Spanish King forthwith and that, furthermore, he should then and there announce publicly his allegiance to the new power.—Whatever the Aztec might have felt during the weeks of Cortez' slow advance upon his capital from the seashore, nothing at the present moment seemed to disturb his aristocratic reserve. He had thought and he had made up his mind. Without semblance of anger, fear or impatience; without humility or protest but with the force bred of a determination to face at any cost a situation fast going beyond his control, he spoke again. He explained that his people were not the aborigines of the land but that they had emigrated there in times past and ended by accepting the Spanish Monarch as his rightful and hereditary master. After due announcements and explanations had been made to the people Cortez became the acknowledged regent, in the name of Castile and the true church, for all that country.

ELIZABETH BISHOP

Brazil, January 1, 1502

Elizabeth Bishop (1911–1979), named poet laureate of the United States in 1949, is best known for *North and South* (1946); Pulitzer Prize–winning *A Cold Spring* (1955); *Questions of Travel* (1965); and *Geography III* (1976), which includes two of her most anthologized poems, "In the Waiting Room" and "One Art." Orphaned at age five, Bishop led a peripatetic life: moving as a child from Massachusetts to Nova Scotia and living as an adult in France, Spain, Ireland, Italy, North Africa, Key West, and above all, Brazil. She had planned on stopping there briefly on her way to Tierra del Fuego in 1951, but ended up staying on for the next fifteen years in a romantic partnership with architect Lota de Macedo Soares. While in Brazil, she came under the influence of Mexican poet Octavio Paz as well as Brazilian poets João Cabral de Melo Neto and Carlos Drummond de Andrade. Her poetry and translations from this period show her trying to come to terms with her status as a foreigner. The selection below recalls the arrival of Portuguese conquistadors more than 400 years before Bishop found herself in the country.

. . . embroidered nature . . . tapestried landscape.
—*Landscape into Art,* by Sir Kenneth Clark

Januaries, Nature greets our eyes
exactly as she must have greeted theirs:
every square inch filling in with foliage—
big leaves, little leaves, and giant leaves,
blue, blue-green, and olive,
with occasional lighter veins and edges,
or a satin underleaf turned over;
monster ferns
in silver-gray relief,

and flowers, too, like giant water lilies
up in the air—up, rather, in the leaves—
purple, yellow, two yellows, pink,
rust red and greenish white;
solid but airy; fresh as if just finished
and taken off the frame.

A blue-white sky, a simple web,
backing for feathery detail:
brief arcs, a pale-green broken wheel,
a few palms, swarthy, squat, but delicate;
and perching there in profile, beaks agape,
the big symbolic birds keep quiet,
each showing only half his puffed and padded,
pure-colored or spotted breast.
Still in the foreground there is Sin:
five sooty dragons near some massy rocks.
The rocks are worked with lichens, gray moonbursts
splattered and overlapping,
threatened from underneath by moss
in lovely hell-green flames,
attacked above
by scaling-ladder vines, oblique and near,
"one leaf yes and one leaf no" (in Portuguese).
The lizards scarcely breathe; all eyes
are on the small, female one, back-to,
her wicked tail straight up and over,
red as a red-hot wire.

Just so the Christians, hard as nails,
tiny as nails, glinting,
in creaking armor, came and found it all,
not unfamiliar:
no lovers' walks, no bowers,
no cherries to be picked, no lute music,
but corresponding, nevertheless,

to an old dream of wealth and luxury
already out of style when they left home—
wealth, plus a brand-new pleasure.
Directly after Mass, humming perhaps
L'Homme armé or some such tune,
they ripped away into the hanging fabric,
each out to catch an Indian for himself—
those maddening little women who kept calling,
calling to each other (or had the birds waked up?)
and retreating, always retreating, behind it.

WILLIAM APESS

Eulogy on King Philip

William Apess (1798–1839), writer and activist, was descended from King Philip of the Wampanoag Nation through his mother, of mixed African, European, and Native American ancestry. After ordaining as a Methodist minister in 1829, he published his autobiography, *A Son of the Forest,* the following year. Preaching to mixed congregations throughout New England in both English and Wampanoag, Apess was one of the key spokesmen for Native American rights. In 1833 he visited Mashpee, the largest Indian town in Massachusetts, to help organize resistance to Massachusetts laws denying native control over natural resources. The Mashpee Revolt of 1833–1834 was covered sympathetically by the *Boston Advocate,* but Apess was jailed for a month. In 1835 he published *The Indian Nullification of the Unconstitutional Laws of Massachusetts,* invoking the 1832 Nullification Crisis on the national level as a template for native rights. His *Eulogy on King Philip,* excerpted here, was delivered and published in Boston in 1836; he disappeared from public life in New England shortly thereafter. He died in New York City in 1839 at the age of forty-one.

I do not arise to spread before you the fame of a noted warrior, whose natural abilities shone like those of the great and mighty Philip of Greece, or of Alexander the Great, or like those of Washington—whose virtues and patriotism are engraven on the hearts of my audience. Neither do I approve of war as being the best method of bowing to the haughty tyrant, Man, and civilizing the world. No, far from me be such a thought. But it is to bring before you beings made by the God of Nature, and in whose hearts and heads he has planted sympathies that shall live forever in the memory of the world, whose brilliant talents shone in the display of natural things, so that the most cultivated, whose powers shown with equal luster, were not able to prepare mantles to cover the burning elements of an uncivilized world. What, then? Shall we cease to mention the mighty of the earth, the noble work of God?

Yet those purer virtues remain untold. Those noble traits that marked the wild man's course lie buried in the shades of night; and who shall stand? I appeal to the lovers of liberty. But those few remaining descendants who now remain as the monument of the cruelty of those who came to improve our race and correct our errors—and as the immortal Washington lives endeared and engraven on the hearts of every white in America, never to be forgotten in time—even such is the immortal Philip honored, as held in memory by the degraded but yet grateful descendants who appreciate his character; so will every patriot, especially in this enlightened age, respect the rude yet all accomplished son of the forest, that died a martyr to his cause, though unsuccessful, yet as glorious as the American Revolution. Where, then, shall we place the hero of the wilderness?

Justice and humanity for the remaining few prompt me to vindicate the character of him who yet lives in their hearts and, if possible, melt the prejudice that exists in the hearts of those who are in the possession of his soil, and only by the right of conquest—is the aim of him who proudly tells you, the blood of a denominated savage runs in his veins. It is, however, true that there are many who are said to be honorable warriors, who, in wisdom of their civilized legislation, think it no crime to wreak their vengeance upon whole nations and communities, until the fields are covered with blood and the rivers turned into purple fountains, while groans, like distant thunder, are heard from the wounded and the tens of thousands of the dying, leaving helpless families depending on their cares and sympathies for life; while a loud response is heard floating through the air from the ten thousand

Indian children and orphans, who are left to mourn the honorable acts of a few—civilized men.

Now, if we have common sense and ability to allow the difference between the civilized and the uncivilized, we cannot but see that one mode of warfare is as just as the other; for while one is sanctioned by authority of the enlightened and cultivated men, the other is an agreement according to the pure laws of nature, growing out of natural consequences; for nature has her defense for every beast of the field; even the reptiles of the earth and the fishes of the sea have their weapons of war. But thou frail man was made for a nobler purpose—to live, to love, and adore his God, and do good to his brother—for this reason, and this alone, the God of heaven prepared ways and means to blast anger, man's destroyer, and cause the Prince of Peace to rule, that man might swell those blessed notes. My image is of God; I am not a beast.

But as all men are governed by animal passions who are void of the true principles of God, whether cultivated or uncultivated, we shall now lay before you the true character of Philip, in relation to those hostilities between himself and the whites; and in so doing, permit me to be plain and candid.

The first inquiry is: Who is Philip? He was the descendant of one of the most celebrated chiefs in the known world, for peace and universal benevolence toward all men; for injuries upon injuries, and the most daring robberies and barbarous deeds of death that were ever committed by the American Pilgrims, were with patience and resignation borne, in a manner that would do justice to any Christian nation or being in the world—especially when we realize that it was voluntary suffering on the part of the good old chief. His country extensive, his men numerous, so as the wilderness was enlivened by them, say, a thousand to one of the white men, and they also sick and feeble—where, then, shall we find one nation submitting so tamely to another, with such a host at their command? For injuries of much less magnitude have the people called Christians slain their brethren, till they could sing, like Samson: With a jawbone of an ass have we slain our thousands and laid them in heaps. It will be well for us to lay those deeds and depredations committed by whites upon Indians before the civilized world, and then they can judge for themselves.

THOMAS JEFFERSON

Letter to General Lafayette, June 16, 1792

Thomas Jefferson (1843–1826), principal author of the Declaration of Independence (1776) and third president of the United States (1801–1809), was an Enlightenment polymath who spoke five languages and contributed to the fields of philosophy, archeology, botany, music, mathematics, and engineering as well as law, his chosen profession. Jefferson also served as vice president (1797–1801) and secretary of state (1790–1793). In his later years he founded the University of Virginia (1819), designing the campus around a library rather than a chapel. In 1780, as governor of Virginia, he received many queries from the French diplomat François Barbé-Marbois about the physical and social conditions of his home state. *Notes on the State of Virginia* (1785) was the result: an extensive compilation of scientific and demographic data and a meditation on the detrimental effects of slavery on whites as well as blacks. Jefferson was minister to France from 1785 to 1789, the year the French Revolution started. In the letters below, he pays tribute to Marquis de Lafayette's fight against the "monster aristocracy" and its "associate monarchy" while keeping a wary eye on "king-jobbers," blacks, and "Indian neighbors" back home.

Behold you, then, my dear friend, at the head of a great army, establishing the liberties of your country against a foreign enemy. May heaven favor your cause, and make you the channel thro' which it may pour its favors. While you are exterminating the monster aristocracy, & pulling out the teeth & fangs of its associate monarchy, a contrary tendency is discovered in some here. A sect has shewn itself among us, who declare they espoused our new constitution, not as a good & sufficient thing itself, but only as a step to an English constitution, the only thing good & sufficient in itself, in their eye. It is happy for us that these are preachers without followers, and that our people are firm & constant in their republican purity. You will wonder to be told that it is from the Eastward chiefly that these champions for a king, lords & commons come. They get some important associates from New York, and are puffed off by a tribe of Agioteurs which have been hatched in a bed of corruption made up after the model of their beloved

England. Too many of these stock jobbers & king-jobbers have come into our legislature, or rather too many of our legislature have become stock jobbers & king-jobbers. However the voice of the people is beginning to make itself heard, and will probably cleanse their seats at the ensuing election.—The machinations of our old enemies are such as to keep us still at bay with our Indian neighbors.—What are you doing for your colonies? They will be lost if not more effectually succoured. Indeed no future efforts you can make will ever be able to reduce the blacks. All that can be done in my opinion will be to compound with them as has been done formerly in Jamaica. We have been less zealous in aiding them, lest your government should feel any jealousy on our account. But in truth we as sincerely wish their restoration, and their connection with you, as you do yourselves. We are satisfied that neither your justice nor their distresses will ever again permit their being forced to seek at dear & distant markets those first necessaries of life which they may have at cheaper markets placed by nature at their door, & formed by her for their support.—What is become of Mde de Tessy and Mde de Tott? I have not heard of them since they went to Switzerland. I think they would have done better to have come & reposed under the Poplars of Virginia. Pour into their bosoms the warmest effusions of my friendship & tell them they will be warm and constant unto death. Accept of them also for Mde de la Fayette & your dear children—but I am forgetting that you are in the field of war, & they I hope in those of peace.

THOMAS JEFFERSON

Letter to James Monroe, July 14, 1793

Dear Sir,

. . . The situation of the St. Domingo fugitives (aristocrats as they are) calls aloud for pity and charity. Never was so deep a tragedy presented to the feelings of man. I deny the power of the general government to apply money to such a purpose, but I deny it with a bleeding heart. It belongs to the state governments. Pray urge ours to be liberal. The Executive should hazard themselves more on such an occasion, and the legislative when it meets ought to approve and extend it. It will have a great effect in doing away the impression of other disobligations towards France.—I become daily more and more convinced that all the West India islands will remain in the hands of the people of colour, and a total expulsion of the whites sooner or later take place. It is high time we should foresee the bloody scenes which our children certainly, and possibly ourselves (South of Patowmac) have to wade through, and try to avert them.—We have no news from the continent of Europe later than the 1st. of May.—My love to Mrs. Monroe. Tell her they are paving the street before your new house. Adieu. Yours affectionately.

VICTOR SÉJOUR

The Mulatto

trans. Philip Barnard

Victor Séjour (1817–1874) was the author of the earliest known work of fiction by an African American. Born in New Orleans to a wealthy, free, mixed-race father from Saint-Domingue and a free African American mother, he was educated at a private school. Moving to Paris for education and work in his teens, he got to know the publisher of the black-owned journal *La Revue des Colonies*. In 1837 that journal published his first work, "Le Mulâtre," the story of a slave who takes revenge on his master (and father) for the death of his wife. Not translated from French to English until the late twentieth century, "Le Mulâtre" was initially all but unknown to American readers. His journey to literary acclaim—by way of Paris—would be a path subsequently followed by a long list of African American writers. The excerpt below, which opens the story, sets the stage for the tale of vengeance.

The first rays of dawn were just beginning to light the black mountaintops when I left the Cape for Saint-Marc, a small town in St. Domingue, now known as Haiti. I had seen so many exquisite landscapes and thick, tall forests that, truth to tell, I had begun to believe myself indifferent to these virile beauties of creation. But at the sight of this town, with its picturesque vegetation, its bizarre and novel nature, I was stunned; I stood dumb-struck before the sublime diversity of God's works. The moment I arrived, I was accosted by an old negro, at least seventy years of age; his step was firm, his head held high, his form imposing and vigorous; save the remarkable whiteness of his curly hair, nothing betrayed his age. As is common in that country, he wore a large straw hat and was dressed in trousers of coarse gray linen, with a kind of jacket made from plain batiste.

"Good day, Master," he said, tipping his hat when he saw me.

"Ah! There you are . . .," and I offered him my hand, which he shook in return.

"Master," he said, "that's quite noble-hearted of you. . . . But you know, do you not, that a negro's as vile as a dog; society rejects him; men detest him; the laws curse him. . . . Yes, he's a most unhappy being, who hasn't even the consolation of always being virtuous. . . . He may be born good, noble, and generous; God may grant him a great and loyal soul; but despite all that, he often goes to his grave with bloodstained hands, and a heart hungering after yet more vengeance. For how many times has he seen the dreams of his youth destroyed? How many times has experience taught him that his good deeds count for nothing, and that he should love neither his wife nor his son; for one day the former will be seduced by the master, and his own flesh and blood will be sold and transported away despite his despair. What, then, can you expect him to become? Shall he smash his skull against the paving stones? Shall he kill his torturer? Or do you believe the human heart can find a way to bear such misfortune?"

The old negro fell silent a moment, as if awaiting my response.

"You'd have to be mad to believe that," he continued, heatedly. "If he continues to live, it can only be for vengeance; for soon he shall rise . . . and, from the day he shakes off his servility, the master would do better to have a starving tiger raging beside him than to meet that man face to face." While the old man spoke, his face lit up, his eyes sparkled, and his heart pounded forcefully. I would not have believed one could discover that much life and power beneath such an aged exterior. Taking advantage of this moment of excitement, I said to him: "Antoine, you promised you'd tell me the story of your friend Georges."

"Do you want to hear it now?"

"Certainly . . ." We sat down, he on my trunk, myself on my valise. Here is what he told me:

"Do you see this edifice that rises so graciously toward the sky and whose reflection seems to rise from the sea; this edifice that in its peculiarity resembles a temple and in its pretense a palace? This is the house of Saint-M***. Each day, in one of this building's rooms, one finds an assemblage of hangers-on, men of independent means, and the great plantation owners. The first two groups play billiards or smoke the delicious cigars of Havana, while the third purchases negroes; that is, free men who have been torn from their country by ruse or by force, and who have become, by violence, the goods, the property of their fellow men. . . . Over here we have the husband without the wife; there, the sister without the brother; farther on, the mother without the children. This makes you shudder? Yet this loathsome commerce goes on continuously. Soon, in any case, the offering is a young Senegalese woman, so beautiful that from every mouth leaps the exclamation: 'How pretty!' Everyone there wants her for his mistress, but not one of them dares dispute the prize with the young Alfred, now twenty-one years old and one of the richest planters in the country.

" 'How much do you want for this woman?'

" 'Fifteen hundred piasters,' replied the auctioneer.

" 'Fifteen hundred piasters,' Alfred rejoined dryly.

" 'Yes indeed, Sir.'

" 'That's your price?'

" 'That's my price.'

" 'That's awfully expensive.'

" 'Expensive?' replied the auctioneer, with an air of surprise. 'But surely you see how pretty she is; how clear her skin is, how firm her flesh is. She's eighteen years old at the most. . . .' Even as he spoke, he ran his shameless hands all over the ample and half-naked form of the beautiful African.

" 'Is she guaranteed?' asked Alfred, after a moment of reflection.

" 'As pure as the morning dew,' the auctioneer responded. But, for that matter, you yourself can. . . .'

" 'No no, there's no need,' said Alfred, interrupting him. 'I trust you.'

" 'I've never sold a single piece of bad merchandise,' replied the vendor, twirling his whiskers with a triumphant air. When the bill of sale had been signed and all formalities resolved, the auctioneer approached the young slave.

'This man is now your master,' he said, pointing toward Alfred.

" 'I know it,' the negress answered coldly.

" 'Are you content?'

" 'What does it matter to me . . . him or some other . . .'

" 'But surely. . . .' stammered the auctioneer, searching for some answer.

" 'But surely what?' said the African, with some humor. 'And if he doesn't suit me?'

" 'My word, that would be unfortunate, for everything is finished. . . .'

" 'Well then, I'll keep my thoughts to myself.'

"Ten minutes later, Alfred's new slave stepped into a carriage that set off along the chemin des *guêpes*, a well-made road that leads out into those delicious fields that surround Saint-Marc like young virgins at the foot of the altar. A somber melancholy enveloped her soul, and she began to weep. The driver understood only too well what was going on inside her, and thus made no attempt to distract her. But when he saw Alfred's white house appear in the distance, he involuntarily leaned down toward the unfortunate girl and, with a voice full of tears, said to her: 'Sister, what's your name?'

" 'Laïsa,' she answered, without raising her head.

"At the sound of this name, the driver shivered. Then, gaining control of his emotions, he asked: 'Your mother?'

" 'She's dead. . . .'

" 'Your father?'

" 'He's dead. . . .'

" 'Poor child,' he murmured. 'What country are you from, Laïsa?'

" 'From Senegal. . . .'

"Tears rose in his eyes; she was a fellow countrywoman.

" 'Sister,' he said, wiping his eyes, 'perhaps you know old Chambo and his daughter. . . .'

" 'Why?' answered the girl, raising her head quickly.

" 'Why?' continued the driver, in obvious discomfort, 'well, old Chambo is my father, and . . .'

" 'My God,' cried out the orphan, cutting off the driver before he could finish. 'You are?'

" 'Jacques Chambo.'

" 'You're my brother!'

" 'Laïsa!'

"They threw themselves into each other's arms. They were still embracing when the carriage passed through the main entrance to Alfred's property. The overseer was waiting. . . . 'What's this I see,' he shouted, uncoiling an immense whip that he always carried on his belt; 'Jacques kissing the new arrival before my very eyes. What impertinence!' With this, lashes began to fall on the unhappy man, and spurts of blood leaped from his face."

HENRY DAVID THOREAU

Resistance to Civil Government

Henry David Thoreau (1817–1862), naturalist, poet, and abolitionist, is best known for *Walden* (1854), an experiment in "simple living"; and for "Resistance to Civil Government" (or "Civil Disobedience"), an essay he wrote after he was jailed for one night in July 1846 for refusing to pay the poll tax as a protest against slavery and the Mexican-American War. Thoreau's doctrine of nonviolent resistance has inspired followers from Tolstoy to Gandhi to Martin Luther King, Jr. He was born in Concord, Massachusetts, educated at Harvard, and widely read in geology, evolutionary biology, and Eastern religion and philosophy, as demonstrated in *A Week on the Concord and Merrimack Rivers* (1849) and in his faithfully kept journals. In 1859, after a late-night excursion to count tree rings during a rain storm, Thoreau contracted bronchitis and died after three years of declining health. When asked whether he had made his peace with God, he is said to have replied: "I didn't know we had quarreled." Thoreau did quarrel with the state, however, as we can see in this excerpt from "Resistance to Civil Government."

Under a government which imprisons any unjustly, the true place for a just man is also a prison. The proper place to-day, the only place which Massachusetts has provided for her freer and less desponding spirits, is in her prisons, to be put out and locked out of the State by her own act, as they have already put themselves out by their principles. It is there that the fugitive slave, and the Mexican prisoner on parole, and the Indian come to plead the wrongs of his race, should find them; on that separate, but more free and honorable ground, where the State places those who are not with her, but against her, the only house in a slave State in which a free man can abide with honor. If any think that their influence would be lost there, and their voices no longer afflict the ear of the State, that they would not be as an enemy within its walls, they do not know by how much truth is stronger than error, nor how much more eloquently and effectively he can combat injustice who has experienced a little in his own person. Cast your whole vote, not a strip of paper merely, but your whole influence. A minority is powerless while it conforms to the majority; it is not even a minority then; but it is irresistible, when it clogs by its whole weight. If the alternative is to keep all just men in prison, or give up war and slavery, the State will not hesitate which to choose. If a thousand men were not to pay their tax-bills this year, that would not be a violent and bloody measure, as it would be to pay them, and enable the State to commit violence and shed innocent blood. This is, in fact, the definition of a peaceable revolution, if any such is possible. If the tax-gatherer, or any other public officer, asks me, as one has done, "But what shall I do?" my answer is, "If you really wish to do anything, resign your office." When the subject has refused allegiance, and the officer has resigned his office, then the revolution is accomplished. But even suppose blood should flow. Is there not a sort of blood shed when the conscience is wounded? Through this wound a man's real manhood and immortality flow out, and he bleeds to an everlasting death. I see this blood flowing now.

MARGARET FULLER

Dispatch 29

Margaret Fuller (1810–1850), author, translator, and journalist, is best known for her seminal work, *Woman in the Nineteenth Century* (1845). Born in Cambridge, Massachusetts, Fuller became prominent in the

Transcendentalist circles, editing the journal *The Dial* (1840–1842), and conducting "conversations" as a form of adult education. In 1844 she was hired by Horace Greeley to serve as the first female editor of the *New York Tribune*, and later as its first female foreign correspondent. Her dispatches about the political upheavals in Europe were among her most memorable. Fuller was in Italy from 1847 to 1849, where she witnessed the birth of the short-lived Roman Republic while forming a romantic partnership with an Italian nobleman and revolutionary, Count Giovanni Ossoli. The couple and their son were on their way back to the United States when they suffered a shipwreck just 100 yards from Fire Island, New York. Neither Fuller's body nor her completed manuscript about the Roman Republic was ever recovered. In the excerpt below, from an 1849 dispatch, her hopes for Italy are tempered by a clear-eyed realism.

Mazzini, in his exile, remained absolutely devoted to his native country. Because, though feeling as few can that the interests of humanity in all nations are identical, he felt also that, born of a race so suffering, so much needing devotion and energy, his first duty was to that. The only powers he acknowledged were *God and the People*, the special scope of his acts the unity and independence of Italy. Rome was the theme of his thoughts, but, very early exiled, he had never seen that home to which all the orphans of the soul so naturally turn. Now he entered it as a Roman citizen, elected representative of the people by universal suffrage. His motto, *Dio e Popolo*, is put upon the coin with the Roman eagle; unhappily this first-issued coin is of brass, or else of silver, with much alloy. *Dii, avertite omen*, and may peaceful days turn it all to pure gold!

On his first entrance to the house, Mazzini, received with fervent applause and summoned, to take his place beside the President, spoke as follows:—

"It is from me, colleagues, that should come these tokens of applause, these tokens of affection, because the little good I have not done, but tried to do, has come to me from Rome. Rome was always a sort of talisman for me; a youth, I studied the history of Italy, and found, while all the other nations were born, grew up, played their part in the world, then fell to reappear no more in the same power, a single city was privileged by God to die only to rise again greater than before, to fulfil a mission greater than the first. I saw the Rome of the Empire extend her conquests from the confines of Africa to the confines of Asia. I saw Rome perish, crushed by the barbarians, by those whom even yet the world, calls barbarians. I saw her rise again, after having chased away these same barbarians, reviving in its sepulchre the germ of Civilization. I saw her rise more great for conquest, not with arms, but with words,—rise in the name of the Popes to repeat her grand mission. I said in my heart, the city which alone in the world has had two grand lives, one greater than the other, will have a third. After the Rome which wrought by conquest of arms, the Rome which wrought by conquest of words, must come a third which shall work by virtue of example. After the Rome of the Emperors, after the Rome of the Popes, will come the Rome of the People. The Rome of the People is arisen; do not salute with applauses, but let us rejoice together! I cannot promise anything for myself, except concurrence in all you shall do for the good of Rome, of Italy, of mankind. Perhaps we shall have to pass through great crises; perhaps we shall have to fight a sacred battle against the only enemy that threatens us,—Austria. We will fight it, and we will conquer. I hope, please God, that foreigners may not be able to say any more that which so many of them repeat to-day, speaking of our affairs,—that the light which, comes from Rome is only an *ignis fatuus* wandering among the tombs. The world shall see that it is a starry light, eternal, pure, and resplendent as those we look up to in the heavens!"

On a later day he spoke more fully of the difficulties that threaten at home the young republic, and said:—

"Let us not hear of Right, of Left, of Centre; these terms express the three powers in a constitutional monarchy; for us they have no meaning; the only divisions for us are of Republicans or non-Republicans,—or of sincere men and temporizing men. Let us not hear so much of the Republicans of to-day and of yesterday; I am a Republican of twenty years' standing. Entertaining such hopes for Italy, when many excellent, many sincere men held them as Utopian, shall I denounce these men because they are now convinced of their practicability?"

This last I quote from memory. In hearing the gentle tone of remonstrance with those of more petty mind, or influenced by the passions of the partisan, I was forcibly reminded of the parable by Jesus, of the vineyard and the discontent of the laborers that those who came at the eleventh hour "received also a penny." Mazzini also is content that all should fare alike as brethren, if only they will come into the vineyard. He is not an orator, but the simple conversational tone of his address is in refreshing contrast with the boyish rhetoric and academic swell common to Italian speakers in the present unfledged state. As they have freer use of the power of debate, they will become more simple and manly. The speech of Mazzini is laden with thought,—it goes straight to the mark by the shortest path, and moves without effort, from the irresistible impression of deep conviction and fidelity in the speaker. Mazzini is a man of genius, an elevated thinker; but the most powerful and first impression from his presence must always be of the religion of his soul, of his *virtue*, both in the modern and antique sense of that word.

If clearness of right, if energy, if indefatigable perseverance, can steer the ship through this dangerous pass, it will be done. He said, "We will conquer"; whether Rome will, this time, is not to me certain, but such men as Mazzini conquer always,—conquer in defeat. Yet Heaven grant that no more blood, no more corruption of priestly government, be for Italy. It could only be for once more, for the strength, of her present impulse would not fail to triumph at last; but even one more trial seems too intolerably much, when I think of the holocaust of the broken hearts, baffled lives, that must attend it.

STEPHEN CRANE

Stephen Crane's Vivid Story of the Battle of San Juan

Stephen Crane (1871–1900) is best known for *Maggie: A Girl of the Streets* (1893) and *The Red Badge of Courage* (1895), a novel that he wrote by consulting history books, as the Civil War had ended six years before he was born. Sent on assignment to the Spanish-American War, he became a roving reporter for several news syndicates. En route to Cuba in January

1897, his ship, the *Commodore,* sank off the coast of Florida, leaving him and three others floundering in a ten-foot dinghy for a day and a half. His short story "The Open Boat" recounts that ordeal.

Crane covered the Greco-Turkish War and spent time in England, socializing with Henry James and Joseph Conrad before finally arriving in Cuba to witness the most famous action of the Spanish-American War, the Battle of San Juan. The excerpt below offers a not exactly reassuring account of that battle. Crane died at the age of 28 in a German sanatorium, but short stories such as "The Blue Hotel" and "The Bride Comes to Yellow Sky" and his distinctive style of reporting would leave a tangible legacy on authors such as Ernest Hemingway.

In front of Santiago, July 4, via Old Point Comfort, Va., July 13.—The action at San Juan on July 1 was, particularly speaking, a soldiers' battle. It was like Inkerman, where the English fought half leaderless all day in a fog. Only the Cuban forest was worse than any fog.

No doubt when history begins to grind out her story we will find that many a thundering, fine, grand order was given for that day's work; but after all there will be no harm in contending that the fighting line, the men and their regimental officers, took the hill chiefly because they knew they could take it, some having no orders and others disobeying whatever orders they had.

In civil life the newspapers would have called it a grand, popular movement. It will never be forgotten as long as America has a military history.

A line of intrenched hills held by men armed with a weapon like the Mauser is not to be taken by a front attack of infantry unless the trenches have first been heavily shaken by artillery fire. Any theorist will say that it is impossible, and prove it to be impossible. But it was done, and we owe the success to the splendid gallantry of the American private soldier.

As near as one can learn headquarters expected little or no fighting on the 1st. Lawton's division was to go by the Caney road, chase the Spaniards out of that interesting village, and then, wheeling half to the left, march down to join the other divisions in some kind of attack on San Juan at daybreak on the 2d.

But somebody had been entirely misinformed as to the strength and disposition of the Spanish forces at Caney, and instead of taking Lawton six minutes to capture the town it took him nearly all day, as well it might.

The other divisions lying under fire, waiting for Lawton, grew annoyed at a delay which was, of course, not explained to them, and suddenly arose and took the formidable hills of San Juan. It was impatience suddenly exalted to one of the sublime passions.

Lawton was well out toward Caney soon after daybreak, and by 7 o'clock we could hear the boom of Capron's guns in support of the infantry. The remaining divisions—Kent's and Wheeler's—were trudging slowly along the muddy trail through the forest.

When the first gun was fired a grim murmur passed along the lean column. "They're off!" somebody said.

The marching was of necessity very slow and even then the narrow road was often blocked. The men, weighted with their packs, cartridge belts and rifles, forded many streams, climbed hills, slid down banks and forced their way through thickets.

Suddenly there was a roar of guns just ahead and a little to the left. This was Grimes's battery going into action on the hill which is called El Paso. Then, all in a moment, the quiet column moving forward was opposed by men carrying terrible burdens. Wounded Cubans were being carried to the rear. Most of them were horribly mangled.

The second brigade of dismounted American cavalry had been in support of the battery, its position being directly to the rear. Some Cubans had joined there. The Spanish shrapnel fired at the battery was often cut too long, and passing over burst amid the supports and the Cubans.

The loss of the battery, the cavalry and the Cubans from this fire was forty men in killed and wounded, the First regular cavalry probably suffering most grievously. Presently there was a lull in the artillery fire, and down through spaces in the trees we could see the infantry still plodding with its packs steadily toward the front.

The artillerymen were greatly excited. Some showed with glee fragments of Spanish shells which had come dangerously near their heads. They had gone through their ordeal and were talking over it lightly.

In the meantime Lawton's division, some three miles away, was making plenty of noise. Caney is just at the base of a high willow-green, crinkled mountain, and Lawton was making his way over little knolls which might be termed foothills. We could see the great white clouds of smoke from Capron's guns and hear their roar punctuating the incessant drumming of the infantry. It was plain even then that Lawton was having considerably more of a fete than anybody had supposed previously.

MARK TWAIN

Incident in the Philippines

Mark Twain (1835–1910), born Samuel Langhorne Clemens, worked as a typesetter, printer, and steamboat pilot before becoming a writer. In his journalistic sketches, *The Celebrated Jumping Frog of Calaveras County* (1867) and *Roughing It* (1872), and in his celebrated novels, *The Adventures of Tom Sawyer* (1876), *The Adventures of Huckleberry Finn* (1884), and *Pudd'nhead Wilson* (1894), Twain put frontier humor and Mississippi River culture front and center. His wider travels were reflected in *The Innocents Abroad* (1869), *A Connecticut Yankee in King Arthur's Court* (1889), and *Following the Equator* (1897). In 1894 Twain went into bankruptcy due to a failed investment in the Paige typesetting machine. His bleakest works date from that period: *The Man That Corrupted Hadleyburg* (1900), *What Is Man?* (1906), and *The Mysterious Stranger* (1916). The U.S. military intervention in the Philippines also added to that bleakness. From 1901 to 1910 Twain served as vice president of the American Anti-Imperialist League. His antiwar story "The War Prayer," rejected by *Harper's* in 1905, remained unpublished in his lifetime. His account of the Moro Massacre, *Incident in the Philippines*, excerpted here, was likewise unpublished until 1924.

This incident burst upon the world last Friday in an official cablegram from the commander of our forces in the Philippines to our Government at Washington. The substance of it was as follows: A tribe of Moros, dark-skinned savages, had fortified themselves in the bowl of an extinct crater not many miles from Jolo; and as they were hostiles, and bitter against us because we have been trying for eight years to take their liberties away from them, their presence in that position was a menace. Our commander, Gen. Leonard Wood, ordered a reconnaissance. It was found that the Moros numbered six hundred, counting women and children; that their crater bowl was in the summit of a peak or mountain twenty-two hundred feet above sea level, and very difficult of access for Christian troops and artillery. Then General Wood ordered a surprise, and went along himself to see the order carried out. Our troops climbed the heights by devious and difficult trails, and even took some artillery with them. The kind of artillery is not specified, but in one place it was hoisted up a sharp acclivity by tackle a distance of some three hundred feet. Arrived at the rim of the crater, the battle began. Our soldiers numbered five hundred and forty. They were assisted by auxiliaries consisting of a detachment of native constabulary in our pay—their numbers not given—and by a naval detachment, whose numbers are not stated. But apparently the contending parties were about equal as to number—six hundred men on our side, on the edge of the bowl; six hundred men, women and children in the bottom of the bowl. Depth of the bowl, 50 feet.

Gen. Wood's order was, "Kill or capture the six hundred."

The battle began—it is officially called by that name—our forces firing down into the crater with their artillery and their deadly small arms of precision; the savages furiously returning the fire, probably with brickbats—though this is merely a surmise of mine, as the weapons used by the savages are not nominated in the cablegram. Heretofore the Moros have used knives and clubs mainly; also ineffectual trade—muskets when they had any.

The official report stated that the battle was fought with prodigious energy on both sides during a day and a half, and that it ended with a complete victory for the American arms. The completeness of the victory for the American arms. The completeness of the victory is established by this fact: that of the six hundred Moros not one was left alive. The brilliancy of the victory is established by this other fact, to wit: that of our six hundred heroes only fifteen lost their lives.

General Wood was present and looking on. His order had been. "Kill *or* capture those savages." Apparently our little army considered that the "or" left them authorized to kill *or* capture according to taste, and that their taste had remained what it has been for eight years, in our army out there—the taste of Christian butchers.

The official report quite properly extolled and magnified the "heroism" and "gallantry" of our troops; lamented the loss of the fifteen who perished, and elaborated the wounds of thirty-two of our men who suffered injury, and even minutely and faithfully described the nature of the wounds, in the interest of future historians of the United States. It mentioned that a private had one of his elbows scraped by a missile, and the private's name was mentioned. Another private had the end of his nose scraped by a missile. His name was also mentioned—by cable, at one dollar and fifty cents a word.

Next day's news confirmed the previous day's report and named our fifteen killed and thirty-two wounded *again*, and once more described the wounds and gilded them with the right adjectives.

Let us now consider two or three details of our military history. In one of the great battles of the Civil War ten per cent. of the forces engaged on the two sides were killed and wounded. At Waterloo, where four hundred thousand men were present on the two sides, fifty thousand fell, killed and wounded, in five hours, leaving three hundred and fifty thousand sound and all right for further adventures. Eight years ago, when the pathetic comedy called the Cuban War was played, we summoned two hundred and fifty thousand men. We fought a number of showy battles, and when the war was over we had lost two hundred and sixty-eight men out of our two hundred and fifty thousand, in killed and wounded in the field, and just *fourteen times as many* by the gallantry of the army doctors in the hospitals and camps. We did not exterminate the Spaniards—far from it. In each engagement we left an average of *two per cent.* of the enemy killed or crippled on the field.

Contrast these things with the great statistics which have arrived from that Moro crater! There, with six hundred engaged on each side, we lost fifteen men killed outright, and we had thirty-two wounded—counting that nose and that elbow. The enemy numbered six hundred—including women and children—and we abolished them utterly, leaving not even a baby alive to cry for its dead mother. *This is incomparably the greatest victory that was ever achieved by the Christian soldiers of the United States.*

Now then, how has it been received? The splendid news appeared with splendid display-heads in every newspaper in this city of four million and thirteen thousand inhabitants, on Friday morning. But there was not a single reference to it in the editorial columns of any one of those newspapers. The news appeared again in all the evening papers of Friday, and again those papers were editorially silent upon our vast achievement. Next day's additional statistics and particulars appeared in all the morning papers, and still without a line of editorial rejoicing or a mention of the matter in any way. These additions appeared in the evening papers of that same day (Saturday) and again without a word of comment. In the columns devoted to correspondence, in the morning and evening papers of Friday and Saturday, nobody said a word about the "battle." Ordinarily those columns are teeming with the passions of the citizen; he lets no incident go by, whether it be large or small, without pouring out his praise or blame, his joy or his indignation about the matter in the correspondence column. But, as I have said, during those two days he was as silent as the editors themselves. So far as I can find out, there was only one person among our eighty millions who allowed himself the privilege of a public remark on this great occasion—that was the President of the United States. All day Friday he was as studiously silent as the rest. But on Saturday he recognized that his duty required him to say something, and he took his pen and performed that duty. If I know President Roosevelt—and I am sure I do—this utterance cost him more pain and shame than any other that ever issued from his pen or his mouth. I am far from blaming him. If I had been in his place my official duty would have compelled me to say what he said. It was a convention, an old tradition, and he had to be loyal to it. There was no help for it. This is what he said:

> Washington, March 10. Wood, Manila: I congratulate you and the officers and men of your command upon the brilliant feat of arms wherein you and they so well upheld the honor of the American flag. (Signed) Theodore Roosevelt.

His whole utterance is merely a convention. Not a word of what he said came out of his heart. He knew perfectly well that to pen six hundred helpless and weaponless savages in a hole like rats in a trap and massacre them in detail during a stretch of a day and a half, from a safe position on the heights above, was no brilliant feat of arms—and would not have been a brilliant feat of arms even if Christian America, represented by its salaried soldiers, had shot them down with Bibles and the Golden Rule instead of bullets. He knew perfectly well that our uniformed assassins had *not* upheld the honor of the American flag, but had done as they have been doing continuously for eight years in the Philippines—that is to say, they had dishonored it.

The next day, Sunday,—which was yesterday—the cable brought us additional news—still more splendid news—still more honor for the flag. The first display-head shouts this information at us in the stentorian capitals: "WOMEN SLAIN MORO SLAUGHTER."

"Slaughter" is a good word. Certainly there is not a better one in the Unabridged Dictionary for this occasion.

The next display line says:

"With Children They Mixed in Mob in Crater, and All Died Together."

They were mere naked savages, and yet there is a sort of pathos about it when that word *children* falls under your eye, for it always brings before us our perfectest symbol of innocence and helplessness; and by help of its deathless eloquence color, creed and nationality vanish away and we see only that they are children—merely children. And if they are frightened and crying and in trouble, our pity goes out to them by natural impulse. We see a picture. We see the small forms. We see the terrified faces. We see the tears. We see the small hands clinging in supplication to the mother; but we do not see those children that we are speaking about. We see in their places the little creatures whom we know and love.

The next heading blazes with American and Christian glory like to the sun in the zenith:

"Death List is Now 900."
I was never so enthusiastically proud of the flag till now!

JOHN ASHBERY

Memories of Imperialism

John Ashbery (born 1927) has written more than twenty volumes of poetry in a style at once casual and oblique, seemingly prosaic and yet impossible to pin down. Educated at Harvard, he started out as a copywriter before traveling to France on a Fulbright scholarship in the 1950s. He lived there for ten years, working as the European art editor of the *New York Herald Tribune* while translating French murder mysteries to make ends meet. Returning to New York in 1963, he continued as an art critic for *Newsweek* and became friends with Andy Warhol. His poetry—from *Some Trees* (1956) to *The Tennis Court Oath* (1962) to *Three Poems* (1972), which contains long prose sections—was controversial but won major awards, including the Pulitzer Prize, the National Book Award, and the National Book Critics Circle Award for *Self-Portrait in a Convex Mirror* (1975). Ashbery also coauthored a novel, *A Nest of Ninnies* (1969). His art criticism is collected in *Reported Sightings* (1989); his Charles Eliot Norton Lectures in *Other Traditions* (2000). In the poem selected here, George Dewey, an American admiral who fought in the Spanish-American War, is whimsically mixed up with Melvil Dewey, the inventor of the Dewey Decimal System.

Dewey took Manila
and soon after invented the decimal system
that keeps libraries from collapsing even unto this day.
A lot of mothers immediately started naming their male
    offspring "Dewey,"
which made him queasy. He was already having second
    thoughts about imperialism.
In his dreams he saw library books with milky numbers
on their spines floating in Manila Bay.
Soon even words like "vanilla" or "mantilla" would cause him
    to vomit.
The sight of a manila envelope precipitated him
into his study, where all day, with the blinds drawn,
he would press fingers against temples, muttering "What have I done?"
all the while. Then, gradually, he began feeling a bit better.
The world hadn't ended. He'd go for walks in his old
    neighborhood,
marveling at the changes there, or at the lack of them. "If
    one is
to go down in history, it is better to do so for two things
rather than one," he would stammer, none too meaningfully.

One day his wife took him aside
in her boudoir, pulling the black lace mantilla from her head
and across her bare breasts until his head was entangled in
   it.
"Honey, what am I supposed to say?" "Say nothing, you big
   boob.
Just be glad you got away with it and are famous."
   "Speaking of
boobs . . ." "Now you're getting the idea. Go file those books
on those shelves over there. Come back only when you're finished."

EDITH WHARTON

Fighting France

Edith Wharton (1862–1937) wrote more than twenty novels as well as short stories, poetry, and nonfictional works, combining a sharp wit with a keen insight into the foibles of the privileged. Born to a wealthy New York family of English and Dutch ancestry, Wharton traveled widely through Europe as a child. Her first published book was *The Decoration of Houses*, cowritten with architect Ogden Codman, Jr. Among her most notable works are *The House of Mirth* (1905), *Ethan Frome* (1911), the Pultizer Prize–winning *The Age of Innocence* (1920), and an autobiography, *A Backward Glance* (1934). After her divorce, Wharton settled permanently in France in 1913 and did extensive volunteer work for the Allies during World War I. In 1916 she was named a Chevalier de la Légion d'honneur by the French government. Wharton died in France in 1937. This excerpt from *Fighting France* (1918) shows Wharton traveling through the war-ravaged countryside and paying a visit to a village church converted to a field hospital, where she was struck by the fervor of the singing and the lack of response from the wounded.

We came back to the high-road, and he asked us if we should like to see the church. It was about three o'clock, and in the low porch the curé was ringing the bell for vespers. We pushed open the inner doors and went in. The church was without aisles, and down the nave stood four rows of wooden cots with brown blankets. In almost every one lay a soldier—the doctor's "worst cases"—few of them wounded, the greater number stricken with fever, bronchitis, frost-bite, pleurisy, or some other form of trench-sickness too severe to permit of their being carried farther from the front. One or two heads turned on the pillows as we entered, but for the most part the men did not move.

The curé, meanwhile, passing around to the sacristy, had come out before the altar in his vestments, followed by a little white acolyte. A handful of women, probably the only "civil" inhabitants left, and some of the soldiers we had seen about the village, had entered the church and stood together between the rows of cots; and the service began. It was a sunless afternoon, and the picture was all in monastic shades of black and white and ashen grey: the sick under their earth-coloured blankets, their livid faces against the pillows, the black dresses of the women (they seemed all to be in mourning) and the silver haze floating out from the little acolyte's censer. The only light in the scene—the candle—gleams on the altar, and their reflection in the embroideries of the curé's chasuble—were like a faint streak of sunset on the winter dusk.

For a while the long Latin cadences sounded on through the church; but presently the curé took up in French the Canticle of the Sacred Heart, composed during the war of 1870, and the little congregation joined their trembling voices in the refrain:

"*Sauvez, sauvez la France,*
Ne l'abandonnez pas!"

The reiterated appeal rose in a sob above the rows of bodies in the nave: "*Sauvez, sauvez la France,*" the women wailed it near the altar, the soldiers took it up from the door in stronger tones; but the bodies in the cots never stirred, and more and more, as the day faded, the church looked like a quiet grave-yard in a battle-field.

RITA DOVE

The Return of Lieutenant James Reese Europe

Rita Dove (born 1952) served as poet laureate of the United States from 1993–1995 and was awarded the 2011 National Medal of Arts by President Obama. Her first collection of poetry, *The Yellow House on the Corner* (1980), was followed by many others, including *Museum* (1983), *On the Bus with Rosa Parks* (1999), and most recently, *Sonata Mulattica* (2009). With *Thomas and Beulah* (1986), she became the second African American poet to win the Pulitzer Prize. She has also written short stories, a book of essays, a novel, and a play, **The Darker Face of the Earth,** performed at the Kennedy Center in Washington, D.C., and the Royal National Theatre in London. Her song cycle, *Seven for Luck,* was premiered by the Boston Symphony Orchestra. In "The Return of Lieutenant James Reese Europe," from *American Smooth* (2004), Dove imagines the return of the acclaimed African American band leader from World War I to a New York that "didn't want us when we left" and "didn't want us coming back." For that New York, he would only play a "brisk French march," saving the real thing—jazz—for 110th Street and Lenox Avenue, the entry to Harlem.

(Victory Parade, New York City, February 1919.)

We trained in the streets: the streets where we came from.
We drilled with sticks, boys darting between bushes, shouting—
that's all you thought we were good for. We trained anyway.
In camp we had no plates or forks. First to sail, first to
join the French,
first to see combat with the shortest training time.

My, the sun is looking fine today.

We toured devastation, American good will
in a forty-four piece band. Dignitaries smiled; the wounded
settled back to dream. That old woman in St. Nazaire

who tucked up her skirts so she could "walk the dog."
German prisoners tapping their feet as we went by.
Miss Flatiron with your tall cool self: How do.

You didn't want us when we left but we went.
You didn't want us coming back but here we are,
stepping right up white-faced Fifth Avenue in a phalanx
(*no prancing, no showing of teeth, no swank*)
past the Library lions, eyes forward, tin hats aligned—

a massive, upheld human shield.

No jazz for you: We'll play a brisk French march
and show our ribbons, flash our *Croix de Guerre*
(yes, we learned French, too) all the way
until we reach 110th Street and yes! take our turn
onto Lenox Avenue and all those brown faces and then—

Baby, Here Comes Your Daddy Now!

MURIEL RUKEYSER

Mediterranean

Muriel Rukeyser (1913–1980), poet, journalist, and translator, was born
in New York City. As literary editor of Vassar's *Student Review* in 1931,
she covered the Scottsboro trial, the landmark case in Alabama involving the right to a fair trial of nine black youths accused of rape. She was
on assignment in Barcelona in 1936 to cover the People's Olympiad, an
alternative to the Nazis' Berlin Olympics, and witnessed the outbreak
of the Spanish Civil War. Back in the United States, she traveled to
Gauley Bridge, West Virginia, to investigate the Hawk's Nest Incident, an
industrial disaster resulting in an epidemic of silicosis. The testimonies

of the miners and their families, doctors, and social workers made up "The Book of the Dead," the centerpiece of her best-known work, *U.S. 1* (1938). As president of PEN in the 1970s, Rukeyser traveled to South Korea to protest the death sentence of the dissident poet Kim Chi-ha. In this poem from *Mediterranean* (1938), she describes her evacuation from Barcelona in the company of Belgian, Hungarian, and American volunteers in the International Brigades.

I

At the end of July, exile. We watched the gangplank go
cutting the boat away, indicating: sea.
Barcelona, the sun, the fire-bright harbor, war.
Five days.

Here at the rail, foreign and refugee,
we saw the city, remembered that zero of attack,
chase in the groves, snares through the olive hills,
rebel defeat: leaders, two regiments,
broadcasts of victory, tango, surrender.
The truckride to the city, barricades,
bricks pried at corners, rifle-shot in street,
car-burning, bombs, blank warnings, fists up, guns
busy sniping, the torn walls, towers of smoke.
And order making, committees taking charge, foreigners
commanded out by boat.

I saw the city, sunwhite flew on glass,
trucewhite from window, the personal lighting found
eyes on the dock, sunset-lit faces of singers,
eyes, goodbye into exile. Saw where Columbus rides
black-pillared: discovery, turn back, explore
a new-found Spain, coast-province, city-harbor.
Saw our parades ended, the last marchers on board
listed by nation.

I saw first of those faces going home into war
the brave man. Otto Boch, the German exile, knowing
he quieted tourists during machine-gun battle,
he kept his life straight as a single issue—
left at that dock we left, his gazing Breughel face,
square forehead and eyes, strong square breast fading,
the narrow runner's hips diminishing dark.
I see this man, dock, war, a latent image.

The boat *Ciudad di Ibiza*, built for two hundred,
loaded with five hundred, manned by loyal sailors,
chartered by Belgians when consulates were helpless,
through a garden of gunboats, margin of the port,
entered: Mediterranean.

LANGSTON HUGHES

Harlem Swing and Spanish Shells

Langston Hughes (1902–1967), a key figure of the Harlem Renaissance, was a newspaper columnist, short story writer, translator, and playwright as well as a poet. By the age of eighteen, he had already published his most celebrated poem, "The Negro Speaks of Rivers" (1921), invoking not only the Mississippi but also the Euphrates, the Congo, and the Nile. Many critical periods of his life were spent abroad, beginning with the summers he spent in Mexico as a teenager visiting his estranged father. After one year at Columbia University in 1920, he worked as a seaman in Europe and West Africa. He was part of a black delegation to the Soviet Union in 1932, traveling on to Central Asia, China, Japan, and Korea. He corresponded with poets from French Madagascar, French Guinea, Haiti, Cuba, and Mexico and translated their work. In 1937 Hughes reported on the Spanish Civil War for the *Baltimore Afro-American*. In "Harlem Swing and Spanish Shells," he describes decorous human conduct and the vibrant rhythms of jazz amid the extreme scarcity of food in a Madrid under siege. On a more disturbing note in "General Franco's Moors," he writes of the uncanny feeling of seeing black soldiers fighting on the Fascist side.

One of Franco's ways of getting back at besieged Madrid for holding out so tenaciously was to broadcast daily, from his powerful radio towers at Burgos or Seville, the luncheon and dinner menus of the big hotels there, the fine food that the Falangists were eating, and the excellent wines they drank. (Rioja and the best of wine areas were in Fascist hands.) One could almost hear rebel diners smacking their lips on the radio.

Since food was scarce in Madrid, I did not torture myself listening to Franco's succulent broadcasts. But I found myself thinking a great deal about hamburgers, hot dogs, sugared doughnuts and ice cream—things one can get on almost any American corner—not to speak of more substantial items like steak. In Madrid, when I got there, even with the proper ration cards, there was next to nothing to buy. The city was almost surrounded by Franco's troops, who were trying to starve the people out. I, after missing my first breakfast in the city, never missed another one.

Breakfast at the Alianza consisted of a single roll and "Malta coffee"—burnt grain, pulverized and brewed into a muddy liquid. Sometimes there was milk, but no sugar. Guillén and I had brought from Paris several bottles of saccharin tablets which we shared with the others as a sweetener. After breakfast one had the whole day uninterrupted by meals. I spent much of my time trying to discover bars that served tidbits with drinks. There were several that tried to do so each day, circumstances permitting, so by making the rounds between bombardments, I could manage sometimes to eat a small lunch of knickknacks before night. One very sedate old wine house on Alcala Zamora was still serving ancient expensive sherry—for very rare old sherry was all it had left in its cellars. Here they would attempt every day at five to serve something to go with the sherry—often only chestnuts or green almonds. But sometimes from the slaughter house, the venerable proprietor would secure the hearts, liver and lights of various animals and boil them, then slice them into little hunks to be speared with a toothpick. Each person might have a small saucer of these innards with his sherry. Almost all the writers at the Alianza were to be found in this dusky wood-panel old bar in the late afternoon talking about literature and trying not to seem unduly disturbed if the proprietor was unable to furnish anything that day but rare old sherry.

Dinner at the Alianza was beautifully served every evening and delicious, for the club had an excellent cook, who did her best to make what little she could purchase appetizing. She would create a wonderful soup out of almost nothing but a pot of water, a few herbs and some rancid olive oil. It became a very special soup if someone left a few crumbs or crusts of bread on the breakfast table. She would toast and fry these in olive oil at night and put them into the soup. Beans she could flavor superbly. Once in a blue moon we might have meat, a little cube, or a very thin slice for each person. Sometimes, but rarely, there was fresh fish from Valencia. I shall never forget one night when we had fish; we had also a very special guest. He was a venerable Spanish scholar, soft-spoken and grey-haired, who had arrived in Madrid from Valencia, probably on the same truck that brought the city's ration of fish that day. Our distinguished guest had not been in Madrid before during the Civil War, so he had never experienced such slim food rations, since in Valencia people still ate fairly well. And there, of course, came plenty of fish directly from the sea.

When our ration of fish arrived on the table at the Alianza—a dozen beautifully fried but quite small smelts—and the platter was passed to our distinguished guest first, he simply raked all the fish into his own plate, thinking them a single service. As polite as Spaniards generally are, at this moment two or three persons at the table could not resist a groan of anguish. Someone even blurted out before thinking, "Ay, Señor, you've taken all the fish."

Our hostess, María Teresa León, who presided over the table, quickly and graciously said, "Oh, but they're yours, sir, prepared just for you." However, the bewildered guest could not help but notice the sad faces at the table, so he said, "But won't you all share mine?"

By now everyone had gotten their company manners back, and politely refused. "Oh, thank you, no, those are for you, dear friend, sweet visitor. *Bon apetit!* Eat well!"

A dozen little fish normally would have been a rather small serving for even one person in Spain—just a starter preceding the meat course. In Valencia one person might even in war time have that many fish for a meal. But in Madrid, where everything had to come into the city by trucks using precious gasoline, and over a shell-raked road, it was another matter. Our embarrassed guest entreated in vain that we share his fish. No, we would not! We stuck to the fiction that they were prepared *just* for him. Fortunately, a bowl of *garbanzos,* big old Spanish cowpeas, arrived on the table, so we each had a helping of those for dinner, plus an onion. I never ate so many raw onions in my life as I did that summer. Onions and grapes were the only things to eat that were at all plentiful in Madrid. Sometimes the grapes were very sour and green, but we ate them voraciously.

Beans and onions and grapes at the Alianza were all elegantly brought to table in priceless old china belonging to the marquis who was with Franco in Burgos. I suppose he has gotten all his beautiful dishes back now after the war, as well as his lovely tapestries and priceless El Grecos on the walls. As head of the Alianza, Rafael Alberti was most careful of its belongings. And everybody's heart bled when a cup or something was broken, which didn't happen often, but when it did the fault usually lay with the club's collective son, Luis, a war orphan the Alianza had adopted. Luis was a gentle boy of sixteen who tried to be as careful as he could, but it seemed his fate to almost always be tripping over a rung near a Venetian mirror, dropping something, or tearing the page of an old book just by looking at it. The writers and artists in the house nicknamed the boy, El Destroyer. But because he had seen his whole family wiped out in a bombing raid on his village, nobody scolded him. Usually María Teresa just asked him to *please* be very careful.

At first I thought perhaps the youngster was just careless, until I saw a series of little mishaps, one after another, overtake him through no fault of his own; the lad was accident prone. One night I witnessed what must have been for an adolescent, the most embarrassing moment of his life. This was the evening when the main salon of the mansion, seldom used, had been opened in honor of the visit to Madrid of two American Congressmen, Henry O'Connell of Montana and James T. Bernard from Minnesota. For these American dignitaries the intellectuals of wartime Madrid held a reception at the Alianza. Everybody put on their best clothes for the occasion. After we had all shaken hands with the visiting Americans, there was to be an hour of music. The large drawing room was crowded with visitors, including General Miaja, the defender of Madrid. All went well until the very moment when the music was to begin. As the Congressmen took their seats, the rest of the assemblage found places, too, including El Destroyer. He sat down unobtrusively on one of the little antique golden Louis XV chairs in an out-of-the-way corner near the tail of the grand piano. This chair, generations old, must have held many people in its time. But of all nights, tonight was the night the chair decided to cease performing its function. Just as the first note was about to be struck on the piano and the dignified soprano faced her quiet listeners, with an unduly loud splintering of its tiny legs, the Louis XV chair suddenly gave way beneath the young Spaniard. It sank to the floor with a loud crash, carrying with it an astonished adolescent.

El Destroyer loved American jazz. But fortunately my records were locked away safe from breakage, with the marquis's symphonies in the recreation house across the courtyard from the mansion itself. This room had a splendid record player with modern amplification and was seldom used except during a very heavy shelling of the city. The shells generally came from the west where Franco's artillery was situated. This recreation house was on the western side of the court, protected by a much taller building adjoining it. Shells would have to penetrate this larger building before striking the recreation rooms. So this house was considered by the residents of the Alianza as the safest place to be during a *bombardeo*. When heavy shells began to whistle too near our mansion, or explode within wall-trembling distance, Maria Teresa would get the key to the game room and we would all gather there and listen to music until the bombardment ceased. Before I came, Harry Dunham told me, they had listened mostly to Beethoven, Brahms, or Wagnerian overtures. But when I appeared with a box full of swing music, folks would call for Benny Goodman, Duke Ellington, Lunceford or Charlie Barnet. Certainly in intensity and volume my records were much better than the marquis's symphonies for drowning out the sound of Franco's shells exploding in the streets outside.

The first heavy night shelling of Madrid after my arrival occurred at about two o'clock in the morning. Busy on an article for the *Afro-American,* I had not yet gone to bed, and was rather fascinated to watch from my window artillery flashes in the distance, then a split second later to hear a shell whistling overhead. Artillery bombardments never frightened me nearly so much as air raids. There were no baleful warning sirens, screeching eerily, to make the flesh crawl as there were before air raids. The big guns simply started to go off—and that was that. But this night shells soon began to fall near the Alianza. Suddenly a projectile landed at our very corner with a terrific explosion, like a thousand tons of dynamite. I jumped up from my typewriter and started downstairs.

Usually at the Alianza no one bothered to get out of bed during a late bombardment. But this bombardment was so intense that almost everyone gathered for company across the court in the recreation hall. As usual, someone began to play records to drown out the sound of the explosions. The amplifier was turned up very loud—so loud in fact, that unless a shell had fallen in the courtyard, we could hardly have heard it. The automatic record player would repeat a disc innumerable times if one wished. So that night of the big bombardment, the Jimmie Lunceford record we kept going continuously until almost dawn was "Organ Grinder's Swing."

LANGSTON HUGHES

General Franco's Moors

"Imagine," said the Madrileños, "that rebel Franco bringing Mohammedans to Spain to fight Christians! The Crusaders would turn over in their graves. The Moors are back in Spain."

With Dick Mowrer and Leland Stowe, I visited a prison hospital in Madrid and saw my first Moor. We had gone to interview some captured German aviators and Italian ground troops. The Germans were in one ward and the Italians in another. The Italians were the most talkative. They said they had come to Spain because Mussolini had sent them. They had no choice in the matter, and they seemed to have no idea what the war was about—or if they did have, they were careful not to express themselves. They were amiable young fellows, stocky and rough-looking, probably peasants at home or unskilled workers. The Germans, on the other hand, were much less communicative. They had been sent to fight communism, they said, and yes, they bombed cities full of women and children. An airman had to take orders, *nein?* But one of them said that now he knew what a bombardment felt like, as he lay there in this prison hospital that had been struck by fourteen shells.

It was a hot day and smelly in the hospital wards. Since I didn't understand German or Italian well, and the other reporters were dragging out their interviews a very long time, I decided to walk down the corridor and see if I could find some water. If I missed anything, Stowe or Mowrer would tell me later. The hospital hall was empty. But as I got almost to the end where the hall turned, around the corner came one of the darkest, tallest men I have ever seen in my life. His blackness was accentuated by a white hospital gown flopping about his bare legs, and a white bandage around his head. Not having seen a Negro since I'd been in Madrid, the sudden sight of this very dark face almost startled me out of my wits. There at the corner of the corridor the man and I would have collided, had I not stopped in my tracks as he passed me without a word, silently like a black ghost.

I was a bit ashamed of myself for having been startled at the unexpected sight of a dark face in a hospital I had thought filled only with white prisoners. I thought of how once, when I had been walking with some other fellows along a bayou in Louisiana, a white woman had looked out of her hut and cried. "You colored boys get away from here. I'm scared of you." Now, here I was—a Negro myself—suddenly frightened by another dark face!

When I got back to the German ward and asked the nurse about the man I had seen, she said there were a number of Moors in another part of the hospital. While Mowrer and Stowe continued to talk to the Germans, I went with the nurse to find them. In a big room with three rows of cots, a number of Moors sat on their beds in white wrappings and bandages, while others lay suffering quietly, too badly wounded to be up. It was almost impossible for me to carry on any sort of conversation with them. They spoke little or no Spanish and I had no interpreter with me. But finally I came across a small boy who had been wounded at the Battle of Brunete. He looked to be a lad of ten or eleven, a bright smiling child, who spoke Spanish.

"Where did you come from?" I asked.

He named a town I'd never heard of in Morocco.

"How old are you?"

"Thirteen," he said.

"And how did you happen to be fighting in Spain?"

"I came with my mother," he said.

"Your mother?" I exclaimed, for that was the first time I had heard of Moorish women being brought to Spain. The rebels, I learned later, imported women as well as men—women to accompany the troops, to wash and cook for them behind the lines.

"What happened to your mother?"

The little boy closed his eyes. "She was killed at Brunete," he said.

The Moorish troops were colonial conscripts, or men from the Moroccan villages enticed into the army by offers of what seemed to them very good pay. Franco's personal bodyguard consisted of Moorish soldiers, tall picturesque fellows in flowing robes and winding turbans. Before I left home American papers had carried photographs of turbanned Mohammedan troops marching in the streets of Burgos, Seville and Malaga. And a United Press dispatch from Gibraltar that summer said:

Arabs have been crossing the Straits of Gibraltar from Spanish Morocco to Algeciras and Malaga at the rate of 300 to 400 a day, according to reliable information reaching here. General Franco intends to mass 50,000 new Arab troops in Spain so that he can maintain the strength of the Nationalist army should the Italian volunteers be withdrawn.

According to Madrid papers these shiploads of Moorish mercenaries from Larache provided a strange union of the Cross and the Crescent against Spanish democracy. The Falangist papers reaching Madrid were most religious, even running in their advertisements slogans such as VIVA CRISTO REY! VIVA FRANCO! as if Christ and the General were of equal importance. On the cover of the book, *España en la Cruz*, published in rebel territory, the map of Spain was pictured crucified on an enormous cross by the nails of Marxism, Judaism and Masonry, which the book claimed formed the core of the Loyalist government. Yet the Franco insurrectionists, in spite of their Christian cast, had encamped thousands of pagan Moors at Casa del Campo. And General Queipo de Llano was said to have promised one girl in Madrid to each twenty Moors. But I could not find that the enemy's use of these colored troops had brought about any increased feeling of color consciousness on the part of the people of Spain. I was well received everywhere I went, and the Negroes in the International Brigades reported a similar reception.

Negroes were not strange to Spain, nor did they attract an undue amount of attention. In the cities no one turned around to look twice. Most Spaniards had seen colored faces, and many are quite dark themselves. Distinct traces of Moorish blood from the days of the Mohammedan conquest remain in the Iberian Peninsula. Copper-colored Gypsies like La Niña de los Peines are common. There were, too, quite a number of colored Portuguese living in Spain. And in both Valencia and Madrid I saw pure-blooded Negroes from the colonies in Africa, as well as many Cubans who had migrated to Spain.

All the Negroes, of whatever nationality, to whom I talked, agreed that there was not the slightest trace of color prejudice in Spain. In that respect they said it was even better than France because in Paris, charming city that it is, some of the big hotels catering to tourists will not register dark-skinned guests. Negro jazz musicians told me that they enjoyed performing in Spain where audiences are most cordial. I found, shortly after my arrival, that one of the most popular variety stars in Madrid was El Negro Aquilino, a Cuban, who played both jazz and flamenco on the saxophone. Aquilino was then in his third month at the Teatro Calderon, and appeared on the same bill with the famous Pastora Imperio, the great dancer who remained on the Loyalist side. Aquilino traveled all over government Spain, and was a great favorite with the soldiers for whom he played at the front. When I went backstage to interview him for my paper, I asked him about color in Spain. He said, "Color? *No le hace nada en España*—it doesn't matter."

Sometimes, amusingly enough, American Negroes in Brigade uniforms were asked if they were Moors fighting on the Loyalist side. One young Negro, Walter Cobb, had a big scare behind the lines on the Aragon front where he was the only American with a French brigade. Cobb spoke both French and Spanish.

"I have to keep in practice with my languages in this man's country," he said. "If I hadn't known Spanish in the last action, I'd have been taken for a Moor and made a prisoner. Man, I was driving a captured Franco truck that we took at Belchite one night, bringing it back behind our own lines to be repaired, and I hadn't had a chance to paint out the Falangist markings on it. I hadn't gone but a few kilometers in the dark before some Loyalist soldiers on patrol duty, Spanish boys, stopped me at a crossroads and threw their flashlights on the truck. When they saw me, dark as I am, and saw that truck with those Fascist insignias on it, they thought sure I was a Moor that had got lost and come across the lines by accident. They yelled at me to jump down quick with my hands up, and they held their guns cocked at my head until I got off that truck. Man, I started talking Spanish right away, explained I was an International. So they let me show them my papers and tell them how we captured that truck from the Fascists, and that it belonged to us now. Then, man, they almost hugged me! But suppose I didn't keep in practice with my Spanish? As much like a Moor as I look, I might have been dead, driving a Franco truck! It pays to *habla español*."

In Arguelles, I saw two posters in a classroom for the Spanish soldiers of the 14th Battalion training to fight the Moors. One poster said: LIKE THE SPANISH PEASANTS, THE INDUSTRIOUS AND DECENT MOOR DOES NOT TAKE UP A GUN, HE TILLS THE SOIL. And the other poster declared: THE MOORS ON THE SIDE OF THE FALANGISTS DO NOT KNOW THEY ARE FIGHTING AGAINST THE REAL SPANISH REVOLUTION. WORKERS, HELP US! RESPECT THE MOORISH PRISONERS.

The International Brigaders were, of course, aware of the irony of the colonial Moors—victims themselves of oppression in North Africa—fighting against a Republic that had been seeking to work out a liberal policy toward Morocco. To try to express the feelings of some of the Negro fighting men in this regard, I wrote these verses in the form of a letter from an American Negro in the Brigades to a relative in Dixie:

INTERNATIONAL BRIGADES, LINCOLN BATTALION, SOMEWHERE IN SPAIN, 1937

Dear Brother at home:
We captured a wounded Moor today.
He was just as dark as me.
I said, Boy, what you doin' here,
Fightin' against the free?
He answered something in a language
I couldn't understand.
But somebody told me he was sayin'
They grabbed him in his land
And made him join the Fascist army
And come across to Spain.
And he said he had a feelin'
He'd never get back home again.
He said he had a feelin'
This whole thing wasn't right.
He said he didn't know

These folks he had to fight.
And as he lay there dyin'
In a village we had taken,
I looked across to Africa
And I seen foundations shakin'—
For if a free Spain wins this war,
The colonies, too, are free—
Then something wonderful can happen
To them Moors as dark as me.
I said, Fellow, listen,
I guess that's why old England
And I reckon Italy, too,
Is afraid to let Republic Spain
Be good to me and you—
Because they got slaves in Africa
And they don't want 'em free.
Listen, Moorish prisoner—
Here, shake hands with me!
I knelt down there beside him
And I took his hand,
But the wounded Moor was dyin'
So he didn't understand.

PHILIP LEVINE

To P.L., 1916–1930.
A Solder of the Republic

Philip Levine (1928–2015), the eighteenth poet laureate of the United States, was strongly associated with working-class Detroit, writing gritty, fiercely unsentimental poetry. After going through the public schools and Wayne State University, he took a number of industrial jobs, including the night shift at the Chevrolet Gear and Axle factory, reading and writing in his off hours. In 1953 he studied with John Berryman and Robert Lowell at the Iowa Writers' Workshop, publishing his debut collection, *On the Edge*, in 1963. He wrote many other works, including *News of the World* (2009); *Breath* (2004); *The Mercy* (1999); the Pulitzer Prize–winning *The Simple Truth* (1994); the National Book Award–winning *What Work Is* (1991); *A Walk with Tom Jefferson* (1988); and *Ashes* (1979), which won the National Book Award and the National Book Critics Circle Award. He also translated from the Spanish *Off the Map: Selected Poems of Gloria Fuertes* (1984) and *Tarumba: The Selected Poems of Jaime Sabines* (2007). This selection from *They Feed They Lion* (1972) pays tribute to the Spanish Civil War by refusing to romanticize it.

Gray earth peeping through snow,
you lay for three days
with one side of your face
frozen to the ground. They tied your cheek
with the red and black scarf
of the Anarchists, and bundled you
in canvas, and threw you away.
Before that an old country woman
of the Aragon, spitting on her thumb
rubbing it against her forefinger,
stole your black Wellingtons,
the gray hunting socks, and the long
slender knife you wore
in a little leather scabbard
riding your right hip. She honed it,
ran her finger down the blade, and laughed
though she had no meat to cut,
blessing your tight fists
that had fallen side by side
like frozen faces on your hard belly
that was becoming earth. (Years later
she saw the two faces

at table, and turned from the bread
and the steaming oily soup, turned
to the darkness of the open door,
and opened her eyes to darkness
so that they might be filled with anything
but those two faces squeezed
in the blue of the snow and snow and snow.)
She blessed your feet, still pink,
with hard yellow shields of skin
at heel and toe, and she laughed
scampering across the road, into
the goat field, and up the long hill,
the boots bundled in her skirts,
and the gray hunting socks, and the knife.
For seven weeks she wore the boots
stuffed with rags at toe and heel,
she thought she understood
why you lay down to rest
even in snow, and gave them to a nephew,
and the gray socks too.
The knife is still used, the black handle
almost white, the blade
worn thin since there is meat to cut.
Without laughter she is gone
ten years now,
and on the road to Huesca in spring
there is no one to look for you
among the wild jonquils, the curling
grasses at the road side,
and the blood red poppies, no one
to look on the farthest tip
of wind breathing down from the mountains
and shaking the stunted pines you hid among.

GERTRUDE STEIN

Brewsie and Willie

Gertrude Stein (1874–1946) wrote novels, poems, plays, and essays that challenged the genres they invoke. After studying philosophy and psychology at Harvard under William James and publishing her first essay, "Normal Motor Automatism," as an undergraduate, Stein enrolled at the Johns Hopkins Medical School before moving to Europe with her brother Leo. Her long expatriate career was marked by close friendships with artists such as Henri Matisse and Pablo Picasso. Her most popular work, *The Autobiography of Alice B. Toklas* (1933), written in the chatty tones of her lifelong companion, offers a bemused account of the Parisian scene, a departure from the abstract, riddling style that characterized earlier works such as *Three Lives* (1909) and *Tender Buttons* (1914). The volunteer work that she and Toklas did during World War I is also detailed in that faux-autobiography. The extent of her collaboration with the Vichy regime during World War II has recently come under scrutiny. This excerpt from *Brewsie and Willie* (1946), Stein's last work, inspired by her contact with G.I.s, makes fun of the muddle-headedness of jingoistic sentiments.

You know Willie, said Brewsie, I think we are all funny, pretty funny, about this fraternisation business, now just listen. They did not have to make any anti-fraternisation ruling for the German army in France because although the Germans did their best to fraternise, no French woman would look or speak to them or recognise their existence. I kind of wonder would our women be like French or be like Germans, if the horrible happened and our country was conquered and occupied.

WILLIE: Well I wouldn't want any American woman to be like a Frenchwoman.

BREWSIE: No you would want them to be like the Germans, sleep with the conquerors.

WILLIE: You get the hell out of here, Brewsie. No American woman would sleep with a foreigner.

BREWSIE: But you admire the Germans who do. Which do you want American women to be like.

WILLIE: I know what I dont want them to be like, I dont want them to be like any lousy foreigner.

BREWSIE: But all your fathers and mothers were lousy foreigners.

WILLIE: You get the hell out of here, Brewsie. What's that to you, I am going to sleep with any German wench who'll sleep with me and they all will.

BREWSIE: Sure they all will but all the same if the horrible happened and our country was defeated and occupied, how about it.

WILLIE: Well our country isnt going to be defeated and occupied, that's all there is to that.

BREWSIE: Yes but you never can tell in a war.

WILLIE: And that's the reason there aint going to be any more war not if I can help it.

BREWSIE: But if you cant help it.

WILLIE: I'll see to it that I do help it, there aint going to be any more war.

BREWSIE: But that's what they said last time and hell here we are.

WILLIE: Well did I say we werent here, we're here all right, you betcha we're here, and I am going to sleep with any German girl who'll sleep with me, and they all will and that's what I call fraternisation, and they let us do it and we're doing it.

T. S. ELIOT

"Little Gidding," from *Four Quartets*

T. S. [Thomas Stearns] Eliot (1888–1965), awarded the 1948 Nobel Prize for "his outstanding, pioneer contribution to present-day poetry," was born in St. Louis and educated at Harvard, the Sorbonne, and Oxford, studying philosophy and Sanskrit. He gave shape and impetus to the Modernist movement with the publication of "The Love Song of J. Alfred Prufrock"

(1917). This was followed by "The Waste Land" (1922), heavily edited by Ezra Pound and dedicated to that poet. With its celebrated opening line— "April is the cruelest month"—"The Waste Land" is often cited as the most influential poem of the twentieth century, the counterpart to James Joyce's *Ulysses*, published the same year. "The Hollow Men" (1925), "Ash Wednesday" (1930), and *Four Quartets* (1945) are among his best-known subsequent works, along with plays such as *Murder in the Cathedral* (1935) and *The Cocktail Party* (1949), winner of the 1950 Tony Award for best play. The excerpt here is from "Little Gidding," a section of *Four Quartets* set against the London Blitz, described by Eliot in religious language as the descent of the "dark dove" with its "flame of incandescent terror."

Ash on an old man's sleeve
Is all the ash the burnt roses leave.
Dust in the air suspended
Marks the place where a story ended.
Dust inbreathed was a house—
The walls, the wainscot and the mouse,
The death of hope and despair,
This is the death of air.

KURT VONNEGUT

Slaughterhouse-Five

Kurt Vonnegut (1922–2007) is best known for novels such as *Cat's Cradle* (1963), *Slaughterhouse-Five* (1969), and *Breakfast of Champions* (1973), a heady brew of sardonic wit, narrative salvo, and science fiction. Born in Indianapolis to third-generation German American parents, Vonnegut joined the U.S. Army while studying at Cornell. After being captured in 1944 at the Battle of the Bulge when his infantry division, the 106th, was cut off, he was held as a prisoner of war in an underground meat locker in Dresden when that city was firebombed. That event, the emotional pivot of *Slaughterhouse-Five*, would reappear in at least six other novels. Many of his characters also recur, notably Kilgore Trout, a pulp science fiction writer. Vonnegut did graduate work in anthropology at the University of Chicago, turning in *Cat's Cradle* as his master's thesis. He was also a serious graphic artist, evident in the felt-tip pen illustrations in *Breakfast for Champions* and the album cover he designed for the rock band Phish: *Hook, Line, and Sinker.* This selection from *Slaughterhouse-Five* offers a terse report on the destruction of Dresden.

He was down in the meat locker on the night that Dresden was destroyed. There were sounds like giant footsteps above. Those were sticks of high-explosive bombs. The giants walked and walked. The meat locker was a very safe shelter. All that happened down there was an occasional shower of calcimine. The Americans and four of their guards and a few dressed carcasses were down there, and nobody else. The rest of the guards had, before the raid began, gone to the comforts of their own homes in Dresden. They were all being killed with their families.

So it goes.

The girls that Billy had seen naked were all being killed, too, in a much shallower shelter in another part of the stockyards.

So it goes.

A guard would go to the head of the stairs every so often to see what it was like outside, then he would come down and whisper to the other guards. There was a firestorm out there. Dresden was one big flame. The one flame ate everything organic, everything that would burn.

It wasn't safe to come out of the shelter until noon the next day. When the Americans and their guards did come out, the sky was black with smoke. The sun was an angry little pinhead. Dresden was like the moon now, nothing but minerals. The stones were hot. Everybody else in the neighborhood was dead.

So it goes.

The guards drew together instinctively, rolled their eyes. They experimented with one expression and then another, said nothing, though their mouths were often open. They looked like a silent film of a barbershop quartet.

"So long forever," they might have been singing, "old fellows and pals; So long forever, old sweethearts and pals—God bless 'em—"

JONATHAN SAFRAN FOER

Extremely Loud and Incredibly Close

Jonathan Safran Foer (born 1977) grew up in Washington, D.C., the son of Albert Foer, a lawyer, and the Polish-born Esther Safran Foer, a child of Holocaust survivors. With the encouragement of his teacher Joyce Carol Oates, he published his Princeton Creative Writing senior thesis as his first novel, *Everything Is Illuminated* (2002). His second novel, *Extremely Loud and Incredibly Close* (2005), tells the story of 9/11 through the feverish voice of nine-year-old Oskar Schell, interwoven with the World War II story of Oskar's grandparents, and sprinkled throughout with visual material from photographs of doorknobs to a fourteen-page flip book at the end. Foer taught fiction writing at Yale in 2008 and now teaches in the Graduate Writing Program at New York University. He wrote a nonfiction work, *Eating Animals*, in 2009, followed by his third novel, *Tree of Codes* (2010), a "sculptural object" created by carving out words from his favorite novel, Bruno Schulz's *Street of Crocodiles*. This excerpt is from *Extremely Loud and Incredibly Close*, a searing account of the destruction of Dresden.

One hundred planes flew overhead, massive, heavy planes, pushing through the night like one hundred whales through water, they dropped clusters of red flares to light up the blackness for whatever was to come next, I was alone on the street, the red flares fell around me, thousands of them, I knew that something unimaginable was about to happen, I was thinking of Anna, I was overjoyed. I ran downstairs four steps at a time, they saw the look on my face, before I had time to say anything—what would I have said?—we heard a horrible noise, rapid, approaching explosions, like an applauding audience running toward us, then they were atop us, we were thrown to the corners, our cellar filled with fire and smoke, more powerful explosions, the walls lifted from the floor and separated just long enough to let light flood in before banging back to the ground, orange and blue explosions, violet and white, I later read that the first bombing lasted less than half an hour, but it felt like days and weeks, like the world was going to end, the bombing stopped as matter of factly as it had began, "Are you OK?" "Are you OK?" "Are you OK?" We ran out of the cellar, which was flooded with yellow-gray smoke, we didn't recognize anything, I had been on the stoop just half an hour before, and now there was no stoop in front of no house on no street, only fire in every direction, all that remained of our house was a patch of the facade that stubbornly held up the front door, a horse on fire galloped past, there were burning vehicles and carts with burning refugees, people were screaming, I told my parents I had to go find Anna, my mother told me to stay with them, I said I would meet them back at our front door, my father begged me to stay, I grabbed the doorknob and it took the skin off my hand, I saw the muscles of my palm, red and pulsing, why did I grab it with my other hand? My father shouted at me, it was the first time he had ever shouted at me, I can't write what he shouted, I told them I would meet them back at our door, he struck me across the face, it was the first time he had ever struck me, that was the last time I saw my parents. On my way to Anna's house, the second raid began, I threw myself into the nearest cellar, it was hit, it filled with pink smoke and gold flames, so I fled into the next cellar, it caught fire, I ran from cellar to cellar as each previous cellar was destroyed, burning monkeys screamed from the trees, birds with their wings on fire sang from the telephone wires over which desperate calls traveled, I found another shelter, it was filled to the walls, brown smoke pressed down from the ceiling like a hand, it became more and more difficult to breathe, my lungs were trying to pull the room in through my mouth, there was a silver explosion, all of us tried to leave the cellar at once, dead and dying people were trampled, I walked over an old man, I walked over children, everyone was losing everyone, the bombs were like a waterfall, ran through the streets, from cellar to cellar, and saw terrible things: legs and necks, I saw a woman whose blond hair and green dress were on fire, running with a silent baby in her arms, I saw humans melted into thick pools of liquid, three or four feet deep in places, I saw bodies crackling like embers, laughing, and the remains of masses of people who had tried to escape the firestorm by jumping head first into the lakes and ponds, the parts of their bodies that were submerged in the water were still intact, while the parts that protruded above water were charred beyond recognition, the bombs kept falling, purple, orange and white, I kept running, my hands kept bleeding, through the sounds of collapsing buildings I heard the roar of that baby's silence. I passed the zoo, the cages had been ripped open, everything was everywhere, dazed animals cried in pain and confusion, one of the keepers was calling out for help, he was a strong man, his eyes had been burnt closed, he grabbed my arm and asked me if I knew how to fire a gun, I told him I had to get to someone, he handed me his rifle and said, "You've got to find the carnivores," I told him I wasn't a good shot, I told him I didn't know which were carnivores and which weren't, he said, "Shoot everything," I don't know how many animals I killed, I killed an elephant, it had been thrown twenty yards from its cage, I pressed the rifle to the back of its head and wondered, as I squeezed the trigger, Is it necessary to kill this animal? I killed an ape that was perched on the stump of a fallen tree, pulling its hair as it surveyed the destruction, I killed two lions, they were standing side by side facing west, were they related, were they friends, mates, can lions love? I killed a cub that was climbing atop a massive dead bear, was it climbing atop its parent? I killed a camel with twelve bullets, I suspected it wasn't a carnivore, but I was killing everything, everything had to be killed, a rhinoceros was banging its head against a rock, again and again, as if to put itself out of its suffering, or to make itself suffer, I fired at it, it kept banging its head, I fired again, it banged harder, I walked up to it and pressed the gun between its eyes, I killed it, I killed a zebra, I killed a giraffe, I turned the water of the sea lion's tank red, an ape approached me, it was the ape I had shot before, I'd thought I'd killed it, it walked up to me slowly, its hands covering its ears, what did it want from me, I screamed, "What do you want from me?" I shot it again, where I thought its heart was, it looked at me, in its eyes I was sure I saw some form of understanding, but I didn't see forgiveness, I tried to shoot the vultures, but I wasn't a good enough shot, later I saw vultures fattening themselves on the human carnage, and I blamed myself for everything.

ART SPIEGELMAN

Maus

Art Spiegelman (born 1948), named by *Time* magazine as one of the "Top 100 Most Influential People" in 2005, is best known for *Maus*, a Holocaust story told through comics, and the first graphic novel to win a Pulitzer Prize. Born in Stockholm to Polish-Jewish parents, Spiegelman grew up in Queens as a devoted reader of *Mad* magazine. He became part of the Underground Comix movement while designing Wacky Packages for Topps Chewing Gum. In 1980 he and his wife, Françoise Mouly, began co-editing *Raw*, showcasing the work of avant-garde cartoonists such as Charles Burns. *Maus* was turned down by many publishers before Pantheon finally agreed to publish the first six chapters, entitled *Maus: A Survivor's Tale* (1986), followed by *Maus II: And Here My Troubles Began* (1991). These *New York Times* bestsellers inspired an exhibition at the Museum of Modern Art. Spiegelman worked at the *New Yorker* from 1992 to 2001 before leaving to work full-time on *In the Shadow of No Towers* (2004), his response to 9/11, another demonstration of his belief that comics are fully equipped to take on catastrophic events. In this excerpt from *Maus*, schematic divisions—Jews as mice, Germans as cats, and ethnic Poles as pigs—get tangled up when Anja encounters rats while hiding in the cellar.

SHE TOLD ME THESE TWO ACQUAINTANCES VISITED OFTEN TO HER ON THURSDAY EVENINGS... TODAY WAS MAYBE A MONDAY...

I DON'T GET IT... WASN'T HUNGARY AS DANGEROUS AS POLAND?

NO. FOR A LONGER TIME IT WAS **BETTER** THERE IN HUNGARY FOR THE JEWS... BUT THEN, NEAR THE VERY FINISH OF THE WAR, THEY ALL GOT PUT **ALSO** TO AUSCHWITZ.

I WAS THERE, AND I SAW IT. THOUSANDS - HUNDREDS OF THOUSANDS OF JEWS FROM HUNGARY...

SO MANY, IT WASN'T EVEN ROOM ENOUGH TO BURY THEM ALL IN THE OVENS.

BUT AT THAT TIME, WHEN I WAS THERE WITH KAWKA, WE COULDN'T **KNOW** THEN.

SO.... I WENT NEXT DAY TO DEKERTA STREET TO BUY FOOD...

OH GOD! OH GOD! MR. SPIEGELMAN, YOU'RE ALIVE! I'M SO GLAD TO SEE YOU!

MRS. MOTO-NOWA!

PRAISE MARY, YOU'RE SAFE! I COULDN'T **SLEEP**, I FELT SO GUILTY ABOUT CHASING YOU AND YOUR WIFE OUT.

I WANTED TO FIND A NEW CONNECTION TO HIDE US. BUT **REALLY** I DIDN'T THINK TO FIND AGAIN **HER**.

THE GESTAPO NEVER EVEN CAME TO MY HOUSE. I JUST PANICKED FOR NOTHING. PLEASE COME BACK AGAIN.

ANJA WAS GLAD OF GOING BACK. AND MOTONOWA ALSO...ALWAYS I PAID HER NICELY.

AND THAT SAME NIGHT WE SAID GOODBYE TO KAWKA AND WENT AGAIN TO SZOPIENICE.

BUT, THEN, MOTONOWA STOPPED TO COME DOWN.

IT'S BEEN 3 DAYS SINCE SHE BROUGHT ANY FOOD.

HERE...HAVE ANOTHER CANDY...

I HAD STILL CANDIES I ORGANIZED ON DEKERTA. ONLY *THIS* WE HAD TO EAT.

ALSO, HERE WE HAD NO PLACE WHERE TO WASH, SO ANJA GOT ON ALL HER SKIN A TERRIBLE RASH.

I DON'T KNOW WHAT'S WORSE- THE HUNGER OR THE ITCHING.

DON'T SCRATCH! IT ONLY- SHH!

CLIK

THE DOOR.

I'M SORRY I COULDN'T GET DOWN BEFORE...MY HUSBAND IS GETTING SUSPICIOUS.

HE ASKED WHY I GO TO THE CELLAR SO OFTEN. HE EVEN ASKED IF I WAS HIDING JEW$ HERE! ...HE WAS *JOKING*, BUT STILL...

ARE YOU ALL RIGHT HERE?

THERE ARE *RATS*, GIANT RATS! THEY'RE HORRIBLE!

WELL- YOU'RE BETTER OFF WITH THE RATS THAN WITH THE GESTAPO... AT LEAST THE RATS WON'T *KILL* YOU!

MMM...

AND SHE WAS RIGHT. WE WERE HAPPY EVEN TO HAVE *THESE* CONDITIONS.

AFTER THE TEN DAYS HER HUSBAND LEFT, AND SHE TOOK US BACK.

IT'S GOOD TO BE "HOME" EH, VLADEK?

IT'S A LOT NICER THAN THAT CELLAR.

BUT I DIDN'T FEEL SAFE HERE. IT WAS TOO MANY WAYS SOMEBODY COULD FIND US OUT. I WANTED TO GO BETTER TO HUNGARY.

SO, WHEN IT CAME THURSDAY, I WENT IN THE DIRECTION TO TAKE A STREETCAR TO SEE KAWKA IN SOSNOWIEC.

I HAD TO PASS WHERE SOME CHILDREN WERE PLAYING.

LOOK!

A JEW! A JEW!

THEY RAN SCREAMING HOME.

HELP! MOMMY! A JEW!!

A JEW!

THE MOTHERS ALWAYS TOLD SO: "BE CAREFUL! A JEW WILL CATCH YOU TO A BAG AND EAT YOU!" ... SO THEY TAUGHT TO THEIR CHILDREN.

I APPROACHED OVER TO THEM...

HEIL HITLER.

QUICK, THE MOTHERS CAME OUTSIDE TO SEE WHAT WAS!

IF I RAN AWAY THEY, WOULD SEE: "YES, IT *IS* A JEW HERE."

DON'T BE AFRAID, LITTLE ONES. I'M NOT A JEW. I WON'T HURT YOU.

SORRY, MISTER. YOU KNOW HOW KIDS ARE ... HEIL HITLER.

SO I CAME OUT WELL FROM THIS...

BUT THE EXPERIENCE COST ME REALLY A LOT OF HAIRS.

JORIE GRAHAM

Soldatenfriedhof

Jorie Graham (born 1950), poet and Boylston Professor of Oratory and
Rhetoric at Harvard, was born in New York, raised in Rome, and educated in Paris. She received an MFA from the Iowa Writers' Workshop.
Best known for her distinctive verse form, indentation, and spacing, her
poetry collections include *Hybrids of Plants and Ghosts* (1980), *The End
of Beauty* (1987), *Region of Unlikeness* (1991), *P L A C E* (2012), and the
Pulitzer Prize–winning *The Dream of the Unified Field: Selected Poems
1974–1992* (1995). Graham was awarded a MacArthur Fellowship in 1990.
She served as the chancellor of the Academy of American Poets from 1997
to 2003. The poem below, "Soldatenfriedhof," is from *Overlord* (2005), the
code name for the Battle of Normandy, the Allied operation that successfully invaded German-occupied France in June 1944. Visiting Normandy
sixty years later, the speaker in the poem tries to use a computer in the
German cemetery to locate the countless Kleins buried there.

"To find a fallen person," it says, "push green key."
Fill in name, last name, first name, I put in
Klein. 210 Kleins in the Soldatenfriedhof.
I scroll. Klein stays the same.
The first name changes, rank, row, plot.
No. The graveyard changes too. At 88 Kleins in
Colleville (U.S. graveyard). At 93 he's in the British one (Bayeux).
Have you found your fallen person says the program
when I go back to the home page. No slot for
nationality. None for religion. Just date of
birth
then rank, row, plot, and field come forth. I'm staring at
the soundless
screen. Keys very large for easy use.
Back through the doorway there's the
field. 21,222 German soldiers. Some named, some not.

Inside the office now a wide face looking up.
When is the last time a new man was found, I ask.
Here it is full, he says, people now go to St. André.
So there are no new bodies being found?
Oh no. No, no. Just last month eight—
here look, pulling a red file from a stack.
Look and it's open here, you'll see.
A name, a question mark, a print of teeth of which two
(lost after death) marked "lost after death." A plastic
baggie holds an oval metal tag, almost
illegible, now placed into
my hand. The other baggie he snaps open: here:
a button: we mostly tell them from the buttons:
this was a paratrooper: you can see from
the size, the color of the casing. The sleeve
of something other than time, I think,
slides open to reveal, nested, as in a pod, this seed, hard, dark, how does he
make out its
identity—a paratrooper—a German one each people's
buttons different—if it's a German, we get called if he is ours
we begin work whatever clothing still exists part of
a boot,
a lace, can get you back
the person—a metal clip—the stitching of a kind of
cloth. There were so many kinds of fiber then. Then
as much soil as we can get—bone fragments when there are—
how fast flesh turns to soil again—that is why clothing is
so good.
Where there are teeth too it is good—
we will be able to notify the family.
There is great peace in knowing your person is found.
Mostly in spring when the land is plowed.
Sometimes when they widen roads.
Many were put in with the apple trees.
One feels, from the way they are placed, the burying
was filled with kindness. I don't really know why, but it is
so. I turn the oval in my hand. Soil on it still, inside the chiseled number-

group, deeper

in the 3's and 8's, so that it's harder to make out the whole.

The boy is 17 he says.

What if he hadn't been found.

What if he is now found.

What does he re-enter.

Champigny-St.-André will receive

some earth, jaw, teeth, buttons, dog tag, an

insignia, hair, bones of most of one

right hand. When more than one have been found

together, the official of the graves registration department

—this man with soft large hands holding the folder out—

portions out enough human remains

to make up as many people as possible.

The possible person: a tooth is enough. Anything

will do

really, he says looking up, almost inaudibly.

With whom is he pleading.

Behind him now the field where in 1947 American bodies, and parts-of,
    put here

temporarily,

were dug up and moved for the final time

to their last resting place, to the American Normandy war memorial—

and these available German parts and wholes pulled from their

holding grounds and placed in openings Americans

released.

Forgive me says the man still in his seat,

I have been rude, I did not mean (gets up)

my name is————, here is my card.

May I hold the button a moment longer?

You from under the apple orchard,

you still not found in my field,

and the mole hacking through,

and the rabbits at dawn eating,

and the bird I cannot identify,

you, meaninglessness,

speak out—what do you hate—what do you hate—

WILLIAM FAULKNER

Two Soldiers

William Faulkner (1897–1962), awarded the 1949 Nobel Prize in Literature, is best known for *The Sound and the Fury* (1929), *As I Lay Dying* (1930), *Light in August* (1932), and *Absalom, Absalom!* (1936)—difficult, Modernist works with complex narrative structures. He also received the Pulitzer Prize for *A Fable* (1954) and *The Reivers* (1962) and the National Book Award for his *Collected Stories* (1951), from which "Two Soldiers" is excerpted. Raised, educated, and living most of his life in Oxford, Mississippi, Faulkner is often exclusively identified with the fictional Yoknapatawpha County, based on Lafayette Country near Oxford. However, he also spent considerable time in New Orleans in the 1920s, and as a screenwriter in Hollywood throughout the 1930s and 1940s. Between 1954 and 1961, he lectured in Japan, the Philippines, Greece, Iceland, and Latin America under the sponsorship of the State Department. In this excerpt, two brothers learned about the attack on Pearl Harbor as announced over the radio in Mississippi.

Me and Pete would go down to Old Man Killegrew's and listen to his radio. We would wait until after supper, after dark, and we would stand outside Old Man Killegrew's parlor window, and we could hear it because Old Man Killegrew's wife was deaf, and so he run the radio as loud as it would run, and so me and Pete could hear it plain as Old Man Killegrew's wife could, I reckon, even standing outside with the window closed.

And that night I said, "What? Japanese? What's a pearl harbor? and Pete said, "Hush."

And so we stood there, it was cold, listening to the fellow in the radio talking, only I couldn't make no heads nor tails neither out of it. Then the fellow said that would be all for a while, and me and Pete walked back up the road to home, and Pete told me what it was. Because he was nigh twenty and he had done finished the Consolidated last June and he knowed a heap: about them Japanase dropping bombs on Pearl Harbor and that Pearl Harbor was across the water.

"Across what water? I said. Across that Government reservoy up at Oxford?"

"Naw," Pete said. "Across the big water. The Pacific Ocean."

We went home. Maw and pap was already asleep, and me and Pete laid in the bed, and I still couldn't understand where it was, and Pete told me again—the Pacific Ocean.

"What's the matter with you?" Pete said. "You're going on nine years old. You been in school now ever since September. Ain't you learned nothing yet?"

"I reckon we ain't got as fer as the Pacific Ocean yet," I said.

We was still sowing the vetch then that ought to been all finished by the fifteenth of November, because pap was still behind, just like he had been ever since me and Pete had knowed him. And we had firewood to git in, too, but every night me and Pete would go down to Old Man Killegrew's and stand outside his parlor window in the cold and listen to his radio; then we would come back home and lay in the bed and Pete would tell me what it was. That is, he would tell me for a while. Then he wouldn't tell me. It was like he didn't want to talk about it no more. He would tell me to shut up because he wanted to go to sleep, but he never wanted to go to sleep.

He would lay there, a heap stiller than if he was asleep, and it would be something, I could feel it coming out of him, like he was mad at me even, only I knowed he wasn't thinking about me, or like he was worried about something, and it wasn't that neither, because he never had nothing to worry about. He never got behind like pap, let alone stayed behind. Pap give him ten acres when he graduated from the Consolidated, and me and Pete both reckoned pap was durn glad to get shut of at least ten acres, less to have to worry with himself; and Pete had them ten acres all sowed to vetch and busted out and bedded for the winter, and so it wasn't that. But it was something. And still we would go down to Old Man Killegrew's every night and listen to his radio, and they was at it in the Philippines now, but General MacArthur was holding um. Then we would come back home and lay in the bed, and Pete wouldn't tell me nothing or talk at all. He would just lay there still as a ambush and when I would touch him, his side or his leg would feel hard and still as iron, until after a while I would go to sleep.

Then one night—it was the first time he had said nothing to me except to jump on me about not chopping enough wood at the wood tree where we was cutting—he said, "I got to go."

"Go where? "I said.

"To that war," Pete said.

"Before we even finish gettin' in the firewood?"

"Firewood, hell," Pete said.

"All right," I said. "When we going to start?"

But he wasn't even listening. He laid there, hard and still as iron in the dark. "I got to go," he said. "I jest ain't going to put up with no folks treating the Unity States that way."

"Yes," I said. "Firewood or no firewood, I reckon we got to go."

This time he heard me. He laid still again, but it was a different kind of still.

"You? "he said. "To a war?"

"You'll whup the big uns and I'll whup the little uns," I said.

Then he told me I couldn't go. At first I thought he just never wanted me tagging after him, like he wouldn't leave me go with him when he went sparking them girls of Tull's. Then he told me the Army wouldn't leave me go because I was too little, and then I knowed he really meant it and that I couldn't go nohow noways. And somehow I hadn't believed until then that he was going himself, but now I knowed he was and that he wasn't going to leave me go with him a-tall.

"I'll chop the wood and tote the water for you-all then!" I said. "You got to have wood and water!"

NORMAN MAILER

The Naked and the Dead

Norman Mailer (1923–2007) won wide acclaim with his first novel, *The Naked and the Dead* (1948), which was partly based on his World War II experience in the Philippines. Fiction mixed with nonfiction would always be his signature style. Mailer helped found the *Village Voice* and promoted a "New Journalism," combining autobiography, social commentary, and eyewitness reports, showcased in *Armies of the Night* (1968), a colorful account of the 1967 March on the Pentagon, and

The Executioner's Song (1979), a novelization of the life of murderer Gary Gilmore. Both received the Pulitzer Prize. Mailer took up many causes, from anti–Vietnam War activism to later support for Salman Rushdie under threat of a fatwa. His novels, including *Ancient Evenings* (1983), featuring Egypt in 1100 BCE, and *Harlot's Ghost* (1991), a history of the CIA, were consistent best-sellers. This excerpt from *The Naked and the Dead* asks why the maiming of an insect is disturbing when humans are killed with relative ease.

Back at 2d Battalion, Wyman had just wounded an insect. It was a long hairy caterpillar with black and gold coloring, and he had jabbed a twig into its body. The caterpillar began to run about in circles and then flopped over on its back. It was struggling desperately to right itself until Wyman held his burning cigarette near the insect's back. The insect writhed, and lay prostrate again, its back curled into an L and its legs thrashing helplessly in the air. It looked as if it were trying desperately to breathe.

Ridges had watched this with displeasure, his long dumpy face wrinkled in a scowl. "That ain't the right way to treat a bug," he said.

Wyman was absorbed in the convulsions of the insect, and the interruption irritated him. He felt a trace of shame. "What do you mean, Ridges? What the hell's so important about a bug?"

"Shoot," Ridges sighed, "'tain't doin' you no harm. Jus' mindin' its own business."

Wyman turned to Goldstein. "The preacher's gettin' all excited over a bug." He laughed sarcastically, and then said, "Killin' one of Gawd's creatures, huh?"

Goldstein shrugged. "Every man has his own viewpoint," he said gently.

Ridges lowered his head stubbornly. "Not sayin' 'tain't hard to make fun of a man if he believes in the written Word."

"You eat meat, don't ya?" Wyman demanded. He was pleased to have the better arguments, for usually he felt inferior to most of the men in the squad. "Where the hell's it say you can eat meat but you can't kill a bug?"

"Meat ain't the same. Y' don' eat a bug."

Wyman poured a little dirt over the caterpillar and watched it struggle to free itself. "I don't see you caring if you kill a Jap or two," he said.

"They're *heathen*," Ridges said.

"Excuse me," Goldstein said, "but I don't think you're quite right. I was reading an article a few months ago which said there were over a hundred thousand Christians in Japan."

Ridges shook his head. "Well, Ah wouldn' want to be killing one of them," he said.

"But you'll have to," Wyman said. "Whyn't you admit you're wrong?"

"The Lord'll keep me from shooting a Christian," Ridges said stubbornly. "Aaaaah."

"That's what Ah believe," Ridges said. Actually, he was quite upset. The writhing of the insect had recalled to him the way the bodies of the Japanese had looked the morning after they had tried to cross the river. They had seemed the same as the animals who had died on his father's farm. He had told himself that it was because they were heathen, but now after Goldstein's statement he was confused. One hundred thousand was a vast number to him; he assumed that was at least half the people in Japan, and now he was thinking that some of the dead men he had seen in the river must have been Christians. He brooded over it for a moment or two, and then understood. It was very simple to him.

"You believe man got a soul?" he asked Wyman.

"I don't know. What the hell is a soul?"

Ridges chuckled. "Shoot, you ain't so smart as you think y'are. The soul's what leaves a man after he dies—that's what goes up t' heaven. That's why he looks so bad when you see him jus' lyin' in the river, it's because he ain't what he was before. That somethin' that's important, his soul, that's gone from him."

"Who the hell knows," Wyman said. He felt philosophical.

The insect was dying under the last handful of earth he had poured over it.

JOHN HERSEY

Hiroshima

John Hersey (1914–1993) was one of the earliest practitioners of New Journalism, fusing fictional narrative with nonfiction reporting. He was born in Tientsin, China, the child of missionary parents, and spoke Chinese as his first language. He eventually attended Yale and Clare College, Cambridge. In 1937 Hersey began writing for *Time* magazine, covering both Asia and Europe during World War II. The concise clarity of works such as *Men on Bataan* (1942) and *Into the Valley* (1943) led the *New York Times* to call him a "new Hemingway." His first novel, *A Bell for Adano*, featuring an Italian American soldier in Sicily, won the Pulitzer Prize in 1945. It was followed by *The Wall* (1950), an equally successful novel about the razing of the Warsaw ghetto. On assignment in Japan in 1946, he found a text written by a Jesuit missionary who had survived the atomic bomb. Using this, and interviewing other survivors, he wrote *Hiroshima*, first published in the *New Yorker* (1946) and then as a book, to immediate acclaim. Einstein is said to have ordered a thousand copies. In the excerpt below, Hersey describes Hiroshima doctors struggling to cope with the magnitude of the disaster.

The night was hot, and it seemed even hotter because of the fires against the sky, but the younger of the two girls Mr. Tanimoto and the priests had rescued complained to Father Kleinsorge that she was cold. He covered her with his jacket. She and her older sister had been in the salt water of the river for a couple of hours before being rescued. The younger one had huge, raw flash burns on her body; the salt water must have been excruciatingly painful to her. She began to shiver heavily, and again said it was cold. Father Kleinsorge borrowed a blanket from someone nearby and wrapped her up, but she shook more and more, and said again, "I am so cold," and then she suddenly stopped shivering and was dead.

Mr. Tanimoto found about twenty men and women on the sandspit. He drove the boat onto the bank and urged them to get aboard. They did not move and he realized that they were too weak to lift themselves.

He reached down and took a woman by the hands, but her skin slipped off in huge, glovelike pieces. He was so sickened by this that he had to sit down for a moment. Then he got out into the water and, though a small man, lifted several of the men and women, who were naked, into his boat. Their backs and breasts were clammy, and he remembered uneasily what the great burns he had seen during the day had been like: yellow at first, then red and swollen, with the skin sloughed off, and finally, in the evening, suppurated and smelly. With the tide risen, his bamboo pole was now too short and he had to paddle most of the way across with it. On the other side, at a higher spit, he lifted the slimy living bodies out and carried them up the slope away from the tide. He had to keep consciously repeating to himself, "These are human beings." It took him three trips to get them all across the river. When he had finished, he decided he had to have a rest, and he went back to the park.

As Mr. Tanimoto stepped up the dark bank, he tripped over someone, and someone else said angrily, "Look out! That's my hand." Mr. Tanimoto, ashamed of hurting wounded people, embarrassed at being able to walk upright, suddenly thought of the naval hospital ship, which had not come (it never did), and he had for a moment a feeling of blind, murderous rage at the crew of the ship, and then at all doctors. Why didn't they come to help these people?

Dr. Fujii lay in dreadful pain throughout the night on the floor of his family's roofless house on the edge of the city. By the light of a lantern, he had examined himself and found: left clavicle fractured; multiple abrasions and lacerations of face and body, including deep cuts on the chin, back, and legs; extensive contusions on chest and trunk; a couple of ribs possibly fractured. Had he not been so badly hurt, he might have been at Asano Park, assisting the wounded.

By nightfall, ten thousand victims of the explosion had invaded the Red Cross Hospital, and Dr. Sasaki, worn out, was moving aimlessly and dully up and down the stinking corridors with wads of bandage and bottles of Mercurochrome, still wearing the glasses he had taken from the wounded nurse, binding up the worst cuts as he came to them. Other doctors were putting compresses of saline solution on the worst burns. That was all they could do. After dark, they worked by the light of the city's fires and by candles the ten remaining nurses held for them. Dr. Sasaki had not looked outside the hospital all day; the scene inside was so terrible and so compelling that it had not occurred to him to ask any questions about what had happened beyond the windows and doors. Ceilings and partitions had fallen; plaster, dust, blood, and vomit were everywhere. Patients were dying by the hundreds, but there was nobody to carry away the corpses. Some of the hospital staff distributed biscuits and rice balls, but the charnel-house smell was so strong that few were hungry. By three o'clock the next morning, after nineteen straight hours of his gruesome work, Dr. Sasaki was incapable of dressing another wound. He and some other survivors of the hospital staff got straw mats and went outdoors—thousands of patients and hundreds of dead were in the yard and on the driveway—and hurried around behind the hospital and lay down in hiding to snatch some sleep. But within an hour wounded people had found them; a complaining circle formed around them: "Doctors! Help us! How can you sleep?" Dr. Sasaki got up again and went back to work. Early in the day, he thought for the first time of his mother, at their country home in Mukaihara, thirty miles from town. He usually went home every night. He was afraid she would think he was dead.

LESLIE MARMON SILKO

Ceremony

Leslie Marmon Silko (born 1948), best known as a novelist, is also a poet and essayist producing haunting portraits of Native American life through a combination of hard-nosed realism, indigenous myths, and ecological mediations. Born of mixed heritage in Albuquerque, Silko grew up on the outskirts of the Laguna Pueblo reservation. Prohibited from using the Keresan language of her grandmother and aunts while at school, she nonetheless excelled, graduating from the University of New Mexico in 1969. She established herself as a key Native American writer with her first novel, *Ceremony* (1977), which featured Tayo, a traumatized World War II veteran returning to the Laguna reservation and the power of ritual. This was followed by *Storyteller* (1981) and *The Almanac* *of the Dead* (1991), the latter a sprawling novel ranging over five centuries and several continents, written with the support of her 1983 MacArthur Fellowship. Her other works include *Delicacy and Strength of Lace* (1986), her correspondence with the poet James Wright; *Garden in the Dunes* (1999); and *The Turquoise Ledge: A Memoir* (2010). In this excerpt from *Ceremony*, Tayo suffers a nightmarish paralysis, conflating friend and foe as he sees his Uncle Josiah in a Japanese soldier.

Sometimes the Japanese voices came first, angry and loud, pushing the song far away, and then he could hear the shift in his dreaming, like a slight afternoon wind changing its direction, coming less and less from the south, moving into the west, and the voices would become Laguna voices, and he could hear Uncle Josiah calling to him, Josiah bringing him the fever medicine when he had been sick a long time ago. But before Josiah could come, the fever voices would drift and whirl and emerge again—Japanese soldiers shouting orders to him, suffocating damp voices that drifted out in the jungle steam, and he heard the women's voices then; they faded in and out until he was frantic because he thought the Laguna words were his mother's, but when he was about to make out the meaning of the words, the voice suddenly broke into a language he could not understand; and it was then that all the voices were drowned by the music—loud, loud music from a big juke box, its flashing red and blue lights pulling the darkness closer.

He lay there early in the morning and watched the high small window above the bed; dark gray gradually became lighter until it cast a white square on the opposite wall at dawn. He watched the room grow brighter then, as the square of light grew steadily warmer, more yellow with the climbing sun. He had not been able to sleep for a long time—for as long as all things had become tied together like colts in single file when he and Josiah had taken them to the mountain, with the halter rope of one colt tied to the tail of the colt ahead of it, and the lead colt's rope tied to the wide horn on Josiah's Mexican saddle. He could still see them now—the creamy sorrel, the bright red bay, and the gray roan—their slick summer coats reflecting the sunlight as it came up from behind the yellow mesas, shining on them, strung out behind Josiah's horse like an old-time pack train. He could get no rest as long as the memories were tangled with the present, tangled up like colored threads from old Grandma's wicker sewing basket when he was a child, and he had carried them outside to play and they had spilled out of his arms into the summer weeds and rolled away in all directions, and then he had hurried to pick them up before Auntie found him. He could feel it inside his skull—the tension of little threads being pulled and how it was with tangled things, things tied together, and as he tried to pull them apart and rewind them into their places, they snagged and tangled even more. So Tayo had to sweat through those nights when thoughts became entangled; he had to sweat to think of something that wasn't unraveled or tied in knots to the past— something that existed by itself, standing alone like a deer. And if he could hold that image of the deer in his mind long enough, his stomach might shiver less and let him sleep for a while. It worked as long as the deer was alone, as long as he could keep it a gray buck on an unrecognized hill; but if he did not hold it tight, it would spin away from him and become the deer he and Rocky had hunted. That memory would unwind into the last day when they had sat together, oiling their rifles in the jungle of some nameless Pacific island. While they used up the last of the oil in Rocky's pack, they talked about the deer that Rocky had hunted, and the corporal next to them shook his head, and kept saying he had dreamed the Japs would get them that day.

The humid air turned into sweat that had run down the corporal's face while he repeated his dream to them. That was the first time Tayo had realized that the man's skin was not much different from his own. The skin. He saw the skin of the corpses again and again, in ditches on either side of the long muddy road—skin that was stretched shiny and dark over bloated hands; even white men were darker after death. There was no difference when they were swollen and covered with flies. That had become the worst thing for Tayo: they looked too familiar even when they were alive. When the sergeant told them to kill all the Japanese soldiers lined up in front of the cave with their hands on their heads, Tayo could not pull the trigger. The fever made him shiver, and the sweat was stinging his eyes and he couldn't see clearly; in that instant he saw Josiah standing there; the face was dark from the sun, and the eyes were squinting as though he were about to smile at Tayo. So Tayo stood there, stiff with nausea, while they fired at the soldiers, and he watched his uncle fall, and he *knew* it was Josiah; and even after Rocky started shaking him by the shoulders and telling him to stop crying, it was *still* Josiah lying there. They forced medicine into Tayo's mouth, and Rocky pushed him toward the corpses and told him to look, look past the blood that was already dark like the jungle mud, with only flecks of bright red still shimmering in it. Rocky made him look at the corpse and said, "Tayo, this is a *Jap*! This is a *Jap* uniform!" And then he rolled the body over with his boot and said, "Look, Tayo, look at the face," and that was when Tayo started screaming because it wasn't a Jap, it was Josiah, eyes shrinking back into the skull and all their shining black light glazed over by death.

The sergeant had called for a medic and somebody rolled up Tayo's sleeve; they told him to sleep, and the next day they all acted as though nothing had happened. They called it battle fatigue, and they said hallucinations were common with malarial fever.

Rocky had reasoned it out with him; it was impossible for the dead man to be Josiah, because Josiah was an old Laguna man, thousands of miles from the Philippine jungles and Japanese armies. "He's probably up on some mesa right now, chopping wood," Rocky said. He smiled and shook Tayo's shoulders. "Hey, I know you're homesick. But, Tayo, we're *supposed* to be here. This is what we're supposed to do."

Tayo nodded, slapped at the insects mechanically and staring straight ahead, past the smothering dampness of the green jungle leaves. He examined the facts and logic again and again, the way Rocky had explained it to him; the facts made what he had seen an impossibility. He felt the shivering then; it began at the tips of his fingers and pulsed into his arms. He shivered because all the facts, all the reasons made no difference any more; he could hear Rocky's words, and he could follow the logic of what Rocky said, but he could not feel anything except a swelling in his belly, a great swollen grief that was pushing into his throat.

CHANG-RAE LEE

A Gesture Life

Chang-Rae Lee (born 1965), novelist and professor of Creative Writing, for many years at Princeton and now at Stanford, emigrated to the United States from Korea at the age of three. He received a BA from Yale and an MFA from the University of Oregon, working briefly as a Wall

Street financial analyst before turning to writing. Lee's first novel, *Native Speaker* (1995), which received the PEN/Hemingway Award, tests the degree of assimilation in two characters: a Korean American industrial spy seemingly without accent, and a Korean American politician running for office in New York whose accent seems to vary involuntarily. This unstable claim to identity is further explored in Lee's next four novels: *A Gesture Life* (1999), about an elderly Japanese American army medic from World War II; *Aloft* (2004), about the unraveling world of an Italian American; *The Surrendered* (2010), about the persistence of war trauma; and *On Such a Full Sea* (2014), about a post-catastrophe America colonized by a new China. This excerpt from *A Gesture Life* recounts the experience of the army medic with the "comfort women" servicing the Japanese army.

In fact, it was all but finished. The comfort house, which is how it was known, was a narrow structure with five not-quite-square doorways, each with a rod across the top for a sheet for privacy. The whole thing was perhaps as long as a large transport truck, ten or so meters. There were five compartments, of course, one for each of the girls; these were tiny, windowless rooms, no more than the space of one and a half tatami mats, not even wide enough for a tall man to lie across without bending his knees. In the middle of each space was a wide plank of wood, fashioned like a bench seat but meant for lying down on, with one's feet as anchors on either side. At the other end, where the shoulders would be, the plank was widest, and then it narrowed again for the head, so that its shape was like the lid of a coffin. This is how they would receive the men. After their duties were over, they would sleep where they could in the compartment. They would take their meals with the older Japanese woman, who was already living in her own small tent behind the comfort house. She would prepare their food and keep hold of their visitors' tickets and make sure they had enough of the things a young woman might need to keep herself in a minimally respectable way.

I alone was responsible for their health. Captain Ono had briefed me fully. Well-being aside, I was to make certain they could perform their duties for the men in the camp. The greatest challenge, of course, would be venereal disease. It was well known what an intractable problem this was in the first years of fighting, particularly in Manchuria, when it might happen that two of every three men were stricken and rendered useless for battle. In those initial years there had been houses of comfort set up by former prostitutes shipped in from Japan by Army-sanctioned merchants, and the infection rate was naturally high. Now that the comfort stations were run under military ordinances and the women not professionals but rather those who had unwittingly enlisted or been conscripted into the wartime women's volunteer corps, to contribute and sacrifice as all did, the expectation was that the various diseases would be kept more or less in check. Certainly, it was now the men who were problematic, and there was stiff penalty and corporal punishment for anyone known to be infected and not seeking treatment. I had one of the sergeants announce final call for the camp in this regard, as I hoped to quarantine anyone who might infect a girl, who in turn would certainly transmit it back among the men many times over, but it was very close to the time of their visits and only two men came forward complaining of symptoms, both of whom were in the ward already.

I was also to examine the girls and state their fitness for their duties. I was surprised that Captain Ono had given me this responsibility, though of course he had already completed an exam for the personal sake of the commander. But as there were procedural considerations, it was up to me to ask the older woman, who was called Mrs. Matsui, to bring them to the examination and surgery room of the ward.

I had put on a doctor's coat and was sitting at the desk with several folders of paperwork that needed completing for the Captain. I usually did this work for him, though it wasn't part of my stated tasks, but that afternoon I found I had no real patience for it. The intense heat of the day seemed to bound and treble inside the room, and the stiff white coat was yet another layer atop my regular uniform. I hadn't eaten anything yet that day, because of the sticking temperature and the crabbed feeling of an incipient illness, which I knew was due partly to my shock at events of the previous night, as well as the anticipation of this present moment, which should be nothing at all for an experienced medic but was unnerving all the same.

The woman, Mrs. Matsui, poked her head through the open doorway and bowed several times quickly. She was pale and pock-faced and dressed in the tawdry, over-shiny garb of a woman who had obviously once been in the trade. She was clearly, too, a full Japanese, and the fact of this bothered me now, to see her cheapness against the line of modest girls that trailed her.

They were all fairly young, ranging from sixteen to twenty-one. At the head of them was a tallish girl with a dark mole on her cheek. She was pretty, in an easily recognizable sort of way, with arched eyebrows and a full, deep-hued mouth. The two beside her were more retiring in their appearance, their eyes averted from me and everything else; they seemed to be clinging to each other, though they weren't touching at all. The next girl, I realized, was the one who had hidden beneath the commander's hut. She had firm hold of the hand of the girl behind her, her eyes unfocused, as if she were blind.

Her sister, whom I had not seen up close until then, was the only one of them who gazed directly at me. She did not stare or hold my sight; rather she met my eyes as someone might on any public bus or trolley car, though her regard was instantly fixing and cold. She had a wide, oval-shaped face, and there was still some faint bruising along the side of her jaw and upper neck. She had been housed with the captain while the rest of them had gone on to entertain the commander; the doctor had reserved her, implying to the commander that she was not a virgin like the others, who would offer him the salubrious and then other ineffable effects of his taking their maidenhood, which to a soldier is like an amulet of life and rebirth.

But in the end, I believe, it was not that the doctor thought her to be simply beautiful. For it is a fact well evidenced that there were many attractive, even lovely girls that one could have as a soldier of an occupying army. It was a more particular interest than that, and one I think perhaps he himself could not (and would not) describe. Like a kind of love, which need not be romantic or sexual but is a craving all the same, the way a young boy can so desire something that he loves it with the fiercest intensity, some toy or special ball, until the object becomes him, and he, it. Early the first morning after the girls' arrival I chanced upon him going into this very room, and in passing the closed door I heard him asking questions of someone concerning parentage and birthplace and education. A female voice had answered him clearly and evenly, and I knew it must be the fifth girl, the one called "Kkutaeh."

I told Mrs. Matsui to ready them for examination and she ordered them to remove their clothing. They were slow to do so and she went up to the girl with the mole and tore at her hair. The girl complied and the rest of them began to disrobe. I did not watch them. I stood at the table with a writing board and the sheets of paper for recording their medical histories and periodic examinations. There was special paperwork for everything, and it was no different for the young women of the comfort house. The girl with the mole came to me first. I nodded to the table and she lifted herself up gingerly. She was naked and in the bright afternoon light coming from the slatted window her youthful skin was practically luminous, as though she were somehow lit from inside. For a moment I was transfixed by the strangeness of it all, the sheer exposed figure of the girl and then the four others who stood covering themselves with their hands, their half-real, half-phantom nearness, which I thought must be like the allure of pornography for Corporal Endo. But then Mrs. Matsui came around the front of the girl on the exam table and without prompting from me spread her knees apart.

"You'll probably see they're all a bit raw today," she said hoarsely, like a monger with her morning's call. "Nothing like the first time, right? But you'll believe me when I say they'll be used to it by tomorrow."

PHILIP K. DICK

The Man in the High Castle

Philip K. Dick (1928–1982) was instrumental in giving science fiction philosophical depth and mainstream appeal. After briefly studying German at UC Berkeley, he went on to produce a unique corpus, a realism of unreal worlds. In signature works such as *The Man in the High Castle* (1962), *The Three Stigmata of Palmer Eldritch* (1965), *Do Androids Dream of Electric Sheep?* (1968), *Ubik* (1969), *Flow My Tears, The Policeman Said* (1974), *A Scanner Darkly* (1977), and *VALIS* (1981), Dick offers alternate histories and parallel universes, playing with a planet turned hallucinatory as he explores the fragile boundaries between human and nonhuman, reality and simulacra. Many of his books have been made into films, notably *Blade Runner* (1982), *Total Recall* (1990), *Minority Report* (2002), *Paycheck* (2003), and *A Scanner Darkly* (2006). This excerpt from *The Man in the High Castle* features a parallel universe in which World War II was won by Germany and Japan.

Guiltily, he woke himself. Too much to plan; no time for a midday doze. Was he absolutely properly dressed to enter the Nippon Times Building? Possibly he would faint in the high-speed elevator. But he had motion-illness tablets with him, a German compound. The various modes of address . . . he knew them. Whom to treat politely, whom rudely. Be brusque with the doorman, elevator operator, receptionist, guide, any janitorial person. Bow to any Japanese, of course, even if it obliged him to bow hundreds of times. But the *pinocs*. Nebulous area. Bow, but look straight through them as if they did not exist. Did that cover every situation, then? What about a visiting foreigner? Germans often could be seen at the Trade Missions, as well as neutrals.

And then, too, he might see a slave.

German or South ships docked at the port of San Francisco all the time, and blacks occasionally were allowed off for short intervals. Always in groups of fewer than three. And they could not be out after nightfall; even under Pacific law, they had to obey the curfew. But also slaves unloaded at the docks, and these lived perpetually ashore, in shacks under the wharves, above the waterline. None would be in the Trade Mission offices, but if any unloading were taking place—for instance, should he carry his own bags to Mr. Tagomi's office? Surely not. A slave would have to be found, even if he had to stand waiting an hour. Even if he missed his appointment. It was out of the question to let a slave see him carrying something; he had to be quite careful of that. A mistake of that kind would cost him dearly; he would never have place of any sort again, among those who saw.

In a way, Childan thought, I would almost enjoy carrying my own bags into the Nippon Times Building in broad daylight. What a grand gesture. It is not actually illegal; I would not go to jail. And I would show my real feelings, the side of a man which never comes out in public life. But . . .

I could do it, he thought, if there weren't those damn black slaves lurking around; I could endure those above me seeing it, their scorn—after all, they scorn me and humiliate me every day. But to have those beneath see me, to feel their contempt. Like this *chink* peddling away ahead of me. If I hadn't taken a pedecab, if he had seen me trying to *walk* to a business appointment . . .

One had to blame the Germans for the situation. Tendency to bite off more than they could chew. After all, they had barely managed to win the war, and at once they had gone off to conquer the solar system, while at home they had passed edicts which . . . well, at least the idea was good. And after all, they had been successful with the Jews and Gypsies and Bible Students. And the Slavs had been rolled back two thousand years' worth, to their heartland in Asia. Out of Europe entirely, to everyone's relief. Back to riding yaks and hunting with bow and arrow. And those great glossy magazines printed in Munich and circulated around to all the libraries and newsstands . . . one could see the full-page color pictures for oneself: the blue-eyed, blond-haired Aryan settlers who now industriously tilled, culled, plowed, and so forth in the vast grain bowl of the world, the Ukraine. Those fellows certainly looked happy. And their farms and cottages were clean. You didn't see pictures of drunken dull-witted Poles any more, slouched on sagging porches or hawking a few sickly turnips at the village market. All a thing of the past, like rutted dirt roads that once turned to slop in the rainy season, bogging down the carts.

But Africa. They had simply let their enthusiasm get the better of them there, and you had to admire that, although more thoughtful advice would have cautioned them to perhaps let it wait a bit until, for instance, Project Farmland had been completed. Now *there* the Nazis had shown genius; the artist in them had truly emerged. The Mediterranean Sea bottled up, drained, made into tillable farmland, through the use of atomic power— what daring! How the sniggerers had been set back on their heels, for instance certain scoffing merchants along Montgomery Street. And as a matter of fact, Africa had almost been successful . . . but in a project of that sort, *almost* was an ominous word to begin to hear. Rosenberg's well-known powerful pamphlet issued in 1958; the word had first shown up, then. *As to the Final Solution of the African Problem, we have almost achieved our objectives. Unfortunately, however—*

Still, it had taken two hundred years to dispose of the American aborigines, and Germany had almost done it in Africa in fifteen years. So no criticism was legitimately in order. Childan had, in fact, argued it out recently while having lunch with certain of those other merchants. They expected miracles, evidently, as if the Nazis could remold the world by magic. No, it was science and technology and that fabulous talent for hard work; the Germans never stopped applying themselves. And when they did a task, they did it *right*.

THOMAS McGRATH

Ode for the American Dead in Asia

Thomas McGrath (1916–1990), born and raised on a North Dakota farm, was profoundly shaped by the Great Depression and the experience of the Dust Bowl during the 1930s. After graduating from the University of North Dakota, he served in the U.S. Army during World War II before earning a Rhodes Scholarship to Oxford. After a brief stint as a labor organizer, he devoted most of his early life to teaching. It was not until 1953, when he was summoned by the House Un-American Activities Committee and as a result lost his job at Los Angeles State College, that his literary career began in earnest. His first publication, the book-length poem *Letter to an Imaginary Friend* (1962), is a highly personal yet representative portrait of the Left. In "Ode for the American Dead in Asia" (1988), McGrath mourns those who perished in Korea and Vietnam, "leeched and tumbled to / a tomb of footnotes," while insisting with clear-eyed realism that those footnotes are the natural expressions of a "culture that was mined for war."

1.

God love you now, if no one else will ever,
Corpse in the paddy, or dead on a high hill
In the fine and ruinous summer of a war
You never wanted. All your false flags were
Of bravery and ignorance, like grade school maps:
Colors of countries you would never see—
Until that weekend in eternity
When, laughing, well armed, perfectly ready to kill
The world and your brother, the safe commanders sent
You into your future. Oh, dead on a hill,
Dead in a paddy, leeched and tumbled to
A tomb of footnotes. We mourn a changeling: you:
Handselled to poverty and drummed to war
By distinguished masters whom you never knew.

2.

The bee that spins his metal from the sun,
The shy mole drifting like a miner ghost
Through midnight earth—all happy creatures run
As strict as trains on rails the circuits of
Blind instinct. Happy in your summer follies,
You mined a culture that was mined for war:
The state to mold you, church to bless, and always
The elders to confirm you in your ignorance.
No scholar put your thinking cap on nor
Warned that in dead seas fishes died in schools
Before inventing legs to walk the land.
The rulers stuck a tennis racket in your hand,
An Ark against the flood. In time of change
Courage is not enough: the blind mole dies,
And you on your hill, who did not know the rules.

3.

Wet in the windy counties of the dawn
The lone crow skirls his draggled passage home:
And God (whose sparrows fall aslant his gaze,
Like grace or confetti) blinks and he is gone,
And you are gone. Your scarecrow valor grows
And rusts like early lilac while the rose
Blooms in Dakota and the stock exchange
Flowers. Roses, rents, all things conspire
To crown your death with wreaths of living fire.
And the public mourners come: the politic tear
Is cast in the Forum. But, in another year,
We will mourn you, whose fossil courage fills
The limestone histories: brave: ignorant: amazed:
Dead in the rice paddies, dead on the nameless hills.

MYUNG MI KIM

Under Flag

Myung Mi Kim (born 1957), born in South Korea, came to the United States with her family at the age of nine. Raised in the Midwest and earning an MFA from the University of Iowa, Kim has taught at San Francisco State University and the University at Buffalo. Her poetry collections include *Under Flag* (1991), *The Bounty* (1996) and, more recently, *River Antes* (2006) and *Penury* (2009). Using fragmentary language and seemingly unrelated vignettes, she explores the sense of dislocation shared by many displaced populations. In this excerpt from *Under Flag*, Kim chronicles the Korean War as an apparently random sequence of haunting images, alternating between civilians struggling to hold on to their traditional way of life and the conspicuous—though not always effective—presence of high-tech weapons like the Bell H-13 D helicopter, an observation vehicle surveying the horrors unfolding on the ground.

On this side of the sea the rancor of their arrival
Where invasion occurs according to schedule
Evacuees, a singular wave set against stubbed bluffs
Rigor of those who carry households on their backs
Above: victims.
Below: Chonui, a typical Korean town. In the distance,
a 155-mm shell has exploded.
Of elders who would have been sitting in the warmest part
of the house with comforters draped around their shoulders
peeling tangerines
Of an uncle with shrapnel burrowing into shinbone
for thirty years
A wave of much white cloth
Handfull of millet, a pair of never worn shoes, one chicken
grabbed by the neck, ill-prepared for carrying,
carrying through
Not to have seen it yet inheriting it

Drilled at the core for mineral yield and this, once depleted,
never to be replaced
At dawn the next morning, firing his machine gun, Corporal Leonard H.
was shot and instantly killed while stopping the Reds' last attempt
to overrun and take the hilltop
The demoralized ROK troops disappeared but the handful of Americans,
completely surrounded, held out for seven hours against continuous
attack, until all ammunition was exhausted
General D.'s skillful direction of the flight was fully as memorable
as his heroic personal participation with pistol and bazooka
Grumman F9F
Bell H-130s
Shooting Stars
Flying Cheetahs
They could handle them if they would only use the weapons we have
give them properly, said Colonel Wright.
Lockheed F-04 Starfire
Lockheed F-803
Bell H-13 Sioux
Bell H-13 Ds

JAY CANTOR

The Death of Che Guevara

Jay Cantor (born 1948) is best known for *The Death of Che Guevara* (1983), a minutely researched historical novel centered on Ernesto "Che" Guevara, the legendary guerrilla leader whose name has become synonymous with revolution throughout Latin America and the world. To meet the challenge of writing about this iconic figure, Cantor experimented with multiple genres and different kinds of evidence, weaving letters, journal entries, Party communiqués, and folk songs into his psychological speculations, the better to "find the inner within the flat *outer* world."

This narrative experimentation also drives his second work, *Krazy Kat* (1988), a High Modernist riff on the comic strip, as well as his gargantuan third novel, *Great Neck* (2003), about the private dramas of multitudes. In this selection from *The Death of Che Guevara*, Cantor offers an audio portrait of Fidel Castro as a tactician of silence.

Fidel is silent. The afternoon of our talk, after the ride from the airport in which we each shouted and punched the air, ended in silence, that to some uncanny silence of his, when he joins the world of mineral things, when the most talkative of men, whose life is a stream, river, torrent vapor cloud stream, etc., of words, shuts up; when his gestures, too, his hand reaching out and upward to punctuate a point, to squeeze a shoulder, come to an end. His hands lie open by his sides.

We sat facing each other, neither of us speaking, on the crow's-nest platform he had built in the middle of his room. (To reach it we walked up a circular metal stairway that winds about a thick metal pole. The pole supports the wooden platform.) Fidel sat in a rounded wooden desk chair on rollers (a triumph for someone to have gotten up that ladder), and I made myself comfortable in a small straight-backed wooden chair. We were eight feet off the ground, talking, smoking; not talking. I looked down at his room. His single bed was neatly made, the blue and red blanket tucked tight. (He rarely sleeps here. Uneasy in Havana, he travels all over the island, wandering, in a caravan of jeeps. And in Havana he prefers others' beds.) Iron weights were scattered on the floor, dumbbells, a rowing machine, baseball bats, baseball and boxing gloves, the wide white cross-weave of a trampoline. Fidel does not want to get fat; or old; or die. The trampoline was useless for exercise, though; books were piled all over it. Books were everywhere, books on farming, on soil science, on cattle raising, books on crop hybridization, books half read, books stacked on the seat of the rowing machine, with red ribbon place-markers sticking out from their pages. Books on the red reclining chair and on the wobbly leopard-skin footrest, books opened and spread face down on the floor, their spines cracking. Scattered about among the wilderness of books were the musical instruments he has tried to play from time to time—a guitar, a bright new brass trumpet, an accordion. (A one-man mariachi band!) For a bad moment I looked about, at the scattered books on agriculture, and the musical instruments he had abandoned (each time he gave up on the project before he had learned to play even a simple tune. Not enough time, not enough patience. There is only one instrument for him: the crowded plaza, his orchestra); and I thought of the factories—my ministry's responsibility—many of them idle or half used, hobbled for lack of raw materials or trained workers, or spare parts. The Revolution was an old engraving I saw once, as a child: a pensive bearded man, a broken god, with a ruined city in the background, a collection of useless instruments around him, a magic square whose impotent charm means nothing beyond itself, a pile of books under his elbow on the spectral unproductive science of alchemy, that promises so much and accomplishes nothing; only one tool: a reaper, instrument of some dubious harvest.

I looked back at Fidel. His eyes were distant, tired. He'd been up the night before, perhaps discussing my arrival, perhaps with a woman. His hands lay on his lap (he'd moved them when I looked away. It made me smile; he didn't respond). He was still now. Immobile. Mineral.

I was exhausted by my plane trip, and would usually have been fretful. I had a clammy smell. But I knew my thoughts. I stretched my legs out and looked at my boots. I put my hands in my lap. I sat.

This silence of his was tactical. (All of Fidel's actions, all his gestures are—or by his genius could later be gathered up into—a tactic.) It was a rare tactic, but not unfamiliar. Occasionally, in committee meetings, in planning sessions (earlier ones, when consent was still often at issue) he would do this immobility business, as if his motor ("the little motor that sets the big motor—the masses—in motion") had run down, finally, for good and all. His hands, which had been busy curling and uncurling the thick hair of his sideburns, fell, as if he'd died, to his sides. His mouth fell open a bit, almost doltishly, if it hadn't been for the intelligence of his eyes, which looked as if they were seeing something puzzling, distasteful. The others chattered on for a bit, until they saw him; then, one by one, they too grew quiet; waited.

His silence was another manner of argument (silence is argument carried on by other means). When he had said all he could think to say (and that meant hours), when he had run out of rhetoric, examples, dialectical twists, and you—a broad, bearded comrade from the mountains, a too-open man—were still obstinate, obdurate, unconvinced, then he would sit like this. You thought the Revolution had promised land to the peasants, land they would own, land they would work themselves. Now Fidel was talking of reserving land for state farms, cooperative enterprises. You glared at those around the table. You were in uniform; some of them wore suit jackets. They weren't comrades; they were shit. No one looked back at you. Fidel's silence meant, "examine your motives"; it meant, "I do not know why you are so obstinate, it's something dark in you that you won't admit to us, perhaps because you haven't admitted it to yourself; some desire for personal power, some petit-bourgeois prejudice; some mulish pride that keeps you attached to your mistake. But I am more obdurate than you. We'll sit here until you discover your error. Or, if you fail, I will end this meeting in silence."

And perhaps you would discover your blindness; or perhaps his silence was (in so many ways) too terrifying to be abided—as if you thought he (or someone) was dying. He, the principle of Revolution, was being absorbed into the nonhuman world. You would do what you must to bring him back, to save him (or someone). You would indeed (and why not call your motive concern, loyalty, love for him whether he was right or wrong?). For perhaps there was, you felt, a glacial change going on within that silence, a change that would be irreversible; a mountain was being gouged from the land by the slow progress of a huge silent mass of ice. You were falling away from him, you were falling down that mountain, out of his confidence. He might smile suddenly and end the meeting. We would get up and leave the high-ceilinged room; and it would be far too late. You would find yourself at a distance from him, in a province, in exile, in jail, dead. His silence prefigured an abandonment, an absence, a death. Maybe yours.

But to revive him now, to bring him back up the chain of being from rock to man, required a lot of talk from you. You could not anymore simply acquiesce in his plan. You must indicate thoroughly your hidden motive, now discovered, for disagreement. You must show that you had apprehended the flaw in your character, and so seen your theoretical mistake. You must display your understanding of his idea: economies of scale, creation of a new man, destruction of the petit-bourgeois element. You must elaborate for a while on why you now agreed—hard to do, for he had exhausted most of the means of elaboration himself. Perhaps you could use anecdotes from the war: when we had redistributed expropriated cattle to the peasants they had immediately slaughtered and eaten them, afraid the cows would be taken away again. Only state cooperatives could prevent this. I had seen you, a courageous man, drag a wounded comrade from a field strafed by gunfire, but sweat covered your body now as you showed yourself before your comrades. I could smell it: an acrid unpleasant odor. You clasped your fingers together with strain, in prayer, as I had seen you do when you first tried to learn to read. Again, words were failing to come to you. Comrades stared at the light from the high windows, or the discolored rectangles on the wall where the portraits of Cuba's betrayers had hung. (I, however, watched you perform. You caught my eye and I smiled and nodded. You hated me ever after.) You went on till he spoke, for his silence was a waste of snow you might have to wander in till your heart froze in confusion and terror.

And often, as the holdout heard himself talk, he found that he now agreed with Fidel, not simply for show, but deeply. (Or was this pride's ruse to save one's dignity?) Even as you nervously spoke (I have been told) you found that something recalcitrant in you had melted. Fidel *was* right. Of course he was right. Who better could interpret that exacting god, the Revolution? You turned about before our eyes; he had turned you; you wanted even to thank him; you saw things freshly. You didn't feel you had abandoned your position exactly (something you would never have done in a battle, when the enemy was clearly uniformed, when you thought you had known what you were fighting for); rather you simply couldn't find your old position from your new perspective.

MICHAEL HERR

Dispatches

Michael Herr (born 1940), war correspondent of *Esquire Magazine* (1967–1969), arrived in Vietnam just after the North Vietnamese Tet Offensive shattered any hope of a quick U.S. military victory. *Dispatches* (1977)—praised by John Le Carré as "the best book I have ever read on men and war in our time"—captures that historical moment with an almost surreal realism, pioneering the out-of-control psychology and detail-obsessed style of the "nonfictional novel," a genre shared with

Truman Capote and Norman Mailer. Herr went on to collaborate on the screenplays of two films on Vietnam: Francis Ford Coppola's *Apocalypse Now* (1979) and Stanley Kubrick's *Full Metal Jacket* (1987). In the following selection from *Dispatches*, he writes about a strange episode at Khe Sanh: the inability of a young U.S. Marine at the end of his tour to leave according to plan, as a suddenly paralyzing fear has made it impossible for him to reach the plane waiting at the end of a deadly airstrip.

He was smiling on this last morning of his tour. His gear was straight, his papers in order, his duffel packed, and he was going through all of the last-minute business of going home, the back-slapping and goosing; the joshing with the Old Man ("Come on, you know you're gonna miss this place." "Yes sir, Oh wow!"); the exchanging of addresses; the odd, fragmented reminiscences blurted out of awkward silences. He had a few joints left, wrapped up in a plastic bag (he hadn't smoked them, because, like most Marines at Khe Sanh, he'd expected a ground attack, and he didn't want to be stoned when it came), and he gave these to his best friend, or, rather, his best surviving friend. His oldest friend had been blown away in January, on the same day that the ammo dump had been hit. He had always wondered whether Gunny, the company gunnery sergeant, had known about all the smoking. After three wars Gunny probably didn't care much; besides, they all knew that Gunny was into some pretty cool shit himself. When he dropped by the bunker they said goodbye, and then there wasn't anything to do with the morning but to run in and out of the bunker for a look at the sky, coming back in every time to say that it really ought to clear enough by ten for the planes to get in. By noon, when the goodbyes and take-cares and get-a-little-for-me's had gone on for too long by hours, the sun started to show through the mist. He picked up his duffel and a small AWOL bag and started for the airstrip and the small, deep slit trench on the edge of the strip.

Khe Sanh was a very bad place then, but the airstrip there was the worst place in the world. It was what Khe Sanh had instead of a V-ring, the exact, predictable object of the mortars and rockets hidden in the surrounding hills, the sure target of the big Russian and Chinese guns lodged in the side of CoRoc Ridge, eleven kilometers away across the Laotian border. There was nothing random about the shelling there, and no one wanted anything to do with it. If the wind was right, you could hear the NVA .50-calibers starting far up the valley whenever a plane made its approach to the strip, and the first incoming artillery would precede the landings by seconds. If you were waiting there to be taken out, there was nothing you could do but curl up in the trench and try to make yourself small, and if you were coming in on the plane, there was nothing you could do, nothing at all.

There was always the debris of one kind of aircraft or another piled up on or near the strip, and sometimes the damage would cause the strip to be closed off for hours while the Seabees or the 11th Engineers did the clearing. It was so bad, so predictably bad, that the Air Force stopped flying in their star transport, the C-130, and kept to the smaller, more maneuverable C-123. Whenever possible, loads were parachuted in on pallet drops from 1,500 feet, pretty blue-and-yellow chutes, a show, dropping down around the perimeter. But obviously, passengers had to be flown in or picked up on the ground. These were mostly replacements, guys going to or returning from R&R's, specialists of one kind or another, infrequent brass (most staff from Division and higher made their own travel arrangements for Khe Sanh) and a lot of correspondents. While a planeload of passengers tensed and sweated and made the run for the trench over and over in their heads, waiting for the cargo hatch to drop, ten to fifty Marines and correspondents huddled down in the trench, worked their lips futilely to ease the dryness, and then, at the exact same instant, they would all race, collide, stampede, exchanging places. If the barrage was a particularly heavy one, the faces would all distort in the most simple kind of panic, the eyes going wider than the eyes of horses caught in a fire. What you saw was a translucent blur, sensible only at the immediate center, like a swirly-chic photograph of Carnival, and you'd glimpse a face, a shell fragment cased in white sparks, a piece of gear somehow suspended in air, a drift of smoke, and you'd move around the flight crews working the heavy cargo strapping, over scout dogs, over the casually arranged body bags that always lay not far from the strip, covered with flies. And men would still be struggling on or off as the aircraft turned slowly to begin the taxi before the most accelerated take-off the machine had it in it to make. If you were on board, that first movement was an ecstasy. You'd all sit there with empty, exhausted grins, covered with the impossible red dust that laterite breaks down to, dust like scales, feeling the delicious afterchill of the fear, that one quick convulsion of safety. There was no feeling in the world as good as being airborne out of Khe Sanh.

On this last morning, the young Marine caught a ride from his company position that dropped him off fifty meters from the strip. As he moved on foot he heard the distant sound of the C-123 coming in, and that was all he heard. There was hardly more than a hundred-foot ceiling, scary, bearing down on him. Except for the approaching engines, everything was still. If there had been something more, just one incoming round, he might have been all right, but in that silence the sound of his own feet moving over the dirt was terrifying to him. He later said that this was what made him stop. He dropped his duffel and looked around. He watched the plane, his plane, as it touched down, and then he ran leaping over some discarded sandbags by the road. He lay out flat and listened as the plane switched loads and took off, listened until there was nothing left to listen to. Not a single round had come in.

Back at the bunker there was some surprise at his return, but no one said anything. Anyone can miss a plane. Gunny slapped him on the back and wished him a better trip the next time out. That afternoon he rode in a jeep that took him all the way to Charlie Med, the medical detachment for Khe Sanh that had been set up insanely close to the strip, but he never got himself past the sandbagging outside of the triage room.

"Oh no, you raggedy-assed bastard," Gunny said when he got back to the outfit. But he looked at him for a long while this time.

"Well," the kid said. "Well . . ."

The next morning two of his friends went with him to the edge of the strip and saw him into the trench. ("Goodbye," Gunny said. "And that's an order.") They came back to say that he'd gotten out for sure this time. An hour later he came up the road again, smiling. He was still there the first time I left Khe Sanh, and while he probably made it out eventually, you can't be sure.

YUSEF KOMUNYAKAA

Tu Do Street

Yusef Komunyakaa (born 1947) was born James William Brown in Bogalusa, Louisiana, the son of a carpenter, and later reclaimed the name *Komunyakaa*, the original name of his grandfather, a stowaway from Trinidad. He served in Vietnam from 1969 to 1970, working as correspondent and editor of *The Southern Cross*, an army newspaper. His poetry about the Vietnam War, much of which is collected in *Dien Cai Dau* (1988), is among his most haunting and unforgettable. Komunyakaa co-translated *The Insomnia of Fire* (1995) by the Vietnamese poet Nguyen Quang Thieu. Much of his poetry, from *Copacetic* (1984) and *I Apologize for the Eyes in My Head* (1986), to the Pulitzer Prize–winning *Neon Vernacular* (1994), to *Talking Dirty to the Gods* (2000) and *Warhorses* (2008), incorporates the textures of colloquial speech and the rhythms of blues and jazz. He coedited *The Jazz Poetry Anthology* (1991) and published a collection of essays, *Blue Notes* (2000). Also a playwright, he has written and produced *Gilgamesh: A Verse Play* (2006). The poem selected here, "Tu Do Street" from *Dien Cai Dau*, meditates on the way war is both gun and music, brutally dividing but also involuntarily unifying.

Music divides the evening.
I close my eyes & can see
men drawing lines in the dust.
America pushes through the membrane
of mist & smoke, & I'm a small boy
again in Bogalusa. *White Only*
signs & Hank Snow. But tonight
I walk into a place where bar girls
fade like tropical birds. When
I order a beer, the mama-san
behind the counter acts as if she
can't understand, while her eyes

skirt each white face, as Hank Williams
calls from the psychedelic jukebox.
We have played Judas where
only machine-gun fire brings us
together. Down the street
black GIs hold to their turf also.
An off-limits sign pulls me
deeper into alleys, as I look
for a softness behind these voices
wounded by their beauty & war.
Back in the bush at Dak To
& Khe Sanh, we fought
the brothers of these women
we now run to hold in our arms.
There's more than a nation
inside us, as black & white
soldiers touch the same lovers
minutes apart, tasting
each other's breath,
without knowing these rooms
run into each other like tunnels
leading to the underworld.

W. S. MERWIN

The Asians Dying

W. S. [William Stanley] Merwin (born 1927), the seventeenth U.S. poet laureate, combines many linguistic traditions to create a unique poetic fabric. After publishing his first book, *A Mask for Janus* (1952), chosen by W. H. Auden for the Yale Younger Poets Prize, he worked and traveled throughout Europe in the 1950s. His return to the United States marked a shift toward a more irregular metric, beginning with *Green* *with Beasts* (1956), *The Drunk in the Furnace* (1960), and continuing through his antiwar volumes, *The Lice* (1967) and the Pulitzer Prize–winning *The Carrier of Ladders* (1970). In 1976 Merwin moved to Hawaii to study with the Zen master Robert Aitken. His poetry since then has been intensely environmentally minded, including *The Rain in the Trees* (1988); *The Folding Cliffs* (1998), a novel in verse inspired by the history of Hawaii; and *The Shadow of Sirius* (2008), which won a second Pulitzer Prize. Merwin has also translated the poetry of Federico García Lorca and Pablo Neruda, Euripides's *Iphigeneia at Aulis* (1978), Dante's *Purgatorio* (2000), the poetry of the Russian poet Osip Mandelstam (2004), *Sir Gawain and the Green Knight* (2004), and *Collected Haiku of Yosa Buson* (2013). "The Asians Dying," from *The Second Four Books of Poetry*, is his best-known antiwar poem.

When the forests have been destroyed their darkness remains
The ash the great walker follows the possessors
Forever
Nothing they will come to is real
Nor for long
Over the watercourses
Like ducks in the time of the ducks
The ghosts of the villages trail in the sky
Making a new twilight

Rain falls into the open eyes of the dead
Again again with its pointless sound
When the moon finds them they are the color of everything

The nights disappear like bruises but nothing is healed
The dead go away like bruises
The blood vanishes into the poisoned farmlands
Pain the horizon
Remains
Overhead the seasons rock
They are paper bells
Calling to nothing living

The possessors move everywhere under Death their star
Like columns of smoke they advance into the shadows
Like thin flames with no light
They with no past
And fire their only future

MAXINE HONG KINGSTON

China Men

Maxine Hong Kingston (born 1940) was awarded the 1997 National Humanities Medal by President Clinton and the 2013 National Medal of Arts by President Obama. Born in Stockton, California, to immigrant parents from Canton, China, she graduated from UC Berkeley in 1962 and taught creative writing there from 1990 until her retirement in 2003. Best known for books combining fiction and nonfiction—*The Woman Warrior: Memoirs of a Girlhood among Ghosts* (1976) and *China Men* (1980)—she also wrote a novel, *Tripmaster Monkey: His Fake Book* (1989). *The Woman Warrior* was awarded the National Book Critics Circle Award, followed by the National Book Award for *China Men,* and the PEN West Award for *Tripmaster Monkey.* Her more recent works include *To Be the Poet* (2002), *The Fifth Book of Peace* (2003), and *I Love a Broad Margin to My Life* (2011). This excerpt from *China Men* recounts the experiences of the narrator's brother in Vietnam, where he makes a separate peace with a war that he is drafted into but is ambivalent about.

So here he was on an aircraft carrier from whose flight deck hour after hour corps of planes took off. He could not take naps, his bunk was directly beneath the rocket launchers. Even using binoculars, he did not see much of the shore. Hanoi was an hour away by plane. He did not see the bombs drop out of the planes, whether they fell like long white arrows, or whether they turned and turned, flashing in the sun. During loading, when they were locked into place, they looked like neatly rolled joints; they looked like long grains of rice; they looked like pupae and turds. He never heard cries under the bombing. They were not attacking the enemy with surprise bombings but routine bombings or "air operations" in twelve-hour shifts. When the sister ship got there, there would be bombings through the night, round-the-clock bombings. The pilots flew out there, unloaded their quota, and came back. It took intelligence and imagination to think that they were in Vietnam in the middle of the heaviest American bombing. A man he'd eaten lunch with did not show up for dinner, and that meant the man's plane had gone down. He had to imagine his death because he saw no blood, no body. The pilots either came back or they did not come back. There were no wounded. Sometimes a pilot would say that he had returned with a dead co-pilot in the cockpit. The sailors did not mourn the pilots, an arrogant, strut-ting class who volunteered for the bombings. Nobody was drafted to drop bombs. "Extra dessert tonight," the sailors said. "He asked for it," they said. "Hot shot." "Gung ho." When the pilots returned alive, it was no different from a practice run. No celebrations and no mournings, just business, a job. An officer was assigned to sort the dead man's personal effects; he censored those things too embarrassing to send to the family, such as photographs of Asian women.

The brother did touch foot on Vietnam by visiting a base near Saigon. He did not explore the city. He met some infantrymen who told him that when they were ordered to patrol the jungle they made a lot of noise, clanged equipment, talked loud. The enemy did the same, everybody warn-ing one another off. Once in a while, to keep some hawk officer happy, they fired rounds into the trees.

The brother was formally asked by his Commanding Officer to train as a pilot. He had the test scores, the potential, but he said No.

The pilots often invited their shipmates for the bombings. "Want to come along?" "Come on. Take a ride. Come along for the ride." The brother said No, "No, not me," many times. Then one day he said, "Sure. Why not? When? Sure, I'll come along for the ride." He put on a parachute and walked with the pilot and co-pilot across the flight deck on to the plane. He felt overheated, his head crammed into the helmet and his body pulled backward by the parachute. He had to duck through the door. Stuffed into his low seat, which was tilted toward the ceiling, he found with effort the seat belts and buckled himself in. The door slid shut. It was not too late to ask out. The plane was still lined up behind others waiting for takeoff. He could say he'd changed his mind and cause only a minor inconvenience. He wouldn't be embarrassed. The engine revved. He wasn't, after all, committing a worse act by riding on the plane than riding on the ship. The plane accelerated on its short runway, left the deck, and climbed over the water, the horizon slanting, dipping, and rising. Then there was the steadiness one feels riding in any plane, train, or car. The instruments, needles, dials, and lights made no alarming flashes or jumps. He put on a headset and heard familiar numbers and letters. Once he got up against the gravity and looked out of the windshield, which was narrow like a pair of wraparound glasses. All that he witnessed was heavy jungle and, in the open skies, other planes that seemed to appear and disappear quickly, shiny planes and their decals and formations. The bombs must have gone off behind them. Some air turbulence might have been a bomb ejected. He heard no explosion. There did seem to be some turns and banks like a ride in any small plane. The plane turned in the direction from which they seemed to have come— he could tell by the sun now on the other side—and they were descending and landing. The plane caught in the wires, not needing the net. The door opened, and he climbed out. "Smooth run," said the pilot. "Yeah, smooth," said the co-pilot. The brother felt no different from before, but he made a decision never to go again.

JOAN DIDION

Salvador

Joan Didion (born 1934), novelist, screenwriter, and one of the most important journalists of the past decades, is usually associated with the subjective reporting style of New Journalism. In essay collections such as *Slouching towards Bethlehem* (1968) and *The White Album* (1979), she emerged as a key interpreter of California's counterculture and the legacies of the 1960s. Much of her subsequent work has focused on American intervention in the political turmoil of Latin America. In novels like *The Last Thing He Wanted* (1996), set on a small island off Costa Rica during the Iran-Contra scandal, and *A Book of Common Prayer* (1977), set in the fictional South American locale "Boca Grande," Didion weaves the intricacies of global politics into the haunting voices of her protagonists. After a two-week trip in 1982 with her husband, John Gregory Dunne, she wrote *Salvador* (1983), a nonfictional work excerpted here. Like Norman Mailer on WWII and Herr on Vietnam, Didion blends historical fact with visceral reaction to create the nightmarish landscape of an oppressive military regime.

Terror is the given of the place. Black-and-white police cars cruise in pairs, each with the barrel of a rifle extruding from an open window. Roadblocks materialize at random, soldiers fanning out from trucks and taking positions, fingers always on triggers, safeties clicking on and off. Aim is taken as if to pass the time. Every morning *El Diario de Hoy* and *La Prensa Gráfica* carry cautionary stories. "*Una madre y sus dos hijos fueron asesinados con arma cortante (corvo) por ocho sujetos desconocidos el lunes en la noche*": a mother and her two sons hacked to death in their beds by eight *desconocidos*, unknown men. The same morning's paper: the unidentified body of a young man, strangled, found on the shoulder of a road. Same morning, different story: the unidentified bodies of three young men, found on another road, their faces partially destroyed by bayonets, one face carved to represent a cross.

It is largely from these reports in the newspapers that the United States embassy compiles its body counts, which are transmitted to Washington in a weekly dispatch referred to by embassy people as "the grim-gram." These counts are presented in a kind of tortured code that fails to obscure what is taken for granted in El Salvador, that government forces do most of the killing. In a January 15 memo to Washington, for example, the embassy issued a "guarded" breakdown on its count of 6,909 "reported" political murders between September 16, 1980, and September 15, 1981. Of these 6,909, 922 were "believed committed by security forces," 952 "believed committed by leftist terrorists," 136 "believed committed by rightist terrorists," and 4,889 "committed by unknown assailants," the famous *desconocidos* favored by those San Salvador newspapers still publishing. (By whom the remaining ten were committed is unclear.) The memo continued:

The uncertainty involved here can be seen on the fact that responsibility cannot be fixed in the majority of cases. We note, however, that it is generally believed in El Salvador that a large number of the unexplained killings are carried out by the security forces, officially or unofficially. The Embassy is aware of dramatic claims that have been made by one interest group or another in which the security forces figure as the primary agents of murder here. El Salvador's tangled web of attack and vengeance, traditional criminal violence and political mayhem make this an impossible charge to sustain. In saying this, however, we make no attempt to lighten the responsibility for the deaths of many hundreds, and perhaps thousands, which can be attributed to the security forces. . . .

The body count kept by what is generally referred to in San Salvador as "the Human Rights Commission" is higher than the embassy's, and documented periodically by a photographer who goes out looking for bodies. The bodies he photographs are often broken into unnatural positions, and the faces to which the bodies are attached (when they are attached) are equally unnatural, sometimes unrecognizable as human faces, obliterated by acid or beaten to a mash of misplaced ears and teeth or slashed ear to ear and invaded by insects. "*Encontrado en Antiguo Cuscatlán el día 25 de marzo 1982: camison de dormir celeste,*" the typed caption reads on one photograph: found in Antiguo Cuscatlán March 25, 1982, wearing a sky-blue night shirt. The captions are laconic. Found in Soyapango May 21, 1982. Found in Mejicanos June 11, 1982. Found at El Playón May 30, 1982, white shirt, purple pants, black shoes.

The photograph accompanying that last caption shows a body with no eyes, because the vultures got to it before the photographer did. There is a special kind of practical information that the visitor to El Salvador acquires immediately, the way visitors to other places acquire information about the currency rates, the hours for the museums. In El Salvador one learns that vultures go first for the soft tissue, for the eyes, the exposed genitalia, the open mouth. One learns that an open mouth can be used to make a specific point, can be stuffed with something emblematic; stuffed, say, with a penis, or, if the point has to do with land title, stuffed with some of the dirt in question. One learns that hair deteriorates less rapidly than flesh, and that a skull surrounded by a perfect corona of hair is not an uncommon sight in the body dumps.

All forensic photographs induce in the viewer a certain protective numbness, but dissociation is more difficult here. The disfigurement is too routine. The locations are too near, the dates too recent. There is the presence of the relatives of the disappeared: the women who sit every day in this cramped office on the grounds of the archdiocese, waiting to look at the spiral-bound photo albums in which the photographs are kept. These albums have plastic covers bearing soft-focus color photographs of young Americans in dating situations (strolling through autumn foliage on one album, recumbent in a field of daisies on another), and the women, looking for the bodies of their husbands and brothers and sisters and children, pass them from hand to hand without comment or expression.

One of the more shadowy elements of the violent scene here [is] the death squad. Existence of these groups has long been disputed, but not by many Salvadorans. . . . Who constitutes the death squads is yet another difficult question. We do not believe that these squads exist as permanent formations but rather as ad hoc vigilante groups that coalesce according to perceived need. Membership is also uncertain, but in addition to civilians we believe that both on- and off-duty members of the security forces are participants. This was unofficially confirmed by right-wing spokesman Maj. Roberto D'Aubuisson who stated in an interview in early 1981 that security force members utilize the guise of the death squad when a potentially embarrassing or odious task needs to be performed.
—*from the confidential but later declassified January 15, 1982, memo previously cited, drafted for the State Department by the political section at the embassy in San Salvador*

The dead and pieces of the dead turn up in El Salvador everywhere, everyday, as taken for granted as in a nightmare, or a horror movie. Vultures of course suggest the presence of a body. A knot of children on the street suggests the presence of a body. Bodies turn up in the brush of vacant lots, in the garbage thrown down ravines in the richest districts, in public rest rooms, in bus stations. Some are dropped in Lake Ilopango, a few miles east of the city, and wash up near the lakeside cottages and clubs frequented by what remains in San Salvador of the sporting bourgeoisie. Some still turn up at El Playón, the lunar lava field of rotting human flesh visible at one time or another on every television screen in America but characterized as recently as June in the *El Salvador News Gazette*, an English-language weekly edited by an American named Mario Rosenthal, as an "uncorroborated story . . . dredged up from the files of leftist propaganda." Others turn up at Puerta del Diablo, above Parque Balboa, a national *Turicentro* still described, in the April-July 1982 issue of *Aboard TACA*, the magazine provided passengers on the national airline of El Salvador, as "offering excellent subjects for color photography."

JUNOT DÍAZ

The Brief Wondrous Life of Oscar Wao

Junot Díaz (born 1968), fiction writer and Creative Writing professor at MIT, is best known for his Pulitzer Prize–winning novel, *The Brief Wondrous Life of Oscar Wao* (2007). He has also published two collections of short stories, *Drown* (1997) and *This Is How You Lose Her* (2012). Díaz was named a MacArthur Fellow in 2012. Born in the Dominican Republic, he moved with his family to the United States in 1974 and has remained active in many community groups, from the VONA/Voices Summer Workshops, which he cofounded, to the Partido de los Trabajadores Dominicanos (Dominican Workers' Party), to Freedom University, a volunteer organization in Georgia that provides post-secondary education for undocumented immigrants. *The Brief Wondrous Life of Oscar Wao*, written in a streetwise Spanglish with footnotes and asides, fuses realism with magical realism, capturing both the New Jersey suburban landscape and the ghost-filled world of the Dominican Republic under Rafael Trujillo. This excerpt from the opening of the novel meditates on the New World curse called the "fukú."

They say it came first from Africa, carried in the screams of the enslaved; that it was the death bane of the Taínos, uttered just as one world perished and another began; that it was a demon drawn into Creation through the nightmare door that was cracked open in the Antilles. *Fukú americanus*, or more colloquially, fukú—generally a curse or a doom of some kind; specifically the Curse and the Doom of the New World. Also called the fukú of the Admiral because the Admiral was both its midwife and one of its great European victims; despite 'discovering' the New World the Admiral died miserable and syphilitic, hearing (dique) divine voices. In Santo Domingo, the Land He Loved Best (what Oscar, at the end, would call the Ground Zero of the New World), the Admiral's very name has become synonymous with both kinds of fukú, little and large; to say his name aloud or even to hear it is to invite calamity on the heads of you and yours. No matter what its name or provenance, it is believed that the arrival of Europeans on Hispaniola unleashed the fukú on the world, and we've all been in the shit ever since. Santo Domingo might be fukú's Kilometer Zero, its port of entry, but we are all of us its children, whether we know it or not.

But the fukú ain't just ancient history, a ghost story from the past with no power to scare. In my parents' day the fukú was real as shit, something your everyday person could believe in. Everybody knew someone who'd been eaten by a fukú, just like everybody knew somebody who worked up in the Palacio. It was in the air, you could say, though, like all the most important things on the Island, not something folks really talked about. But in those elder days, fukú had it good; it even had a hypeman of sorts, a high priest, you could say: Our then dictator-for-life Rafael Leónidas Trujillo Molina. For those of you who missed your mandatory two seconds of Dominican history: Trujillo, one of the twentieth century's most infamous dictators, ruled the Dominican Republic between 1930 and 1961 with an implacable ruthless brutality. A portly, sadistic, pig-eyed mulato who bleached his skin, wore platform shoes, and had a fondness for Napoleon-era haberdashery, Trujillo (also known as El Jefe, the Failed Cattle Thief, and Fuckface) came to control nearly every aspect of the DR's political, cultural, social, and economic life through a potent (and familiar) mixture of violence, intimidation, massacre, rape, co-optation, and terror; treated the country like it was a plantation and he was the master. At first glance, he was just your prototypical Latin American caudillo, but his power was terminal in ways that few historians or writers have ever truly captured or, I would argue, imagined. He was our Sauron, our Arawn, our Darkseid, our Once and Future Dictator, a personaje so outlandish, so perverse, so dreadful that not even a sci-fi writer could have made his ass up. Famous for changing ALL

THE NAMES of ALL THE LAND MARKS in the Dominican Republic to honor himself (Pico Duarte became Pico Trujillo, and Santo Domingo de Guzman, the first and oldest city in the New World, became Ciudad Trujillo); for making ill monopolies out of every slice of the national patrimony (which quickly made him one of the wealthiest men on the planet); for building one of the largest militaries in the hemisphere (dude had bomber wings, for fuck's sake); for fucking every hot girl in sight, even the wives of his subordinates, thousands upon thousands upon thousands of women; for expecting, no, *insisting* on absolute veneration from his pueblo (tellingly, the national slogan was 'Dios y Trujillo'); for running the country like it was a Marine boot camp; for stripping friends and allies of their positions and properties for no reason at all; and for his almost *supernatural* abilities. Outstanding accomplishments include: the 1937 genocide against the Haitian and Haitian-Dominican community; one of the longest, most damaging U.S.-backed dictatorships in the Western Hemisphere (and if we Latin types are skillful at anything it's tolerating U.S.-backed dictators, so you know this was a hard-earned victory, the chilenos and the argentinos are still appealing); the creation of the first modern kleptocracy (Trujillo was Mobutu before Mobutu was Mobutu); the systematic bribing of American senators; and, last but not least, the forging of the Dominican peoples into a modern state (did what his Marine trainers, during the Occupation, were unable to do).

No one knows whether Trujillo was the Curse's servant or its master, its agent or its principal, but it was clear he and it had an understanding, that them two was *tight*. It was believed, even in educated circles, that anyone who plotted against Trujillo would incur a fukú most powerful, down to the seventh generation and beyond. If you even thought a bad thing about Trujillo, *fuá*, a hurricane would sweep your family out to *sea, fuá*, a boulder would fall out of a clear sky and squash you, *fuá*, the shrimp you ate today was the cramp that killed you tomorrow. Which explains why everyone who tried to assassinate him always got done, why those dudes who finally did buck him down all died so horrifically.

PHILIP ROTH

Operation Shylock

Philip Roth (born 1933) won wide recognition with his irreverent novel, *Goodbye, Columbus* (1959), and the controversial *Portnoy's Complaint* (1969), the monologue of a "lust-ridden, mother-addicted, young Jewish bachelor." Some thirty other works followed, including the Pulitzer Prize–winning *American Pastoral* (1997), *The Human Stain* (2000), and *The Plot Against America* (2004). Though most of his novels are set in the United States, Roth has also lived in London and Rome. In 1974 he helped launch the Penguin "Writers from the Other Europe" series, introducing American readers to East European writers such as Milan Kundera. In the *Prague Orgy* (1985), Roth's alter ego, Nathan Zuckerman, travels to Czechoslovakia. Later in his career, Roth turned his attention to the conflict in the Middle East with *Operation Shylock* (1993). Set during the First Intifada in the late 1980s, this hallucinatory novel features Palestinians, Israeli Jews, and their counterparts in Europe and the United States. The excerpt here recounts a half-comic, half-nightmarish visit to the Israeli-occupied Gaza Strip.

"Hey!" I shouted. "Hey, you! Where are you?"

When there was no reply, I opened the driver's door and felt around for the ignition: *he'd left the keys.* I got in and shut the door and, without hesitating, started the car, accelerating hard in neutral to prevent it from stalling. Then I pulled onto the road and tried to build up speed—there must be a checkpoint *somewhere!* But I hadn't driven fifty feet before the driver appeared in the dim beam of the headlights waving one hand for me to stop and clutching his trousers around his knees with the other. I had to swerve wildly to avoid hitting him, and then, instead of stopping to let him get back in and drive me the rest of the way, I gunned the motor and pumped the gas pedal but nothing was able to get the thing to pick up speed and, only seconds later, the motor conked out.

Back behind me in the road I saw the flashlight wavering in the air, and in a few minutes the old driver was standing, breathless, beside the car.

I got out and handed him the keys and he got back in and, after two or three attempts, started the motor, and we began to move off, jerkily at first, but then everything seemed to be all right and we were driving along once again in what I decided to believe was the right direction.

"You should have said you had to shit. What was I supposed to think when you just stopped the car and disappeared?"

"Sick," he answered. "Stomach."

"You should have told me that. I misunderstood."

"Are you a Zionist?"

"Why do you keep *asking* that? If you mean Meir Kahane, then I am not a Zionist. If you mean Shimon Peres . . ." But why was I favoring with an answer this harmless old man with bowel problems, answering him seriously in a language he understood only barely . . . where the hell *was* my sense of reality? "Drive, please," I said, "Jerusalem. Just get me to Jerusalem. And without talking!"

But we hadn't got more than three or four miles closer to Jerusalem when he drove the car over to the shoulder, shut off the engine, took up the flashlight, and got out. This time I sat calmly in the back seat while he found himself some spot off the road to take another crap. I even began to laugh aloud at how I had exaggerated the menacing side of all this, when suddenly I was blinded by headlights barreling straight toward the taxi. Just inches from the front bumper, the other vehicle stopped, although I had braced for the impact and may even have begun to scream. Then there was noise everywhere, people shouting, a second vehicle, a third, there was a burst of light whitening everything, a second burst and I was being dragged out of the car and onto the road. I didn't know which language I was hearing, I could discern virtually nothing in all that incandescence, and I didn't know what to fear more, to have fallen into the violent hands of marauding Arabs or a violent band of Israeli settlers. "English!" I shouted, even as I tumbled along the surface of the highway. "I speak English!"

I was up and doubled over the car fender and then I was yanked and spun around and something knocked glancingly against the back of my skull and then I saw, hovering enormously overhead, a helicopter. I heard myself shouting, "Don't hit me, God damn it, I'm a Jew!" I'd realized that these were just the people I'd been looking for to get me safely back to my hotel.

I couldn't have counted all the soldiers pointing rifles at me even if I could have managed successfully to count—more soldiers even than there'd been in the Ramallah courtroom, helmeted and armed now, shouting instructions that I couldn't have heard, even if their language was one I understood, because of the noise of the helicopter.

"I hired this taxi in Ramallah!" I shouted back to them. "The driver stopped to shit!"

"Speak English!" someone shouted to me.

"THIS IS ENGLISH! HE STOPPED TO MOVE HIS BOWELS!"

"Yes? Him?"

"The driver! The Arab driver!" But where was he? Was I the only one they'd caught? *There was a driver!*

"Too late at night!"

"Is it? I didn't know."

"Shit?" a voice asked.

"Yes—we stopped for the driver to shit, he was only flashing the flashlight—"

"To shit!"

"Yes!"

Whoever had been asking the questions began to laugh. "That's all?" he shouted.

"As far as I know, *yes*. I could be wrong."

"You are!"

Just then one of them approached, a young, heavyset soldier, and he had a hand extended toward mine. In his other hand was a pistol. "Here." He gave me my wallet. "You dropped this."

"Thank you."

"This is quite a coincidence," he said politely in perfect English, "I just today, this afternoon, finished one of your books."

MICHAEL CHABON

The Yiddish Policemen's Union

Michael Chabon (born 1963), writer of novels, comics, children's books, and screenplays, won instant acclaim with *The Mysteries of Pittsburgh*

(1988), his UC Irvine master's thesis. Other books and genres followed, including the Pulitzer Prize–winning *The Amazing Adventures of Kavalier & Clay* (2000), a roving epic about two Jewish cousins who created a popular comics series just before World War II; and *The Yiddish Policemen's Union* (2007), an alternate history detective novel which won the Hugo, Nebula, and Sidewise Awards. Other works include the *Gentlemen of the Road* (2007), a 15-part serialized novel that ran in the *New York Times Magazine*; and *Telegraph Avenue* (2012), another action-packed, genre-bending creation, a tribute to the San Francisco Bay Area, especially Berkeley, where he now lives. Chabon's works are characterized by extensive graphics, playful allusions, and nods to genre fiction as well as to authors such as Jorge Luis Borges, Gabriel García Márquez, F. Scott Fitzgerald, and William Faulkner. This excerpt from *The Yiddish Policemen's Union* introduces us to Sitka, Alaska, which, in this counterfactual fabrication was settled by Jewish refugees during World War II.

In the street the wind shakes rain from the flaps of its overcoat. Landsman tucks himself into the hotel doorway. Two men, one with a cello case strapped to his back, the other cradling a violin or viola, struggle against the weather toward the door of Pearl of Manila across the street. The symphony hall is ten blocks and a world away from this end of Max Nordau Street, but the craving of a Jew for pork, in particular when it has been deep-fried, is a force greater than night or distance or a cold blast off the Gulf of Alaska. Landsman himself is fighting the urge to return to room 505, and his bottle or slivovitz, and his World's Fair souvenir glass.

Instead, he lights a papiros. After a decade of abstinence, Landsman took up smoking again not quite three years ago. His then-wife was pregnant at the time. It was a much-discussed and in some quarters a long-desired pregnancy—her first—but not a planned one. As with many pregnancies that are discussed too long there was a history of ambivalence in the prospective father. At seventeen weeks and a day—the day Landsman bought his first package of Broadways in ten years they got a bad result. Some but not all of the cells that made up the fetus, code-named Django, had an extra chromosome on the twentieth pair. A mosaicism, it was called. It might cause grave abnormalities. It might have no effect at all. In the available literature, a faithful person could find encouragement, and a faithless one ample reason to despond. Landsman's view of things—ambivalent, despondent, and with no faith in anything—prevailed. A doctor with half a dozen laminaria dilators broke the seal on the life of Django Landsman. Three months later, Landsman and his cigarettes moved out of the house on Tshernovits Island that he and Bina had shared for nearly all the fifteen years of their marriage. It was not that he couldn't live with the guilt. He just couldn't live with it and Bina, too.

An old man, pushing himself like a rickety hand cart, weaves a course toward the door of the hotel. A short man, under five feet, dragging a large valise. Landsman observes the long white coat, worn open over a white suit with a waistcoat, and the wide brimmed white hat pulled down over his ears. A white beard and sidelocks, wispy and thick at the same time. The valise an ancient chimera of stained brocade and scratched hide. The whole right side of the man's body sags five degrees lower than the left, where the suitcase, which must contain the old boy's entire collection of lead ingots, weighs it down. The man stops and raises a finger, as if he has a question to pose of Landsman. The wind toys with the man's whiskers and with the brim of his hat. From his beard, arm pits, breath, and skin, the wind plucks a rich smell of stale tobacco and wet flannel and the sweat of a man who lives in the street. Landsman notes the color of the man's antiquated boots, yellowish ivory, like his beard, with sharp toes and buttons running up the sides.

Landsman recalls that he used to see this nut a lot, back when he was arresting Tenenboym for petty theft and possession. The yid was no younger then and is no older now. People used to call him Elijah, because he turned up in all kinds of unlikely spots, with his pushke box and his indefinable air of having something important to say.

"Darling," he says to Landsman now. "This is the Hotel Zamenhof, no?"

His Yiddish sounds a bit exotic to Landsman, flavored with Dutch maybe. He is bent and frail, but his face, apart from crow's-feet around the blue eyes, looks youthful and unlined. The eyes themselves hold a match flame of eagerness that puzzles Landsman. The prospect of a night at the Zamenhof does not often give rise to such anticipation.

"That's right." Landsman offers Elijah the Prophet a Broadway, and the little man takes two and tucks one into the reliquary of his breast pocket. "Hot and cold water. Licensed shammes right on the premises."

"Are you the manager, sweetness?"

Landsman can't help smiling at that. He steps aside, gesturing toward the door. "The manager's inside," he says.

But the little man just stands there getting rained on, his beard fluttering like a flag of truce. He gazes up at the faceless face of the Zamenhof, gray in the murky streetlight. A narrow pile of dirty white brick and slit windows, three or four blocks off the tawdriest stretch of Monastir Street, the place has all the allure of a dehumidifier. Its neon sign blinks on and off, tormenting the dreams of the losers across the street at the Blackpool.

"The Zamenhof," the old man says, echoing the intermittent letters on the neon sign. "Not the Zamenhof. The Zamenhof."

Now the latke, a rookie named Netsky, comes jogging up, holding on to his round, flat, wide-brimmed patrolman's hat.

"Detective," the latke says, out of breath, and then gives the old man a squint and a nod. "Evening, Grandpa. Right, uh, Detective, sorry, I just got the call, I was hung up for a minute there." Netsky has coffee on his breath and powdered sugar on the right cuff of his blue coat. "Where's the dead yid?"

"In two-oh-eight," Landsman says, opening the door for the latke, then turning back to the old man. "Coming in, Grandpa?"

"No," Elijah says, with a hint of mild emotion that Landsman can't quite read. It might be regret, or relief, or the grim satisfaction of a man with a taste for disappointment. The flicker trapped in the old man's eyes has given way to a film of tears. "I was only curious. Thank you, Officer Landsman."

"It's Detective now," Landsman says, startled that the old man has retrieved his name. "You remember me, Grandpa?"

"I remember everything, darling." Elijah reaches into a hip pocket of his bleach yellow coat and takes out his pushke, a wooden casket, about the size of a box meant for index cards, painted black. On the front of the box, Hebrew words are painted: L'ERETZ YISROEL.

Cut into the top of the box is a narrow slit for coins or a folded dollar bill. "A small donation?" Elijah says.

The Holy Land has never seemed more remote or unattainable than it does to a Jew of Sitka. It is on the far side of the planet, a wretched place ruled by men united only in their resolve to keep out all but a worn fistful of small-change Jews. For half a century, Arab strongmen and Muslim partisans, Persians and Egyptians, socialists and nationalists and monarchists, pan-Arabists and pan-Islamists, traditionalists and the Party of Ali, have all sunk their teeth into Eretz Yisroel and worried it down to bone and gristle. Jerusalem is a city of blood and slogans painted on the wall, severed heads on telephone poles. Observant Jews around the world have not abandoned their hope to dwell one day in the land of Zion. But Jews have been tossed out of the joint three times now—in 586 BCE, in 70 CE and with savage finality in 1948. It's hard even for the faithful not to feel a sense of discouragement about their chances of once again getting a foot in the door.

Landsman gets out his wallet and pokes a folded twenty into Elijah's pushke. "Lots of luck," he says.

The little man hoists his heavy valise and starts to shuffle away. Landsman reaches out and pulls at Elijah's sleeve, a question formulating in his heart, a child's question about the old wish of his people for a home. Elijah turns with a look of practiced wariness. Maybe Landsman is some kind of troublemaker. Landsman feels the question ebb away like the nicotine in his bloodstream.

"What you got in the bag, Grandpa?" Landsman says. "Looks heavy."

"It's a book."

"One book?"

"It's very big."

"Long story?"

"Very long."

"What's it about?"

"It's about Messiah," Elijah says. "Now please take your hand off of me."

Landsman lets go. The old man straightens his back and raises his head. The clouds on his eyes blow over, and he looks angry, disdainful, and not in the least old.

"Messiah is coming," he says. It isn't quite a warning and yet somehow as a promise of redemption, it lacks a certain warmth.

"That works out well," Landsman says, jerking his thumb toward the hotel lobby. "As of tonight we have a vacancy."

Elijah looks hurt, or maybe just disgusted. He opens the black box and looks inside. He takes out the twenty-dollar bill that Landsman gave him and hands it back. Then he picks up his suitcase, settles his floppy white hat down over his head, and trudges off into the rain.

Landsman crumples the twenty and drops it into his hip pocket. He grinds his papiros under his shoe and goes into the hotel.

"Who's the nut?" Netsky says.

"They call him Elijah. He's harmless," says Tenenboym from behind the steel mesh of the reception window. "You used to see him around sometimes. Always pimping for Messiah." Tenenboym clacks a gold toothpick against his molars. "Listen, Detective, I'm not supposed to say anything. But I might as well tell you. Management is sending out a letter tomorrow."

"I can't wait to hear this," Landsman says.

"The owners sold out to a Kansas City concern."

"They're tossing us."

"Maybe," Tenenboym says. "Maybe not. Nobody's status is clear. But it's not out of the question that you might have to move out."

"Is that what it's going to say in the letter?"

Tenenboym shrugs. "The letter's all written in lawyer."

Landsman puts Netsky the latke on the front door. "Don't tell them what they heard or saw," he reminds him. "And don't give them a hard time, even if they look like they could use one."

Menashe Shpringer, the criminalist working the graveyard shift, blows into the lobby in a black coat and fur hat, with a rattling of rain. In one hand Shpringer carries a dripping umbrella. With the other he tows a chrome caddy to which his black vinyl toolbox and a plastic bin, with holes for handles, are strapped with bungee cord. Shpringer is a fireplug, his bowed legs and simian arms affixed to his neck without apparent benefit of shoulders. His face is mostly jowl and his ridged forehead looks like one of those domed beehives you see representing Industry in medieval woodcuts. The bin is blazoned with the single word EVIDENCE in blue letters.

"Are you leaving town?" Shpringer says. It's not an uncommon greeting these days. A lot of people have left town in the past couple of years, fled the District for the short roster of places that will welcome them, or that have tired of hearing about pogroms secondhand and are hoping to throw one for themselves. Landsman says that as far as he knows, he is not going anywhere. Most of the places that will take Jews require that you have a near relative living there. All of Landsman's nearest relatives are dead or facing Reversion themselves.

"Then let me say goodbye to you now, forever," Shpringer says. "Tomorrow night at this time I will be basking in the warm Saskatchewan sun."

"Saskatoon?" Landsman guesses.

"Thirty below they had today," Shpringer says.

"That was the high."

"Look at it this way," Landsman says. "You could be living in this dump."

"The Zamenhof." In his memory, Shpringer pulls Landsman's file, and frowns at its contents. "That's right. Home sweet home, eh?"

"It suits me in my current style of life."

Shpringer smiles a thin smile from which almost every trace of pity has been erased.

"Which way to the dead man?" he says.

NAOMI SHIHAB NYE

For Mohammed Zeid of Gaza, Age 15

Naomi Shihab Nye (born 1952), the daughter of a Palestinian refugee and American mother, is a poet familiar with politically explosive borders. Born in St. Louis, she returned with her family to Ramallah on the West Bank when she was fourteen, moving back to San Antonio a year later. Her ties to the Texas-Mexican border as well as the Middle East inform much of her poetry. *Different Ways to Pray* (1980) and *Hugging the Jukebox* (1982) explore the faiths and rituals that both connect and divide different human populations. Beginning with *Yellow Glove* (1986), followed by *The Red Suitcase* (1994) and her best-known volume, *Fuel* (1998), the Middle East becomes increasingly central to her poetry. Nye was elected a Chancellor of the Academy of American Poets in 2009. She has also written many children's books, including *Habibi* (1997), which won the Jane Addams Children's Book Award. In 2013 Nye received both the Robert Creeley Award and the NSK Neustadt Prize for Children's Literature. This selection from *You and Yours* (2005) features a child at the mercy of a bullet.

There is no *stray* bullet, sirs.
No bullet like a worried cat
crouching under a bush,
no half-hairless puppy bullet
dodging midnight streets.
The bullet could not be a pecan

plunking the tin roof,
not hardly, no fluff of pollen
on October's breath,
no humble pebble at our feet.

So don't gentle it, please.

We live among stray thoughts,
tasks abandoned midstream.
Our fickle hearts are fat
with stray devotions, we feel at home
among bits and pieces,
all the wandering ways of words.

But this bullet had no innocence, did not
wish anyone well, you can't tell us otherwise
by naming it mildly, this bullet was never the friend
of life, should not be granted immunity
by soft saying—friendly fire, straying death-eye,
why have we given the wrong weight to what we do?

Mohammed, Mohammed, deserves the truth.
This bullet had no secret happy hopes,
it was not singing to itself with eyes closed
under the bridge.

II. Food

S ection II, "Food," is organized around three interlocking topics, celebrating its tastes and smells, but also calling attention to the large-scale forces that bring it to the table, while not losing sight of the flights of the imagination that it has nourished. We start from an unusual place, with scarcity and hunger as a longstanding and ongoing problem, one of the material conditions linking the United States to the rest of the world. We then turn to its more familiar guise, food in all its abundance and variety: the buying, cooking, and eating of it; the ways it encodes memories of individual lives while serving as a site for cultural understanding and cross-fertilization. We end with selections meditating on the interplay between edible food and the not edible but equally pleasurable food for thought, a teasing paradox that fires the intellect as well as whets the appetite.

A cluster of three texts—an excerpt from Cabeza de Vaca's *La Relación* (1542); Mary Rowlandson's captivity narrative, *The Sovereignty and Goodness of God* (1682); and Louise Erdrich's poem, "Captivity" (2003)—open this section. The first was originally written in Spanish; the other two in styles reflecting the three-hundred-year gap separating them. In spite of these obvious differences, these three nonetheless speak in one voice when it comes to the shortage of food and the compulsions of hunger. Scarcity emerges here as a foundational fact, the point of convergence for authors who otherwise have little in common: a sixteenth-century Spanish explorer surviving a shipwreck, a seventeenth-century Puritan woman sharing the scanty supplies of her Indian captors, and a twentieth-century Native

American knowledgeable about hunger on the reservation. Surprisingly, also in this company is a fourth author, a man who would go on to become the governor of New York and then the twenty-sixth president of the United States. Theodore Roosevelt, in *Rough Riders* (1899), offers a spirited account of what inedible rations and missing basics can do to the morale of the troops, reminding us that food, then and now, is a necessity of life, its bodily imperatives not negotiable, allowing for shared enjoyment cutting across cultural divides, and missed in much the same way when there is not enough.

Food shortage is, of course, especially endemic during war, making the selections here a logical sequel to those in Section I, with many echoes and cross-references. In this spirit, we proceed to look at food as a lens on war in a variety of contexts: e. e. cummings's gastronomic experiences under French detention during World War I; Amy Tan's focus on the small detail of the chestnut during the Nanking Massacre; Ha Jin's description of the starving Chinese soldiers during the Korean War. These are striking instances. And yet the lack of food, as a form of psychic debasement, accompanied by a retributive violence that inversely mirrors it, is not limited only to the combat zone. It seems more widespread and elemental. Sharon Olds's poem, "The Food-Thief," framed by the drought in Uganda, asks us to think of stealing and punishing as the two faces of a compulsion dictated by our bodily needs. It is a bleak view of humanity. To balance things out, we turn to a world radically different from our own, a fantasy created by Ursula K. Le Guin as an alternative and counterpoint to what we take for granted. For Le Guin, the frigid and seemingly barren environment of the planet Winter need not spell disaster or even a stunted gastronomic life. Her *The Left Hand of Darkness* challenges us to be inventive in what we eat.

To think about scarcity and hunger as a cultural and political—as well as physiological—problem is to think about the complex place of the human body in a global field. This is no less true when food is present in great variety and abundance. "Stubb's Supper," a chapter from Melville's *Moby-Dick*, shows humans and sharks comically mirroring each other in their shared voraciousness, and in their shared economy of domination and subjection. This ubiquitous sharkishness is made even more explicit in the colonial context of Jack London's "The Water Baby." On a more somber note, Upton Sinclair's description of the odors and sounds greeting the immigrant workers as they approach the Chicago stockyards, followed by Ruth Ozeki's fictional media campaign to sell American beef to Japanese housewives, make it clear that food is big business, a scale of operation dwarfing any individual laborer or consumer. And yet food can at the same time be intimate, memory-laden, whether as family recipes, or as still remembered, still cherished tastes and smells from the old country. Bringing these into contact with the recipes, the tastes and smells that come with new languages and cultures, they fuse the near with the far, the inherited with the acquired. Willa Cather's portrait of two French missionaries in New Mexico, speaking French on Christmas Day and trying to find New World substitutes for their French ingredients; and Jhumpa Lahiri's oblique portrait of the Pakistan-Bangladesh war, refracted through the home-cooked but TV-dominated Indian dinners in suburban Boston, remind us that there are many layers of reality packed into food, many worlds condensed and recalled in the small rituals of cooking and eating. These and other selections give us a world minutely savored and multiply situated, in which food is both taste and process.

ÁLVAR NÚÑEZ CABEZA DE VACA

La Relación

trans. Rolena Adorno and Patrick Charles Pautz

Álvar Núñez Cabeza de Vaca (c. 1490–1558), Spanish explorer and writer, was one of the four survivors of the 1527 Narváez expedition, among the first Europeans to make the trek across present-day Florida, Texas, and Mexico. His account of this eight-year journey, *La Relación*, describes in great detail the many indigenous tribes and cultures that he met along the way. It also tells the story of his personal transformation from a colonial treasurer to a trader and faith healer sought out by the native inhabitants. In the following passage, a naked and starving Cabeza de Vaca survives the cold by traveling with a lighted torch and a load of wood to make a fire, looking for the Avavares Indians, who feed him prickly pears, the only food they have. In integrating himself into these indigenous communities, Cabeza de Vaca enacts a form of cross-cultural encounter that allows Indians and Europeans to meet on an equal footing and share resources, a practice sadly not adopted by most of his compatriots.

That same night that we arrived, some Indians came to Castillo and said to him that they suffered a malady of the head, begging him to cure them. And after he had made the sign of the cross over them and commended them to God, at that point the Indians said that all the sickness had left them. And they went to their houses and brought many prickly pears and a piece of venison, a thing that we could not identify. And when this news was spread among them, many other sick people came that night to be cured. And each one brought a piece of venison. And there were so many of them that we did not know where to put the meat. We gave great thanks to God because each day his mercy and blessings were increasing. And after the cures were completed, they began to dance and make their *areitos* and celebrations, which lasted until sunrise of the following day. And the celebration held on account of our arrival lasted for three days. And at the end of them, we asked them about the land that lay ahead, and about the people that we would find in it, and the sources of food that were in it. They responded to us that throughout that entire land there were many prickly pears, but that the season was already over, and that there were no people because they had all gone to their homes, having already collected the prickly pears, and that the land was very cold and in it there were very few hides. Seeing that winter and cold weather were already upon us, we decided to spend it with these Indians. Five days after we had arrived there, they left to hunt for other prickly pears where there were other people of different nations and tongues. And traveling five days with very great hunger because there were no prickly pears nor any other fruit along the route, we arrived at a river where we put up our houses. And after setting them up, we went to look for the fruit of some trees, which is like [the fruit of] a vetch. And since through all this land there are no trails, I stopped to investigate it more fully; the people returned and I remained alone, and going to look for them, that night I got lost. And it pleased God that I found a tree aflame, and warmed by its fire I endured the cold that night, and in the morning I gathered a load of firewood, and I took two firebrands and again looked for the people. And I continued in this manner for five days, always with my lighted torch and load of wood, so that if my fire died in a place where there was no firewood (since in many areas there was none), I would have the means to make other firebrands and I would not remain without a light, because against the cold I had no other recourse since I went naked as I was born. And for the night I had this defense, that is, I went to the groves of the wood near the rivers, and stopped in them before sunset. And in the earth I dug a pit with the butt of a timber and in it I threw a great deal of firewood from the trees that grow in great quantity there. And I gathered much dry wood fallen from the trees, and around that pit I placed four fires like the points of a cross. And I made an effort and took care to rekindle the fire from time to time, and from the long grass that grows there I made some bundles to cover myself in that hole. And in this way I protected myself from the cold of night. And during one of them, the fire fell on the grass with which I was covered. And while I was sleeping in the pit the fire began to burn fiercely, and despite the great haste that I made to get out, my hair nevertheless received the sign of the danger in which I had been. In this entire time I did not eat a mouthful of food, nor did I find anything that I could eat, and since my feet were bare, they bled a great deal. And God took pity upon me, that in all this time the north wind did not blow, because otherwise it would have been impossible for me to survive. And at the end of five days, I arrived at a bank of a river where I found my Indians, for they and the Christians had already taken me for dead, and they were convinced that some viper had bitten me. All took great pleasure in seeing me, especially the Christians, and they told me that until then, they had traveled with great hunger, that this was the reason they had not searched for me, and that night they gave me to eat some of the prickly pears they had. And the next day we departed from there and went to where we found many prickly pears with which all satisfied their great hunger. And we gave many thanks to our Lord because his succor never failed us.

MARY ROWLANDSON

The Sovereignty and Goodness of God

Mary Rowlandson (c. 1637–1711) is best known for *The Sovereignty and Goodness of God* (1682), a best-selling colonial captivity narrative that stands as one of the foundational works of American literature. Rowlandson emigrated from England to the Massachusetts Bay Colony in the mid-seventeenth century, marrying the Reverend John Rowlandson in 1656 and settling in the frontier town of Lancaster. Her narrative, beginning with the Narragansett and Wampanoag attack on that town, comprises a series of twenty "removes" detailing her trek with her captors. True to her Puritan faith, Rowlandson crafts the arc of her suffering and return as the trial and ultimate triumph of her religious devotion. Here, her vacillating attitude toward indigenous food tells a complex story of doctrinal rigidity modified by the need for human contact and the pressures of extreme hunger. While thanking God for making formerly repulsive food palatable, she is sometimes so driven by hunger as to behave in ways seemingly un-Christian.

THE NINTH REMOVE

. . . My son was ill, and I could not but think of his mournful looks, and no Christian friend was near him, to do any office of love for him, either for soul or body. And my poor girl, I knew not where she was, nor whether she was sick, or well, or alive, or dead. I repaired under these thoughts to my Bible (my great comfort in that time) and that Scripture came to my hand, "Cast thy burden upon the Lord, and He shall sustain thee" (Psalm 55.22). But I was fain to go and look after something to satisfy my hunger, and going among the wigwams, I went into one and there found a squaw who showed herself very kind to me, and gave me a piece of bear. I put it into my pocket, and came home, but could not find an opportunity to broil it, for fear they would get it from me, and there it lay all that day and night in my stinking pocket. In the morning I went to the same squaw, who had a kettle of ground nuts boiling. I asked her to let me boil my piece of bear in her kettle, which she did, and gave me some ground nuts to eat with it: and I cannot but think how pleasant it was to me. I have sometime seen bear baked very handsomely among the English, and some like it, but the thought that it was bear made me tremble. But now that was savory to me that one would think was enough to turn the stomach of a brute creature. One bitter cold day I could find no room to sit down before the fire. I went out, and could not tell what to do, but I went in to another wigwam, where they were also sitting round the fire, but the squaw laid a skin for me, and bid me sit down, and gave me some ground nuts, and bade me come again; and told me they would buy me, if they were able, and yet these were strangers to me that I never saw before. . . .

THE EIGHTEENTH REMOVE

We took up our packs and along we went, but a wearisome day I had of it. As we went along I saw an Englishman stripped naked, and lying dead upon the ground, but knew not who it was. Then we came to another Indian town, where we stayed all night. In this town there were four English children, captives; and one of them my own sister's. I went to see how she did, and she was well, considering her captive condition. I would have tarried that night with her, but they that owned her would not suffer it. Then I went into another wigwam, where they were boiling corn and beans, which was a lovely sight to see, but I could not get a taste thereof. Then I went to another wigwam, where there were two of the English children; the squaw was boiling horses feet; then she cut me off a little piece, and gave one of the English children a piece also. Being very hungry I had quickly eat up mine, but the child could not bite it, it was so tough and sinewy, but lay sucking, gnawing, chewing and slabbering of it in the mouth and hand. Then I took it of the child, and eat it myself, and savory it was to my taste. Then I may say as Job 6.7, "The things that my soul refused to touch are as my sorrowful meat." Thus the Lord made that pleasant refreshing, which another time would have been an abomination. Then I went home to my mistress's wigwam; and they told me I disgraced my master with begging, and if I did so any more, they would knock me in the head. I told them, they had as good knock me in head as starve me to death.

LOUISE ERDRICH

Captivity

Louise Erdrich (born 1954), novelist and poet, was born in Minnesota to a German American father and a French and Chippewa mother. The meaning of mixed heritage is explored in many of her works. Her writing has garnered much praise—*Love Medicine* won the 1984 National Book Critics Circle Award, *The Round House* the 2012 National Book Award—but has also sparked controversy. In a 1986 review of *The Beet Queen*, Leslie Marmon Silko (also included in this volume) objected to Erdrich's postmodern style, arguing that its technical virtuosity comes at the expense of historical truth. In "Captivity" from *Original Fire* (2003), we see an example of this technical daring. Erdrich rewrites Mary Rowlandson's *The Sovereignty and Goodness of God*, imagining an erotic attachment between captive and captor while playing fast and loose with her evidence. The epigram to the poem comes in fact not from Rowlandson, but John Gyles's *Memoirs of Odd Adventures, Signal Deliverances, Etc* (1736); the "bisquit" he dare not eat is offered not by a Native American but by a Jesuit interested in buying him. Taking liberties in this way, Erdrich shows that what passes for historical truth is often accompanied by complex fictions.

~~~~~~

He (my captor) gave me a bisquit, which I put in my pocket, and not daring to eat it, buried it under a log, fearing he had put something in it to make me love him.

—From the narrative of the captivity of Mrs. Mary Rowlandson, who was taken prisoner by the Wampanoag when Lancaster, Massachusetts, was destroyed, in the year 1676

The stream was swift, and so cold
I thought I would be sliced in two.
But he dragged me from the flood
by the ends of my hair.
I had grown to recognize his face.
I could distinguish it from the others.
There were times I feared I understood
his language, which was not human,
and I knelt to pray for strength.

We were pursued by God's agents
or pitch devils, I did not know.
Only that we must march.
Their guns were loaded with swan shot.
I could not suckle and my child's wail
put them in danger.
He had a woman
with teeth black and glittering.
She fed the child milk of acorns.
The forest closed, the light deepened.

I told myself that I would starve
before I took food from his hands
but I did not starve.
One night
he killed a deer with a young one in her

and gave me to eat of the fawn.
It was so tender,
the bones like the stems of flowers,
that I followed where he took me.
The night was thick. He cut the cord
that bound me to the tree.

After that the birds mocked.
Shadows gaped and roared
and the trees flung down
their sharpened lashes.
He did not notice God's wrath.
God blasted fire from half-buried stumps.
I hid my face in my dress, fearing He would burn us all
but this, too, passed.

Rescued, I see no truth in things.
My husband drives a thick wedge
through the earth, still it shuts
to him year after year.
My child is fed of the first wheat.
I lay myself to sleep
on a Holland-laced pillowbeer.
I lay to sleep.
And in the dark I see myself
as I was outside their circle.

They knelt on deerskins, some with sticks,
and he led his company in the noise
until I could no longer bear
the thought of how I was.
I stripped a branch
and struck the earth,
in time, begging it to open
to admit me
as he was
and feed me honey from the rock.

THEODORE ROOSEVELT

The Rough Riders

Theodore Roosevelt (1858–1919), the twenty-sixth president of the United States, also served as the governor of New York and the vice president under President McKinley; he received the Nobel Peace Prize in 1906. Born to wealth in New York City, he championed the "Square Deal" for the average citizen, and throughout his long career advocated regulating business and breaking up monopolies, eventually leaving the Republican Party to launch the Progressive Party in 1912. Focusing on the Panama Canal in his foreign policy, he spoke out domestically on conservation and greatly expanded the national park system. His prolific writing career began with his Harvard senior thesis, eventually published as *The Naval War of 1812* (1882), followed by many other works including his autobiography, *Theodore Roosevelt* (1913), and a four-volume history of the American frontier, *The Winning of the West* (1889–1896). *The Rough Riders* (1899), excerpted here, is his account of the Spanish-American War (1898), during which he helped form and served under the first U.S. Volunteer Cavalry Regiment and experienced firsthand the inedible food endured by soldiers on the front line.

COLONEL REPORT TO THE SECRETARY OF WAR (SEPTEMBER 10, 1898)

We were two weeks on the troop-ship Yucatan, and as we were given twelve days' travel rations, we of course fell short toward the end of the trip, but eked things out with some of our field rations and troop stuff. The quality of the travel rations given to us was good, except in the important item of meat. The canned roast beef is worse than a failure as part of the rations, for in effect it amounts to reducing the rations by just so much, as a great majority of the men find it uneatable. It was coarse, stringy, tasteless, and very disagreeable in appearance, and so unpalatable that the effort to eat it made some of the men sick. Most of the men preferred to be hungry rather than eat it. If cooked in a stew with plenty of onions and potatoes—i.e., if only one ingredient in a dish with other more savory ingredients—it could be eaten, especially if well salted and peppered; but, as usual (what I regard as a great mistake), no salt was issued with the travel rations, and of course no potatoes and onions. There were no cooking facilities on the transport. When the men obtained any, it was by bribing the cook. Toward the last, when they began to draw on the field rations, they had to eat the bacon raw. On the return trip the same difficulty in rations obtained.—i.e., the rations were short because the men could not eat the canned roast beef, and had no salt. We purchased of the ship's supplies some flour and pork and a little rice for the men, so as to relieve the shortage as much as possible, and individual sick men were helped from private sources by officers, who themselves ate what they had purchased in Santiago. As nine-tenths of the men were more or less sick, the unattractiveness of the travel rations was doubly unfortunate. It would have been an excellent thing for their health if we could have had onions and potatoes, and means for cooking them. Moreover, the water was very bad, and sometimes a cask was struck that was positively undrinkable. The lack of ice for the weak and sickly men was very much felt. Fortunately there was no epidemic, for there was not a place on the ship where patients could have been isolated.

During the month following the landing of the army in Cuba the food-supplies were generally short in quantity, and in quality were never such as were best suited to men undergoing severe hardships and great exposure in an unhealthy tropical climate. The rations were, I understand, the same as those used in the Klondike. In this connection, I call especial attention to the report of Captain Brown, made by my orders when I was Brigade-Commander, and herewith appended. I also call attention to the report of my own Quartermaster. Usually we received full rations of bacon and hardtack. The hardtack, however, was often mouldy, so that parts of cases, and even whole cases, could not be used. The bacon was usually good. But bacon and hardtack make poor food for men toiling and fighting in trenches under the midsummer sun of the tropics. The ration of coffee was often short, and that of sugar generally so; we rarely got any vegetables. Under these circumstances the men lost strength steadily, and as the fever speedily attacked them, they suffered from being reduced to a bacon and hardtack diet. So much did the shortage of proper food tell upon their health that again and again officers were compelled to draw upon their private purses, or upon the Red Cross Society, to make good the deficiency of the Government supply. Again and again we sent down improvised pack-trains composed of officers' horses, of captured Spanish cavalry ponies, or of mules which had been shot or abandoned but were cured by our men. These expeditions—sometimes under the Chaplain, sometimes under the Quartermaster, sometimes under myself, and occasionally under a trooper—would go to the sea-coast or to the Red Cross head-quarters, or, after the surrender, into the city of Santiago, to get food both for the well and the sick. The Red Cross Society rendered invaluable aid. For example, on one of these expeditions I personally brought up 600 pounds of beans; on another occasion I personally brought up 500 pounds of rice, 800 pounds of cornmeal, 200 pounds of sugar, 100 pounds of tea, 100 pounds of oatmeal, 5 barrels of potatoes, and two of onions, with cases of canned soup and condensed milk for the sick in hospitals. Every scrap of the food thus brought up was eaten with avidity by the soldiers, and put new heart and strength into them. It was only our constant care of the men in this way that enabled us to keep them in any trim at all. As for the sick in the hospital, unless we were able from outside sources to get them such simple delicacies as rice and condensed milk, they usually had the alternative of eating salt pork and hardtack or going without. After each fight we got a good deal of food from the Spanish camps in the way of beans, peas, and rice, together with green coffee, all of which the men used and relished greatly. In some respects the Spanish rations were preferable to ours, notably in the use of rice. After we had been ashore a month the supplies began to come in in abundance, and we then fared very well. Up to that time the men were under-fed, during the very weeks when the heaviest drain was being made upon their vitality, and the deficiency was only partially supplied through the aid of the Red Cross, and out of the officers' pockets and the pockets of various New York friends who sent us money. Before, during, and immediately after the fights of June 24th and July 1st, we were very short of even the bacon and hardtack. About July 14th, when the heavy rains interrupted communication, we were threatened with famine, as we were informed that there was not a day's supply of provisions in advance nearer than the sea-coast; and another twenty-four hours' rain would have resulted in a complete breakdown of communications, so that for several days we should have been reduced to a diet of mule-meat and mangos. At this time, in anticipation of such a contingency, by foraging and hoarding we got a little ahead, so that when our supplies were cut down for a day or two we did not suffer much, and were even able to furnish a little aid to the less fortunate First Illinois Regiment, which was camped next to us. Members of the Illinois Regiment were offering our men $1 apiece for hardtacks.

e. e. cummings

The Enormous Room

e. e. [Edward Estlin] cummings (1894–1962), born in Cambridge, Massachusetts, and educated at Harvard, began experimenting with words at an early age, influenced by the Dada and Surrealist movements no less than by Ezra Pound and Gertrude Stein. Compulsive punning, play with numbers and typography, unusual punctuation and idiosyncratic breaking of words—all these contribute to the intensely visual nature of his poetry, beginning with early volumes such as & (1925) and is 5 (1926) and continuing throughout his career. Cummings was also a painter, playwright, essayist, and novelist. His first published work, *The Enormous Room* (1922), recounts his detention during World War I in a French internment camp, along with his friend William Slate Brown (referred to as B.), on an unfounded charge of treasonable correspondence. In this excerpt, Cummings describes with a mixture of humor and horror the behavior of the prisoners at mealtime.

"A la soupe les hommes."

The cry was lost in a tremendous confusion, a reckless thither-and-hithering of humanity, every one trying to be at the door, spoon in hand, before his neighbor. B. said calmly, extracting his own spoon from beneath his *paillasse*, on which we were seated: "They'll give you yours downstairs, and when you get it you want to hide it or it'll be pinched"—and in company with Monsieur Bragard, who had refused the morning promenade, and whose gentility would not permit him to hurry when it was a question of such a low craving as hunger, we joined the dancing, roaring throng at the door. I was not too famished myself to be unimpressed by the instantaneous change which had come over The Enormous Room's occupants. Never did Circe herself cast upon men so bestial an enchantment. Among these faces convulsed with utter animalism I scarcely recognized my various acquaintances. The transformation produced by the *planton's* shout was not merely amazing; it was uncanny, and not a little thrilling. These eyes bubbling with lust, obscene grins sprouting from contorted lips, bodies unclenching and clenching in unctuous gestures of complete savagery, convinced me by a certain insane beauty. Before the arbiter of their destinies some thirty creatures, hideous and authentic, poised, cohering in a sole chaos of desire; a fluent and numerous cluster of vital inhumanity. As I contemplated this ferocious and uncouth miracle, this beautiful manifestation of the sinister alchemy of hunger, I felt that the last vestige of individualism was about utterly to disappear, wholly abolished in a gamboling and wallowing throb.

The beefy-neck bellowed:

"Est-ce que vous êtes tous ici?"

A shrill roar of language answered. He looked contemptuously around him, upon the thirty clamoring faces each of which wanted to eat him— puttees, revolver and all. Then he cried:

"Allez, descendez."

Squirming, jostling, fighting, roaring, we poured slowly through the doorway. Ridiculously. Horribly. I felt like a glorious microbe in huge, absurd din irrevocably swathed. B. was beside me. A little ahead Monsieur Auguste's voice protested. Count Bragard brought up the rear.

When we reached the corridor nearly all the breath was knocked out of me. The corridor being wider than the stairs allowed me to inhale and look around. B. was yelling in my ear:

"Look at the Hollanders and the Belgians! They're always ahead when it comes to food!"

Sure enough: John the Bathman, Harree and Pompom were leading this extraordinary procession. Fritz was right behind them, however, and pressing the leaders hard. I heard Monsieur Auguste crying in his child's voice:

"*Si tout-le-monde veut marcher dou-ce-ment nous allons ar-ri-ver plus tôt! Il faut pas faire comme ça!*"

Then suddenly the roar ceased. The mêlée integrated. We were marching in orderly ranks. B. said:

"The *Surveillant!*"

At the end of the corridor, opposite the kitchen window, there was a flight of stairs. On the third stair from the bottom stood (teetering a little slowly back and forth, his lean hands joined behind him and twitching regularly, a képi tilted forward on his cadaverous head so that its visor almost hid the weak eyes sunkenly peering from under droopy eyebrows, his pompous rooster-like body immaculately attired in a shiny uniform, his puttees sleeked, his *croix* polished)—The Fencer. There was a renovated look about him which made me laugh. Also his pose was ludicrously suggestive of Napoleon reviewing the armies of France.

Our column's first rank moved by him. I expected it to continue ahead through the door and into the open air, as I had myself done in going from *les douches* to *le cour;* but it turned a sharp right and then sharp left, and I perceived a short hall, almost hidden by the stairs. In a moment I had passed the Fencer myself and entered the hall. In another moment I was in a room, pretty nearly square, filled with rows of pillars. On turning into the hall the column had come almost to a standstill. I saw now that the reason for this slowing-down lay in the fact that on entering the room every man in turn passed a table and received a piece of bread from the chef. When B. and I came opposite the table the dispenser of bread smiled pleasantly and nodded to B., then selected a large hunk and pushed it rapidly into B.'s hands with an air of doing something which he shouldn't. B. introduced me, whereupon the smile and selection was repeated.

"He thinks I'm a German," B. explained in a whisper, "and that you are a German too." Then aloud, to the cook: "My friend here needs a spoon. He just got here this morning and they haven't given him one."

The excellent person at the bread table hereupon said to me: "You shall go to the window and say I tell you to ask for spoon and you will catch one spoon"—and I broke through the waiting line, approached the kitchen-window, and demanded of a roguish face within:

"*Une cuillère, s'il vous plaît.*"

The roguish face, which had been singing in a high faint voice to itself, replied critically but not unkindly:

"*Vous êtes un nouveau?*"

I said that I was, that I had arrived late last night.
It disappeared, reappeared, and handed me a tin spoon and cup, saying:

"*Vous n'avez pas de tasse?*"—"*Non,*" I said.

"*Tiens. Prends ça. vite.*" Nodding in the direction of the *Surveillant,* who was standing all this time on the stairs behind me.
I had expected from the cook's phrase that something would be thrown at me which I should have to catch, and was accordingly somewhat relieved at the true state of affairs. On re-entering the *salle à manger* I was greeted by many cries and wavings, and looking in their direction perceived *tout le monde* uproariously seated at wooden benches which were placed on either side of an enormous wooden table. There was a tiny gap in one bench where a place had been saved for me by B. with the assistance of Monsieur Auguste, Count Bragard, Harree and several other fellow-convicts. In a moment I had straddled the bench and was occupying the gap, spoon and cup in hand, and ready for anything.
The din was perfectly terrific. It had a minutely large quality. Here and there, in a kind of sonal darkness, solid sincere unintelligible absurd wisps of profanity heavily flickered. Optically the phenomenon was equally remarkable: seated waggingly swaying corpse-like figures, swaggering, pounding with their little spoons, roaring hoarse unkempt. Evidently *Monsieur le Surveillant* had been forgotten. All at once the roar bulged unbearably. The roguish man, followed by the *chef* himself, entered with a suffering waddle, each of them bearing a huge bowl of steaming something. At least

six people immediately rose, gesturing and imploring: *"Ici"*—*"Mais non, ici"*—*"Mettez le ici"*—

The bearers plumped their burdens carefully down, one at the head of the table and one in the middle. The men opposite the bowls stood up. Every man seized the empty plate in front of him and shoved it into his neighbour's hand; the plates moved toward the bowls, were filled amid uncouth protestations and accusations—*"Mettez plus que ça"*—*"C'est pas juste, alors"*—*"Donnez-moi encore des pommes"*—*"Nom de Dieu, il n'y en a pas assez"*—*"Cochon, qu'est-ce qu'il veut?"*—"Shut up"—"Gott-fer-dummer"—and returned one by one. As each man received his own, he fell upon it with a sudden guzzle.

Eventually, in front of me, solemnly sat a faintly-smoking urine-colored circular broth, in which soggily hung half-suspended slabs of raw potato. Following the example of my neighbors, I too addressed myself to *La Soupe*. I found her luke-warm, completely flavorless. I examined the hunk of bread. It was almost bluish in color; in taste mouldy, slightly sour. "If you crumb some into the soup," remarked B., who had been studying my reactions from the corner of his eye, "they both taste better." I tried the experiment. It was a complete success. At least one felt as if one were getting nourishment. Between gulps I smelled the bread furtively. It smelled rather much like an old attic in which kites and other toys gradually are forgotten in a gentle darkness.

B. and I were finishing our soup together when behind and somewhat to the left there came the noise of a lock being manipulated. I turned and saw in one corner of the *salle à manger* a little door, shaking mysteriously. Finally it was thrown open, revealing a sort of minute bar and a little closet filled with what appeared to be groceries and tobacco; and behind the bar, standing in the closet, a husky competent-looking lady. "It's the canteen," B. said. We rose, spoon in hand and breadhunk stuck on spoon, and made our way to the lady. I had, naturally, no money; but B. reassured me that before the day was over I should see the *Gestionnaire* and make arrangements for drawing on the supply of ready cash which the gendarmes who took me from Gré had confided to the *Surveillant's* care; eventually I could also draw on my account with Norton-Harjes in Paris; meantime he had *quelques sous* which might well go into chocolate and cigarettes. The large lady had a pleasant quietness about her, a sort of simplicity, which made me extremely desirous of complying with B.'s suggestion. Incidentally I was feeling somewhat uncertain in the region of the stomach, due to the unique quality of the lunch which I had just enjoyed, and I brightened at the thought of anything as solid as chocolate. Accordingly we purchased (or rather B. did) a *paquet jaune* and a cake of something which was not Menier. And the remaining *sous* we squandered on a glass apiece of red acrid *pinard,* gravely and with great happiness pledging the hostess of the occasion and then each other.

With the exception of ourselves hardly anyone patronized the canteen, noting which I felt somewhat conspicuous. When, however, Harree, Pompom and John the Bathman came rushing up and demanded cigarettes my fears were dispelled. Moreover the *pinard* was excellent.

"Come on! Arrange yourselves!" the bull-neck cried hoarsely as the five of us were lighting up; and we joined the line of fellow-prisoners with their breads and spoons, gaping, belching, trumpeting fraternally, by the doorway.

"*Tout le monde en haut!*" this *planton* roared.

Slowly we fled through the tiny hall, past the stairs (empty now of their Napoleonic burden), down the corridor, up the creaking, gnarled, damp flights, and (after the inevitable pause in which the escort rattled chains and locks) into The Enormous Room.

This would be about ten-thirty.

AMY TAN

The Kitchen God's Wife

Amy Tan (born 1952) made a name for herself with her first book, *The Joy Luck Club* (1987), which details the lives of four Chinese American families in San Francisco through stories told by players in a *mahjong* game. Generational conflict between mother and daughter is a persistent theme in her work, from *The Kitchen God's Wife* (1991) and *The Hundred Secret Senses* (1995) to *The Bonesetter's Daughter* (2001) and *The Valley of Amazement* (2013). *Saving Fish from Drowning* (2005), however, recounts the tribulations of a group lost on an expedition in the Burmese jungles.

Tan has also written children's books, including *Sagwa: The Chinese Siamese Cat* (1994), made into an animation series and aired on PBS. She plays in a rock band, the Rock Bottom Remainders, with several other writers. This excerpt from *The Kitchen God's Wife* frames the large-scale violence of World War II through the focus on a roasted chestnut, held in the hand throughout the horror and chaos of the Nanking Massacre.

Hulan and I had followed the sweet smoke of roasting chestnuts, and we were now standing in front of a sidewalk vendor. He was stirring a basket filled with dark nuggets. It was three hours since we had eaten our breakfast, so Hulan and I agreed: A handful would be good for warming our hands.

"You've come just in time," the vendor said. "I added the honey just half an hour ago, when the shells cracked open." He poured six chestnuts each into two newspaper cones.

I had just peeled one open, was about to put the steaming chestnut into my mouth, when—a shout in the street: "Japanese planes! Disaster is coming!" And then we heard the airplanes, faraway sounds, like thunder coming.

All those people, all those vendors—they began to push and run. The basket of chestnuts tipped over. Chickens were squawking, beating against their cages. Hulan grabbed my hand and we were running too, as if we could go faster than those planes could fly. The airplane noise became louder, until they were over our backs, roaring like elephants. And we knew the bullets and bombs were coming. Then everyone around us began to fall at the same time, just like wheat in a field blown down by the same wind. I was falling too. Hulan was pushing me down. But because my stomach was so big, I had to lie curled up on my side. "Now we are dying!" Hulan cried.

My face was turned to the ground, my hands over my head. If people were screaming, we could not tell—the planes were roaring so loud above us. Hulan's hands were shaking as she held my shoulders. Or maybe it was my body that was making her shake.

And then the sounds seemed to be going away. I could feel my heart beating fast, so I knew I was still alive. I lifted my head just as others lifted theirs. I felt so lucky. I felt so grateful. I could hear people crying, "Thank you, Goddess of Mercy! Thank you!" Then we heard the airplanes coming back. And all those praises to the goddess turned into curses. We lowered our heads, and I thought that those curses would be my last memory. The planes flew back and forth, back and forth, and people's heads were going up and down, up and down, as if we were bowing to those Japanese planes.

I was so angry. I was so scared. I wanted to get up and run. But my body was too numb to rise. And although I was fierce in my desire to live, my thoughts were only of death, perhaps because people around me were now crying and chanting, "Amitaba, Amitaba"—already calling upon Buddha's guide to the next world.

I thought, Have we already died? How do I know? It seemed to me my breath had stopped, yet my thoughts were still racing, my hands could still feel the cold, hard ground. And I could still hear the airplane sounds, which now—eh?—now seemed to be moving farther and farther away.

The chanting stopped. But we all stayed down, so quiet, not moving. After many long minutes, I heard somebody whispering. I could feel people around me uncurling themselves. Someone was moaning. A baby was crying. I did not want to look up, to see what had happened. Hulan was shaking me. "Are you hurt? Get up!" I could not move. I could not trust my own senses.

"Get up!" cried Hulan. "What has happened to you?"

Hulan was helping me stand. We all rose slowly, the same field of wheat, now unbending. And we all whispered the same thought: "No blood." Then Hulan shouted: "No blood! Only snow!" At least that's what she thought it was at first. And because she said that, that's what I thought at first too. Big flakes of snow covered the street, lay on the backs of people crouched on the ground.

And when I looked up, I saw the snow falling from the sky, each flake as big as a sheet of paper. A pedicab driver in front of us picked up one of those flakes, and it was a sheet of thin paper. He handed it to me. "What does it say?"

The paper showed a happy drawing of a Japanese soldier with a little Chinese girl sitting on his shoulders. "Japanese government," I said. "If we do not resist, good treatment will be given to everyone, nothing to fear. If we resist, trouble follows for everyone."

And then I heard a Chinese soldier screaming in the street. He was kicking the paper snow, like a crazy man. "Lies! Lies!" he cried. "That's what they said in Shanghai. Look what they did to us! This is what is left of our army! Only rags to mop up China's blood!"

An old woman began to scold him. "Be quiet! Behave! You have to behave, or we will all be in trouble." But the soldier continued to shout. The old woman spit on his feet, picked up her bags, and hurried away. Now everyone began to talk, and then others began to shout, and soon the whole street was filled with frightened voices.

I tell you, that day, when this fear sickness spread, everyone became a different person. You don't know such a person exists inside of you until you become *taonan*. I saw people grabbing for food, stealing things. Vendors walked away from their steaming pots. I saw fights and arguments, children lost and crying, people pushing to get into a bus, then emptying out of the bus when they saw the streets were too full for anyone to move forward.

Hulan asked the pedicab driver in front of us to take us home. But as soon as he got off his seat to help us in, a bigger man knocked him down, jumped on the pedicab, and drove off. And before I could even say, "How terrible," a beggar boy ran up to me and tried to tear my purse from my hands. Hulan beat him off.

Suddenly someone cried, "Run! Run!" And everyone behind this voice began to move forward, a crowd of people coming toward us. A barrel of ice and fish was knocked over, as if it were a light vase. A woman fell down and cried—such a horrible cry, lasting for so long until it disappeared under hundreds of feet. Hulan twisted my arm, made me turn around, pushing me along in the same direction as the crowd. And then we were swallowed up in the wave, carried between other people's shoulders. I could feel elbows and knees punching into my back, into my big stomach. And then the space around us grew even tighter, and we were squashed together, moving in one breath, one current.

Hulan had one hand on my shoulder and was pushing me forward. "Hurry-go, hurry-go," she murmured behind my back, as if she were praying. "Hurry-go, hurry-go," she said with each step. Suddenly the crowd burst onto a wide boulevard, and I was no longer crushed between people. People were now running in different directions.

"This way, this way," Hulan said. I felt her hand slip off my shoulder.

"Which way?" I called back to her. "Hulan!"

No answer.

"Hulan! Hulan!" I shouted. I turned around and people rushed by me, but there was no Hulan. I turned forward again. She was not there either.

And in that crowd, all alone, all the fears I had been holding inside fell out. I started swimming against all those people rushing toward me, looking right and left, down below. She was gone.

"Ma! Ma!" I was crying. And I was amazed that those were the words coming out of my throat. "Ma! Ma!" As if she could have saved me, the mother who had abandoned me so long ago.

I was so stupid that day. I could have been knocked over, stepped on, and killed like so many other people. Someone could have knocked the baby right out of my body. Yet I was walking through the crowd, calling for my mother, looking for Hulan.

If you asked me how many minutes, how many hours went by before I was found, I could not tell you. When my senses came back, this was all I knew: I was sitting on a bench, staring at a chestnut in my hand. I had found it in my hand, the same chestnut I had peeled before the airplanes came. I wanted to laugh and cry, that this was what I had held onto when I almost died. And I was about to throw it away, when I considered I should still hold onto it. These are the kinds of important thoughts you have when your world changes so suddenly. The city gone mad, Hulan disappeared—should you keep a cold chestnut or not?

"Eh, sister! I hope you have one for me!" It was like a voice waking me out of a bad dream.

I saw Hulan riding up to me on a pedicab. Can you imagine! She was joking after a terrible disaster, joking when I had thought she was dead! I ran to her with a happy cry.

"Get in fast," she said, and held out her arm to pull me in. I threw the chestnut away, then struggled into the little backseat. Hulan pedaled off. She handed a stick back to me, the leg of a stool or chair.

"If anyone tries to steal this pedicab from us, beat them away!" she shouted. "You have to do this, understand? Beat them away!"

HA JIN

War Trash

Ha Jin (born 1956), the penname for Jin Xuefei, is a novelist, poet, essayist, and short story writer. Born in Liaoning, China, and joining the People's Liberation Army at the age of 13, he was on a fellowship at Brandeis University when the Tiananmen Square Massacre occurred and decided to remain in the United States, eventually receiving his PhD and writing in English from that point on. Since then Ha Jin has produced an impressive corpus, mostly set in China and detailing the hardships and predicaments of ordinary people, including *Ocean of Words* (1996), *Under the Red Flag* (1997), *The Bridegroom* (2000), and *Nanjing Requiem* (2011). *A Map of Betrayal* (2014), a multi-generational spy novel with a narrative arc extending from the United States to China, marks a new departure. Ha Jin was awarded the PEN/Faulkner Award twice: for *Waiting* (1999) and *War Trash* (2004), his two best-known works. The latter, excerpted here, tells the story of the Korean War through the physical and emotional desperation of a soldier in the Chinese People's Volunteer Army, culminating in the image of the inedible, rotting horsemeat.

After a month of hiding in the daytime and trying in vain to find a rift in the enemy's encirclement, our team was reduced to thirty-four men. Whenever someone was killed or disappeared, I couldn't help but think about my promises to my mother and Julan. It seemed unlikely I would be able to make it home. But in spite of my fear and sadness, I forced myself to appear cheerful, especially in the presence of Commissar Pei, who always insisted that at all costs we must survive. Some of the remaining officers were familiar with guerrilla tactics. Our team leader, Yan Wenjin, the director of the divisional security section, had led dozens of guerrillas in both the war against the Japanese and the civil war. But we were in a foreign country now. Without the knowledge of its language, its terrain, and its people, how could we get the civilians' support that was the basis of guerrilla warfare?

Hunger was our most pressing problem. During the day we picked wild grapes and berries on the mountain, though we dared not move about conspicuously. The wild fruits, tiny and bitter, numbed our tongues and made a greenish saliva dribble out from the corners of our mouths. Commissar Pei couldn't eat what we gathered because of his ulcer, but he encouraged us to search for fruits and herbs for ourselves.

One morning Yan Wenjin ran over and beamed, "There's a dead horse in the woods!"

We all went over to take a look. The horse, a Mongolian sorrel, had been dead for some days. Its hair had begun to fall off, and the gun wound in its chest festered with rings of maggots like a large white chrysanthemum. Flies droned over it madly even though a man wielded a leafy branch to drive them away. Yet we were elated to find the carcass and immediately set about looking for bayonets, wooden shell boxes, and steel helmets. I went up a slope with two men to search the area beyond a patch of dwarf fir trees. As we walked, flocks of crows took off, cawing fitfully. Behind a low rise we came across four dead South Korean soldiers. In the middle of them lay a Chinese soldier, whose head was smashed and whose face was gone, eaten up by birds. Around him were scattered splinters of wooden grenade handles. Clearly he had detonated the grenades and died together with the enemy. We carried his body into a cavity under a juniper and covered him with stones and green branches. After saluting him, we went back with two bayonets and an empty box that had contained mortar shells. We had also found a brass lighter in a Korean man's pocket. The other groups brought back a bayonet, three helmets, and some wooden cartridge boxes too. From God knows where one man returned with a dented field cauldron.

Immediately they started butchering the horse. The air turned putrid as dark sticky blood dripped onto the ground. Soon, large chunks of the meat were being boiled in the cauldron, which had been propped on a horseshoe of rocks. Dr. Wang limped over. Frowning, he had a look at the carcass and then with a pair of tweezers poked the horsemeat in the pot. He said in a thin voice, "The meat is rotten. You'll get poisoned if you eat it."

Disappointed, we walked away to wash our bloody hands in a puddle of rainwater. Some men couldn't stop swearing.

To solve the problem of hunger, Yan Wenjin offered to go down the mountain with five men to search for grain. Commissar Pei let them go. They left after sunset, and we waited for them anxiously. But for five days we heard nothing from them. Later in the prison camp I learned that they had ambushed an American truck transporting a squad of GIs and some supplies. Three of them had been killed by a machine gun, and Yan Wenjin had been hit in the stomach and died on the way to the hospital. After that failed attempt, smaller groups were sent down the mountain to search for food, but none of them ever came back. By chance, I had seen through binoculars how three of our men fell into the enemy's hands. It was overcast that morning, but the air was clear. As our comrades were approaching the foot of the southern hill, suddenly about twenty GIs with two wolf dogs appeared in front of them. Our men swung aside, dashing away in different directions, but the Americans caught up with them and brought them down, some kicking them furiously and some stomping on their chests. For a moment a cloud of dust obscured the human figures. When I could see again, the dogs were springing at our men and tearing at their limbs. Viewed from the distance of one and a half miles, the whole scene was eerily quiet, without a single shot fired. Horrified, I reported the loss to Commissar Pei. His face fell, and for hours he didn't speak a word.

SHARON OLDS

The Food-Thief

Sharon Olds (born 1942) has published more than ten volumes of poetry, her cascading lines ranging from obsessive family romance to fiery war protest. Born in San Francisco and educated at Stanford and Columbia (writing her PhD thesis on Emerson's prosody), she has offended some with her sexual and political candor but has also received many awards, including the Pulitzer Prize and the T. S. Eliot Prize for *Stag's Leap* (2012) and the National Book Critics Circle Award for *The Dead and the Living* (1983). In 2005 Olds was invited by First Lady Laura Bush to the National Book Festival; she declined in an open letter published in *The Nation*, saying in closing that she "could not stomach" the "thought of the clean linens at your table, the shining knives and the flames of the candles," when the United States was responsible for so much "blood, wounds and fire" in the world. In "The Food-Thief," from her third book of poetry,

The Gold Cell (1987), Olds depicts with dry-eyed realism both the desperation of the one who steals and the furor of those who punish him.

~~~~~~

They drive him along the road in the steady
conscious way they drove their cattle
when they had cattle, when they had homes and
living children. They drive him with pliant
peeled sticks, snapped from trees
whose bark cannot be eaten—snapped,
not cut, no one has a knife, and the trees that can be
eaten have been eaten leaf and trunk and the
long roots pulled from the ground and eaten.
They drive him and beat him, a loose circle of
thin men with sapling sticks,
driving him along slowly, slowly
beating him to death. He turns to them
with all the eloquence of the body, the
wrist turned out and the vein up his forearm
running like a root just under the surface, the
wounds on his head ripe and wet as a
rich furrow cut back and cut back at
plough-time to farrow a trench for the seed, his
eye pleading, the iris black and
gleaming as his skin, the white a dark
occluded white like cloud-cover on the
morning of a day of heavy rain.
His lips are open to his brothers as the body of a
woman might be open, as the earth itself was
split and folded back and wet and
seedy to them once, the lines on his lips
fine as the thousand tributaries of a
root-hair, a river, he is asking them for life
with his whole body, and they are driving his body
all the way down the road because
they know the life he is asking for—
it is their life.

URSULA K. LE GUIN

The Left Hand of Darkness

Ursula K. Le Guin (born 1929) is best known for her speculative fiction, depicting futuristic worlds in which gender, kinship, politics, and the natural environment appear in ways strikingly different from our own, making cross-cultural contact both difficult and necessary. Le Guin grew up in Berkeley, the daughter of anthropologists Alfred Kroeber and Theodora Kroeber. Educated at Radcliffe College and Columbia University, she gave up graduate work to raise a family after meeting her future husband, historian Charles Le Guin, while on a Fulbright research trip to France. Unable to get published between 1951 and 1961, she would eventually become the only author to win both the Hugo and Nebula awards for two consecutive books—*The Left Hand of Darkness* (1969) and *The Dispossessed* (1974)—while receiving no fewer than twenty-one Locus Awards, voted by magazine subscribers, as well as the 2014 National Book Foundation Medal for Distinguished Contribution to American Letters. In 2000 the Library of Congress made her a "living legend." This excerpt from *The Left Hand of Darkness* explores alternative food sources in a frigid environment.

He glanced at me, and drank down his cup of tea. Tea it might as well be called; brewed from roasted perm-grain, orsh is a brown, sweetsour drink, strong in vitamins A and C, sugar, and a pleasant stimulant related to lobeline. Where there is no beer on Winter there is orsh; where there is neither beer nor orsh, there are no people.

"It will be hard," he said, setting down his cup. "Very hard. Without luck, we will not make it."

"I'd rather die up on the Ice than in that cesspool you got me out of."

He cut off a chunk of dried breadapple, offered me a slice, and sat meditatively chewing. "We'll need more food," he said.

"What happens if we do make it to Karhide—to you, I mean? You're still proscribed."

He turned his dark, otter's glance on me. "Yes. I suppose I'd stay on this side."

"And when they found you'd helped their prisoner escape—?"

"They needn't find it." He smiled, bleak, and said, "First we have to cross the Ice."

I broke out, "Listen, Estraven, will you forgive what I said yesterday—"

"Nusuth." He stood up, still chewing, put on his hieb, coat, and boots, and slipped otterlike out the self-sealing valved door. From outside he stuck his head back in: "I may be late, or gone overnight. Can you manage here?"

"Yes."

"All right." With that he was off. I never knew a person who reacted so wholly and rapidly to a changed situation as Estraven. I was recovering, and willing to go; he was out of thangen; the instant that was all clear, he was off. He was never rash or hurried, but he was always ready. It was the secret, no doubt, of the extraordinary political career he threw away for my sake; it was also the explanation of his belief in me and devotion to my mission. When I came, he was ready. Nobody else on Winter was.

Yet he considered himself a slow man, poor in emergencies.

Once he told me that, being so slow-thinking, he had to guide his acts by a general intuition of which way his "luck" was running, and that this intuition rarely failed him. He said it seriously; it may have been true. The Foretellers of the Fastnesses are not the only people on Winter who can see ahead. They have tamed and trained the hunch, but not increased its certainty. In this matter the Yomeshta also have a point: the gift is perhaps not strictly or simply one of foretelling, but is rather the power of seeing (if only for a flash) everything at once: seeing whole.

I kept the little heater-stove at its hottest setting while Estraven was gone, and so got warm clear through for the first time in—how long? I thought it must be Thern by now, the first month of winter and of a new Year One, but I had lost count in Pulefen.

The stove was one of those excellent and economical devices perfected by the Gethenians in their millennial effort to outwit cold. Only the use of a fusion-pack as power source could improve it. Its bionic-powered battery was good for fourteen months' continuous use, its heat output was intense, it was stove, heater, and lantern all in one, and it weighed about four pounds. We would never have got fifty miles without it. It must have cost a good deal of Estraven's money, that money I had loftily handed over to him in Mishnory. The tent, which was made of plastics developed for weather-resistance and designed to cope with at least some of the inside water-condensation that is the plague of tents in cold weather; the pesthry-fur sleeping-bags; the clothes, skis, sledge, food-supplies, everything was of the finest make and kind, lightweight, durable, expensive. If he had gone to get more food, what was he going to get it with?

He did not return till nightfall next day. I had gone out several times on snowshoes, gathering strength and getting practice by waddling around the slopes of the snowy vale that hid our tent. I was competent on skis, but not much good on snowshoes. I dared not go far over the hilltops, lest I lose my backtrack; it was wild country, steep, full of creeks and ravines, rising fast to the cloud-haunted mountains eastward. I had time to wonder what I would do in this forsaken place if Estraven did not come back.

He came swooping over the dusky hill—he was a magnificent skier—and stopped beside me, dirty and tired and heavy-laden. He had on his back a huge sooty sack stuffed full of bundles: Father Christmas, who pops down the chimneys of old Earth. The bundles contained kadik-germ, dried bre-adapple, tea, and slabs of the hard, red, earthy-tasting sugar that Gethenians refine from one of their tubers.

"How did you get all this?"

"Stole it," said the one-time Prime Minister of Karhide, holding his hands over the stove, which he had not yet turned down; he, even he, was cold. "In Turuf. Close thing." That was all I ever learned. He was not proud of his exploit, and not able to laugh at it. Stealing is a vile crime on Winter; indeed the only man more despised than the thief is the suicide.

"We'll use up this stuff first," he said, as I set a pan of snow on the stove to melt. "It's heavy." Most of the food he had laid in previously was "hyper-food" rations, a fortified, dehydrated, compressed, cubed mixture of high-energy foods—the Orgota name for it is gichy-michy, and that's what we called it, though of course we spoke Karhidish together. We had enough of it to last us sixty days at the minimal standard ration: a pound a day apiece. After he had washed up and eaten, Estraven sat a long time by the stove that night figuring out precisely what we had and how and when we must use it. We had no scales, and he had to estimate, using a pound box of gichy-michy as standard. He knew, as do many Gethenians, the caloric and nutritive value of each food; he knew his own requirements under various conditions, and how to estimate mine pretty closely. Such knowledge has high survival-value, on Winter.

When at last he had got our rations planned out, he rolled over onto his bag and went to sleep. During the night I heard him talking numbers out of his dreams: weights, days, distances . . .

We had, very roughly, eight hundred miles to go. The first hundred would be north or northeast, going through the forest and across the northernmost spurs of the Sembensyen range to the great glacier, the ice-sheet that covers the double-lobed Great Continent everywhere north of the 45th parallel, and in places dips down almost to the 35th. One of these southward extensions is in the region of the Fire-Hills, the last peaks of the Sembensyens, and that region was our first goal. There among the mountains, Estraven reasoned, we should be able to get onto the surface of the ice-sheet, either descending onto it from a mountain-slope or climbing up to it on the slope of one of its effluent glaciers. Thereafter we would travel on the Ice itself, eastward, for some six hundred miles. Where its edge trends north again near the Bay of Guthen we would come down off it and cut southeast a last fifty or a hundred miles across the Shenshey Bogs, which by then should be ten or twenty feet deep in snow, to the Karhidish border.

HERMAN MELVILLE

"Stubb's Supper," from *Moby-Dick*

Herman Melville (1819–1891), novelist and poet, now stands as a towering figure of American literature, and *Moby-Dick* (1851) as a world classic, with one of the most famous opening lines: "Call me Ishmael." Best known in the nineteenth century for sea adventures such as *Typee* (1846), Melville spent a good part of his early life as a sailor, a career that included a Pacific voyage on the whaler *Acushnet* (1841–1842). Later he also embarked on a six-month tour of England and the Mediterranean (1856). His writings feature a wide range of settings, from the Marquesas Islands in *Typee* to the Liverpool slums in *Redburn* (1849) to the Holy Land in his long poem, *Clarel* (1876). For Melville, the world is oceanic and interconnected, both for good and for ill. He returned to this theme in his last, unfinished story, "Billy Budd, Sailor," published posthumously in 1924 and later made into an opera by Benjamin Britten, with the libretto by E. M. Forster. In this excerpt, "Stubb's Supper," from *Moby-Dick*, Melville shows the kinship between humans and nonhumans through Stubb, the *Pequod*'s second mate, feasting on the whale he killed more sharkishly than the sharks themselves.

"A steak, a steak, ere I sleep! You, Daggoo! overboard you go, and cut me one from his small!"

Here be it known, that though these wild fishermen do not, as a general thing, and according to the great military maxim, make the enemy defray the current expenses of the war (at least before realizing the proceeds of the voyage), yet now and then you find some of these Nantucketers who have a genuine relish for that particular part of the Sperm Whale designated by Stubb; comprising the tapering extremity of the body.

About midnight that steak was cut and cooked; and lighted by two lanterns of sperm oil, Stubb stoutly stood up to his spermaceti supper at the capstan-head, as if that capstan were a sideboard. Nor was Stubb the only banqueter on whale's flesh that night. Mingling their mumblings with his own mastications, thousands on thousands of sharks, swarming round the dead leviathan, smackingly feasted on its fatness. The few sleepers below in their bunks were often startled by the sharp slapping of their tails against the hull, within a few inches of the sleepers' hearts. Peering over the side you could just see them (as before you heard them) wallowing in the sullen, black waters, and turning over on their backs as they scooped out huge globular pieces of the whale of the bigness of a human head. This particular feat of the shark seems all but miraculous. How at such an apparently unassailable surface, they contrive to gouge out such symmetrical mouthfuls, remains a part of the universal problem of all things. The mark they thus leave on the whale, may best be likened to the hollow made by a carpenter in countersinking for a screw.

Though amid all the smoking horror and diabolism of a sea-fight, sharks will be seen longingly gazing up to the ship's decks, like hungry dogs round a table where red meat is being carved, ready to bolt down every killed man that is tossed to them; and though, while the valiant butchers over the deck-table are thus cannibally carving each other's live meat with carving-knives all gilded and tasselled, the sharks, also, with their jewel-hilted mouths, are quarrelsomely carving away under the table at the dead meat; and though, were you to turn the whole affair upside down, it would still be pretty much the same thing, that is to say, a shocking sharkish business enough for all parties; and though sharks also are the invariable outriders of all slave ships crossing the Atlantic, systematically trotting alongside, to be handy in case a parcel is to be carried anywhere, or a dead slave to be decently buried; and though one or two other like instances might be set down, touching the set terms, places, and occasions, when sharks do most socially congregate, and most hilariously feast; yet is there no conceivable time or occasion when you will find them in such countless numbers, and in gayer or more jovial spirits, than around a dead sperm whale, moored by night to a whaleship at sea. If you have never seen that sight, then suspend your decision about the propriety of devil-worship, and the expediency of conciliating the devil.

But, as yet, Stubb heeded not the mumblings of the banquet that was going on so nigh him, no more than the sharks heeded the smacking of his own epicurean lips.

"Cook, cook!—where's that old Fleece?" he cried at length, widening his legs still further, as if to form a more secure base for his supper; and, at the same time darting his fork into the dish, as if stabbing with his lance; "cook, you cook!—sail this way, cook!"

The old black, not in any very high glee at having been previously roused from his warm hammock at a most unseasonable hour, came shambling along from his galley, for, like many old blacks, there was something the matter with his knee-pans, which he did not keep well scoured like his other pans; this old Fleece, as they called him, came shuffling and limping along, assisting his step with his tongs, which, after a clumsy fashion, were made of straightened iron hoops; this old Ebony floundered along, and in obedience to the word of command, came to a dead stop on the opposite side of Stubb's sideboard; when, with both hands folded before him, and resting on his two-legged cane, he bowed his arched back still further over, at the same time sideways inclining his head, so as to bring his best ear into play.

"Cook," said Stubb, rapidly lifting a rather reddish morsel to his mouth, "don't you think this steak is rather overdone? You've been beating this steak too much, cook; it's too tender. Don't I always say that to be good, a whale-steak must be tough? There are those sharks now over the side, don't you see they prefer it tough and rare? What a shindy they are kicking up! Cook, go and talk to 'em; tell 'em they are welcome to help themselves civilly, and in moderation, but they must keep quiet. Blast me, if I can hear my own voice. Away, cook, and deliver my message. Here, take this lantern," snatching one from his sideboard; "now then, go and preach to 'em!'"

Sullenly taking the offered lantern, old Fleece limped across the deck to the bulwarks; and then, with one hand dropping his light low over the sea, so as to get a good view of his congregation, with the other hand he solemnly flourished his tongs, and leaning far over the side in a mumbling voice began addressing the sharks, while Stubb, softly crawling behind, overheard all that was said.

"Fellow-critters: I'se ordered here to say dat you must stop dat dam noise dare. You hear? Stop dat dam smackin' ob de lips! Massa Stubb say dat you can fill your dam bellies up to de hatchings, but by Gor! you must stop dat dam racket!"

"Cook," here interposed Stubb, accompanying the word with a sudden slap on the shoulder,—"Cook! why, damn your eyes, you mustn't swear that way when you're preaching. That's no way to convert sinners, cook!"

"Who dat? Den preach to him yourself," sullenly turning to go.

"No, cook; go on, go on."

"Well, den, Belubed fellow-critters:"—

"Right!" exclaimed Stubb, approvingly, "coax 'em to it; try that," and Fleece continued.

"Do you is all sharks, and by natur wery woracious, yet I zay to you, fel-low-critters, dat dat woraciousness—'top dat dam slappin' ob de tail! How you tink to hear, spose you keep up such a dam slappin' and bitin' dare?"

"Cook," cried Stubb, collaring him, "I won't have that swearing. Talk to 'em gentlemanly."

Once more the sermon proceeded.

"Your woraciousness, fellow-critters, I don't blame ye so much for; dat is natur, and can't be helped; but to gobern dat wicked natur, dat is de pint. You is sharks, sartin; but if you gobern de shark in you, why den you be angel; for all angel is not'ing more dan de shark well goberned. Now, look here, bred'ren, just try wonst to be cibil, a helping yourselbs from dat whale. Don't be tearin' de blubber out your neighbour's mout, I say. Is not one shark dood right as toder to dat whale? And, by Gor, none on you has de right to dat whale; dat whale belong to some one else. I know some o' you has berry brig mout, brigger dan oders; but den de brig mouts sometimes has de small bellies; so dat de brigness of de mout is not to swaller wid, but to bit off de blubber for de small fry ob sharks, dat can't get into de scrouge to help demselves."

"Well done, old Fleece!" cried Stubb, "that's Christianity; go on."

"No use goin' on; de dam willains will keep a scougin' and slappin' each oder, Massa Stubb; dey don't hear one word; no use a-preaching to such dam g'uttons as you call 'em, till dare bellies is full, and dare bellies is bottomless; and when dey do get 'em full, dey wont hear you den; for den dey sink in the sea, go fast to sleep on de coral, and can't hear noting at all, no more, for eber and eber."

"Upon my soul, I am about of the same opinion; so give the benediction, Fleece, and I'll away to my supper."

Upon this, Fleece, holding both hands over the fishy mob, raised his shrill voice, and cried—

"Cussed fellow-critters! Kick up de damndest row as ever you can; fill your dam bellies 'till dey bust—and den die."

"Now, cook," said Stubb, resuming his supper at the capstan; "stand just where you stood before, there, over against me, and pay particular attention."

"All 'dention," said Fleece, again stooping over upon his tongs in the desired position.

"Well," said Stubb, helping himself freely meanwhile; "I shall now go back to the subject of this steak. In the first place, how old are you, cook?"

"What dat do wid de 'teak," said the old black, testily.

"Silence! How old are you, cook?"

"'Bout ninety, dey say," he gloomily muttered.

"And you have lived in this world hard upon one hundred years, cook, and don't know yet how to cook a whale-steak?" rapidly bolting another mouthful at the last word, so that morsel seemed a continuation of the question. "Where were you born, cook?"

"'Hind de hatchway, in ferry-boat, goin' ober de Roanoke."

"Born in a ferry-boat! That's queer, too. But I want to know what country you were born in, cook!"

"Didn't I say de Roanoke country?" he cried sharply.

"No, you didn't, cook; but I'll tell you what I'm coming to, cook. You must go home and be born over again; you don't know how to cook a whale-steak yet."

"Bress my soul, if I cook noder one," he growled, angrily, turning round to depart.

"Come back here, cook;—here, hand me those tongs;—now take that bit of steak there, and tell me if you think that steak cooked as it should be? Take it, I say"—holding the tongs towards him—"take it, and taste it."

Faintly smacking his withered lips over it for a moment, the old negro muttered, "Best cooked 'teak I eber taste; joosy, berry joosy."

"Cook," said Stubb, squaring himself once more; "do you belong to the church?"

"Passed one once in Cape-Down," said the old man sullenly.

"And you have once in your life passed a holy church in Cape-Town, where you doubtless overheard a holy parson addressing his hearers as his beloved fellow-creatures, have you, cook! And yet you come here, and tell me such a dreadful lie as you did just now, eh?" said Stubb. "Where do you expect to go to, cook?"

"Go to bed berry soon," he mumbled, half-turning as he spoke.

"Avast! heave to! I mean when you die, cook. It's an awful question. Now what's your answer?"

"When dis old brack man dies," said the negro slowly, changing his whole air and demeanor, "he hisself won't go nowhere; but some bressed angel will come and fetch him."

"Fetch him? How? In a coach and four, as they fetched Elijah? And fetch him where?"

"Up dere," said Fleece, holding his tongs straight over his head, and keeping it there very solemnly.

"So, then, you expect to go up into our main-top, do you, cook, when you are dead? But don't you know the higher you climb, the colder it gets? Main-top, eh?"

"Didn't say dat t'all," said Fleece, again in the sulks.

"You said up there, didn't you? and now look yourself, and see where your tongs are pointing. But, perhaps you expect to get into heaven by crawling through the lubber's hole, cook; but, no, no, cook, you don't get there, except you go the regular way, round by the rigging. It's a ticklish business, but must be done, or else it's no go. But none of us are in heaven yet. Drop your tongs, cook, and hear my orders. Do ye hear? Hold your hat in one hand, and clap t'other a'top of your heart, when I'm giving my orders, cook. What! that your heart, there?—that's your gizzard! Aloft! aloft!—that's it—now you have it. Hold it there now, and pay attention."

"All 'dention," said the old black, with both hands placed as desired, vainly wriggling his grizzled head, as if to get both ears in front at one and the same time.

"Well then, cook, you see this whale-steak of yours was so very bad, that I have put it out of sight as soon as possible; you see that, don't you? Well, for the future, when you cook another whale-steak for my private table here, the capstan, I'll tell you what to do so as not to spoil it by overdoing. Hold the steak in one hand, and show a live coal to it with the other; that done, dish it; d'ye hear? And now to-morrow, cook, when we are cutting in the fish, be sure you stand by to get the tips of his fins; have them put in pickle. As for the ends of the flukes, have them soused, cook. There, now ye may go."

But Fleece had hardly got three paces off, when he was recalled.

"Cook, give me cutlets for supper to-morrow night in the mid-watch. D'ye hear? away you sail, then.—Halloa! stop! make a bow before you go.— Avast heaving again! Whale-balls for breakfast—don't forget."

"Wish, by gor! whale eat him, 'stead of him eat whale. I'm bressed if he ain't more of shark dan Massa Shark hisself," muttered the old man, limping away; with which sage ejaculation he went to his hammock.

JACK LONDON

The Water Baby

Jack London (1876–1916) is best known for his fiction set in the Klondike: *The Call of the Wild* (1903), *White Fang* (1906), and the short story "To Build a Fire" (1908). But he also covered the Russo-Japanese war for the *San Francisco Examiner*, wrote extensively about the South Pacific, and experimented with what would now be called science fiction (including a story on germ warfare, "The Scarlet Plague," also included in this volume). A lifelong political activist, London combined a keen awareness of systemic global forces with a special sympathy for the underdog. Stories such as "The Mexican," "The Chinago," and "Koolau the Leper" include Mexican, Asian, and Hawaiian characters. "The Water Baby," published in 1918 in *Cosmopolitan* and excerpted here, stages an encounter between a Hawaiian-speaking narrator and a crafty old fisherman, Kohokumu, who proceeds to tell a story about an equally crafty young boy, Keikiwai, "half fish himself and talking the language of fishes," who is able to procure lobsters for the king by tricking sharks into eating each other rather than himself.

~~~~~~

"There will be no more bites for a while," he announced. "The fish sharks are prowling around, and we shall have to wait until they are gone. And so that the time shall not be heavy, I will sing you the canoe-hauling song to Lono. You remember:

> " 'Give to me the trunk of the tree, O Lono!
> Give me the tree's main root, O Lono!
> Give me the ear of the tree, O Lono!—' "

"For the love of mercy, don't sing!" I cut him short. "I've got a headache, and your singing hurts. You may be in devilish fine form to-day, but your throat is rotten. I'd rather you talked about dreams, or told me whoppers."

"It is too bad that you are sick, and you so young," he conceded cheerily. "And I shall not sing any more. I shall tell you something you do not know and have never heard; something that is no dream and no whopper, but is what I know to have happened. Not very long ago there lived here, on the beach beside this very lagoon, a young boy whose name was Keikiwai, which, as you know, means Water Baby. He was truly a water baby. His gods were the sea and fish gods, and he was born with knowledge of the language of fishes, which the fishes did not know until the sharks found it out one day when they heard him talk it.

"It happened this way. The word had been brought, and the commands, by swift runners, that the king was making a progress around the island, and that on the next day a luau was to be served him by the dwellers here of Waihee. It was always a hardship, when the king made a progress, for the few dwellers in small places to fill his many stomachs with food. For he came always with his wife and her women, with his priests and sorcerers, his dancers and flute players and hula singers, and fighting men and servants, and his high chiefs with their wives, and sorcerers and fighting men and servants.

"Sometimes, in small places like Waihee, the path of his journey was marked afterward by leanness and famine. But a king must be fed, and it is not good to anger a king. So, like warning in advance of disaster, Waihee heard of his coming, and all food-getters of field and pond and mountain and sea were busied with getting food for the feast. And behold, everything was got, from the choicest of royal taro to sugar-cane joints for the roasting, from opihis to limu, from fowl to wild pig and poi-fed puppies—everything save one thing. The fishermen failed to get lobsters.

"Now be it known that the king's favorite food was lobster. He esteemed it above all *kao-kao* (food), and his runners had made special mention of it. And there were no lobsters, and it is not good to anger a king in the belly of him. Too many sharks had come inside the reef. That was the trouble. A young girl and an old man had been eaten by them. And of the young men who dared dive for lobsters, one was eaten, and one lost an arm, and another lost one hand and one foot.

"But there was Keikiwai, the Water Baby, only eleven years old, but half fish himself and talking the language of fishes. To his father the head men came, begging him to send the Water Baby to get lobsters to fill the king's belly and divert his anger.

"Now this, what happened, was known and observed. For the fishermen and their women, and the taro growers and the bird catchers, and the head men, and all Waihee, came down and stood back from the edge of the rock where the Water Baby stood and looked down at the lobsters far beneath on the bottom.

"And a shark, looking up with its cat's eyes, observed him, and sent out the shark call of 'fresh meat' to assemble all the sharks in the lagoon. For the sharks work thus together, which is why they are strong. And the sharks answered the call till there were forty of them, long ones and short ones and lean ones and round ones, forty of them by count; and they talked to one another, saying: 'Look at that titbit of a child, that morsel delicious of human-flesh sweetness without the salt of the sea in it, of which salt we have too much, savory and good to eat, melting to delight under our hearts as our bellies embrace it and extract from it its sweet.'

"Much more they said, saying: 'He has come for the lobsters. When he dives in he is for one of us. Not like the old man we ate yesterday, tough to dryness with age, nor like the young men whose members were too hard-muscled, but tender, so tender that he will melt in our gullets ere our bellies receive him. When he dives in, we will all rush for him, and the lucky one of us will get him, and, gulp, he will be gone, one bite and one swallow, into the belly of the luckiest one of us.'

"And Keikiwai, the Water Baby, heard the conspiracy, knowing the shark language; and he addressed a prayer, in the shark language, to the shark god Moku-halii, and the sharks heard and waved their tails to one another and winked their cat's eyes in token that they understood his talk. And then he said: 'I shall now dive for a lobster for the king. And no hurt shall befall me, because the shark with the shortest tail is my friend and will protect me.'

"And, so saying, he picked up a chunk of lava rock and tossed it into the water, with a big splash, twenty feet to one side. The forty sharks rushed for the splash, while he dived, and by the time they discovered they had missed him, he had gone to the bottom and come back and climbed out, within his hand a fat lobster, a wahine lobster, full of eggs, for the king.

" 'Ha!' said the sharks, very angry. 'There is among us a traitor. The titbit of a child, the morsel of sweetness, has spoken, and has exposed the one among us who has saved him. Let us now measure the length of our tails!'

"Which they did, in a long row, side by side, the shorter-tailed ones cheating and stretching to gain length on themselves, the longer-tailed ones cheating and stretching in order not to be out-cheated and out-stretched. They were very angry with the one with the shortest tail, and him they rushed upon from every side and devoured till nothing was left of him.

"Again they listened while they waited for the Water Baby to dive in. And again the Water Baby made his prayer in the shark language to Moku-halii, and said: 'The shark with the shortest tail is my friend and will protect me.' And again the Water Baby tossed in a chunk of lava, this time twenty feet away off to the other side. The sharks rushed for the splash, and in their haste ran into one another, and splashed with their tails till the water was all foam and they could see nothing, each thinking some other was swallowing the titbit. And the Water Baby came up and climbed out with another fat lobster for the king.

"And the thirty-nine sharks measured tails, devouring the one with the shortest tail, so that there were only thirty-eight sharks. And the Water Baby continued to do what I have said, and the sharks to do what I have told you, while for each shark that was eaten by his brothers there was another fat lobster laid on the rock for the king. Of course, there was much quarreling and argument among the sharks when it came to measuring tails; but in the end it worked out in rightness and justice, for, when only two sharks were left, they were the two biggest of the original forty.

"And the Water Baby again claimed the shark with the shortest tail was his friend, fooled the two sharks with another lava chunk, and brought up another lobster. The two sharks each claimed the other had the shorter tail, and each fought to eat the other, and the one with the longer tail won—"

"Hold, O Kohokumu!" I interrupted. "Remember that that shark had already—" "I know just what you are going to say," he snatched his recital back from me. "And you are right. It took him so long to eat the thirty-ninth shark, for inside the thirty-ninth shark were already the nineteen other sharks he had eaten, and inside the fortieth shark were already the nineteen other sharks he had eaten, and he did not have the appetite he had started with. But do not forget he was a very big shark to begin with.

"It took him so long to eat the other shark, and the nineteen sharks inside the other shark, that he was still eating when darkness fell and the people of Waihee went away home with all the lobsters for the king. And didn't they find the last shark on the beach next morning dead and burst wide open with all he had eaten?"

Kohokumu fetched a full stop and held my eyes with his own shrewd ones.

"Hold, O Lakana!" he checked the speech that rushed to my tongue. "I know what next you would say. You would say that with my own eyes I did not see this, and therefore that I do not know what have been telling you. But I do know, and I can prove it. My father's father knew the grandson of the Water Baby's father's uncle. Also, there, on the rocky point to which I point my finger now, is where the Water Baby stood and dived. I have dived for lobsters there myself. It is a great place for lobsters. Also, and often, have I seen sharks there. And there, on the bottom, as I should know, for I have seen and counted them, are the thirty-nine lava rocks thrown in by the Water Baby as I have described."

"But—" I began.

"Ha!" he baffled me. "Look! While we have talked the fish have begun again to bite."

He pointed to three of the bamboo poles erect and devil-dancing in token that fish were hooked and struggling on the lines beneath. As he bent to his paddle, he muttered, for my benefit:

"Of course I know. The thirty-nine lava rocks are still there. You can count them any day for yourself. Of course I know, and I know for a fact."

UPTON SINCLAIR

The Jungle

Upton Sinclair (1878–1968) is best known for his muckraking novel *The Jungle* (1906), based on his research while working incognito at the Chicago stockyards. The public furor that followed its publication led directly to the passage of the Pure Food and Drug Act and the Meat Inspection Act later that year. Sinclair continued these exposés in *The Metropolis* (1908), *The Moneychangers* (1908), *King Coal* (1917), *The Brass Check* (1919), and *Oil!* (1927). By his death in 1968, he had written more than eighty books, twenty plays, and hundreds of articles dealing with virtually every social ill in the United States. He also started the California chapter of the American Civil Liberties Union, and ran twice, though unsuccessfully, on the Socialist ticket: in 1920 for the House of Representatives, and in 1922 for the Senate. In 1934 he was the Democratic Party nominee for governor of California, another unsuccessful campaign. He did win the Pulitzer Prize for Fiction in 1943 for *Dragon's Teeth*. In this excerpt from *The Jungle*, Sinclair writes about the sights and odors that greeted the Lithuanian immigrants as their train approached the stockyards.

A full hour before the party reached the city they had begun to note the perplexing changes in the atmosphere. It grew darker all the time, and upon the earth the grass seemed to grow less green. Every minute, as the train sped on, the colors of things became dingier; the fields were grown parched and yellow, the landscape hideous and bare. And along with the thickening smoke they began to notice another circumstance, a strange, pungent odor. They were not sure that it was unpleasant, this odor; some might have called it sickening, but their taste in odors was not developed, and they were only sure that it was curious. Now, sitting in the trolley car, they realized that they were on their way to the home of it—that they had traveled all the way from Lithuania to it. It was now no longer something far off and faint, that you caught in whiffs; you could literally taste it, as well as smell it—you could take hold of it, almost, and examine it at your leisure. They were divided in their opinions about it. It was an elemental odor, raw and crude; it was rich, almost rancid, sensual, and strong. There were some who drank it in as if it were an intoxicant; there were others who put their handkerchiefs to their faces. The new emigrants were still tasting it, lost in wonder, when suddenly the car came to a halt, and the door was flung open, and a voice shouted—"Stockyards!"

They were left standing upon the corner, staring; down a side street there were two rows of brick houses, and between them a vista: half a dozen chimneys, tall as the tallest of buildings, touching the very sky—and leaping from them half a dozen columns of smoke, thick, oily, and black as night. It might have come from the center of the world, this smoke, where the fires of the ages still smolder. It came as if self-impelled, driving all before it, a perpetual explosion. It was inexhaustible; one stared, waiting to see it stop, but still the great streams rolled out. They spread in vast clouds overhead, writhing, curling; then, uniting in one giant river, they streamed away down the sky, stretching a black pall as far as the eye could reach.

Then the party became aware of another strange thing. This, too, like the color, was a thing elemental; it was a sound, a sound made up of ten thousand little sounds. You scarcely noticed it at first—it sunk into your consciousness, a vague disturbance, a trouble. It was like the murmuring of the bees in the spring, the whisperings of the forest; it suggested endless activity, the rumblings of a world in motion. It was only by an effort that one could realize that it was made by animals, that it was the distant lowing of ten thousand cattle, the distant grunting of ten thousand swine.

WILLA CATHER

Death Comes for the Archbishop

Willa Cather (1873–1947), best known for her novels about the Midwest, grew up in Red Cloud, Nebraska, where her family moved in 1883. Following her graduation from the University of Nebraska in 1895, she embarked on a career in journalism, eventually becoming the managing editor of *McClure's*, a popular New York–based magazine. At the urging of friend and mentor Sarah Orne Jewett, Cather began to try her hand at fiction. Her first novel, *Alexander's Bridge* (1912), was followed by her Prairie Trilogy: *O Pioneers!* (1913), *The Song of the Lark* (1915), and *My Ántonia* (1918). Beginning in 1902, Cather regularly spent time in France; she was in Paris when *One of Ours* was awarded the Pulitzer Prize in 1923. At the same time, the American Southwest also became an important setting for her, notably in *The Professor's House* (1925) and *Death Comes for the Archbishop* (1927), featured here. In this excerpt, Cather's love of France and her fascination with the Southwest come together to give us two French missionaries in New Mexico, indulging themselves in the French language and French cuisine on Christmas Day.

"Monseigneur est servi! Alors, Jean, veux-tu apporter les bougies?"

The Bishop carried the candles into the dining-room, where the table was laid and Father Vaillant was changing his cook's apron for his cassock. Crimson from standing over an open fire, his rugged face was even homelier than usual—though one of the first things a stranger decided upon meeting Father Joseph was that the Lord had made few uglier men. He was short, skinny, bow-legged from a life on horseback, and his countenance had little to recommend it but kindliness and vivacity. He looked old, though he was then about forty. His skin was hardened and seamed by exposure to weather in a bitter climate, his neck scrawny and wrinkled like an old man's. A bold, blunt-tipped nose, positive chin, a very large mouth,—the lips thick and succulent but never loose, never relaxed, always stiffened by effort or working with excitement. His hair, sunburned to the shade of dry hay, had originally been tow-coloured; "Blanchet" ("Whitey") he was always called at the Seminary. Even his eyes were near-sighted, and of such a pale, watery blue as to be unimpressive. There was certainly nothing in his outer case to suggest the fierceness and fortitude and fire of the man, and yet even the thick-blooded Mexican half-breeds knew his quality at once. If the Bishop returned to find Santa Fé friendly to him, it was because everybody believed in Father Vaillant—homely, real, persistent, with the driving power of a dozen men in his poorly-built body.

On coming into the dining-room, Bishop Latour placed his candlesticks over the fire-place, since there were already six upon the table, illuminating the brown soup-pot. After they had stood for a moment in prayer, Father Joseph lifted the cover and ladled the soup into the plates, a dark onion soup with croutons. The Bishop tasted it critically and smiled at his companion. After the spoon had travelled to his lips a few times, he put it down and leaning back in his chair remarked,

"Think of it, Blanchet; in all this vast country between the Mississippi and the Pacific Ocean, there is probably not another human being who could make a soup like this."

"Not unless he is a Frenchman," said Father Joseph. He had tucked a napkin over the front of his cassock and was losing no time in reflection.

"I am not deprecating your individual talent, Joseph," the Bishop continued, "but, when one thinks of it, a soup like this is not the work of one man. It is the result of a constantly refined tradition. There are nearly a thousand years of history in this soup."

Father Joseph frowned intently at the earthen pot in the middle of the table. His pale, near-sighted eyes had always the look of peering into distance. "C'est ça, c'est vrai," he murmured. "But how," he exclaimed as he filled the Bishop's plate again, "how can a man make a proper soup without leeks, that king of vegetables? We cannot go on eating onions for ever."

After carrying away the soupière, he brought in the roast chicken and pommes sautées. "And salad, Jean," he continued as he began to carve. "Are we to eat dried beans and roots for the rest of our lives? Surely we must find time to make a garden. Ah, my garden at Sandusky! And you could snatch me away from it! You will admit that you never ate better lettuces in France. And my vineyard; a natural habitat for the vine, that. I tell you, the shores of Lake Erie will be covered with vineyards one day. I envy the man who is drinking my wine. Ah well, that is a missionary's life; to plant where another shall reap."

As this was Christmas Day, the two friends were speaking in their native tongue. For years they had made it a practice to speak English together, except upon very special occasions, and of late they conversed in Spanish, in which they both needed to gain fluency.

ALICE B. TOKLAS

The Alice B. Toklas Cookbook

Alice B. Toklas (1877–1967) was born in San Francisco and met Gertrude Stein the day she arrived in Paris. Soon the two presided over a salon at 27 rue de Fleurus, attracting expatriate American authors such as Ernest Hemingway, Ezra Pound, and Paul Bowles and avant-garde painters such as Picasso, Matisse, Juan Gris, and Braque. Toklas was Stein's lover, cook, typist, proofreader, and muse; her name was immortalized when Stein published her memoir under the title of *The Autobiography of Alice B. Toklas* (1933), the only book Stein wrote that was instantly popular. Toklas published her own memoir in the form of *The Alice B. Toklas Cookbook* (1954), mixing recipes with wry observations. Its most famous recipe was for "Haschich Fudge," a mixture of fruit, nuts, spices, and "canibus sativa," or marijuana, a concoction that inspired Peter Sellers's 1968 film, *I Love You, Alice B. Toklas*. Monique Truong's *The Book of Salt* (2003), also excerpted in this volume, is another spinoff from the *Cookbook*. In the following selection, Toklas offers four different recipes for gazpacho, each reflecting its own history and geography.

From murder to detection is not far. And here is a note on tracking a soup to its source. It was as a result of eating *gazpacho* in Spain lately that I came to the conclusion that recipes through conquests and occupations have travelled far.

After the first ineffable *gazpacho* was served to us in Malaga and an entirely different but equally exquisite one was presented in Seville the recipes for them had unquestionably become of greater importance than Grecos and Zurbarans, than cathedrals and museums. Surely the Calle de las Sierpes, the liveliest, most seductive of streets, would produce the cookbook that would answer the burning consuming question of how to prepare a *gazpacho*. Down the narrow Sierpes where only pedestrians are permitted to pass, with its de luxe shops of fans, boots and gloves, toys and sweets, its smart men's clubs on either side whose members sit three tables deep sipping iced drinks and evaluating the young ladies who pass, at the end of the street was the large book shop remembered from a previous visit forty years before. Cook-books without number, exactly eleven, were offered for inspections but not a *gazpacho* in any index. Oh, said the clerk, *gazpachos* are only eaten in Spain by peasants and Americans. Choosing the book that seemed to have the fewest French recipes, I hurried back to Zurbaran and Greco, to museums and cathedrals.

At Cordoba there was another and suaver *gazpacho*, at Segovia one with a more vulgar appeal, outrageously coarse. There was nothing to do but to resign oneself to an experimental laboratory effort as soon as a kitchen was available.

Upon the return from Spain, my host at Cannes, a distinguished Polish-American composer, a fine *gourmet* and experienced cook, listened to the story of the futile chase for *gazpacho* recipes, for their possible ingredients.

Ah, said he, but you are describing a *chlodnik*, the Polish iced soup. Before he had time to prepare it for us a Turkish guest arrived and he hearing about the *gazpachos* and the *chlodnik* said, You are describing a Turkish *cacik*.

Perhaps, said I. It was confusing. He said he would prepare a *cacik* for us. It was to be sure an iced soup, but the Turk had not the temperament of a great cook, he should not have accepted olive oil as a substitute for the blander oil of sesame.

Then we had the *chlodnik*, a really great dish worthy of its Spanish cousins. But that was not the end.

There was the Greek *tarata*. Yes indeed, it was confusing, until one morning it occurred to me that it was evident each one of these frozen soups was not a separate creation. Had the Poles passed the recipe to their enemy the Turks at the siege of Vienna or had it been brought back to

Poland much earlier than that from Turkey or Greece? Or had it been brought back by a crusader from Turkey? Had it gone to Sicily from Greece and then to Spain? It is a subject to be pursued. Well, here are the seven Mediterranean soups.

Gazpacho of Malaga (Spanish)

- 4 cups veal broth cooked with 2 cloves garlic and a large Spanish onion.
- 1 large tomato, peeled, with its seeds removed, and cut in minute cubes.
- 1 small cucumber, peeled, with its seeds removed, and cut in minute cubes.
- 1/2 sweet red pepper, skin and seed removed, cut in minute cubes.
- 4 Tablespoons cooked rice.
- 2 Tablespoons olive oil.

Mix thoroughly and serve ice-cold. Sufficient for 4 though double the quantity may not be too much!

Gazpacho of Seville

In a bowl put 4 crushed cloves of garlic, 1 teaspoon salt, 1/2 teaspoon powdered Spanish pepper, and the pulp of 2 medium-sized tomatoes, crushed.

Mix these ingredients thoroughly and add drop by drop 4 Tablespoons olive oil. Add 1 Spanish onion cut in tissue-paper-thin slices; 1 sweet red or green pepper, seeds removed and cut in minute cubes; 1 cucumber; and 4 Tablespoons fresh white breadcrumbs.

Add 3 cups water, mix thoroughly. Serve ice-cold.

Gazpacho of Cordoba

- 2 cloves of crushed garlic.
- 2 cucumbers peeled, seeds removed and minutely cubed.
- 2 Tablespoons olive oil.
- 2 cups water.
- 2 cups heavy cream.
- 2 teaspoons cornflour.
- 1 teaspoon salt.

Mix thoroughly the first three ingredients. Bring the water to a boil with the salt. Mix the cornflour with 3 additional tablespoons water, add to the boiling water. When the cornflour is cooked and the water thickened pour it over the garlic, cucumbers and oil. Let it cool and gradually add the cream. Serve ice-cold.

Gazpacho of Segovia

- 4 cloves garlic, pressed.
- 1 teaspoon ground Spanish pepper.
- 1 teaspoon salt.
- 1/2 teaspoon cumin powder.
- 2 Tablespoons finely chopped fresh basil or 3/4 Tablespoon powdered basil.
- 4 Tablespoons olive oil.
- 1 Spanish onion cut in minute cubes.
- 2 tomatoes peeled, seeds removed and cut in minute cubes.
- 2 cucumbers peeled, seeds removed and cut in minute cubes.
- 1 red sweet pepper, seeds removed and cut in minute cubes.
- 2 Tablespoons fresh white breadcrumbs.
- 4 cups water.

Put the first six ingredients in a bowl and add drop by drop the olive oil. When this has become an emulsion add the dry breadcrumbs and the prepared onion, cucumbers and tomatoes. Then add the water. Mix thoroughly. Serve ice-cold.

Chlodnik (Polish)

- 2 ounces lean veal cut in small pieces cooked in water to cover.
- 2 ounces beets cooked until tender and crushed through a sieve. Keep the water in which they were cooked.
- 1 teaspoon chives cut in very small lengths.
- 1 teaspoon powdered dill.
- 10 prawns, can be replaced by 16 large shrimps.
- 1 teaspoon salt, 1 teaspoon pepper.
- 1 cucumber peeled, seeds removed and very thinly sliced.

- 2 cups sour heavy cream.
- 6 hard-boiled eggs sliced.

Add the cucumber to the beets and the water in which they were cooked, then the veal and its juice. Stir in the sour cream gradually, add the dill, salt and pepper, the chives, the prawns or the shrimps. Add the eggs carefully. Serve ice-cold.

Cacik (Turkish)

- 6 cucumbers peeled, seeds removed and cut in slices.
- 6 cups heavy yoghourt.
- 1 teaspoon salt.
- 6 Tablespoons oil of sesame, a bland oil may be substituted.

Mix thoroughly and serve ice-cold.

Tarata (Greek)

- 3 green peppers, skinned and seeds removed.
- 6 egg plants, skinned and seeds removed.

Cook gently in 6 Tablespoons olive oil without browning. Mash fine and mix thoroughly with 4 cups yoghourt. Add 1 teaspoon salt, 1/2 teaspoon pepper, a pinch of cayenne, a pinch of powdered mint, and 2 pressed cloves of garlic. Serve ice-cold.

After this chapter was completed further news of *gazpacho* came from Santiago de Chile in South America. Did the *conquistadores* take the recipe, along with their horses, to the New World? Señora Marta Brunet, a distinguished Chilean writer, is of Spanish or rather Catalan descent and she describes *gazpacho* as a meal of the Spanish muleteers. And meal it seems, in this version, rather than soup.

These muleteers, she says, carry with them on their journeyings a flat earthenware dish—and garlic, olive oil, tomatoes and cucumbers, also dry bread which they crumble. Between two stones by the wayside they grind the garlic with a little salt and then add the oil. This mixture is rubbed all round the inside of the earthenware vessel. Then they slice the tomatoes and cucumbers and put alternating layers of each in the dish, interspersing the layers with layers of breadcrumbs and topping off the four tiers with more breadcrumbs and more oil. This done and prepared, they take a wet cloth, wrap it round the dish and leave it in a sunny place. The evaporation cooks the contents and when the cloth is dry the meal is ready. Too simple, my dear Watson.

MONIQUE TRUONG

The Book of Salt

Monique Truong (born 1968), Saigon-born, brings the vigilance of the intellectual property lawyer to bear on the intricacies of race, sexuality, and geopolitics as they converge on the nexus of food. Her first novel, *The Book of Salt* (2003), winner of the PEN/Robert W. Bingham Prize, was inspired by *The Alice B. Toklas Cookbook*, in which Toklas briefly mentions two "Indochinese" cooks who worked for Gertrude Stein and herself at their Paris salon at 27 rue de Fleurus. From that historical kernel, Truong invented Binh, a gay Vietnamese cook whose complex diasporic sensibility and rich inner life contrast sharply with his limited French vocabulary. In *Bitter in The Mouth* (2010), the outsider status of the young Vietnamese protagonist, Linh-Dao, flows both from her ethnicity and from her synesthesia—her ability to taste words. The following excerpt from *The Book of Salt* offers a gastronomic account of Vietnam under French colonial rule, as Binh watches his brother, Ah Minh, sweating away to make a grand birthday dinner for the wife of the French Governor.

The last time I saw Anh Minh, he was in the garden behind the Governor-General's house with a crew of his strongest men, beating buckets of egg whites and shovels of white sugar in oversized copper bowls. Worktables had been set up just steps away from the door to the kitchen. On a night like this, Anh Minh knew that it was better to labor under the open sky. A breeze might blow through, and the leaves on the branches overhead would fan his men as they worked. On a night like this, the kitchen fans—giant star anises suspended from the ceilings—did little to lessen the heat coming from the ovens. If they had stayed inside, the egg whites, my brother knew, would have cooked solid. He had seen it happen to French chefs, newly arrived, who had no idea what can happen in the kitchens of Vietnam. The egg whites hit the side of the bowl, the wire whisk plunges in, and before the steady stream of sugar can be added, the whites are heavy and scrambled, a calf's brain shattered into useless lumps. In comparison, the garden was an oasis but still far from the ideal temperature for beating air into the whites until they expanded, pillowed, and became unrecogniz-able. Anh Minh compensated by setting each fire-colored bowl in a tray of chipped ice, a fortune disappearing before our eyes. Except for the "whoosh whoosh" of air whisked by taut forearms, there was silence. Sweat beads descended from necks, arms, and hands and collected in the bowls. Their salt, like the copper and the ice, would help the mixture take its shape.

Sixty-two guests were expected that night at Madame's birthday dinner. One hundred twenty-four turban-shaped islands of meringue, crisscrossed by fine lines of caramelized sugar, would bob two by two in crystal bowls brimming with chilled *sabayon* sauce. Anh Minh claimed that this was the one dish that proved that old Chaboux had been worthy of the chef's toque. His replacement, Chef Blériot, must have agreed, as this was the one recipe from the former regime that he followed without change. Even though it was highly unorthodox, said Anh Minh, a clear deviation from the classic recipe for *oeufs à la neige*. "Eggs in the snow," Anh Minh had translated for me, like it was the first line of a poem. He, like Chef Blériot, refused to condemn old Chaboux's actions. "Poor Chaboux," Anh Minh said, "no one had been more surprised by Madame's command than he."

After all, "As if in France!" was Madame's unflinching rallying cry, one that had never failed to set old Chaboux's Gallic heart pounding. "The Governor-General's household has the duty to maintain itself with dignity and distinction. Everything here should be *as if in France!*" Madame com-manded, failing to note that in France she would have only three instead of fifteen to serve her household needs. "As if in France!" ended each sharp command, a punctuation that Madame inserted for our benefit. Even the oldest member of the household staff, the gardener's helper with his stooped back and his moss-grown tongue, could mimic it. Every afternoon when Madame donned her tennis whites and departed for the club, we would let it slip from our lips, an all-purpose complaint, a well-aimed insult, a bitter-filled expletive. Madame's phrase had so many meanings, and we amused ourselves by using them all. Accompanied by our laughter, "As if in France!" barreled through the house, hid itself inside closets, slept behind curtains, until Madame returned, her face flushed from lobbing a little ball to and fro, to reclaim the words as her own. "As if in France!" lost its power over Madame, though, when the topic at hand was her growing distrust of cows' milk. "In this tropical heat," Madame had been told, "it is not unheard of for the milk to spoil as it is leaving the beast's sweaty udder."

"Imagine living among a people who have tasted only mother's milk," the chauffeur overheard Madame exclaiming as she dictated a letter. "Before we arrived," Madame continued, "what the Indochinese called 'milk' was only water poured over crushed dried soybeans!" Madame knew that this would set her sister's head shaking, thinking of how fortunate she was to have married a man with no ambition. Madame ended her letter, which was to be typed by her secretary onto the Governor-General's official stationery, with a few parting lines about the managerial difficulties of overseeing a household staff of fifteen. This, explained the chauffeur, was just in case her sister lingered too long on such unenlightened thoughts.

Madame's orders to old Chaboux were clear. The *crème anglaise*, the surrogate snow, a concoction of egg yolks, sugar, and milk, had to be replaced. For her birthday dinner, Madame wanted her eggs in the snow, but she would not have any of Indochina's milk in the snow. "Simply too much of a risk," she said. "I've heard that the Nationalists have been feeding the cows here a weed so noxious that the milk, if consumed in sufficient amounts, would turn a perfectly healthy woman barren." The "woman" that Madame and old Chaboux had in their minds was, of course, French. Madame added this piece of unsolicited horror and bodily affront to Mother France just in case old Chaboux dared to balk at his task. It was all up to him. He was the intrepid explorer dispatched to honor and to preserve the sanctity of Madame and all Mesdames who would receive the embossed dinner invitations. In a country hovering at the edge of the equator, in a kitchen dried of the milk of his beloved bovine, this beleaguered chef had to do the impossible. Old Chaboux had to find new snow.

"*Sabayon* sauce instead of *crème anglaise!*" Anh Minh repeated the now departed chef's dramatic solution. Every year Minh the Sous Chef's retelling of the ingredients, while guarding their exact proportions as his secret, signaled that the all-night preparation for Madame's dinner had begun. "Over the lowest possible flame, whisk egg yolks with sugar and dry white wine," my brother, standing in a makeshift kitchen lit by stars and a barely present moon, explained the recipe to me one more time, knowing all the while that this would be his final lesson, regretting that in the end it had so little meaning.

NATASHA TRETHEWEY

Kitchen Maid with Supper at Emmaus, or The Mulata after the painting by Diego Velazquez, ca. 1619

Natasha Trethewey (born 1966) is the nineteenth poet laureate of the United States, and the first African American laureate since Rita Dove (1993). Born to a black mother and white father in Gulfport, Mississippi, Trethewey has given special attention to mixed heritage, fusing an autobiographical impulse with a careful attention to craft. *Domestic Work* (2000), her first collection, uses a variety of poetic forms to portray working families, from men on the docks to women hired as domestics. *Bellocq's Ophelia* (2002), an epistolary novella written in verse, fictionalizes the life of a mixed-race prostitute from New Orleans photographed by E. J. Bellocq. *Native Guard*, which won the Pulitzer Prize in 2007, takes its title from the Louisiana Native Guards, a black regiment in the Union Army during the Civil War. Her most recent volume, *Thrall* (2012), from which "Kitchen Maid" is taken, continues in this vein, invoking the bread and wine of the Eucharist to describe the work of the mixed-race or "mulata" servant, at once serving Christ his supper and echoing him in her transubstantiation of matter into spirit.

She is the vessels on the table before her:
the copper pot tipped toward us, the white pitcher
clutched in her hand, the black one edged in red
and upside down. Bent over, she is the mortar
and the pestle at rest in the mortar—still angled
in its posture of use. She is the stack of bowls
and the bulb of garlic beside it, the basket hung
by a nail on the wall and the white cloth bundled
in it, the rag in the foreground recalling her hand.
She's the stain on the wall the size of her shadow—
the color of blood, the shape of a thumb. She is echo
of Jesus at table, framed in the scene behind her:
his white corona, her white cap. Listening, she leans
into what she knows. Light falls on half her face.

OSCAR HIJUELOS

Our House in the Last World

Oscar Hijuelos (1951–2013), the son of working-class Cuban immigrants, was the first Latino writer to win a Pulitzer Prize for Fiction. Born and raised in New York City, he published his first novel, *Our House in the Last World*, in 1983, then *The Mambo Kings Plays Songs of Love* (1989), which won him international acclaim. The works that followed—*Mr. Ives' Christmas* (1995), *Empress of the Splendid Season* (1999), *A Simple Habana Melody* (2002), *Dark Dude* (2008), and *Beautiful Maria of My Soul* (2010)—established him as one of the most notable contemporary authors. *Our House in the Last World* is not focused on politics for the most part, although the excerpt below clearly demonstrates Hijuelos's keen awareness of Cuba's fraught relations to Miami and New York. Its complex global alliances are dramatized here by a chocolate and apricot sundae made by Cuban-American chefs for the Soviet premier Nikita

Khrushchev on his 1961 visit to the United States, and the stacks of garbage bags piled up on the streets of New York, from a party thrown to celebrate Fidel Castro's victorious entry into Havana during the Cuban Revolution.

Down in the cool basement of the hotel restaurant, Alejo Santinio looked over a yellowed newspaper clipping dating back to 1961. He had not looked at it recently, although in the past had always been proud to show it to visitors. And why? Because it was a brief moment of glory. In the newspaper picture Alejo and his friend Diego were in their best dress whites standing before a glittering cart of desserts. Beside them was a fat, cheery beaming face, the Soviet premier Nikita Khrushchev, who was attending a luncheon in his honor at the hotel.

Alejo always told the story: The governor and mayor were there with the premier, who had "great big ears and a bright red nose." The premier had dined on a five-course meal. The waiters and cooks, all nervous wrecks, had fumbled around in the kitchen getting things into order. But outside they managed an orderly composed appearance. After the meal had been served, the cooks drew lots to see who would wheel out the dessert tray. Diego and Alejo won.

Alejo put on his best white uniform and apron and waited in the foyer, chainsmoking nervously, while, outside, news reporters fired off their cameras and bodyguards stood against the walls, watching. Alejo and Diego did not say anything. Alejo was bewildered by the situation: Only in America could a worker get so close to a fat little guy with enormous power. These were the days of the new technology: mushroom-cloud bombs and satellites and missiles. And there he was, a hick from a small town in Cuba, slicked up by America, thinking, "If only my old compañeros could see me now! and my sisters and Mercedes."

When the time came, they went to the freezer, filled up shiny bowls with ice cream, brought out the sauces and hot fudge, and loaded them all onto a dessert cart. Alejo was in charge of cherries. They went out behind the maître d' and stood before the premier's table. They humbly waited as the smiling premier looked over the different cakes, tarts, pies, fruits, sauces, and ice creams. Through a translator the premier asked for a bowl of chocolate and apricot ice cream topped with hot fudge, cocoanut, and a high swirl of fresh whipped cream. This being served, Alejo picked out the plumpest cherry from a bowl and nimbly placed it atop the dessert.

Delighted, the premier whispered to the translator, who said, "The premier wishes to thank you for this masterpiece."

As Diego and Alejo bowed, lightbulbs and cameras flashed all around them. They were ready to wheel the cart back when the premier rose from the table to shake Diego's and Alejo's hands. Then through the translator he asked a few questions. To Alejo: "And where do you come from?"

"Cuba," Alejo answered in a soft voice.

"Oh yes, Cuba," the premier said in halting English. "I would like to go there one day. Cuba." And he smiled and patted Alejo's back and then rejoined the table. A pianist, a violinist, and a cellist played a Viennese waltz.

Afterward reporters came back into the kitchen to interview the two cooks, and the next morning the *Daily News* carried a picture of Alejo, Diego, and Khrushchev with a caption that read: DESSERT CHEFS CALL RUSKY PREMIER HEAP BIG EATER! It made them into celebrities for a few weeks. People recognized Alejo on the street and stopped to talk with him. He even went on a radio show in the Bronx. The hotel gave him a five-dollar weekly raise, and for a while Alejo felt important, and then it played itself out and became the yellowed clipping, stained by grease on the basement kitchen wall.

In Alejo's locker Khrushchev turned up again, on the cover of a *Life* magazine. He was posed, cheek against cheek, with the bearded Cuban premier Fidel Castro. "What was going to happen in Cuba?" Alejo wondered. He shook his head. "How could Cuba have gone 'red'?" It had been more than six years since the fall of Batista on New Year's Eve, 1958, the year of getting rid of the evil in Cuba, and now Alejo and Mercedes were going to sponsor the arrival of Aunt Luisa, her daughters, and a son-in-law, Pedro. They were coming to the United States via *un vuelo de la libertad,* or freedom flight, as the U.S. military airplane trips from Havana to Miami were called. Khrushchev was going to eat up Cuba like an ice cream sundae. Things had gotten out of hand, bad enough for Luisa, who had loved her life in Holguín, to leave. Gone were the days of the happy-go-lucky Cubans who went on jaunts to Miami and New York to have a high time ballroom hopping; gone were the days when Cubans came to the States to make money and see more of the world. Now Cubans were leaving because of Khrushchev's new pal, Fidel Castro, the Shit, as some Cubans called him.

Alejo had supported Castro during the days of the revolution. He had raised money for the pro-Castro Cubans in Miami by hawking copies of the *Sierra Maestra* magazine to pals on the street. This magazine was printed in Miami by pro-Castro Cubans and was filled with pictures of tortured heroes left on the streets or lying in the lightless mortuary rooms with their throats cut and their heads blood-splattered. They were victims of the crooked Batista regime, and now it was time for Batista and his henchmen to go! Alejo was not a political creature, but he supported the cause, of course, to end the injustices of Batista's rule. When someone brought him a box of Cuban magazines to sell, Alejo went down on Amsterdam Avenue and sold them to friends. Alejo always carried one of those magazines in his pocket, and he was persuasive, selling them. In his soft calm voice he would say, "Come on, it's only a dollar and for the cause of your countrymen's freedom!"

And soon he would find himself inviting all the buyers back to his apartment, where they sat in the kitchen drinking and talking about what would save the world: "An honest man with a good heart, out of greed's reach," was the usual consensus. Political talk about Cuba always led to nostalgic talk, and soon Alejo's friends would soften up and bend like orchid vines, glorying in the lost joys of childhood. Their loves and regrets thickened in the room in waves, until they began singing along with their drinking and falling down. With their arms around each other and glasses raised, they toasted Fidel as "the hope for the future."

Alejo and Mercedes had been happy with the success of the revolution. The day Castro entered Havana they threw a party with so much food and drink that the next morning people had to cross into the street to get around the stacks of garbage bags piled on the sidewalk in front of the building. Inside, people were sprawled around everywhere. There were sleepers in the kitchen and in the hall, sleepers in the closet. There was a *dudduhduh* of a skipping needle over a phonograph record. A cat that had come in through the window from the alley was going around eating leftover scraps of food.

Soon the papers printed that famous picture of Castro entering Havana with his cowboy-looking friend, Camilo Cienfuegos, on a tank. They were like Jesus and John the Baptist in a Roman epic movie. The *Sierra Maestra* magazine would later feature a centerfold of Castro as Jesus Christ with his hair long and golden brown, almost fiery in a halo of light. And for the longest time Cubans, Alejo and Mercedes among them, referred to Castro with great reverence and love, as if he were a saint.

CRISTINA GARCÍA

Dreaming in Cuban

Cristina García (born 1958), born in Havana, Cuba, to a Cuban mother and Guatemalan father, moved with her family to New York City while still a child. A graduate of Barnard College and Johns Hopkins University, she eventually settled into a career in journalism after working in Italy and West Germany. She was a reporter and Miami bureau chief for *Time* magazine for more than a decade before writing her first novel, *Dreaming in Cuban* (1992), a multigenerational tale of love, exile, and the painful rifts within a family divided by opposing politics, a theme she shares with Oscar Hijuelos. In more recent works—*The Agüero Sisters* (1997), *Monkey Hunting* (2003), and *A Handbook to Luck* (2007)—García goes further afield, exploring at length the tangled lives of characters from China, El Salvador, and Iran as well as Cuba. The following excerpt from *Dreaming in Cuban* describes the binge-eating of coconut ice cream, perhaps a sly reference to Castro's fondness for ice cream, making a *helado* parlor one of the goals of the Cuban revolution.

There's a bin full of coconuts at the bodega. Felicia trades in her remaining food coupons for every last one, and the grocer throws in a chocolate bar for Ivanito. Then they go door to door, hunting for more coconuts. Ivanito follows his mother as she wanders farther and farther from Palmas Street in her tunic and scuffed pink slippers. Felicia's hair springs from her head like electric wires, and she swings her arms in great arcs, as if her chaos had a rhythm.

They play a game with colors as they walk. "Let's speak in green," his mother says, and they talk about everything that makes them feel green. They do the same with blues and reds and yellows. Ivanito asks her, "If the grass were black, would the world be different?" But Felicia doesn't answer.

His mother collects coconuts from strangers, promising haircuts and manicures in exchange. Others are not so kind. They shout insults at her from their windows and balconies, hiding behind the boughs of acacia trees.

"They're afraid to call me a whore to my face," his mother says disdainfully.

A gaunt mulatta tells Ivanito he smells of death. This scares him but his mother tells him not to worry, that the lady is probably crazy. On the way back, his bag rips and the coconuts scatter in the street like billiard balls. Cars brake and screech but his mother doesn't notice the commotion. Instead, she scolds the coconuts one by one as if they were errant children.

At home, his mother removes her tunic and slippers. She takes a hammer and rusty chisel and shatters each coconut, scraping the blinding white, perfumed flesh from the shells. Ivanito helps her blend the coconut with egg yolks, vanilla, condensed milk, sugar, cornstarch, and salt, and holds the empty tin vegetable-oil containers while she fills them with the mixture. Together they arrange them in the freezer. With the leftover egg whites, she fashions star-shaped meringues, which she serves with the ice cream day after day, for breakfast, lunch, and dinner. His mother believes the coconuts will purify them, that the sweet white milk will heal them.

Felicia's spirits soar as the coconut ice cream diminishes. She makes pronouncements that Ivanito doesn't understand, stays up all night hearing prophecies in her head, forgives her father and ex-husband long lists of past trespasses. She dances for days to her Beny Moré records, her hands in position for an impossibly lanky partner, to "Rebel Heart," her slippers scraping the floor, to "Treat Me As I Am," a buoyant guaracha. There's a Brazilian samba she stamps to in bare feet, waving her arms until she is flushed and exuberant with the rhythm of the drums. When she presses Ivanito to her chest, he can feel her heart jumping like it wants to come out of its cage.

When his sisters return from their camping trip, Ivanito can tell by their faces that something is wrong.

"We've seen Mamá this way before," Milagro whispers.

"What way?" Ivanito asks, but she hushes him.

After Abuela Celia leaves, their mother rips the telephone from the wall and locks them all in the house. Ivanito continues to eat the ice cream his mother serves them but Luz and Milagro dump it in the sink. Undeterred, Felicia stubbornly refills their bowls.

The twins tell Ivanito stories of what happened before he was born. They say their father ran from the house with his head and hands on fire. That Mamá sat on the living-room floor laughing and banging on the walls with metal tongs. That the police came and took her away. That the kitchen curtains burned from the plantains she left frying on the stove.

That night Ivanito stands by his sisters' bedroom window transfixed by the branches of the tamarind tree, so black against the sky. He repeats something he heard his mother say: "The moon glares with a vivid indifference."

His sisters bristle. They tell him that he'll end up crazy like Mamá, that he's starting to show her symptoms. Luz says that families are essentially political and that he'll have to choose sides.

Ivanito senses even then that something has come between them. He will never speak his sisters' language, account for his movements like a cow with a dull bell. He is convinced, although he couldn't say why, that they're united against him, against his happiness with Mamá.

In his room, the wallpaper comes alive in the moonlight. Ivanito imagines the vines and tendrils, taut and violent as a killing rope, snaking along the floor to his bed, wrapping him in place, tighter and tighter, choking off his breath while his sisters sleep.

JAMAICA KINCAID

Annie John

Jamaica Kincaid (born 1949), novelist and essayist, was born Elaine Potter Richardson in St. John's, Antigua, changing her name in 1973 to launch her career as a writer. Antigua's poverty and the British colonial presence are recurring themes in her works, beginning with her short story collection, *At the Bottom of the River* (1983), and continuing through *A Small Place* (1988), *Annie John* (1985), *Lucy* (1990), and *Autobiography of My Mother* (1995). Kincaid was a staff writer for the *New Yorker* from 1976 to 1996. Derek Walcott, 1992 Nobel laureate, says of her prose that "As she writes a sentence, the temperature of it psychologically is that it heads toward its own contraction. It's as if the sentence is discovering itself, discovering how it feels." This selection, from the second chapter of *Annie John*, captures the psychological temperature of a child in just that way, describing the buying, preparing, and consuming of food as minutely observed rituals, making her mother and Antigua both everyday and magical.

When I got up, I placed my bedclothes and my nightie in the sun to air out, brushed my teeth, and washed and dressed myself. My mother would then give me my breakfast, but since, during my holidays, I was not going to school, I wasn't forced to eat an enormous breakfast of porridge, eggs, an orange or half a grapefruit, bread and butter, and cheese. I could get away with just some bread and butter and cheese and porridge and cocoa. I spent the day following my mother around and observing the way she did everything. When we went to the grocer's, she would point out to me the reason she bought each thing. I was shown a loaf of bread or a pound of butter from at least ten different angles. When we went to market, if that day she wanted to buy some crabs she would inquire from the person selling them if they came from near Parham, and if the person said yes my mother did not buy the crabs. In Parham was the leper colony, and my mother was convinced that the crabs ate nothing but the food from the lepers' own plates. If we were then to eat the crabs, it wouldn't be long before we were lepers ourselves and living unhappily in the leper colony.

How important I felt to be with my mother. For many people, their wares and provisions laid out in front of them, would brighten up when they saw her coming and would try hard to get her attention. They would dive underneath their stalls and bring out goods even better than what they had on display. They were disappointed when she held something up in the air, looked at it, turning it this way and that, and then, screwing up her face, said, "I don't think so," and turned and walked away—off to another stall to see if someone who only last week had sold her some delicious christophine had something that was just as good. They would call out after her turned back that next week they expected to have eddoes or dasheen or whatever, and my mother would say, "We'll see," in a very disbelieving tone of voice. If then we went to Mr. Kenneth, it would be only for a few minutes, for he knew exactly what my mother wanted and always had it ready for her. Mr. Kenneth had known me since I was a small child, and he would always remind me of little things I had done then as he fed me a piece of raw liver he had set aside for me. It was one of the few things I liked to eat, and, to boot, it pleased my mother to see me eat something that was so good for me, and she would tell me in great detail the effect the raw liver would have on my red blood corpuscles.

We walked home in the hot midmorning sun mostly without event. When I was much smaller, quite a few times while I was walking with my mother she would suddenly grab me and wrap me up in her skirt and drag me along with her as if in a great hurry. I would hear an angry voice saying angry things, and then, after we had passed the angry voice, my mother would release me. Neither my mother nor my father ever came straight out and told me anything, but I had put two and two together and I knew that it was one of the women that my father had loved and with whom he had had a child or children, and who never forgave him for marrying my mother and having me. It was one of those women who were always trying to harm my mother and me, and they must have loved my father very much, for not once did any of them ever try to hurt him, and whenever he passed them on the street it was as if he and these women had never met.

When we got home, my mother started to prepare our lunch (pumpkin soup with droppers, banana fritters with salt fish stewed in antroba and tomatoes, fungie with salt fish stewed in antroba and tomatoes, or pepper pot, all depending on what my mother had found at market that day). As my mother went about from pot to pot, stirring one, adding something to the other, I was ever in her wake. As she dipped into a pot of boiling something or other to taste for correct seasoning, she would give me a taste of it also, asking me what I thought. Not that she really wanted to know what I thought, for she had told me many times that my taste buds were not quite developed yet, but it was just to include me in everything.

JULIA ALVAREZ

How the García Girls Lost Their Accents

Julia Alvarez (born 1950), born in New York City, was raised in the Dominican Republic until age ten, when her father's opposition to the military dictator Rafael Trujillo made it necessary for the family to leave. The Trujillo regime continued to haunt her two best-known novels, *How the García Girls Lost Their Accents* (1991) and *In the Time of the Butterflies* (1994). In more recent works, however, such as *In the Name* *of Salomé* (2001) and *A Wedding in Haiti* (2012), Alvarez has turned to other settings, including Cuba in the 1960s and Haiti. She began as a poet with *The Other Side* (1995) and *Homecoming* (1984) and has also written roughly a dozen children's books. *How the García Girls Lost Their Accents*, excerpted here, is a tale told in reverse chronology, beginning with the sisters struggling to assimilate in the United States and going back to their former life under Trujillo. The first chapter opens with Yolanda's visit to the Dominican Republic, her first in five years, and the social and political history packed into her search for the fruit she craves: guavas growing in the countryside.

Yolanda pulls up at a cantina, its thatched roof held up by several posts, its floor poured cement, and in its very center, a lone picnic table over which a swarm of flies hover.

Tacked to one of the central posts is a yellowing poster for Palmolive soap. A creamy, blond woman luxuriates under a refreshing shower, her head thrown back in seeming ecstasy, her mouth opened in a wordless cry.

"*¡Buenas!*" Yolanda calls out.

An old woman emerges from a shack behind the cantina, buttoning up a torn housedress. She is followed closely by a little boy, who keeps ducking behind her whenever Yolanda smiles at him. Asking his name drives him further into the folds of the old woman's skirt.

"You must excuse him, doña," the woman apologizes. "He's not used to being among people." People with money who drive through Altamira to the beach resorts on the north coast, she means. "Your name," the old woman repeats, as if Yolanda hasn't asked him in Spanish. The little boy mumbles at the ground. "Speak up!" the old woman scolds, but her voice betrays pride when she speaks up for him. "This little know-nothing is José Duarte, Sánchez y Mella."

Yolanda laughs. A lot of names for such a little boy—the surnames of the country's three liberators!

"Can I serve the doña in any way?" the old woman asks. "*¿Un refresco? ¿Una Coca Cola?*" By the pride in her voice, Yolanda understands the old woman wants to treat her to the best on her menu.

"I'll tell you what I would like." Yolanda gives the tree line beyond the old woman's shack a glance. "Are there any guavas around?"

The old woman's face scrunches up. "*¿Guayabas?*" she murmurs, and thinks to herself a second. "Why, they grow all around, doña. But I can't say as I've seen any lately."

"With your permission—" José Duarte has joined a group of little boys who have come out of nowhere and are milling around the car, boasting how many automobiles they have ridden in. At Yolanda's mention of guavas, he springs forward, pointing across the road towards the summit of the western hills. "I know where there's a whole grove of ripe ones." Behind him, his little companions nod.

"Go on, then!" His grandmother stamps her foot as if she were scatting an animal. "Get the doña some."

A few boys dash across the road and disappear up a steep path on the hillside, but before José can follow, Yolanda calls him back. She wants to go along too. The little boy looks towards his grandmother, unsure of what to think. The old woman shakes her head. The doña will get hot, her nice clothes will get all dirty. José will bring the doña as many guavas as she is wanting.

"But they taste so much better when you've picked them yourself." Yolanda hears the edge in her voice. The old woman has turned into the long arm of her family.

The few boys who have stayed behind with José have again congregated around the car. Each one claims to be guarding it for the doña. It occurs to Yolanda that there is a way to make this a treat all the way around. "What do you say we take the car?" The little boys cheer.

Now that is not a bad idea, the old woman agrees. If the doña insists on going, she can take that dirt road up ahead and then cross over onto the road that is paved all the way to the coffee barns. The old woman points south in the direction of the big house. Many workers take that shortcut to work.

They pile into the car, half a dozen little boys in the back, and José as co-pilot in the passenger seat beside Yolanda. They turn onto a bumpy road off the highway, which grows bumpier and bumpier as it climbs up into wilder, more desolate country. Branches scrape the sides and pebbles pelt the underside of the car. Yolanda wants to turn back, but there is no room. Finally, with a great snapping of twigs and thrashing of branches across the windshield, as if the countryside is loath to release them, the car bursts forth onto smooth pavement and the light of day. On either side of the road are groves of guava trees. The boys who have gone ahead on foot are already pulling down branches and shaking loose a rain of guavas.

Yolanda eats several right on the spot, relishing the slightly bumpy feel of the skin in her hand, devouring the crunchy, sweet white meat. The boys watch her.

The group scatters to harvest the guavas. Yolanda and José, partners, wander far from the path that cuts through the grove. Soon they are bent almost double to avoid getting entangled in the thick canopy of branches overhead. Each addition to Yolanda's beach basket causes a spill from the stash already piled high above the brim.

The way back seems much longer than the way there. Yolanda begins to worry that they are lost, and then, the way worry sprouts worry, it strikes her that they haven't heard or seen the other boys in quite a while. The latticework of branches reveals glimmers of a fading sky. The image of the guard in his elaborate flowering prison flashes through her head. The rustling leaves of the guava trees echo the warnings of her old aunts: you will get lost, you will get kidnapped, you will get raped, you will get killed.

Just ahead, the thicket of guava branches clears, and there is the footpath, and beyond, the gratifying sight of the car still on the side of the road. It is a pleasure to stand upright again. José rests his burden on the ground and straightens his back to full measure. Yolanda looks up at the sky. The sun is low on the western horizon.

"The others must have gone to gather kindling," José observes.

Yolanda glances at her watch—it is past six o'clock. At this rate, she will never make the north coast by nightfall. She hurries José back to the car, where they find a heap of guavas the other boys left behind on the shoulder of the road. Enough guavas to appease even the greediest Island *santo* for life!

They pack the trunk quickly, and climb in, but the car has not gone a foot before it lurches forward with a horrible hobble. Yolanda closes her eyes and lays her head down on the wheel, then glances over at José. His eyes are searching the inside of the car for a clue as to what could have happened. This child won't know how to change a flat tire either.

Soon the sun will set and night will fall swiftly, no lingering dusk as in the States. She explains to José that they have a flat tire and must go back down the road to the big house. Whoever tends to the brown Mercedes will surely know how to change a tire.

"With your permission," José offers. The doña can just wait in the car, and he will be back in no time with someone from the Miranda place.

Miranda, Miranda. . . . Yolanda leans over and gets her aunt's list out of the glove compartment, and sure enough, there they are. *Tía Marina y tío Alejandro Miranda—Altos de Altamira.* A note elaborates that Tío Alejandro was the one *who used to own English saddle horses and taught you four girls to ride.* "All right," she says to the boy. "I'll tell you what." She points to her watch. "If you're back by the time this hand is over here, I'll give you"—she holds up one finger—"a dollar." The boy's mouth falls open. In no time, he has shot out of his side of the car and is headed at a run toward the Miranda place. Yolanda climbs out as well and walks down a pace, until the boy has disappeared in one of the turnings of the road.

From the footpath that cuts through the grove on the opposite side of the road, she hears the sound of branches being thrust aside, twigs snapping underfoot. Two men, one short and dark, and the other slender and light-skinned, emerge. They wear ragged work clothes stained with patches of sweat; their faces are drawn. Machetes hang from their belts.

The men's faces snap awake at the sight of her. Then they look beyond her at the car. The darker man speaks first. "Yours?"

"Is there some problem?" he speaks up again. The taller one is looking her up and down with interest. They are now both in front of her on the road, blocking any escape. Both—she has sized them up as well—are strong and quite capable of catching her if she makes a run for it. Not that she can move, for her legs seem suddenly to have been hammered into the ground beneath her. She considers explaining that she is just out for a drive before dinner at the big house, so that these men will think someone knows where she is, someone will come looking for her if they try to carry her off. But her tongue feels as if it has been stuffed in her mouth like a rag to keep her quiet.

The two men exchange a look—it seems to Yolanda—of collusion.

Then the shorter, darker one speaks up again. "Señorita, are you all right?" He peers at her. He is a short man, no taller than Yolanda, but he gives the impression of being quite large, for he is broad and solid, like something not yet completely carved out of a piece of wood. His companion is slim and tall and of a rich honey-brown color that matches his honey-brown eyes. Anywhere else, Yolanda would find him extremely attractive, but here on a lonely road, with the sky growing darker by seconds, his good looks seem dangerous, a lure to catch her off her guard.

"Can we help you?" the shorter man repeats.

The handsome one smiles knowingly. Two long, deep dimples appear like gashes on either side of his mouth. "*Americana*," he says to the darker man, pointing to the car. "*No comprende.*"

The darker man narrows his eyes and studies Yolanda a moment. "*¿Americana?*" he asks her, as if not quite sure what to make of her.

She has been too frightened to carry out any strategy, but now a road is opening before her. She clasps her hands on her chest—she can feel her pounding heart—and nods. Then, as if the admission itself loosens her tongue, she begins to speak, English, a few words, of apology at first, then a great flood of explanation: how it happens that she is on a back road by herself, her craving for guavas, having never learned to change a flat. The two men stare at her, uncomprehending, rendered docile by her gibberish. Only when she mentions the name Miranda do their eyes light up with respect. She is saved!

Yolanda makes the motions of pumping. The darker man looks at his companion, who shrugs, baffled as well. Yolanda waves for them to follow her. And as if after dragging up roots, she has finally managed to yank them free of the soil they have clung to, she finds she can move her own feet toward the car.

The small group stands staring at the sagging tire a moment, the two men kicking at it as if punishing it for having failed the señorita. They squat by the passenger's side, conversing in low tones. Yolanda leads the men to the rear of the car, where they lift the spare out of its sunken nest—then set to work fitting the interlocking pieces of the jack, unpacking the tools from the deeper hollows of the trunk. They lay their machetes down on the side of the road, out of the way. Above them, the sky is purple with twilight. The sun breaks on the hilltops, spilling its crimson yolk.

Once the flat has been replaced with the spare, the two men lift the deflated tire into the trunk and put away the tools. They hand Yolanda her keys.

"I'd like to give you something," she begins, but the English words are hollow on her tongue. She rummages in her purse and draws out a sheaf of bills, rolls them up and offers them to the men.

The shorter man holds up his hand. Yolanda can see where he has scraped his hand on the pavement and blood has dried dark streaks on his palm. "*No, no, señorita. Nuestro placer.*"

Yolanda turns to the taller one. "Please," she says, urging the bills on him. But he too looks down at the ground—Iluminada's gesture, José's gesture. Quickly, she stuffs the bills in his pocket.

The two men pick up their machetes and raise them to their shoulders like soldiers their guns. The tall man motions towards the big house. "*Directo*, Mirandas." He enunciates the words carefully. Yolanda looks in the direction of his hand. In the faint light of what is left of day, she can barely make out the road ahead. It is as if the guava grove has grown into the road and woven its matt of branches tightly in all directions.

She reaches for each man's hand to shake. The shorter man holds his back at first, as if not wanting to dirty her hand, but finally, after wiping it on the side of his pants, he gives it to Yolanda. The skin feels rough and dry like the bark of trees.

Yolanda climbs into the car while the two men wait a moment on the shoulder to see if the tire will hold. She eases out onto the pavement and makes her way slowly down the road. When she looks for them in her rearview mirror, they have disappeared into the darkness of the guava grove.

EDWIDGE DANTICAT

Breath, Eyes, Memory

Edwidge Danticat (born 1969) grew up in Haiti speaking Creole and French. Moving to Brooklyn at the age of twelve, she published her first work in English two years later, the seed for her MFA thesis at Brown University. Her first novel, *Breath, Eyes, Memory* (1994), was published when she was only twenty-five. This was followed by a short story collection, *Krik? Krak!* (1996), and several other novels: *The Farming of Bones* (1998), *The Dew Breaker* (2004), and *Claire of the Sea Light* (2013). Danticat has also edited an anthology, *Haiti Noire* (2011), and a picture book about the 2010 earthquake, *Tent Life: Haiti* (2011). She received a National Book Critics Circle Award for her memoir, *Brother, I'm Dying*

(2007), and was named a MacArthur Fellow in 2009. *Breath, Eyes, Memory,* excerpted here, is an immigrant story haunted by rape, with traumatic memories extending across two generations. This particular moment, though, simply dwells on the making of a Haitian dish and the way it both brings deep satisfaction and also conjures up the cumulative weight of Haitian economy and family history,

~~~~~~

I asked my grandmother if I could cook supper for us that night.

Tante Atie offered to take me to a private vendor where food was cheaper than the *maché*. She put the leeches in some clean water and we started down the road.

"What are you making for us?" she asked.

"Rice, black beans, and herring sauce," I said.

"Your mother's favorite meal."

"That's what we cooked most often."

We followed a footpath off the road, down to a shallow stream. An old mule was yanking water vines from the edge of the stream while baby crabs freely dashed around its nostrils.

A woman filled a calabash a few feet from where my sandals muddied the water. Tante Atie chatted with the women as she went by. Some young girls were sitting bare-chested in the water, the sun casting darker shadows into their faces. Their hands squirted blackened suds as they pounded their clothes with water rocks.

A dusty footpath led us to a tree-lined cemetery at the top of the hill. Tante Atie walked between the wooden crosses, collecting the bamboo skeletons of fallen kites. She stepped around the plots where empty jars, conch shells, and marbles served as grave markers.

"Walk straight," said Tante Atie, "you are in the presence of family."

She walked around to each plot, and called out the names of all those who had been buried there. There was my great-grandmother, Beloved Martinelle Brigitte. Her sister, My First Joy Sophilus Gentille. My grandfather's sister, My Hope Atinia Ifé, and finally my grandfather, Charlemagne Le Grand Caco.

Tante Atie named them all on sight.

"Our family name, Caco, it is the name of a scarlet bird. A bird so crimson, it makes the reddest hibiscus or the brightest flame trees seem white.

The Caco bird, when it dies, there is always a rush of blood that rises to its neck and the wings, they look so bright, you would think them on fire."

From the cemetery, we took a narrow footpath to the vendor's hut. On either side of us were wild grasses that hissed as though they were full of snakes.

We walked to a whitewashed shack where a young woman sold rice and black beans from the same sisal mat where she slept with her husband.

In the yard, the husband sat under the shade of a straw parasol with a pipe in his mouth and a demijohn at his feet. He was pounding small nails into leather straps and thin layers of polished wood to make sandals.

The hammering echoed in my head until I reached the cane fields. The men were singing about a woman who flew without her skin at night, and when she came back home, she found her skin peppered and could not put it back on. Her husband had done it to teach her a lesson. He ended up killing her.

I was surprised how fast it came back. The memory of how everything came together to make a great meal. The fragrance of the spices guided my fingers the way no instructions or measurements could.

Haitian men, they insist that their women are virgins and have their ten fingers.

According to Tante Atie, each finger had a purpose. It was the way she had been taught to prepare herself to become a woman. Mothering. Boiling. Loving. Baking. Nursing. Frying. Healing. Washing. Ironing. Scrubbing. It wasn't her fault, she said. Her ten fingers had been named for her even before she was born. Sometimes, she even wished she had six fingers on each hand so she could have two left for herself.

I rushed back and forth between the iron pots in the yard. The air smelled like spices that I had not cooked with since I'd left my mother's home two years before.

I usually ate random concoctions: frozen dinners, samples from global cookbooks, food that was easy to put together and brought me no pain. No memories of a past that at times was cherished and at others despised.

By the time we ate, the air was pregnant with rain. Thunder groaned in the starless sky while the lanterns flickered in the hills.

"Well done," Tante Atie said after her fourth serving of my rice and beans.

My grandmother chewed slowly as she gave my daughter her bottle.

"If the wood is well carved," said my grandmother, "it teaches us about the carpenter. Atie, you taught Sophie well."

JHUMPA LAHIRI

When Mr. Pirzada Came to Dine

Jhumpa Lahiri (born 1967), probably best known for her Pulitzer Prize–winning collection of short stories, *The Interpreter of Maladies* (1999), was born in London, raised in Kingston, Rhode Island, and now divides her time between Princeton University and Rome, Italy. Her novels and short stories—*The Lowland* (2013); *Unaccustomed Earth* (2008); and *The Namesake* (2003), made into a popular film—characteristically span several generations, capturing in great detail the fault lines of family life and gesturing toward large-scale historical events only obliquely. In the following story, the 1971 war between India and Pakistan came every night into a suburban Boston home through dinners doubling as TV viewing sessions, shared by an Indian-Bengali family and their guest, Mr. Pirzada from Dacca, soon to be Bangladeshi rather than Pakistani. For the young narrator, Lilia, the distant fate of Mr. Pirzada's wife and seven daughters is oddly linked to the candies that he brought her during each of his visits.

In the autumn of 1971 a man used to come to our house, bearing confections in his pocket and hopes of ascertaining the life or death of his family. His name was Mr. Pirzada, and he came from Dacca, now the capital of Bangladesh, but then a part of Pakistan. That year Pakistan was engaged in civil war. The eastern frontier, where Dacca was located, was fighting for autonomy from the ruling regime in the west. In March, Dacca had been invaded, torched and shelled by the Pakistani army. Teachers were dragged onto streets and shot, women dragged into barracks and raped. By the end of the summer, three hundred thousand people were said to have died. In Dacca Mr. Pirzada had a three-story home, a lectureship in botany at the university, a wife of twenty years, and seven daughters between the ages of six and sixteen whose names all began with the letter A. "Their mother's idea," he explained one day, producing from his wallet a black-and-white picture of seven girls at a picnic, their braids tied with ribbons, sitting cross-legged in a row, eating chicken curry off of banana leaves. "How am I to distinguish? Ayesha, Amira, Amina, Aziza, you see the difficulty."

Each week Mr. Pirzada wrote letters to his wife, and sent comic books to each of his seven daughters, but the postal system, along with most everything else in Dacca, had collapsed, and he had not heard word of them in over six months. Mr. Pirzada, meanwhile, was in America for the year, for he had been awarded a grant from the government of Pakistan to study the foliage of New England. In spring and summer he had gathered data in Vermont and Maine, and in autumn he moved to a university north of Boston, where we lived, to write a short book about his discoveries. The grant was a great honor, but when converted into dollars it was not generous. As a result, Mr. Pirzada lived in a room in a graduate dormitory, and did not own a proper stove or a television set of his own. And so he came to our house to eat dinner and watch the evening news.

At first I knew nothing of the reason for his visits. I was ten years old, and was not surprised that my parents, who were from India, and had a number of Indian acquaintances at the university, should ask Mr. Pirzada to share our meals. It was a small campus, with narrow brick walkways and white pillared buildings, located on the fringes of what seemed to be an even smaller town. The supermarket did not carry mustard oil, doctors did not make house calls, neighbors never dropped by without an invitation, and of these things, every so often, my parents complained. In search of compatriots, they used to trail their fingers, at the start of each new semester, through the columns of the university directory, circling surnames familiar to their part of the world. It was in this manner that they discovered Mr. Pirzada, and phoned him, and invited him to our home.

I have no memory of his first visit, or of his second or his third, but by the end of September I had grown so accustomed to Mr. Pirzada's presence in our living room that one evening, as I was dropping ice cubes into the water pitcher, I asked my mother to hand me a fourth glass from a cupboard still out of my reach. She was busy at the stove, presiding over a skillet of fried spinach with radishes, and could not hear me because of the drone of the exhaust fan and the fierce scrapes of her spatula. I turned to my father, who was leaning against the refrigerator, eating spiced cashews from a cupped fist.

"What is it, Lilia?"

"A glass for the Indian man."

"Mr. Pirzada won't be coming today. More importantly, Mr. Pirzada is no longer considered Indian," my father announced, brushing salt from the cashews out of his trim black beard. "Not since Partition. Our country was divided. 1947."

When I said I thought that was the date of India's independence from Britain, my father said, "That too. One moment we were free and then we were sliced up," he explained, drawing an X with his finger on the countertop, "like a pie. Hindus here, Muslims there. Dacca no longer belongs to us." He told me that during Partition Hindus and Muslims had set fire to each other's homes. For many, the idea of eating in the other's company was still unthinkable.

It made no sense to me. Mr. Pirzada and my parents spoke the same language, laughed at the same jokes, looked more or less the same. They ate pickled mangoes with their meals, ate rice every night for supper with their hands. Like my parents, Mr. Pirzada took off his shoes before entering a room, chewed fennel seeds after meals as a digestive, drank no alcohol, for dessert dipped austere biscuits into successive cups of tea. Nevertheless my father insisted that I understand the difference, and he led me to a map of the world taped to the wall over his desk. He seemed concerned that Mr. Pirzada might take offense if I accidentally referred to him as an Indian, though I could not really imagine Mr. Pirzada being offended by much of anything. "Mr. Pirzada is Bengali, but he is a Muslim," my father informed me. "Therefore he lives in East Pakistan, not India." His finger trailed across the Atlantic, through Europe, the Mediterranean, the Middle East, and finally to the sprawling orange diamond that my mother once told me resembled a woman wearing a sari with her left arm extended. Various cities had been circled with lines drawn between them to indicate my parents' travels, and the place of their birth, Calcutta, was signified by a small silver star. I had been there only once and had no memory of the trip. "As you see, Lilia, it is a different country, a different color," my father said. Pakistan was yellow, not orange. I noticed that there were two distinct parts to it, one much larger than the other, separated by an expanse of Indian territory; it was as if California and Connecticut constituted a nation apart from the U.S.

My father rapped his knuckles on top of my head. "You are, of course, aware of the current situation? Aware of East Pakistan's fight for sovereignty?"

I nodded, unaware of the situation. We returned to the kitchen, where my mother was draining a pot of boiled rice into a colander. My father opened up the can on the counter and eyed me sharply over the frames of his glasses as he ate some more cashews. "What exactly do they teach you at school? Do you study history? Geography?"

"Lilia has plenty to learn at school," my mother said. "We live here now, she was born here." She seemed genuinely proud of the fact, as if it were a reflection of my character. In her estimation, I knew, I was assured a safe life, an easy life, a fine education, every opportunity. I would never have to eat rationed food, or obey curfews, or watch riots from my rooftop, or hide neighbors in water tanks to prevent them from being shot, as she and my father had. "Imagine having to place her in a decent school. Imagine her having to read during power failures by the light of kerosene lamps. Imagine the pressures, the tutors, the constant exams." She ran a hand through her hair, bobbed to a suitable length for her part-time job as a bank teller. "How can you possibly expect her to know about Partition? Put those nuts away."

"But what does she learn about the world?" My father rattled the cashew can in his hand. "What is she learning?"

We learned American history, of course, and American geography. That year, and every year, it seemed, we began by studying the Revolutionary War. We were taken in school buses on field trips to visit Plymouth Rock, and to walk the Freedom Trail, and to climb to the top of the Bunker Hill Monument. We made dioramas out of colored construction paper depicting George Washington crossing the choppy waters of the Delaware River, and we made puppets of King George wearing white tights and a black bow in his hair. During tests we were given blank maps of the thirteen colonies, and asked to fill in names, dates, capitals. I could do it with my eyes closed.

The next evening Mr. Pirzada arrived, as usual, at six o'clock. Though they were no longer strangers, upon first greeting each other, he and my father maintained the habit of shaking hands.

"Come in, sir. Lilia, Mr. Pirzada's coat, please."

He stepped into the foyer, impeccably suited and scarved, with a silk tie knotted at his collar. Each evening he appeared in ensembles of plums, olives, and chocolate browns. He was a compact man, and though his feet were perpetually splayed, and his belly slightly wide, he nevertheless maintained an efficient posture, as if balancing in either hand two suitcases of equal weight. His ears were insulated by tufts of graying hair that seemed to block out the unpleasant traffic of life. He had thickly lashed eyes shaded with a trace of camphor, a generous mustache that turned up playfully at the ends, and a mole shaped like a flattened raisin in the very center of his left cheek. On his head he wore a black fez made from the wool of Persian lambs, secured by bobby pins, without which I was never to see him. Though my father always offered to fetch him in our car, Mr. Pirzada preferred to walk from his dormitory to our neighborhood, a distance of about twenty minutes on foot, studying trees and shrubs on his way, and when he entered our house his knuckles were pink with the effects of crisp autumn air.

"Another refugee, I am afraid, on Indian territory."

"They are estimating nine million at the last count," my father said.

Mr. Pirzada handed me his coat, for it was my job to hang it on the rack at the bottom of the stairs. It was made of finely checkered gray-and-blue wool, with a striped lining and horn buttons, and carried in its weave the faint smell of limes. There were no recognizable tags inside, only a hand-stitched label with the phrase "Z. Sayeed, Suitors" embroidered on it in cursive with glossy black thread. On certain days a birch or maple leaf was tucked into a pocket. He unlaced his shoes and lined them against the baseboard; a golden paste clung to the toes and heels, the result of walking through our damp, unraked lawn. Relieved of his trappings, he grazed my throat with his short, restless fingers, the way a person feels for solidity behind a wall before driving in a nail. Then he followed my father to the living room, where the television was tuned to the local news. As soon as they were seated my mother appeared from the kitchen with a plate of mincemeat kebabs with coriander chutney. Mr. Pirzada popped one into his mouth.

"One can only hope," he said, reaching for another, "that Dacca's refugees are as heartily fed. Which reminds me." He reached into his suit pocket and gave me a small plastic egg filled with cinnamon hearts. "For the lady of the house," he said with an almost imperceptible splay-footed bow.

"Really, Mr. Pirzada," my mother protested. "Night after night. You spoil her."

"I only spoil children who are incapable of spoiling."

It was an awkward moment for me, one which I awaited in part with dread, in part with delight. I was charmed by the presence of Mr. Pirzada's rotund elegance, and flattered by the faint theatricality of his attentions, yet unsettled by the superb ease of his gestures, which made me feel, for an instant, like a stranger in my own home. It had become our ritual, and for several weeks, before we grew more comfortable with one another, it was the only time he spoke to me directly. I had no response, offered no comment, betrayed no visible reaction to the steady stream of honey-filled lozenges, the raspberry truffles, the slender rolls of sour pastilles. I could not even thank him, for once, when I did, for an especially spectacular peppermint lollipop wrapped in a spray of purple cellophane, he had demanded, "What is this thank-you? The lady at the bank thanks me, the cashier at the shop thanks me, the librarian thanks me when I return an overdue book, the overseas operator thanks me as she tries to connect me to Dacca and fails. If I am buried in this country I will be thanked, no doubt, at my funeral."

It was inappropriate, in my opinion, to consume the candy Mr. Pirzada gave me in a casual manner. I coveted each evening's treasure as I would a jewel, or a coin from a buried kingdom, and I would place it in a small keep-sake box made of carved sandalwood beside my bed, in which, long ago in India, my father's mother used to store the ground areca nuts she ate after her morning bath. It was my only memento of a grandmother I had never known, and until Mr. Pirzada came to our lives I could find nothing to put inside it. Every so often before brushing my teeth and laying out my clothes for school the next day, I opened the lid of the box and ate one of his treats.

That night, like every night, we did not eat at the dining table, because it did not provide an unobstructed view of the television set. Instead we huddled around the coffee table, without conversing, our plates perched on the edges of our knees. From the kitchen my mother brought forth the suc-cession of dishes: lentils with fried onions, green beans with coconut, fish cooked with raisins in a yogurt sauce. I followed with the water glasses, and the plate of lemon wedges, and the chili peppers, purchased on monthly trips to Chinatown and stored by the pound in the freezer, which they liked to snap open and crush into their food.

Before eating Mr. Pirzada always did a curious thing. He took out a plain silver watch without a band, which he kept in his breast pocket, held it briefly to one of his tufted ears, and wound it with three swift flicks of his thumb and forefinger. Unlike the watch on his wrist, the pocket watch, he had explained to me, was set to the local time in Dacca, eleven hours ahead. For the duration of the meal the watch rested on his folded paper napkin on the coffee table. He never seemed to consult it.

Now that I had learned Mr. Pirzada was not an Indian, I began to study him with extra care, to try to figure out what made him different. I decided that the pocket watch was one of those things. When I saw it that night, as he wound it and arranged it on the coffee table, an uneasiness possessed me; life, I realized, was being lived in Dacca first. I imagined Mr. Pirzada's daughters rising from sleep, tying ribbons in their hair, anticipating breakfast, preparing for school. Our meals, our actions, were only a shadow of what had already happened there, a lagging ghost of where Mr. Pirzada really belonged.

At six-thirty, which was when the national news began, my father raised the volume and adjusted the antennas. Usually I occupied myself with a book, but that night my father insisted that I pay attention. On the screen I saw tanks rolling through dusty streets, and fallen buildings, and forests of unfamiliar trees into which East Pakistani refugees had fled, seeking safety over the Indian border. I saw boats with fan-shaped sails floating on wide coffee-colored rivers, a barricaded university, newspaper offices burnt to the ground. I turned to look at Mr. Pirzada; the images flashed in miniature across his eyes. As he watched he had an immovable expression on his face, composed but alert, as if someone were giving him directions to an unknown destination.

During the commercial my mother went to the kitchen to get more rice, and my father and Mr. Pirzada deplored the policies of a general named Yahyah Khan. They discussed intrigues I did not know, a catastrophe I could not comprehend. "See, children your age, what they do to survive," my father said as he served me another piece of fish. But I could no longer eat. I could only steal glances at Mr. Pirzada, sitting beside me in his olive green jacket, calmly creating a well in his rice to make room for a second helping of lentils. He was not my notion of a man burdened by such grave concerns. I wondered if the reason he was always so smartly dressed was in preparation to endure with dignity whatever news assailed him, perhaps even to attend a funeral at a moment's notice. I wondered, too, what would happen if suddenly his seven daughters were to appear on television, smiling and waving and blowing kisses to Mr. Pirzada from a balcony. I imagined how relieved he would be. But this never happened.

That night when I placed the plastic egg filled with cinnamon hearts in the box beside my bed, I did not feel the ceremonious satisfaction I normally did. I tried not to think about Mr. Pirzada, in his lime-scented overcoat, connected to the unruly, sweltering world we had viewed a few hours ago in our bright, carpeted living room. And yet for several moments that was all I could think about. My stomach tightened as I worried whether his wife and seven daughters were now members of the drifting, clamoring crowd that had flashed at intervals on the screen. In an effort to banish the image I looked around my room, at the yellow canopied bed with matching flounced curtains, at framed class pictures mounted on white and violet papered walls, at the penciled inscriptions by the closet door where my father recorded my height on each of my birthdays. But the more I tried to distract myself, the more I began to convince myself that Mr. Pirzada's family was in all likelihood dead. Eventually I took a square of white chocolate out of the box, and unwrapped it, and then I did something I had never done before. I put the chocolate in my mouth, letting it soften until the last possible moment, and then as I chewed it slowly, I prayed that Mr. Pirzada's family was safe and sound. I had never prayed for anything before, had never been taught or told to, but I decided, given the circumstances, that it was something I should do. That night when I went to the bathroom I only pretended to brush my teeth, for I feared that I would somehow rinse the prayer out as well. I wet the brush and rearranged the tube of paste to prevent my parents from asking any questions, and fell asleep with sugar on my tongue.

No one at school talked about the war followed so faithfully in my living room. We continued to study the American Revolution, and learned about the injustices of taxation without representation, and memorized passages from the Declaration of Independence. During recess the boys would divide in two groups, chasing each other wildly around the swings and seesaws, Redcoats against the colonies. In the classroom our teacher, Mrs. Kenyon, pointed frequently to a map that emerged like a movie screen from the top of the chalkboard, charting the route of the Mayflower or showing us the location of the Liberty Bell. Each week two members of the class gave a report on a particular aspect of the Revolution, and so one day I was sent to the school library with my friend Dora to learn about the surrender at Yorktown. Mrs. Kenyon handed us a slip of paper with the names of three books to look up in the card catalogue. We found them right away, and sat down at a low round table to read and take notes. But I could not concentrate. I returned to the blond-wood shelves, to a section I had noticed labeled "Asia." I saw books about China, India, Indonesia, Korea. Eventually I found a book titled *Pakistan: A Land and Its People*. I sat on a footstool and opened the book. The laminated jacket crackled in my grip. I began turning the pages, filled with photos of rivers and rice fields and men in military uniforms. There was a chapter about Dacca, and I began to read about its rainfall, and its jute production. I was studying a population chart when Dora appeared in the aisle.

"What are you doing back here? Mrs. Kenyon's in the library. She came to check up on us."

I slammed the book shut, too loudly. Mrs. Kenyon emerged, the aroma of her perfume filling up the tiny aisle, and lifted the book by the tip of its spine as if it were a hair clinging to my sweater. She glanced at the cover, then at me.

"Is this book a part of your report, Lilia?"

"No, Mrs. Kenyon."

"Then I see no reason to consult it," she said, replacing it in the slim gap on the shelf. "Do you?"

As weeks passed it grew more and more rare to see any footage from Dacca on the news. The report came after the first set of commercials, sometimes the second. The press had been censored, removed, restricted, rerouted. Some days, many days, only a death toll was announced, prefaced by a reiteration of the general situation. More poets were executed, more villages set ablaze. In spite of it all, night after night, my parents and Mr. Pirzada enjoyed long, leisurely meals. After the television was shut off, and the dishes washed and dried, they joked, and told stories, and dipped biscuits in their tea. When they tired of discussing political matters they discussed, instead, the progress of Mr. Pirzada's book about the deciduous trees of New England, and my father's nomination for tenure, and the peculiar eating habits of my mother's American coworkers at the bank. Eventually I was sent upstairs to do my homework, but through the carpet I heard them as they drank more tea, and listened to cassettes of Kishore Kumar, and played Scrabble on the coffee table, laughing and arguing long into the night about the spellings of English words. I wanted to join them, wanted, above all, to console Mr. Pirzada somehow. But apart from eating a piece of candy for the sake of his family and praying for their safety, there was nothing I could do. They played Scrabble until the eleven o'clock news, and then, sometime around midnight, Mr. Pirzada walked back to his dormitory. For this reason I never saw him leave, but each night as I drifted off to sleep I would hear them, anticipating the birth of a nation on the other side of the world.

One day in October Mr. Pirzada asked upon arrival, "What are these large orange vegetables on people's doorsteps? A type of squash?"

"Pumpkins," my mother replied. "Lilia, remind me to pick one up at the supermarket."

"And the purpose? It indicates what?"

"You make a jack-o'-lantern," I said, grinning ferociously. "Like this. To scare people away."

"I see," Mr. Pirzada said, grinning back. "Very useful."

The next day my mother bought a ten-pound pumpkin, fat and round, and placed it on the dining table. Before supper, while my father and Mr. Pirzada were watching the local news, she told me to decorate it with markers, but I wanted to carve it properly like others I had noticed in the neighborhood.

"Yes, let's carve it," Mr. Pirzada agreed, and rose from the sofa. "Hang the news tonight." Asking no questions, he walked into the kitchen, opened a drawer, and returned, bearing a long serrated knife. He glanced at me for approval. "Shall I?"

I nodded. For the first time we all gathered around the dining table, my mother, my father, Mr. Pirzada, and I. While the television aired unattended we covered the tabletop with newspapers. Mr. Pirzada draped his jacket over the chair behind him, removed a pair of opal cuff links, and rolled up the starched sleeves of his shirt.

"First go around the top, like this," I instructed, demonstrating with my index finger.

He made an initial incision and drew the knife around. When he had come full circle he lifted the cap by the stem; it loosened effortlessly, and Mr. Pirzada leaned over the pumpkin for a moment to inspect and inhale its contents. My mother gave him a long metal spoon with which he gutted the interior until the last bits of string and seeds were gone. My father, meanwhile, separated the seeds from the pulp and set them out to dry on a cookie sheet, so that we could roast them later on. I drew two triangles against the ridged surface for the eyes, which Mr. Pirzada dutifully carved, and crescents for eyebrows, and another triangle for the nose. The mouth was all that remained, and the teeth posed a challenge. I hesitated.

"Smile or frown?" I asked.

"You choose," Mr. Pirzada said.

As a compromise I drew a kind of grimace, straight across, neither mournful nor friendly. Mr. Pirzada began carving, without the least bit of intimidation, as if he had been carving jack-o'-lanterns his whole life. He had nearly finished when the national news began. The reporter mentioned Dacca, and we all turned to listen: An Indian official announced that unless the world helped to relieve the burden of East Pakistani refugees, India would have to go to war against Pakistan. The reporter's face dripped with sweat as he relayed the information. He did not wear a tie or a jacket, dressed instead as if he himself were about to take part in the battle. He shielded his scorched face as he hollered things to the cameraman. The knife slipped from Mr. Pirzada's hand and made a gash dipping toward the base of the pumpkin.

"Please forgive me." He raised a hand to one side of his face, as if someone had slapped him there. "I am—it is terrible. I will buy another. We will try again."

"Not at all, not at all," my father said. He took the knife from Mr. Pirzada, and carved around the gash, evening it out, dispensing altogether with the teeth I had drawn. What resulted was a disproportionately large hole the size of a lemon, so that our jack-o'-lantern wore an expression of placid astonishment, the eyebrows no longer fierce, floating in frozen surprise above a vacant, geometric gaze.

For Halloween I was a witch. Dora, my trick-or-treating partner, was a witch too. We wore black capes fashioned from dyed pillowcases and conical hats with wide cardboard brims. We shaded our faces green with a broken eye shadow that belonged to Dora's mother, and my mother gave us two burlap sacks that had once contained basmati rice, for collecting candy. That year our parents decided that we were old enough to roam the neighborhood unattended. Our plan was to walk from my house to Dora's, from where I was to call to say I had arrived safely, and then Dora's mother would drive me home. My father equipped us with flashlights, and I had to wear my watch and synchronize it with his. We were to return no later than nine o'clock.

When Mr. Pirzada arrived that evening he presented me with a box of chocolate-covered mints.

"In here," I told him, and opened up the burlap sack. "Trick or treat!" "I understand that you don't really need my contribution this evening," he said, depositing the box. He gazed at my green face, and the hat secured by a string under my chin. Gingerly he lifted the hem of the cape, under which I was wearing a sweater and a zipped fleece jacket. "Will you be warm enough?"

I nodded, causing the hat to tip to one side.

He set it right. "Perhaps it is best to stand still."

The bottom of our staircase was lined with baskets of miniature candy, and when Mr. Pirzada removed his shoes he did not place them there as he normally did, but inside the closet instead. He began to unbutton his coat, and I waited to take it from him, but Dora called me from the bathroom to say that she needed my help drawing a mole on her chin. When we were finally ready my mother took a picture of us in front of the fireplace, and then I opened the front door to leave. Mr. Pirzada and my father, who had not gone into the living room yet, hovered in the foyer. Outside it was already dark. The air smelled of wet leaves, and our carved jack-o'-lantern flickered impressively against the shrubbery by the door. In the distance came the sounds of scampering feet, and the howls of the older boys who wore no costume at all other than a rubber mask, and the rustling apparel of the youngest children, some so young that they were carried from door to door in the arms of their parents.

"Don't go into any of the houses you don't know," my father warned.

Mr. Pirzada knit his brows together. "Is there any danger?"

"No, no," my mother assured him. "All the children will be out. It's a tradition."

"Perhaps I should accompany them?" Mr. Pirzada suggested. He looked suddenly tired and small, standing there in his splayed, stockinged feet, and his eyes contained a panic I had never seen before. In spite of the cold I began to sweat inside my pillowcase.

"Really, Mr. Pirzada," my mother said, "Lilia will be perfectly safe with her friend."

"But if it rains? If they lose their way?"

"Don't worry," I said. It was the first time I had uttered those words to Mr. Pirzada, two simple words I had tried but failed to tell him for weeks, had said only in my prayers. It shamed me now that I had said them for my own sake.

He placed one of his stocky fingers on my cheek, then pressed it to the back of his own hand, leaving a faint green smear. "If the lady insists," he conceded, and offered a small bow.

We left, stumbling slightly in our black pointy thrift-store shoes, and when we turned at the end of the driveway to wave good-bye, Mr. Pirzada was standing in the frame of the doorway, a short figure between my parents, waving back.

"Why did that man want to come with us?" Dora asked.

"His daughters are missing." As soon as I said it, I wished I had not. I felt that my saying it made it true, that Mr. Pirzada's daughters really were missing, and that he would never see them again.

"You mean they were kidnapped?" Dora continued. "From a park or something?"

"I didn't mean they were missing. I meant, he misses them. They live in a different country, and he hasn't seen them in a while, that's all."

We went from house to house, walking along pathways and pressing doorbells. Some people had switched off all their lights for effect, or strung rubber bats in their windows. At the McIntyres' a coffin was placed in front of the door, and Mr. McIntyre rose from it in silence, his face covered with chalk, and deposited a fistful of candy corns into our sacks. Several people told me that they had never seen an Indian witch before. Others performed the transaction without comment. As we paved our way with the parallel beams of our flashlights we saw eggs cracked in the middle of the road, and cars covered with shaving cream, and toilet paper garlanding the branches of trees. By the time we reached Dora's house our hands were chapped from carrying our bulging burlap bags, and our feet were sore and swollen. Her mother gave us bandages for our blisters and served us warm cider and caramel popcorn. She reminded me to call my parents to tell them I had arrived safely, and when I did I could hear the television in the background. My mother did not seem particularly relieved to hear from me. When I replaced the phone on the receiver it occurred to me that the television wasn't on at Dora's house at all. Her father was lying on the couch, reading a magazine, with a glass of wine on the coffee table, and there was saxophone music playing on the stereo. After Dora and I had sorted through our plunder, and counted and sampled and traded until we were satisfied, her mother drove me back to my house. I thanked her for the ride, and she waited in the driveway until I made it to the door. In the glare of her headlights I saw that our pumpkin had been shattered, its thick shell strewn in chunks across the grass. I felt the sting of tears in my eyes, and a sudden pain in my throat, as if it had been stuffed with the sharp tiny pebbles that crunched with each step under my aching feet. I opened the door, expecting the three of them to be standing in the foyer, waiting to receive me, and to grieve for our ruined pumpkin, but there was no one. In the living room Mr. Pirzada, my father, and mother were sitting side by side on the sofa. The television was turned off, and Mr. Pirzada had his head in his hands.

What they heard that evening, and for many evenings after that, was that India and Pakistan were drawing closer and closer to war. Troops from both sides lined the border, and Dacca was insisting on nothing short of independence. The war was to be waged on East Pakistani soil. The United States was siding with West Pakistan, the Soviet Union with India and what was soon to be Bangladesh. War was declared officially on December 4, and twelve days later, the Pakistani army, weakened by having to fight three thousand miles from their source of supplies, surrendered in Dacca. All of these facts I know only now, for they are available to me in any history book, in any library. But then it remained, for the most part, a remote mystery with haphazard clues. What I remember during those twelve days of the war was that my father no longer asked me to watch the news with them, and that Mr. Pirzada stopped bringing me candy, and that my mother refused to serve anything other than boiled eggs with rice for dinner. I remember some nights helping my mother spread a sheet and blankets on the couch so that Mr. Pirzada could sleep there, and high-pitched voices hollering in the middle of the night when my parents called our relatives in Calcutta to learn more details about the situation. Most of all I remember the three of them operating during that time as if they were a single person, sharing a single meal, a single body, a single silence, and a single fear.

In January, Mr. Pirzada flew back to his three-story home in Dacca, to discover what was left of it. We did not see much of him in those final weeks of the year; he was busy finishing his manuscript, and we went to Philadelphia to spend Christmas with friends of my parents. Just as I have no memory of his first visit, I have no memory of his last. My father drove him to the airport one afternoon while I was at school. For a long time we did not hear from him. Our evenings went on as usual, with dinners in front of the news. The only difference was that Mr. Pirzada and his extra watch were not there to accompany us. According to reports Dacca was repairing itself slowly, with a newly formed parliamentary government. The new leader, Sheikh Mujib Rahman, recently released from prison, asked countries for building materials to replace more than one million houses that had been destroyed in the war. Countless refugees returned from India, greeted, we learned, by unemployment and the threat of famine. Every now and then I studied the map above my father's desk and pictured Mr. Pirzada on that small patch of yellow, perspiring heavily, I imagined, in one of his suits, searching for his family. Of course, the map was outdated by then.

Finally, several months later, we received a card from Mr. Pirzada commemorating the Muslim New Year, along with a short letter. He was reunited, he wrote, with his wife and children. All were well, having survived the events of the past year at an estate belonging to his wife's grandparents in the mountains of Shillong. His seven daughters were a bit taller, he wrote, but otherwise they were the same, and he still could not keep their names in order. At the end of the letter he thanked us for our hospitality, adding that although he now understood the meaning of the words "thank you" they still were not adequate to express his gratitude. To celebrate the good news my mother prepared a special dinner that evening, and when we sat down to eat at the coffee table we toasted our water glasses, but I did not feel like celebrating. Though I had not seen him for months, it was only then that I felt Mr. Pirzada's absence. It was only then, raising my water glass in his name, that I knew what it meant to miss someone who was so many miles and hours away, just as he had missed his wife and daughters for so many months. He had no reason to return to us, and my parents predicted, correctly, that we would never see him again. Since January, each night before bed, I had continued to eat, for the sake of Mr. Pirzada's family, a piece of candy I had saved from Halloween. That night there was no need to. Eventually, I threw them away.

ALLEN GINSBERG

One Morning I Took a Walk in China

Allen Ginsberg (1926–1997), born to a Jewish family in New Jersey, studied at Columbia University, where he became friends with William Burroughs and Jack Kerouac, forming the trio that would make up the core of the Beat Movement. In 1957, "Howl" attracted widespread publicity when it became the subject of an obscenity trial at a time when sodomy laws made homosexual acts a crime. Fortunately Judge Clayton W. Horn ruled that "Howl" was not obscene. Ginsberg's participation in nonviolent political protests spanned decades. He also traveled widely, from South America to North Africa and Eastern Europe, from Paris to Kolkata to Beijing, while living modestly, studying Zen Buddhism, and forming close friendships with many, including singer-songwriter Bob Dylan and actor Johnny Depp. Ginsberg received a National Book Award for *The Fall of America* (1974) as well as the Robert Frost Medal (1986), and was decorated as a Chevalier des Arts et des Lettres by the French government in 1993. The selection below, one of Ginsberg's many poems about China, captures the sights and flavors of the food market as a feast of the senses for ordinary people.

Students danced with wooden silvered swords, twirling on hard packed muddy earth
as I walked out Hebei University's concrete North Gate,
across the road a blue capped man sold fried sweet dough-sticks, brown as new boiled doughnuts
in the gray light of sky, past poplar tree trunks, white washed cylinders topped
with red band the height of a boy—Children with school satchels sang & walked past me
Donkeys in the road, one big one dwarf pulling ahead of his brother, hauled a cart of white stones
another donkey dragged a load of bricks, other baskets of dirt—
Under trees at the crossing, vendors set out carts and tables of cigarettes,
mandarin Tangerines, yellow round pears taste crunchy lemony strange,
apples yellow red-pinked, short bananas half black'd green,
few bunches of red grapes—and trays of peanuts, glazed thumbsized crab-apples 6 on a stick,
soft wrinkled yellow persimmons sat dozens spread on a cloth in wet mud by the curb—
cookpots on charcoal near cornerside tables, noodle broth vegetables sprinkled on top

A white headed barber shook out his ragged towel, mirror hung on red nail in the brick wall
where a student sat, black hair clipped at ears straight across the back of his neck
Soft-formed gritty coal pellets lay drying on the sidewalk and down the factory alley, more black mats spread,
Long green cabbages heaped by the buildingside waiting for home pot, or stacked on hand-tractor carts the market verandah a few yards away—
Leeks in a pile, bright orange carrots thick & rare, green unripe tomatoes, parsley, thin celery stalks awful cheap, potatoes & fish—
little & big heads chopped or alive in a tub, tiny fresh babies or aged carp in baskets—
a half pig on a slab, two trotters stick out, a white burlap shroud covered his body cleaved in half—
meat of the ox going thru a grinder, white fat red muscle & sinew together squeezed into human spaghetti—
Bicycles lined up along the concrete walk, trucks pull in & move out delivering cows dead and fresh green-stalked salad—
Downstreet, the dry-goods door—soap, pencils, notebooks, tea, fur coats lying on a counter—
Strawberry jam in rusty-iron topped jars, milk powder, dry cookies with sweetmeats
inside dissolve on the tongue to wash down fragrant black tea—
Ah, the machine shop gateway, brick walled latrine inside the truck yard
—enter, squat on a brick & discharge your earth
or stand & pee in the big hole filled with pale brown squishy droppings an hour before—
Out, down the alleyway across the street a factory's giant smokestack, black cloud-fumes boiling into the sky
gray white with mist I couldn't see that chimney a block away, coming home
past women on bicycles heading downtown their noses & mouths covered with cotton masks.

GERALD VIZENOR

Griever: An American Monkey King in China

Gerald Vizenor (born 1934), novelist, poet, playwright, and essayist, was raised by an Anishinaabe grandmother and a Swedish American mother in Minneapolis and on the White Earth Reservation after his father was murdered when he was two. Spending years in Japan while serving in the army, he invokes the haiku verse form as well as indigenous trickster stories and dream songs, creating a corpus that defies easy classification. His books include a science fiction chronicle, *Bearheart* (1978); nonfictional works such as *Manifest Manners* (1999) and *Fugitive Poses* (2000); as well as the novels *Griever: An American Monkey King in China* (1986), *Hiroshima Bugi* (2003), the American Book Award–winning *Shrouds of White Earth* (2011), and *Blue Ravens* (2014). He often coins new words (such as "survivance," a cross between survival and resistance) to make his point. Vizenor taught for many years at the University of California, Berkeley, while maintaining ties to China and Japan. In this excerpt from *Griever*, a Native American trickster tries to save some chickens in a Tianjin market.

The chicken cutthroat at the counter wore a black rubber apron and an ominous sneer; his cheeks stretched, and his nose flattened. The skin on his hands and face was hard and scabrous, cracked on his lips and thumbs. He reached for a lean hen in one of the wire cages stacked on the street.

With one hand the cutthroat turned the chicken upside down; he laced his fingers around the neck, leg, and one wing of the hen, and with his other hand he whished a stained blade beneath the neck feathers. Dark blood splashed in a metal basin on the wooden counter. Blue flies circled the blood soaked feathers. The bird blinked once, twice, three times, wild near the end; one eye warned the witnesses in the audience. The bird scratched the token earth in space with one free leg; each feather extended in an escape flight from slow death. When the claws curled and the eyes clouded over, the bird was scalded in a barrel and plucked clean on the street. Plumes gathered in the trees, dried on the brick walls, on handcarts pulled through the market. The chicken was tied to the back rack of a bicycle; some naked birds were carried on nooses, their claws seemed outsized.

Cutthroat drank warm chicken blood.

Griever clipped a wedge of cuticle from his right thumb too close. He shivered and a thin line of blood spread beneath the short nail. He pressed his thumb to his lips and tongue and counted the chickens he would liberate that first morning at the market. He counted aloud, seventeen hens stowed in four crude wire cages and one proud cock tied to a short tether.

Griever pinched his ear once more, considered the landscape, holstered his scroll, and sliced through the free market crowd to the chickens. Conversations trailed him to the counter.

"*Wai guo ren, wai guo ren,* the foreign devil, the foreign devil," the cutthroat murmured with suspicion. Few foreigners visited the street market; teachers and other visitors were served their meals at hotels or in special guest houses.

Blood had spilled from the shallow basins and coagulated at the outer rim of the counter near the cages. The hens were nervous. Griever touched his ear, and then pinched his nostrils closed. The brackish smell of boiled feathers tickled his nose and settled deep in his throat. He coughed, pitched his head to the side and spat near the cages; his phlegm curved wide and hit a chicken on the neck. The other hens pecked at the thick spittle as it slid down the soiled white feathers.

The chicken cutthroat turned and waved his short arms like a sorcerer in unnatural flight. Black and white plumes stuck to his rubber apron. Griever overlooked the chickens, spread his arms wide and waved back at the cutthroat. He flapped hard several times, and then, pretending to be surprised, he looked down at his feet, shrugged his shoulders and smiled. At first the cutthroat seemed amused, but when he landed at the counter he snickered over the basins of blood and flashed two bright silver teeth, both incisors. When he spoke, fine lines trailed from his wide mouth like cracks on an old porcelain vessel. He pointed to the foreigner, turned his head to the right, a sudden movement that shifted his black hair, and muttered to his assistant, his epigone, who chortled back, as she poked at the hot coals under the barrel.

Cochin China, the prime cock at the market, posed over the hens. The feathers on his shanks shrouded the crude noose that fastened him to the wire cages. He strutted and danced in place, extended his short wings, shook his wild orange wattle, and carried on as usual, the natural domination of the hens, despite the short tether.

The cutthroat reached for the cock. On the back of his hand there was a large blue star. Griever admired the raw tattoo; he drew uneven angles in space with his middle finger, erased the invisible star, and then started over when the cutthroat untied the tether on the cock.

"Free the birds," said Griever.

"*Ji wang, ji wang*," the cutthroat repeated several times with a pinched smile. The crowd around the counter laughed when he spoke, and laughed more when his assistant chortled over the fire. Cutthroat tipped his head to the crowd.

"How much for the whole flock?"

"*Ji wang, ji wang. . . .*" The cutthroat wrapped the tether around his wrist and pushed the cock down the counter toward the foreign devil.

Cochin China shuddered, flicked his sickle feathers in place, restored his balance once more, a constant struggle with humans, and then the proud cock burst into short flight to the end of the tether and crashed on the blood soaked counter. The hens thrust their heads through twists in the wire cages and clucked in turns, a domestic summons to a primal dance.

Griever leaned back, tapped the toes of his shoes together, and asked the cutthroat how much it would cost to free all the chickens in the cages. He turned his pockets and presented cash, the total advance he had received the night before when he first arrived at the guest house. He spread the bills, tinted pictures of romantic workers and idealized industries, on the counter like a deck of cards.

"Take a card, any card, and count it twice," he said, not knowing the real value of the paper money. The crowd moved closer; several people counted with their fingers. "The best chickens chase the devil," said the trickster. He reached for the cock with one arm and drew him close to his chest; there, he soughed and whistled a tune from "The Stars and Stripes Forever." The cock marched in place and shit on his wrist.

RUTH OZEKI

My Year of Meats

Ruth Ozeki (born 1956), novelist and filmmaker, was born and raised in New Haven, Connecticut, and educated at Smith College. She went on to study classical Japanese literature at Nara University, teaching English at Kyoto Sangyo University and working as a bartender in the city's entertainment district. She entered the film industry after her return to the United States in 1985, working first as an art director and designer in New York, then moving on to television production and to two award-winning films, *Body of Correspondence* (1994) and *Halving the Bones* (1995). Her three novels—*My Year of Meats* (1998), *All Over Creation* (2003), and *A Tale for the Time Being* (2013)—fuse together many different genres to create new and unexpected textures. Going one step further than Allen Ginsberg, Ozeki not only studies Zen Buddhism but is also an ordained priest. This excerpt from *My Year of Meats* combines oddball humor with biting critique of global agribusiness and the media campaign targeting Japanese housewives, selling canned smiles along with American beef.

Akiko

2 kilograms	American beef (rump roast)
1 can	Campbell's Cream of Mushroom Soup
1 package	Lipton's Powdered Onion Soup
1.5 liters	Coca-Cola (*not* Pepsi, please!)

"Rumpu rossuto," Akiko repeated to herself. "Notto Pepsi pleezu." She watched the television screen, where a sturdy American wife held an economy-size plastic bottle of Coca-Cola upside down over a roasting pan. The woman smiled broadly at Akiko, who automatically smiled back. The woman shook the bottle, disgorging its contents in rhythmic spurts onto the red "rumpu rossuto." Under her breath, Akiko pronounced the words again. She liked the sounds, the parallel Japanese *r*'s, with their delicate flick of the tongue across the palate, and the plosive *pu* like a kiss or a fart in the middle of a big American dinner.

She liked the size of things American. Convenient. Economical. Big and simple. Like this wife with the "rumpu." Impatient, she shook the bottle up and down, like a fretful infant unable to make its toy work. A close-up showed the plastic Coke bottle so large it made her fingers look childlike as she squeezed its soft sides. The camera traveled down the foamy brown waterfall of cola until it hit the meat, alive with shiny bubbles. The woman laughed. Her name was Suzie Flowers. What a beautiful name, thought Akiko. Suzie Flowers laughed easily, but Akiko was practicing how to do this too.

Now Suzie was opening a can with her electric can opener. Several children ran through the kitchen and Suzie good-naturedly chased them out with the spatula. Then, never missing a beat, she used the spatula to smear pale mushroom soup over the roast and pat its sides. Pat, pat, pat. She sprinkled the onion soup mix on top and popped it in the oven. Bake at 250° for 3 hours. Easy. Done.

Akiko was so thin her bones hurt. Her watch hung loosely around her wrist and its face never stayed on top. She spun it around and checked the time. The recipe was simple, and if she did her shopping in the morning she would have plenty of time to get to the market and back, marinate the meat, and cook it properly for three hours. She double-checked the ingredients that she had written down on her list and realized she should have a vegetable too. Canned peas, Suzie suggested. Easy. Done. Suzie bent over the oven. Her children pushed between her sturdy, mottled legs and hung off her hem. They must have just poured out, Akiko though, one after the other, in frothy bursts of fertility. It was a disturbing thought, squalid somehow, and made her feel nauseous.

"It's not spite," Akiko muttered, chewing her lip, "or my contrary nature." She tried a smile again at Suzie, tried to feel happy-go-lucky.

GARY SHTEYNGART

Absurdistan

Gary Shteyngart (born 1972), born Igor Semyonovich Shteyngart, came to the United States from Leningrad in 1979. He has written three novels on the lives of Russian immigrants, all darkly extravagant, comic in tone but laced with intimations of personal trauma and global catastrophes. Each has received wide acclaim: *The Russian Debutante's Handbook* (2002) won the Stephen Crane First Fiction Award and the Book-of-the-Month Club First Fiction Award; *Absurdistan* (2006) was chosen one of the ten best books of the year by both the *New York Times Book Review* and *Time* magazine; and *Super Sad True Love Story* (2010) won the Bollinger Everyman Wodehouse Prize for comic literature. His memoir, *Little Failure* (2014), was a finalist for the National Book Critics Circle Award. Shteyngart is also known for his many blurbs, collected on Tumblr. In this selection from *Absurdistan*, he describes the over-the-top food and décor at a restaurant frequented by the super-rich in Russia.

I am Misha Borisovich Vainberg, age thirty, a grossly overweight man with small, deeply set blue eyes, a pretty Jewish beak that brings to mind the most distinguished breed of parrot, and lips so delicate you would want to wipe them with the naked back of your hand.

For many of my last years, I have lived in St. Petersburg, Russia, neither by choice nor by desire. The City of the Czars, the Venice of the North, Russia's cultural capital . . . forget all that. By the year 2001, our St. Leninsburg has taken on the appearance of a phantasmagoric third-world city, our neoclassical buildings sinking into the crap-choked canals, bizarre peasant huts fashioned out of corrugated metal and plywood colonizing the broad avenues with their capitalist iconography (cigarette ads featuring an American football player catching a hamburger with a baseball mitt), and what is worst of all, our intelligent, depressive citizenry has been replaced by a new race of mutants dressed in studied imitation of the West, young women in tight Lycra, their scooped-up little breasts pointing at once to New York and

Shanghai, with men in fake black Calvin Klein jeans hanging limply around their caved-in asses.

The good news is that when you're an incorrigible fatso like me—325 pounds at last count—and the son of the 1,238th richest man in Russia, all of St. Leninsburg rushes out to service you: the drawbridges lower themselves as you advance, and the pretty palaces line up alongside the canal banks, thrusting their busty friezes in your face. You are blessed with the rarest treasure to be found in this mineral-rich land. You are blessed with respect.

On the night of June 15 in the catastrophic year 2001, I was getting plenty of respect from my friends at a restaurant called the Home of the Russian Fisherman on Krestovskiy Island, one of the verdant islands caught in the delta of the Neva River. Krestovskiy is where we rich people pretend to be living in a kind of post-Soviet Switzerland, trudging along the manicured bike paths built 'round our *kottedzhes* and town *khauses*, and filling our lungs with parcels of atmosphere seemingly imported from the Alps.

The Fisherman's gimmick is that you catch your own fish out of a man-made lake, and then for about US$50 per kilo, the kitchen staff will smoke it for you or bake it on coals. On what the police would later call "the night in question," we were standing around the Spawning Salmon pontoon, yelling at our servants, drinking down carafes of green California Riesling, our Nokia *mobilniki* ringing with the social urgency that comes only when the White Nights strangle the nighttime, when the inhabitants of our ruined city are kept permanently awake by the pink afterglow of the northern sun, when the best you can do is drink your friends into the morning.

Let me tell you something: without good friends, you might as well drown yourself in Russia. After decades of listening to the familial agitprop of our parents ("We will die for you!" they sing), after surviving the criminal closeness of the Russian family ("Don't leave us!" they plead), after the crass socialization foisted upon us by our teachers and factory directors ("We will staple your circumcised *khui* to the wall!" they threaten), all that's left is that toast between two failed friends in some stinking outdoor beer kiosk.

"To your health, Misha Borisovich."

"To your success, Dimitry Ivanovich."

"To the army, the air force, and the whole Soviet fleet . . . Drink to the bottom!"

I'm a modest person bent on privacy and lonely sadness, so I have very few friends. My best buddy in Russia is a former American I like to call

Alyosha-Bob. Born Robert Lipshitz in the northern reaches of New York State, this little bald eagle (not a single hair on his dome by age twenty-five) flew to St. Leninsburg eight years ago and was transformed, by dint of alcoholism and inertia, into a successful Russian *biznesman* renamed Alyosha, the owner of ExcessHollywood, a riotously profitable DVD import-export business, and the swain of Svetlana, a young Petersburg hottie. In addition to being bald, Alyosha-Bob has a pinched face ending in a reddish goatee, wet blue eyes that fool you with their near-tears, and enormous flounder lips cleansed hourly by vodka. A skinhead on the metro once described him as a *gnussniy zhid*, or a "vile-looking Yid," and I think most of the populace sees him that way. I certainly did when I first met him as a fellow undergraduate at Accidental College in the American Midwest a decade ago.

Alyosha-Bob and I have an interesting hobby that we indulge whenever possible. We think of ourselves as the Gentlemen Who Like to Rap. Our oeuvre stretches from the old-school jams of Ice Cube, Ice-T, and Public Enemy to the sensuous contemporary rhythms of ghetto tech, a hybrid of Miami bass, Chicago ghetto tracks, and Detroit electronica. The modern reader may be familiar with "Ass-N-Titties" by DJ Assault, perhaps the *seminal* work of the genre.

On the night in question, I got the action started with a Detroit ditty I enjoy on summer days:

> *Aw, shit*
> *Heah I come*
> *Shut yo mouf*
> *And bite yo tongue.*

Alyosha-Bob, in his torn Helmut Lang slacks and Accidental College sweatshirt, picked up the tune:

> *Aw, girl,*
> *You think you bad?*
> *Let me see you*
> *Bounce dat ass.*

Our melodies rang out over the Russian Fisherman's four pontoons (Spawning Salmon, Imperial Sturgeon, Capricious Trout, and Sweet Little

Butterfish), over this whole tiny man-made lake, whatever the hell it's called (Dollar Lake? Euro Pond?), over the complimentary-valet-parking-lot where one of the oafish employees just dented my new Land Rover . . .

And then I heard my manservant, Timofey, ringing his special hand bell. The *mobilnik* fell out of my hand, the Pushkin lover and his girlfriend disappeared from the pontoon, the pontoon itself floated off into another dimension, even Dr. Levine and his soft American ministrations were reduced to a distant hum.

It was feeding time.

With a low bow, manservant Timofey presented me with a tray of blackened sturgeon kebabs and a carafe of Black Label. I fell down on a hard plastic chair that twisted and torqued beneath my weight like a piece of modern sculpture. I bent over the sturgeon, sniffing it with closed eyes as if offering a silent prayer. My feet were locked together, my ankles grinding into each other with expectant anxiety. I prepared for my meal in the usual fashion: fork in my left hand; my dominant right clenched into a fist on my lap, ready to punch anyone who dared take away my food.

I bit into the sturgeon kebab, filling my mouth with both the crisp burnt edges and the smooth mealy interior. My body trembled inside my leviathan Puma tracksuit, my heroic gut spinning counter-clockwise, my two-scoop breasts slapping against each other. The usual food-inspired images presented themselves. Myself, my Beloved Papa, and my young mother in a hollowed-out boat built to resemble a white swan floating past a grotto, triumphant Stalin-era music echoing around us ("Here's my passport! *What* a passport! It's my great red *Soviet* passport!"), Beloved Papa's wet hands rubbing my tummy and skirting the waistband of my shorts, and Mommy's smooth, dry ones brushing against the nape of my neck, a chorus of their hoarse, tired voices saying, "We love you, Misha. We love you, bear cub."

My body fell into a rocking motion like the religious people rock when they're deep in the thrall of their god. I finished off the first kebab and the one after that, my chin oily with sturgeon juices, my breasts shivering as if they'd been smothered with packets of ice. Another chunk of fish fell into my mouth, this one well dusted with parsley and olive oil. I breathed in the smells of the sea, my right fist still clenched, fingers digging into palm, my nose touching the plate, sturgeon extract coating my nostrils, my little circumcised *khui* burning with the joy of release.

And then it was over. And then the kebabs were gone. I was left with an empty plate. I was left with nothing before me. Ah, dear me. Where was I now? An abandoned bear cub without his li'l fishy. I splashed a glass of water on my face and dabbed myself off with a napkin Timofey had tucked into my tracksuit. I picked up the carafe of Black Label, pressed it to my cold lips, and, with a single tilt of the wrist, emptied it into my gullet.

MARIANNE MOORE

Nine Nectarines and Other Porcelain

Marianne Moore (1887–1972), poet, editor, and translator, is widely considered to have been pivotal in creating a transatlantic Modernism. Beginning as a schoolteacher—she taught at the Carlisle Indian School from 1911 to 1915—she eventually served as acting editor for the literary magazine *The Dial* from 1925–1929, publishing works as diverse as the poetry of Rilke and Valery; the philosophy of Benedetto Croce and Bertrand Russell; and the fiction of D. H. Lawrence, Maxim Gorky, and Jean Toomer. Her own work is characterized by its vivid, encyclopedic taxonomies and precise descriptions of animals, plants, and objects. Moore's *Collected Poems* (1951) won both the Pulitzer Prize and the National Book Award. In 1953 she was awarded the Bollingen Prize. A fan of professional baseball, she threw the first pitch for the Yankees in 1968 and was also an admirer of Muhammad Ali, writing the liner notes to his record, *I Am the Greatest!* (1963) In the poem selected here, Moore plays on the relationship between China as a country and china as porcelain to meditate on cultural geography and culinary history.

Arranged by twos as peaches are,
at intervals that all may live—
    eight and a single one, on twigs that
    grew the year before—they look like

a derivative;
    although not uncommonly
the opposite is seen—
nine peaches on a nectarine.
    Fuzzed through slender crescent leaves
        of green or blue or
        both, in the Chinese style, the four

    pairs' half-moon leaf-mosaic turns
out to the sun the sprinkled blush
    of puce-American-Beauty pink
    applied to bees-wax gray by the
uninquiring brush
    of mercantile bookbinding.
Like the peach Yu, the red-
cheeked peach which cannot aid the dead,
    but eaten in time prevents death,
        the Italian
        peach-nut, Persian plum, Ispahan

    secluded wall-grown nectarine,
as wild spontaneous fruit was
    fruit in China first. But was it wild?
    Prudent de Candolle would not say.
We cannot find flaws
    in this emblematic group
        of nine, with leaf window
    unquilted by Curculio—
when someone once depicted on
    this much mended plate,
    in the also accurate
unantlered moose, or Iceland horse,
    or ass, asleep against the old
    thick, lowleaning nectarine that is the
    color of the shrub-tree's brownish
        flower. From manifold
        small boughs, productive as the

magic willow that grew
above the mother's grave and there
on Cinderella what she wished,
a bat is winging. It
is a moonlight scene, bringing
the animal so near, its eyes
are separate from the face—mere
delicately drawn gray discs out from
itself in space. Imperial
happiness lives here
on the peaches of long life
that make it permanent,
a fungus could have meant
long life; a crane, a stork, a dove,
China, with flowers and birds
and half-beasts, became the land
of the best china-making first.

GARY SNYDER

Mu Chi's Persimmons

Gary Snyder (born 1930), poet, essayist, and translator, brings together nature writing, indigenous religions, and Zen Buddhism to create a poetics of the Pacific Rim: spare, concrete, occasionally riddling, and with a deep ecological awareness. Educated at Reed College in Portland, Oregon, he worked as a logger and a forest fire lookout before enrolling at the University of California, Berkeley to study classical Chinese. In 1955 he read "A Berry Feast" at the Six Gallery, inaugurating the San Francisco Renaissance. He also formed close friendships with Allen Ginsberg and Jack Kerouac, serving as the model for Japhy Ryder in Kerouac's *The Dharma Bums* (1958). He then left the United States for a twelve-year stay in Asia, publishing his first book of poetry, *Riprap* (1959), in Japan. This was followed by many other works, including *Myths and Texts* (1960), *Earth House Hold* (1969), *Axe Handles* (1983), *The Practice of the Wild* (1990), and *Mountains and Rivers without End* (1996). In 1975 he won the Pulitzer Prize for *Turtle Island*. He was awarded the Bollingen Prize in 1997 for his corpus as a whole. In the poem selected here, he creates a brainy paradox out of the interplay between the painted persimmon and the "orange goop" of the actual fruit.

There is no remedy for satisfying hunger other than a painted rice cake.
—Dōgen, November, 1242

On a back wall down the hall
lit by a side glass door

is the scroll of Mu Ch'i's great
sumi painting, "Persimmons"

The wind-weights hanging from the
axles hold it still.

The best in the world, I say,
of persimmons.

Perfect statement of emptiness
no other than form

the twig and the stalk still on,
the way they sell them in the
market even now.

—

The original's in Kyoto at a
lovely Rinzai temple where they
show it once a year

this one's a perfect copy from Benrido
I chose the mounting elements myself
with the advice of the mounter

I hang it every fall.

And now, to these overripe persimmons
from Mike and Barbara's orchard.
Napkin in hand,
I bend over the sink
suck the sweet orange goop
that's how I like it
gripping a little twig
those painted persimmons

sure cure hunger.

RICHARD BLANCO

Mango No. 61

Richard Blanco (born 1968) was born in Madrid to a family exiled from Cuba in the wake of the Cuban Revolution, then relocated to Miami with his family while still an infant. He combines the technical instincts of an engineer with the linguistic exuberance of a bilingual speaker, showing readers how words are constantly used and reused, and how American, Cuban, and gay identities are negotiated and renegotiated. Blanco's works include *City of a Hundred Fires* (1998), *Directions to the Beach of the Dead* (2005), and *Looking for the Gulf Motel* (2012). In 2013 he read his poem "One Today" at President Obama's second inauguration, the first immigrant, Latino, and openly gay poet to have that honor. In the following poem, Blanco uses the figure of the *charada*—a pictonumerical lottery game popular throughout Latin America—to convey the lush tangles of a life between margins, skipping giddily from numbered square to square. Gambling here serves as a metaphor for life in America, with family history and world history all packed into the lottery: a messy, mango-sweet game of chance.

~~~~~~

Pescado grande was number 14, while *pescado chico*, was number 12; *dinero*, money, was number 10. This was *la charada*, the sacred and obsessive numerology my *abuela* used to predict lottery numbers or winning trifectas at the dog track. The grocery stores and pawn shops on Flagler street handed out complementary wallet-size cards printed with the entire *charada*, numbers 1 through 100; number 70 was *coco*, number 89 was *melón* and number 61 was mango. Mango was Mrs. Pike, the last *americana* on the block with the best mango tree in the neighborhood. *Mamá* would coerce her in granting us picking rights—after all, *los americanos* don't eat mango, she'd reason. Mango was fruit wrapped in brown paper bags, hidden like ripening secrets in the kitchen oven. Mango was the perfect house warming gift and a marmalade dessert with thick slices of cream cheese at birthday dinners and Thanksgiving. Mangos, watching like amber cat's eyes. Mangos, perfectly still in their speckled maroon shells like giant unhatched eggs. Number 48 was *cucaracha*, number 36 was *bodega*, but mango was my uncle's *bodega*, where everyone spoke only loud Spanish, the precious gold fruit towering in *tres-por-un-peso* pyramids. Mango was mango shakes made with milk, sugar and a pinch of salt—my grandfather's treat at the 8th street market after baseball practice. Number 60 was *sol*, number 18 was *palma*, but mango was my father and I under the largest shade tree at the edges of Tamiami park. Mango was *abuela* and I hunched over the counter covered with the Spanish newspaper, devouring the dissected flesh of the fruit slithering consumed in her rapture and convinced that I absolutely loved mangos. Those messy mangos. Number 79 was *cubano*—us, and number 93 was *revolución*, though I always thought it should be 58, the actual year of the revolution—the reason why, I'm told, we live so obsessively and nostalgically eating number 61's, mangos, here in number 87, *América*.

III. Work, Play, Travel

S ection III, "Work, Play, Travel," begins with Frederick Douglass's letter to William Llyod Garrison, March 27, 1846. Reporting on his visit to Ireland, Douglass wrote that he was heartsick seeing the widespread poverty in Dublin, with "its streets literally alive with beggars." The typical Irish dwelling, the hut, "four mud walls about six feet high," thatched with straw, "without apartments or divisions of any kind—without floor, without windows," made him realize that millions in Ireland were living "in much the same degradation as the American slaves."

Douglass was touring England and Ireland as an abolitionist lecturer, and while he knew that he should stick to his main business, he could not let such misery go by "with my eyes shut, ears stopped, or heart steeled." The "cause of humanity is one the world over," he insisted. Other authors in this section, without putting things quite so explicitly, are also struck by analogous patterns of life traceable across the planet, common threads that bind the fate of one population to another. What happens inside the United States cannot fail to have ripple effects elsewhere, just as the nation itself, for good or ill, has never been immune from occurrences abroad, feeling the impact of catastrophes outside its borders, and registering, in its domestic policies, the promptings and pressures of foreign events.

Global connectivity is explored in this section of the anthology through a triad of terms—work, play, travel—themselves often entangled and compounded, sometimes impossible to separate. Maya Angelou's account of her stay in Ghana, *All God's Children Need Traveling Shoes* (1986), is a case in point. Angelou was in Ghana as a journalist while also working as an administrator at the University of Ghana, joining a small group of African American expatriates, including W. E. B. Du Bois and forming a close friendship with Malcolm X when he visited in 1964. For her many contributions to Ghana, Angelou was honored with a postal stamp. However, as we can see from the excerpt here, not all Ghanaians were appreciative of her. Friction rather than solidarity can be one of the outcomes when the labor force becomes a floating population, in this case pitting black Americans against black Africans, the cultural difference between the two all the more stark for their supposed commonality in skin color.

Rather than shying away from such uncomfortable moments, our anthology dwells on them as important occasions to take stock of the global field as one that allows for no undue optimism, though not without some surprising signs of hope. In "Encounter on the Seine: Black Meets Brown," James Baldwin writes about another fraught meeting: "They face each other, the Negro and the African, over a gulf of three hundred years." Three hundred years, that is, of slavery and the psychological burden of slavery, making it impossible for those who have been through it to be understood by those who have not. Ironically it is against that vexed incomprehension, and against the equally vexing and uncomprehending background of Paris, that Baldwin reaches his deepest insight: that he is the offspring not of Africa but of America, for like every African American, he is a "hybrid," his life made up of the lives of those who have historically oppressed him, "bone of their bone, flesh of their flesh." It is only by embracing this "indescribable complex of tensions" that the "American Negro will make peace with himself." And indeed, even though Baldwin would spend many years abroad, in Paris and Istanbul, he would also make a point of returning to the United States in 1957, to take an active part in the Civil Rights Movement, writing about it in *The Fire Next Time* (1963), and mourning the assassination of three personal friends, Medgar Evers, Malcolm X, and Martin Luther King, Jr. in *No Name in the Street* (1972).

For Baldwin, the historical memories activated by foreign work and travel cast as much light on the United States as on the rest of the world. Other selections—from Melville's account of the "monkey rope" binding Ishmael and Queequeg, to Steinbeck's account of pidgin English discussed by a well-to-do Irish American and a Chinese American cook, to Sherman Alexie's part-whimsical and part-hallowing tribute to Jews and Indians in a baseball game—point to a global field as integral to American literature as the United States itself. One cannot be understood without the other, especially when the subjects themselves are hyphenated.

FREDERICK DOUGLASS

Letter to William Lloyd Garrison, March 27, 1846

Frederick Douglass (c. 1818–1895), born a slave in Maryland, taught himself to read and write, beginning a lifelong commitment to literacy as a path to freedom. Escaping to New York in 1838, he soon became a virtuoso antislavery speaker. In 1845 he published his autobiography, *Narrative of the Life of Frederick Douglass, An American Slave* an instant best-seller. Two expanded versions followed: *My Bondage and My Freedom* (1851) and *The Life and Times of Frederick Douglass* (1881). Fearing recapture from his public appearances, Douglass left the United States to lecture in England and Ireland in 1846–1847. Upon his return, he began editing the *North Star* (later renamed *Frederick Douglass' Paper*), one of the earliest black publications. In 1848 he attended the Seneca Falls Woman's Rights Convention, the first African American to do so. During the Civil War he helped organize the black 54th Regiment from Massachusetts, and after Reconstruction, served as Marshal and Recorder of Deeds of the District of Columbia, then as Minister to Haiti (1889–1891). In this letter to William Lloyd Garrison, Douglass expresses his solidarity with the Irish peasants during the 1846 Potato Famine.

My dear Friend Garrison:

In my letter to you from Belfast, I intimated my intention to say something more about Ireland; and although I feel like fulfilling my promise, the *Liberator* comes to me so laden with foreign correspondence, that I feel some hesitancy about increasing it. I shall, however, send you this, and if it is worth a place in your columns, I need not tell you to publish it. It is the glory of the *Liberator*, that in it the oppressed of every class, color and clime, may have their wrongs fully set forth, and their rights boldly vindicated. Your brave assertion of its character in your last defense of free discussion, has inspired me with a fresh love for the *Liberator*. Though established for the overthrow of the accursed slave system, it is not insensible to other evils that afflict and blast the happiness of mankind. So also, though I am more closely connected and identified with one class of outraged, oppressed and enslaved people,

I cannot allow myself to be insensible to the wrongs and sufferings of any part of the great family of man. I am not only an American slave, but a man, and as such, am bound to use my powers for the welfare of the whole human brotherhood. I am not going through this land with my eyes shut, ears stopped, or heart steeled. I am seeking to see, hear and feel, all that may be seen, heard and felt; and neither the attentions I am receiving here, nor the connections I hold to my brethren in bonds, shall prevent my disclosing the results of my observation. I believe that the sooner the wrongs of the whole human family are made known, the sooner those wrongs will be reached. I had heard much of the misery and wretchedness of the Irish people, previous to leaving the United States, and was prepared to witness much on my arrival in Ireland. But I must confess, my experience has convinced me that the half has not been told. I supposed that much that I heard from the American press on this subject was mere exaggeration, resorted to for the base purpose of impeaching the characters of British philanthropists, and throwing a mantle over the dark and infernal character of American slavery and slaveholders. My opinion has undergone no change in regard to the latter part of my supposition, for I believe a large class of writers in America, as well as in this land, are influenced by no higher motive than that of covering up our national sins, to please popular taste, and satisfy popular prejudice; and thus many have harped upon the wrongs of Irishmen, while in truth they care no more about Irishmen, or the wrongs of Irishmen, than they care about the whipped, gagged, and thumb-screwed slave. They would as willingly sell on the auction-block an Irishman, if it were popular to do so, as an African. For heart, such men have adamant—for consciences, they have public opinion. They are a stench in the nostrils of upright men, and a curse to the country in which they live. The limits of a single letter are insufficient to allow any thing like a faithful description of those painful exhibitions of human misery, which meet the eye of a stranger almost at every step. I spent nearly six weeks in Dublin, and the scenes I there witnessed were such as to make me "blush, and hang my head to think myself a man." I speak truly when I say, I dreaded to go out of the house. The streets were almost literally alive with beggars, displaying the greatest wretchedness—some of them mere stumps of men, without feet, without legs, without hands, without arms—and others still more horribly deformed, with crooked limbs, down upon their hands and knees, their feet lapped around each other, and laid upon their backs, pressing their way through the muddy streets and merciless crowd, casting sad looks to the right and left, in the hope of catching the eye of a passing stranger—the citizens generally having set their faces against giving to beggars. I have had more than a dozen around me at one time, men, women and children, all telling a tale of woe which would move any but a heart of iron. Women, barefooted and bareheaded, and only covered by rags which seemed to be held together by the very dirt and filth with which they were covered—many of these had infants in their arms, whose emaciated forms, sunken eyes and pallid cheeks, told too plainly that they had nursed till they had nursed in vain. In such a group you may hear all forms of appeal, entreaty, and expostulation. A half a dozen voices have broken upon my ear at once: "Will your honor please to give me a penny to buy some bread?" "May the Lord bless you, give the poor old woman a little sixpence." "For the love of God, leave us a few pennies—we will divide them amongst us." "Oh! my poor child, it must starve, for God's sake give me a penny. More power to you! I know your honor will leave the poor creature something. Ah, do! ah, do! and I will pray for you as long as I live." For a time I gave way to my feelings, but reason reminded me that such a course must only add another to the already long list of beggars, and I was often compelled to pass, as if I heeded not and felt not. I fear it had a hardening effect upon my heart, as I found it much easier to pass without giving to the last beggar, than the first. The spectacle that affected me most, and made the most vivid impression on my mind, of the extreme poverty and wretchedness of the poor of Dublin, was the frequency with which I met little children in the street at a late hour of the night, covered with filthy rags, and seated upon cold stone steps, or in corners, leaning against brick walls, fast asleep, with none to look upon them, none to care for them. If they have parents, they have become vicious, and have abandoned them. Poor creatures! they are left without help, to find their way through a frowning world—a world that seems to regard them as intruders, and to be punished as such. God help the poor! An infidel might ask, in view of these facts, with confusing effect—Where is your religion that takes care for the poor—for the widow and fatherless—where are its votaries—what are they doing? The answer to this would be, if properly given, wasting their energies in useless debate on hollow creeds and points of doctrine, which, when settled, neither make one hair white nor black. In conversation with some who were such rigid adherents to their faith that they would scarce be seen in company with those who differed from them in any point of their creed, I have heard them quote the text in palliation of their neglect, "The poor shall not cease out of the land"! During my stay in Dublin, I took occasion to visit the huts of the poor in its vicinity—and of all places to witness human misery, ignorance, degradation, filth and wretchedness, an Irish hut is pre-eminent. It seems to be constructed to promote the very reverse of every thing like domestic comfort. If I were to describe one, it would appear about as follows: Four mud walls about six feet high, occupying a space of ground about ten feet square, covered or thatched with straw—a mud chimney at one end, reaching about a foot above the roof—without apartments or divisions of any kind—without floor, without windows, and sometimes without a chimney—a piece of pine board laid on the top of a box or an old chest—a pile of straw covered with dirty garments, which it would puzzle any one to determine the original part of any one of them—a picture representing the crucifixion of Christ, pasted on the most conspicuous place on the wall—a few broken dishes stuck up in a corner—an iron pot, or the half of an iron pot, in one corner of the chimney—a little peat in the fireplace, aggravating one occasionally with a glimpse of fire, but sending out very little heat—a man and his wife and five children, and a pig. In front of the door-way, and within a step of it, is a hole three or four feet deep, and ten or twelve feet in circumference; into this hole all the filth and dirt of the hut are put, for careful preservation. This is frequently covered with a green scum, which at times stands in bubbles, as decomposition goes on. Here you have an Irish hut or cabin, such as millions of the people of Ireland live in. And some live in worse than these. Men and women, married and single, old and young, lie down together, in much the same degradation as the American slaves. I see much here to remind me of my former condition, and I confess I should be ashamed to lift up my voice against American slavery, but that I know the cause of humanity is one the world over. He who really and truly feels for the American slave, cannot steel his heart to the woes of others; and he who thinks himself an abolitionist, yet cannot enter into the wrongs of others, has yet to find a true foundation for his anti-slavery faith. But, to the subject.

The immediate, and it may be the main cause of the extreme poverty and beggary in Ireland, is intemperance. This may be seen in the fact that most beggars drink whiskey. The third day after landing in Dublin, I met a man in one of the most public streets, with a white cloth on the upper part of his face. He was feeling his way with a cane in one hand, and the other hand was extended, soliciting aid. His feeble step and singular appearance led me to inquire into his history. I was informed that he had been a very intemperate man, and that on one occasion he was drunk, and lying in the street. While in this state of insensibility, a hog with its fangs tore off his nose, and a part of his face! I looked under the cloth, and saw the horrible spectacle of a living man with the face of a skeleton. Drunkenness is still rife in Ireland. The temperance cause has done much—is doing much—but there is much more to do, and, as yet, comparatively few to do it. A great part of the Roman Catholic clergy do nothing about it, while the Protestants may be said to hate the cause. I have been frequently advised to have nothing to do with it, as it would only injure the anti-slavery cause. It was most consoling to me to find that those persons who were most interested in the anti-slavery cause in the United States, were the same that distinguished themselves as the truest and warmest advocates of temperance and every other righteous reform at home. It was a pleasure to walk through the crowd with gentlemen such as the Webbs, Allens and Haughtons, and find them recognized by the multitude as the friends of the poor. My sheet is full.

Always yours,
Frederick Douglass

NATHANIEL HAWTHORNE

The Marble Faun

Nathaniel Hawthorne (1804–1864) counted among his ancestors John Hathorne, the only judge in the Salem witch trials never to repent of his actions. Nathaniel later added a "w" to his own name, perhaps to distance himself from this relative. His father, a sea captain, died of yellow fever near Dutch Guyana in 1808. Hawthorne attended Bowdoin College, where he met future poet Henry Wadsworth Longfellow and future president Franklin Pierce. He wrote a campaign biography for the latter in 1852, and in 1853 was appointed U.S. consul in Liverpool. By this time he had already written his best-known works, intricate portraits of New England life: *The Scarlet Letter* (1850), *Mosses from an Old Manse*

(1846), *The House of the Seven Gables* (1851), and *The Blithedale Romance* (1852), partly based on the Transcendentalist community Brook Farm. This excerpt from *The Marble Faun* (1860) ventures further out, featuring a young woman studying art in Rome who, in her newly gained freedom, paradoxically becomes a copyist rather than an original artist.

This young American girl was an example of the freedom of life which it is possible for a female artist to enjoy at Rome. She dwelt in her tower, as free to descend into the corrupted atmosphere of the city beneath, as one of her companion doves to fly downward into the street;—all alone, perfectly independent, under her own sole guardianship, unless watched over by the Virgin, whose shrine she tended; doing what she liked without a suspicion or a shadow upon the snowy whiteness of her fame. The customs of artist life bestow such liberty upon the sex, which is elsewhere restricted within so much narrower limits; and it is perhaps an indication that, whenever we admit women to a wider scope of pursuits and professions, we must also remove the shackles of our present conventional rules, which would then become an insufferable restraint on either maid or wife. The system seems to work unexceptionally in Rome; and in many other cases, as in Hilda's, purity of heart and life are allowed to assert themselves, and to be their own proof and security, to a degree unknown in the society of other cities.

Hilda, in her native land, had early shown what was pronounced by connoisseurs a decided genius for the pictorial art. Even in her schooldays— still not so very distant—she had produced sketches that were seized upon by men of taste, and hoarded as among the choicest treasures of their portfolios; scenes delicately imagined, lacking, perhaps, the reality which comes only from a close acquaintance with life, but so softly touched with feeling and fancy that you seemed to be looking at humanity with angels' eyes. With years and experience she might be expected to attain a darker and more forcible touch, which would impart to her designs the relief they needed. Had Hilda remained in her own country, it is not improbable that she might have produced original works worthy to hang in that gallery of native art which, we hope, is destined to extend its rich length through many future centuries. An orphan, however, without near relatives, and possessed of a little property, she had found it within her possibilities to come to Italy; that central clime, whither the eyes and the heart of every artist turn, as if pictures could not be made to glow in any other atmosphere, as if statues could not assume grace and expression, save in that land of whitest marble.

Hilda's gentle courage had brought her safely over land and sea; her mild, unflagging perseverance had made a place for her in the famous city, even like a flower that finds a chink for itself, and a little earth to grow in, on whatever ancient wall its slender roots may fasten. Here she dwelt, in her tower, possessing a friend or two in Rome, but no home companion except the flock of doves, whose cote was in a ruinous chamber contiguous to her own. They soon became as familiar with the fair-haired Saxon girl as if she were a born sister of their brood; and her customary white robe bore such an analogy to their snowy plumage that the confraternity of artists called Hilda the Dove, and recognized her aerial apartment as the Dovecote. And while the other doves flew far and wide in quest of what was good for them, Hilda likewise spread her wings, and sought such ethereal and imaginative sustenance as God ordains for creatures of her kind.

We know not whether the result of her Italian studies, so far as it could yet be seen, will be accepted as a good or desirable one. Certain it is, that since her arrival in the pictorial land, Hilda seemed to have entirely lost the impulse of original design, which brought her thither. No doubt the girl's early dreams had been of sending forms and hues of beauty into the visible world out of her own mind; of compelling scenes of poetry and history to live before men's eyes, through conceptions and by methods individual to herself. But more and more, as she grew familiar with the miracles of art that enrich so many galleries in Rome, Hilda had ceased to consider herself as an original artist. No, wonder that this change should have befallen her. She was endowed with a deep and sensitive faculty of appreciation; she had the gift of discerning and worshipping excellence in a most unusual measure. No other person, it is probable, recognized so adequately, and enjoyed with such deep delight, the pictorial wonders that were here displayed. She saw no, not saw, but felt through and through a picture; she bestowed upon it all the warmth and richness of a woman's sympathy; not by any intellectual effort, but by this strength of heart, and this guiding light of sympathy, she went straight to the central point, in which the master had conceived his work. Thus she viewed it, as it were, with his own eyes, and hence her comprehension of any picture that interested her was perfect.

This power and depth of appreciation depended partly upon Hilda's physical organization, which was at once healthful and exquisitely delicate;

and, connected with this advantage, she had a command of hand, a nicety and force of touch, which is an endowment separate from pictorial genius, though indispensable to its exercise.

It has probably happened in many other instances, as it did in Hilda's case, that she ceased to aim at original achievement in consequence of the very gifts which so exquisitely fitted her to profit by familiarity with the works of the mighty old masters. Reverencing these wonderful men so deeply, she was too grateful for all they bestowed upon her, too loyal, too humble, in their awful presence, to think of enrolling herself in their society. Beholding the miracles of beauty which they had achieved, the world seemed already rich enough in original designs, and nothing more was so desirable as to diffuse those self-same beauties more widely among mankind. All the youthful hopes and ambitions, the fanciful ideas which she had brought from home, of great pictures to be conceived in her feminine mind, were flung aside, and, so far as those most intimate with her could discern, relinquished without a sigh. All that she would henceforth attempt and that most reverently, not to say religiously was to catch and reflect some of the glory which had been shed upon canvas from the immortal pencils of old.

So Hilda became a copyist: in the Pinacotheca of the Vatican, in the galleries of the Pam-fili-Doria palace, the Borghese, the Corsini, the Sciarra, her easel was set up before many a famous picture by Guido, Domenichino, Raphael, and the devout painters of earlier schools than these. Other artists and visitors from foreign lands beheld the slender, girlish figure in front of some world-known work, absorbed, unconscious of everything around her, seeming to live only in what she sought to do. They smiled, no doubt, at the audacity which led her to dream of copying those mighty achievements. But, if they paused to look over her shoulder, and had sensibility enough to understand what was before their eyes, they soon felt inclined to believe that the spirits of the old masters were hovering over Hilda, and guiding her delicate white hand. In truth, from whatever realm of bliss and many colored beauty those spirits might descend, it would have been no unworthy errand to help so gentle and pure a worshipper of their genius in giving the last divine touch to her repetitions of their works.

Her copies were indeed marvellous. Accuracy was not the phrase for them; a Chinese copy is accurate. Hilda's had that evanescent and ethereal life—that flitting fragrance, as it were, of the originals—which it is as difficult to catch and retain as it would be for a sculptor to get the very movement and varying color of a living man into his marble bust. Only by watching the efforts of the most skilful copyists—men who spend a lifetime, as some of them do, in multiplying copies of a single picture—and observing how invariably they leave out just the indefinable charm that involves the last, inestimable value, can we understand the difficulties of the task which they undertake.

It was not Hilda's general practice to attempt reproducing the whole of a great picture, but to select some high, noble, and delicate portion of it, in which the spirit and essence of the picture culminated: the Virgin's celestial sorrow, for example, or a hovering angel, imbued with immortal light, or a saint with the glow of heaven in his dying face,—and these would be rendered with her whole soul. If a picture had darkened into an indistinct shadow through time and neglect, or had been injured by cleaning, or retouched by some profane hand, she seemed to possess the faculty of seeing it in its pristine glory. The copy would come from her hands with what the beholder felt must be the light which the old master had left upon the original in bestowing his final and most ethereal touch. In some instances even (at least, so those believed who best appreciated Hilda's power and sensibility) she had been enabled to execute what the great master had conceived in his imagination, but had not so perfectly succeeded in putting upon canvas; a result surely not impossible when such depth of sympathy as she possessed was assisted by the delicate skill and accuracy of her slender hand. In such cases the girl was but a finer instrument, a more exquisitely effective piece of mechanism, by the help of which the spirit of some great departed painter now first achieved his ideal, centuries after his own earthly hand, that other tool, had turned to dust.

Not to describe her as too much a wonder, however, Hilda, or the Dove, as her well-wishers half laughingly delighted to call her, had been pronounced by good judges incomparably the best copyist in Rome. After minute examination of her works, the most skilful artists declared that she had been led to her results by following precisely the same process step by step through which the original painter had trodden to the development of his idea. Other copyists—if such they are worthy to be called—attempt only a superficial imitation. Copies of the old masters in this sense are produced by thousands; there are artists, as we have said, who spend their lives in painting the works, or perhaps one single work, of one illustrious painter over and over again: thus they convert themselves into Guido machines, or Raphaelic machines. Their performances, it is true, are often wonderfully deceptive to a careless eye; but working entirely from the outside, and seeking only to reproduce the surface, these men are sure to leave out that indefinable nothing, that inestimable something, that constitutes the life and soul through which the picture gets its immortality. Hilda was no such machine as this; she wrought religiously, and therefore wrought a miracle.

HENRY JAMES

The American

Henry James (1843–1916), foremost exponent of nineteenth-century realism, grew up traveling throughout Europe with his eccentric father, Henry James Sr., and siblings including William James, the future psychologist, and philosopher. He moved to Europe permanently in 1875, first taking up residence in Paris and immersing himself in the works of Flaubert and Turgenev. After 1876 he made his home in Britain, and began a prodigious career spanning forty years, with a steady outpouring of novels, short stories, essays, and plays. James became a British citizen in 1915, during World War I. Beginning with his early works, *The American* (1877) and *The Europeans* (1878), and continuing through his last novels, *The Wings of the Dove* (1902), *The Ambassadors* (1903), and *The Golden Bowl* (1904), cross-cultural encounters of a vexed kind would be his central subject, traced through a subtle calculus of sensibilities and perceptions. Like *The Marble Faun*, this excerpt from *The American* also features a copyist, in this case a young Frenchwoman, selling a picture to a newly leisured American businessman.

On a brilliant day in May, in the year 1868, a gentleman was reclining at his ease on the great circular divan which at that period occupied the centre of the Salon Carré, in the Museum of the Louvre. This commodious ottoman has since been removed, to the extreme regret of all weak-kneed lovers of the fine arts, but the gentleman in question had taken serene possession of its softest spot, and, with his head thrown back and his legs outstretched, was staring at Murillo's beautiful moon-borne Madonna in profound enjoyment of his posture. He had removed his hat, and flung down beside him a little red guide-book and an opera-glass. The day was warm; he was heated with walking, and he repeatedly passed his handkerchief over his forehead, with a somewhat wearied gesture. And yet he was evidently not a man to whom fatigue was familiar; long, lean, and muscular, he suggested the sort of vigor that is commonly known as "toughness." But his exertions on this particular day had been of an unwonted sort, and he had performed great physical feats which left him less jaded than his tranquil stroll through the Louvre. He had looked out all the pictures to which an asterisk was affixed in those formidable pages of fine print in his Badeker; his attention had been strained and his eyes dazzled, and he had sat down with an aesthetic headache. He had looked, moreover, not only at all the pictures, but at all the copies that were going forward around them, in the hands of those innumerable young women in irreproachable toilets who devote themselves, in France, to the propagation of masterpieces, and if the truth must be told, he had often admired the copy much more than the original. His physiognomy would have sufficiently indicated that he was a shrewd and capable fellow, and in truth he had often sat up all night over a bristling bundle of accounts, and heard the cock crow without a yawn. But Raphael and Titian and Rubens were a new kind of arithmetic, and they inspired our friend, for the first time in his life, with a vague self-mistrust.

An observer with anything of an eye for national types would have had no difficulty in determining the local origin of this undeveloped connoisseur, and indeed such an observer might have felt a certain humorous relish of the almost ideal completeness with which he filled out the national mould. The gentleman on the divan was a powerful specimen of an American. But he was not only a fine American; he was in the first place, physically, a fine man. He appeared to possess that kind of health and strength which, when found in perfection, are the most impressive—the physical capital which the owner does nothing to "keep up." If he was a muscular Christian, it was quite without knowing it. If it was necessary to walk to a remote spot, he walked, but he had never known himself to "exercise." He had no theory with regard to cold bathing or the use of Indian clubs; he was neither an oarsman, a rifleman, nor a fencer—he had never had time for these amusements—and he was quite unaware that the saddle is recommended for certain forms of indigestion. He was by inclination a temperate man; but he had supped the night before his visit to the Louvre at the Café Anglais—some one had told him it was an experience not to be omitted—and he had slept none the less the sleep of the just. His usual attitude and carriage were of a rather relaxed and lounging kind, but when under a special inspiration, he straightened himself, he looked like a grenadier on parade. He never smoked. He had been assured—such things are said—that cigars were excellent for the health, and he was quite capable of believing it; but he knew as little about tobacco as about homeopathy. He had a very well-formed head, with a shapely, symmetrical balance of the frontal and the occipital development, and a good deal of straight, rather dry brown hair. His complexion was brown, and his nose had a bold well-marked arch. His eye was of a clear, cold gray, and save for a rather abundant mustache he was clean-shaved. He had the flat jaw and sinewy neck which are frequent in the American type; but the traces of national origin are a matter of expression even more than of feature, and it was in this respect that our friend's countenance was supremely eloquent. The discriminating observer we have been supposing might, however, perfectly have measured its expressiveness, and yet have been at a loss to describe it. It had that typical vagueness which is not vacuity, that blankness which is not simplicity, that look of being committed to nothing in particular, of standing in an attitude of general hospitality to the chances of life, of being very much at one's own disposal so characteristic of many American faces. It was our friend's eye that chiefly told his story; an eye in which innocence and experience were singularly blended. It was full of contradictory suggestions, and though it was by no means the glowing orb of a hero of romance, you could find in it almost anything you looked for. Frigid and yet friendly, frank yet cautious, shrewd yet credulous, positive yet skeptical, confident yet shy, extremely intelligent and extremely good-humored, there was something vaguely defiant in its concessions, and something profoundly reassuring in its reserve. The cut of this gentleman's mustache, with the two premature wrinkles in the cheek above it, and the fashion of his garments, in which an exposed shirt-front and a cerulean cravat played perhaps an obtrusive part, completed the conditions of his identity. We have approached him, perhaps, at a not especially favorable moment; he is by no means sitting for his portrait. But listless as he lounges there, rather baffled on the aesthetic question, and guilty of the damning fault (as we have lately discovered it to be) of confounding the merit of the artist with that of his work (for he admires the squinting Madonna of the young lady with the boyish coiffure, because he thinks the young lady herself uncommonly taking), he is a sufficiently promising acquaintance. Decision, salubrity, jocosity, prosperity, seem to hover within his call; he is evidently a practical man, but the idea in his case, has undefined and mysterious boundaries, which invite the imagination to bestir itself on his behalf.

As the little copyist proceeded with her work, she sent every now and then a responsive glance toward her admirer. The cultivation of the fine arts appeared to necessitate, to her mind, a great deal of byplay, a great standing off with folded arms and head drooping from side to side, stroking of a dimpled chin with a dimpled hand, sighing and frowning and patting of the foot, fumbling in disordered tresses for wandering hair-pins. These performances were accompanied by a restless glance, which lingered longer than elsewhere upon the gentleman we have described. At last he rose abruptly, put on his hat, and approached the young lady. He placed himself before her picture and looked at it for some moments, during which she pretended to be quite unconscious of his inspection. Then, addressing her with the single word which constituted the strength of his French vocabulary, and holding up one finger in a manner which appeared to him to illuminate his meaning, "*Combien?*" he abruptly demanded.

The artist stared a moment, gave a little pout, shrugged her shoulders, put down her palette and brushes, and stood rubbing her hands.

"How much?" said our friend, in English. "*Combien?*"

"Monsieur wishes to buy it?" asked the young lady in French.

"Very pretty, *splendide. Combien?*" repeated the American.

"It pleases monsieur, my little picture? It's a very beautiful subject," said the young lady.

"The Madonna, yes; I am not a Catholic, but I want to buy it. *Combien?* Write it here." And he took a pencil from his pocket and showed her the fly-leaf of his guide-book. She stood looking at him and scratching her chin with the pencil. "Is it not for sale?" he asked. And as she still stood reflecting, and looking at him with an eye which, in spite of her desire to treat this avidity of patronage as a very old story, betrayed an almost touching incredulity, he was afraid he had offended her. She was simply trying to look indifferent, and wondering how far she might go. "I haven't made a mistake—*pas insulté*, no?" her interlocutor continued. "Don't you understand a little English?"

The young lady's aptitude for playing a part at short notice was remarkable. She fixed him with her conscious, perceptive eye and asked him if he spoke no French. Then, "Donnez!" she said briefly, and took the open guide-book. In the upper corner of the fly-leaf she traced a number, in a minute and extremely neat hand. Then she handed back the book and took up her palette again.

Our friend read the number: "2,000 francs." He said nothing for a time, but stood looking at the picture, while the copyist began actively to dabble with her paint. "For a copy, isn't that a good deal?" he asked at last. "*Pas beaucoup?*"

The young lady raised her eyes from her palette, scanned him from head to foot, and alighted with admirable sagacity upon exactly the right answer. "Yes, it's a good deal. But my copy has remarkable qualities, it is worth nothing less."

The gentleman in whom we are interested understood no French, but I have said he was intelligent, and here is a good chance to prove it. He apprehended, by a natural instinct, the meaning of the young woman's phrase, and it gratified him to think that she was so honest. Beauty, talent, virtue; she combined everything! "But you must finish it," he said. "*Finish*, you know;" and he pointed to the unpainted hand of the figure.

"Oh, it shall be finished in perfection; in the perfection of perfections!" cried mademoiselle; and to confirm her promise, she deposited a rosy blotch in the middle of the Madonna's cheek.

But the American frowned. "Ah, too red, too red!" he rejoined. "Her complexion," pointing to the Murillo, "is—more delicate."

"Delicate? Oh, it shall be delicate, monsieur; delicate as Sèvres *biscuit*. I am going to tone that down; I know all the secrets of my art. And where will you allow us to send it to you? Your address?"

"My address? Oh yes!" And the gentleman drew a card from his pocket-book and wrote something upon it. Then hesitating a moment he said, "If I don't like it when it it's finished, you know, I shall not be obliged to take it."

The young lady seemed as good a guesser as himself. "Oh, I am very sure that monsieur is not capricious," she said with a roguish smile.

"Capricious?" And at this monsieur began to laugh. "Oh no, I'm not capricious. I am very faithful. I am very constant. *Comprenez?*"

"Monsieur is constant; I understand perfectly. It's a rare virtue. To recompense you, you shall have your picture on the first possible day; next week—as soon as it is dry. I will take the card of monsieur." And she took it and read his name: "Christopher Newman." Then she tried to repeat it aloud, and laughed at her bad accent. "Your English names are so droll!"

"Droll?" said Mr. Newman, laughing too. "Did you ever hear of Christopher Columbus?"

"*Bien sûr*! He invented America; a very great man. And is he your patron?"

"My patron?"

"Your patron-saint, in the calendar."

"Oh, exactly; my parents named me for him."

"Monsieur is American?"

"Don't you see it?" monsieur inquired.

"And you mean to carry my little picture away over there?" and she explained her phrase with a gesture.

"Oh, I mean to buy a great many pictures—*beaucoup, beaucoup*," said Christopher Newman.

"The honor is not less for me," the young lady answered, "for I am sure monsieur has a great deal of taste."

"But you must give me your card," Newman said; "your card, you know."

The young lady looked severe for an instant, and then said, "My father will wait upon you."

But this time Mr. Newman's powers of divination were at fault. "Your card, your address," he simply repeated.

"My address?" said mademoiselle. Then with a little shrug, "Happily for you, you are an American! It is the first time I ever gave my card to a gentleman." And, taking from her pocket a rather greasy *porte-monnaie*, she extracted from it a small glazed visiting card, and presented the latter to her patron. It was neatly inscribed in pencil, with a great many flourishes, "Mlle. Noemie Nioche." But Mr. Newman, unlike his companion, read the name with perfect gravity; all French names to him were equally droll.

"And precisely, here is my father, who has come to escort me home," said Mademoiselle Noemie. "He speaks English. He will arrange with you." And she turned to welcome a little old gentleman who came shuffling up, peering over his spectacles at Newman. M. Nioche wore a glossy wig, of an unnatural color which overhung his little meek, white, vacant face, and left it hardly more expressive than the unfeatured block upon which these articles are displayed in the barber's window. He was an exquisite image of shabby gentility. His scant ill-made coat, desperately brushed, his darned gloves, his highly polished boots, his rusty, shapely hat, told the story of a person who had "had losses" and who clung to the spirit of nice habits even though the letter had been hopelessly effaced. Among other things M. Nioche had lost courage. Adversity had not only ruined him, it had frightened him, and he was evidently going through his remnant of life on tiptoe, for fear of waking up the hostile fates. If this strange gentleman was saying anything improper to his daughter, M. Nioche would entreat him huskily, as a particular favor, to forbear; but he would admit at the same time that he was very presumptuous to ask for particular favors.

"Monsieur has bought my picture," said Mademoiselle Noemie. "When it's finished you'll carry it to him in a cab."

"In a cab!" cried M. Nioche; and he stared, in a bewildered way, as if he had seen the sun rising at midnight.

"Are you the young lady's father?" said Newman. "I think she said you speak English."

"Speak English—yes," said the old man slowly rubbing his hands. "I will bring it in a cab."

"Say something, then," cried his daughter. "Thank him a little—not too much."

"A little, my daughter, a little?" said M. Nioche perplexed. "How much?"

"Two thousand!" said Mademoiselle Noemie. "Don't make a fuss or he'll take back his word."

"Two thousand!" cried the old man, and he began to fumble for his snuff-box. He looked at Newman from head to foot; he looked at his daughter and then at the picture. "Take care you don't spoil it!" he cried almost sublimely.

"We must go home," said Mademoiselle Noemie. "This is a good day's work. Take care how you carry it!" And she began to put up her utensils.

"How can I thank you?" said M. Nioche. "My English does not suffice."

"I wish I spoke French as well," said Newman, good-naturedly. "Your daughter is very clever."

"Oh, sir!" and M. Nioche looked over his spectacles with tearful eyes and nodded several times with a world of sadness. "She has had an education—très-supérieure! Nothing was spared. Lessons in pastel at ten francs the lesson, lessons in oil at twelve francs. I didn't look at the francs then. She's an artiste, ah!"

"Do I understand you to say that you have had reverses?" asked Newman.

"Reverses? Oh, sir, misfortunes—terrible."

"Unsuccessful in business, eh?"

"Very unsuccessful, sir."

"Oh, never fear, you'll get on your legs again," said Newman cheerily.

The old man drooped his head on one side and looked at him with an expression of pain, as if this were an unfeeling jest.

"What does he say?" demanded Mademoiselle Noemie. M. Nioche took a pinch of snuff. "He says I will make my fortune again."

"Perhaps he will help you. And what else?"

"He says thou art very clever."

"It is very possible. You believe it yourself, my father?"

"Believe it, my daughter? With this evidence!" And the old man turned afresh, with a staring, wondering homage, to the audacious daub on the easel.

"Ask him, then. if he would not like to learn French."

"To learn French?"

"To take lessons."

"To take lessons, my daughter? From thee?"

"From you!"

"From me, my child? How should I give lessons?"

"*Pas de raisons!* Ask him immediately!" said Mademoiselle Noemie, with soft brevity. M. Nioche stood aghast, but under his daughter's eye he collected his wits, and, doing his best to assume an agreeable smile, he executed her commands. "Would it please you to receive instruction in our beautiful language?" he inquired, with an appealing quaver.

"To study French?" asked Newman, staring.

M. Nioche pressed his finger-tips together and slowly raised his shoulders. "A little conversation!"

"Conversation—that's it!" murmured Mademoiselle Noemie, who had caught the word. "The conversation of the best society."

"Our French conversation is famous, you know," M. Nioche ventured to continue. "It's a great talent."

"But isn't it awfully difficult?" asked Newman, very simply.

"Not to a man of *esprit*, like monsieur, an admirer of beauty in every form!" and M. Nioche cast a significant glance at his daughter's Madonna.

"I can't fancy myself chattering French!" said Newman with a laugh. "And yet, I suppose that the more a man knows the better."

"Monsieur expresses that very happily. *Hélas, oui!*"

"I suppose it would help me a great deal, knocking about Paris, to know the language."

"Ah, there are so many things monsieur must want to say: difficult things!"

"Everything I want to say is difficult. But you give lessons?"

Poor M. Nioche was embarrassed; he smiled more appealingly. "I am not a regular professor," he admitted. "I can't nevertheless tell him that I'm a professor," he said to his daughter.

"Tell him it's a very exceptional chance," answered Mademoiselle Noemie; "an *homme du monde*—one gentleman conversing with another! Remember what you are—what you have been!"

"A teacher of languages in neither case! Much more formerly and much less to-day! And if he asks the price of the lessons?"

"He won't ask it," said Mademoiselle Noemie.

"What he pleases, I may say?"

"Never! That's bad style."

"If he asks, then?"

Mademoiselle Noemie had put on her bonnet and was tying the ribbons. She smoothed them out, with her soft little chin thrust forward. "Ten francs," she said quickly.

"Oh, my daughter! I shall never dare."

"Don't dare, then! He won't ask till the end of the lessons, and then I will make out the bill."

RICHARD WRIGHT

Black Power

Richard Wright (1908–1960), raised in poverty by his maternal grandmother in Jackson, Mississippi, had to leave school to work in Memphis, but managed to publish his first story, "The Voodoo of Hell's Half-Acre," at age sixteen, before moving to Chicago in 1927. His first short story collection, *Uncle Tom's Children* (1938), was widely praised, as was his novel, *Native Son* (1940), the first book by an African American author to be selected by the Book of the Month Club. It was made into a Broadway play the following year, with Orson Welles as director. *Black Boy* (1945), Wright's autobiography, was likewise a best-seller. In 1944 he broke with the Communist Party and moved to Paris, finding new intellectual allies in Jean-Paul Sartre and Albert Camus. He also began exploring racial dynamics within a larger context, notably in *Black Power* (1954), about Ghana, and *The Color Curtain* (1956), about the Bandung Conference of non-aligned nations, hosted by Indonesia in 1955. In this selection from *Black Power*, Wright depicts buying and selling as an impassioned, home-grown phenomenon in Africa, not always comprehensible to outsiders.

The great majority of the Africans buy not from the European stores, but from each other, and one feels, when looking at the bustling activity in the market places, that almost the whole of the population is engaged in buying and selling. Just how this strange method of distributing products came about is a mystery. Perhaps it can be partly explained by the manner in which British firms ship their products to the Gold Coast. The British exporting firm generally deals through a certain *one* firm; that firm in turn sells to another, and *that* firm to *yet* another. . . . An African "mammy" finally enters this elaborate process, buying a huge lot of a certain merchandise, which she, in turn, breaks up and sells in fairly large lots to her customers. And her customers now sell directly to the public or maybe to other sellers who sell to the public. African wives are expected to aid in augmenting the income of the household and they thus take to the streets with their heads loaded with sundry items. . . . Naturally, this fantastic selling and reselling of goods drives the prices up and up until finally poor Africans must pay higher prices than a Britisher for a like product! Capitalism here reaches surrealistic dimensions, for even an ordinary match gains in value if it must afford profit to each hand through which it passes. This frantic concentration of the African mind upon making a profit out of selling a tiny fragment of a bar of soap or a piece of a piece of a piece of cloth is one of the most pathetic sights of the Gold Coast.

Of late there has been an effort to establish co-operatives to eliminate this senseless and self-defeating trading, but a casual glance at Accra's market places reveals that the whole process of buying and selling is anarchy calling for the sharpest wits imaginable. Haggling over a penny enlists the deepest passion, and you have the impression that the African trader is dealing in life-and-death matters. One wonders if such a manner of trading could have grown up in any society other than an illiterate one. It's likely that traditional tribal customs can account to some degree for this seeming preference for direct cash dealing on the part of the African, for his passion for visible, tactile methods of exchange of goods; I don't know. . . . All I know is that the African seems to love a petty financial game of wits and he'll ask you ten times the value of any object he's selling without batting an eye. Of course, the true explanation might be much simpler; the African might have learned all of this innocent chicanery from the Europeans during five hundred years of trading with them. The Portuguese, the Danes, the Swedes, the Germans, the French, and the English had some pretty sharp and unsavory methods of trading cheap trinkets for gold dust, a transaction which allowed for a wide leeway of bargaining. . . . But I leave this question of accounting for the "economic laws" (I don't believe that there's any such thing!) of the Gold Coast to other and more astute minds.

And yet a smart "mammy" will let a moneylender cheat her. . . . Since an African, when he is short of cash, thinks nothing of borrowing as much as he needs to tide him over, the Gold Coast moneylender will charge two, three, or four hundred per cent interest. I was told of a case in which a cocoa farmer borrowed money on his farm and pledged the yield of each year's crop as interest; of course, since his farm did not bring him any income, he could never pay off the principal!

Marriage and adultery too operate on a "cash and carry" basis. Tribal Africans do not like to admit that they buy their wives, but obtaining a wife amounts to no more or less than just that. And if your wife commits adultery, you can be compensated for it. There exists a regular fixed scale of fines to be paid by those either trapped or caught in the act of adultery. Or if your wife runs away, you can claim from her family—that is, the ones from whom you bought her—the return of your money. I'm reliably informed that some chiefs urge their many wives to commit adultery so that they can collect large sums of money by fining the culprits gullible enough to commit fornication with them.

NORMAN RUSH

Mating

Norman Rush (born 1933), best known for his novels and short stories set in Botswana in the 1980s, received both the National Book Award and the 1992 *Irish Times/Aer Lingus* International Fiction Prize for his first novel, *Mating* (1991), told in the first person by an anthropology graduate student chronicling her relation to the founder of an experimental community in the Kalahari Desert. Rush was a conscientious objector during the Korean War and sentenced to two years in jail, though he was released on parole after nine months. For the next fifteen years he worked as a book dealer and teacher, publishing his first story in the *New Yorker* only in 1978. From 1978 to 1983 he and his wife Elsa were in the Peace Corps in Botswana. That experience led to two other works: *Whites* (1986), a collection of short stories; and *Mortals* (2003), a novel about a teacher turned spy. In the following excerpt from *Mating*, the narrator reflects on the Franciscan sisters running a mission in the "still center of nowhere," and their inexplicable sanguineness about the level of nitrates in their drinking water.

The mission was a line of squaredavels along the crest of the high side of the Kang pan. The sisters ran a tiny, overwhelmed clinic and were attempting, without luck so far, to establish a hostel cum primary school for Basarwa children. I enjoyed the sisters, who ceased being at all curious about me when I said the word anthropology. Their eyes glazed. We are not exotic in that part of the world. One of the sisters took me down into the pan to impress me with the severity of the drought. The pan at Kang is pretty deep and I had a recurrence of skepticism about the standard explanation of the origin of the pans, viz. wind action over millennia scouring out these depressions, the proof being that the rim standing most counter to the prevailing wind is supposedly always the highest. They look so much like volcanic or impact craters, though. We went down into the blinding thing. There had been next to no rain for three years. A hand-dug pit at the center of the pan which had been briefly used for watering cattle was now full of bones. We went to it. The floor of the pan was baked and checkered, and walking across it felt like walking on potsherds. In certain cracks you could insert your arm down to the biceps and your fingers would touch a wet substance like paste which would have dried into a rigid plaster coating by the time you pulled your hand out. You had to knock your coated fingers against something hard to get it off.

From an anthropological standpoint I was very interested in there being female Franciscans, women motivated by yet another embalmed male dream to live out their lives in wilderness like this. I have nothing against St. Francis of Assisi, I don't think. I know him by image, exclusively. But it was an anthropologically interesting fact to me that the heavy work of this remote mission was being done exclusively by very nice women. And the same is true for Africa generally, for Lutherans and all the rest of them. Even when a woman gets her own order authorized, like Mother Teresa, it's women who end up doing the cooking and cleaning and nursing and little detachments of men who get to do the fun proselytizing. As I say, I was more interested in the sisters than they were in me. It may be because people who do good, to a self-sacrificial point and on a continuous basis, seem to exist in a kind of light trance a lot of the time. When we were down in the pan I realized I had been waiting for a thing to happen that I'd gotten used to seeing happen among missionary women, *id est* a brief peeping out of the sin of pride. They are consciously determined not to take pride in the afflictions they endure for the love of Christ, but they tend to slip. My guide asked if I had heard the news that a nun had been trampled to death by an elephant in Zambia. I saw the gleam. And I could hear chagrin when honesty compelled her to mention that it was a sister not of their order. I commiserated appropriately, feeling ashamed of the kind of person I am.

It took me a week to get myself outfitted and provisioned for my expedition, and I could have made it take longer. I was protracting the process. Kang was hard to leave. Apparently I wasn't alone in feeling that way, because one of the sisters was in rebellion against a command to return to Racine. The time I spent lending a hand in the clinic also slowed me down by inducing internal questioning along the lines of What would be so terrible about public health as a career for you and What is so compelling about the so-called study of man? What did I think was wrong with the idea of doing something for people whose cheeks looked like pegboard, as opposed to spending my life swimming upstream through the shrinking attention spans of the sons and daughters of the American middle class? I knew I was already too old for medical school.

I knew a woman three years younger who had been told she was too old for veterinary school. The sisters were doing medicine, in effect. And they seemed happy and were living decently, male absence notwithstanding. They were all a little overweight, but were obviously content construing whatever weight they settled at as what God, in the form of interacting genes, diet, and exercise, wanted. It was not on their minds. In America the dominant female types seem to be gaunt women jogging themselves into amenorrhea or women so fat they're barely able to force one thigh past the other when it's time to locomote, like Mom. The problem was that there was no mystery, that I could see, connected with public health. Anthropology, even my rather mundane corner of it, seemed to me to connect with the mystery of everything, by which I think I meant why the world has to be so unpleasant.

What finally stirred me to get moving was the water in Kang. It was cloudy and had an acrid taste. The sisters were aware of it but, I thought, eerily sanguine about it. When I brought it up directly, finally, it was clear they were, it could be said, even rather proud of what they were drinking. It seems the water in Kang is dense with naturally occurring nitrates. The water has been tested by the authorities and found to be spectacularly above the danger level. Everything in the literature suggested that nitrates at this level should cause people to develop a kidney disorder called methemoglobinuria. But there was no sign of the disease among the local people, who had been drinking the water for generations, nor among the nuns. There was no feasible filtering, in any case, nor if there were would it have felt right for them to make use of it when the poor of Kang would not have access to it. It was a medical mystery and a sign that Kang was under divine protection. They said this. So then it was time to bestir myself.

ROBERT HASS

Ezra Pound's Proposition

Robert Hass (born 1941) takes his inspiration from East European and Japanese poets, along with the cadences of Gary Snyder and Allen

Ginsberg. His poetry, meditations on the flora and fauna of California fused with his own confessional impulses, is also consistently internationalist in spirit. In 1984 he began translating the poetry of the Polish Nobel laureate Czeslaw Milosz. *The Essential Haiku: Versions of Bashō, Buson, and Issa* followed in 1994. Hass has won many awards, including the 1996 National Book Critics Circle Award for *Sun Under Wood*, and the 2007 National Book Award for *Time and Materials*, also sharing the Pulitzer Prize the following year for that volume. He was named a MacArthur Fellow in 1984, and from 1995 to 1997 served as poet laureate of the United States, using that office to promote literacy and environmental awareness. Long a poetry teacher at UC Berkeley, he took part in the Occupy Cal demonstration in 2011, writing about it in a *New York Times* op-ed piece, "Poet-Bashing Police." In the poem below, Hass recalls the economic theories of Ezra Pound as he witnesses global capital and child prostitution in Thailand.

Beauty is sexuality, and sexuality
is the fertility of the earth and the fertility
Of the earth is economics. Though he is no recommendation
For poets on the subject of finance,
I thought of him in the thick heat
Of the Bangkok night. Not more than fourteen, she saunters up to you
Outside the Shangri-la Hotel
And says, in plausible English,
"How about a party, big guy?"

Here is more or less how it works:
The World Bank arranges the credit and the dam
Floods three hundred villages, and the villagers find their way
To the city where their daughters melt into the teeming streets,
And the dam's great turbine, beautifully tooled
In Lund or Dresden or Detroit, financed
by Lazard Frères in Paris or the Morgan Bank in New York,
enabled by judicious gifts from Bechtel of San Francisco
or Halliburton in Houston to the local political elite,
Spun by the force of rushing water,

Have become hives of shimmering silver
And, down river, they throw that bluish throb of light
Across her cheekbones and her lovely skin.

ROBERT PINSKY

The Banknote

Robert Pinsky (born 1940) writes with the musical acuity of a former saxophonist, insisting on poetry as an auditory art, one practiced
by ordinary readers as well as poets. Born and raised in Long Branch,
New Jersey, Pinsky says that his exposure to Irish and Italian cultures
expanded his poetic horizons from an early age. His impressive corpus,
which includes *History of My Heart* (1984), *The Want Bone* (1990), *Jersey
Rain* (2000), and *Gulf Music* (2007), explores subjects ranging from jazz
to Stalin to ice hockey and baseball. With Robert Hass, he has translated
the poetry of Czeslaw Milosz (1984); more recently, he published a verse
translation of Dante's *Inferno* (1995). From 1997–2000, he served as poet
laureate of the United States. At home in other media, Pinsky appeared
in a 2002 episode of *The Simpsons*, "Little Girl in the Big Ten"; produced
an interactive fiction game, *Mindwheel* (1984); and released a CD, *Poem-
Jazz* (2012). In the following selection, the first of two in this volume, he
shows the hum of global markets alternating with many other tongues
in Brazil.

Behind profaned walls, calm rituals of exile.
The Brazilian cleaner hums and sponges the table.
A civil quiet between us I will not break

By chanting my gratitude in broken Polish.
She has the courage to be my great-grandfather Ike.
Thanks to his passage a century ahead of hers

I get to sit at the table, I write the check.
To recite this to him through her would be foolish.
Her only language for now is Portuguese,

Though every week she knows more English words.
On the Brazilian equivalent of a dollar bill,
Not only a portrait of Drummond de Andrade

But an entire poem by him: nineteen lines.
It makes the dollar look—Philistine. The poem
Is about a poem he intends to write about

The single diamond made of all our lives.
From gluts, dearths. From markets, forced migrations.
Nossas vidas formam um só diamante.

Sicilian Archimedes could move the universe
If there were a place outside of it to stand.
Locked blind in the diamond, its billion cuts and facets,

Molecules in an obdurate equilibrium
Of pressures, we cannot see the shifting fire.
Words on the banknote; the banknote tints the words.

From Ruth the Moabite, her great-grandson David.
And from Ruth's sister Orpha, Goliath the gentile.
Signature sprayed on steel security shutters

In characters the corrugations disable:
In the unpeace, the breaking of the wards.
The pyramid eye envisions networks of cable,

Gulfs arched, wilderness paved. In the system
Of privilege and deprivation, the employed, the avid:
Fraught in the works, turning the gear of custom.

KAREN TEI YAMASHITA

Through the Arc of the Rain Forest

Karen Tei Yamashita (born 1951), born in Los Angeles, is best known for a genre-bending corpus that could be described as magical realism, science fiction, or postmodern extravaganza. In works such as *Through the Arc of the Rain Forest* (1990), *Brazil-Maru* (1992), and *Tropic of Orange* (1997), the narrative typically spans three continents and features highly unusual protagonists, including a character named Arcangel with the ability to drag the Tropic of Cancer across the U.S.-Mexico border, and an extraterrestrial ball whirling in front of a Japanese expatriate working in Brazil. Yamashita herself spent nine years in Brazil, beginning in 1975, studying the history and anthropology of Japanese immigration. She now teaches creative writing and Asian American literature at the University of California, Santa Cruz, while turning to more clearly Asian American themes in her recent work, as in *I Hotel* (2010). In the following excerpt from *Through the Arc of the Rain Forest*, she casts a satirical eye on the pollsters and news media descending on the newly discovered Matacão in the Amazon forest.

They wept like anything to see
Such quantities of sand:
'If this were only cleared away,'
They said 'it would be grand!'
'If seven maids with seven mops
Swept it for half a year,
Do you suppose' the Walrus said,
'That they would get it clear?'

—Lewis Carroll, *Through the Looking Glass*

Since everyone in this story seems somehow headed for the Matacão, perhaps it would be appropriate to stop for a moment and discuss it. I don't claim to be an expert on the Matacão, but I did gather some interesting facts.

The Matacão has been, since its discovering, a source of curiosity and confusion in the scientific world. Geologists, astronomers, physicists, archaeologists and chemists were suddenly thrown into an unsettling pre-revolutionary state where the basic parameters of scientific truths were undergoing a shift similar to that experienced when Einstein redefined the Newtonian world. Nowadays, scientists cannot present papers or new findings without having to answer the now-common retort, "But what bearing does the Matacão have on your findings?" or "How do you reconcile your hypothesis with the Matacão?"

How or why the Matacão came about is a puzzle for which no clear answers exist. The speculations about its origins have been as varied as the people who came to visit, gasp, grovel, get a tan, pray, relax, study, wonder, hang out, make love, worship, meditate, or pay homage to its existence.

In one comprehensive survey, 18 percent of the people questioned believed that the Matacão was the creation of a highly sophisticated ancient civilization that inhabited the area thousands of years ago. This fraction believed that the Matacão, once penetrated, would produce one of the greatest treasures of ancient civilization. Another 9 percent of those surveyed believed that the Matacão was the result of a hot molten substance within the earth that had managed to seep into the upper layers of the its crust.

A mere 3 percent believed the Matacão was the work of the CIA, that it was one of a number of air bases hidden in the tropical forest for staging short-range raids into Central America and exporting arms to fallen dictators and terrorist freedom-fighters.

About 13 percent believed that the Matacão was a miracle from God, the great foundation for a great church or a new Vatican, while another 11 percent believed that the Matacão possessed supernatural powers, not necessarily from a single God, but beyond the ordinary realm of human reason or contemporary science. Those of the supernatural bent believed that unknown powers that were life-giving and rejuvenating emanated from the Matacão, and that these powers could be used to benefit humanity or to wreak havoc, depending on who was able to harness them. Of course, many of this latter group felt that the powers of the feather were only the tip of the iceberg. A few expressed genuine concern that the free world should maintain control of the Matacão.

But the largest group, 33 percent, believed that the Matacão was of an extraterrestrial nature, a sort of runway prepared for the arrival of aliens. Of these, about half believed that the aliens were of a friendly or benign nature, while the other half believed that military precautions were necessary to prevent invasion. An insignificant number were undecided, and the rest had never heard of the Matacão.

Numerous public and private entities other than GGG Enterprises were funding a variety of scientific research projects on the Matacão. The Brazilian Ministry of the Interior had to create a department to keep track of the projects and to act as a intermediary for overlapping projects. In order to keep a tab on these findings, the government had created a series of legal requirements and official documents to keep the wealth and value of the Matacão within its control. This, in fact, contributed to a growing system of favors and outright graft associated with getting concessions to study areas of the Matacão. Still, a number of congressional members were beginning to argue for greater restrictions on the use and study of the Matacão. Brazil had once before emptied its wealthy gold mines into the coffers of the Portuguese Crown and consequently financed the Industrial Revolution in England. This time, if there was any wealth to be had, it had better remain in Brazil. Some scoffed at the pretensions of certain congresspersons, saying that the treasure of the Matacão might, at best, make a small dent in their continuing interest payments to the International Monetary Fund.

A few of these research studies actually did produce some significant findings. One study, after 5,381 hours of human input and 3,379 hours of computer output, was able to reproduce the complex molecular structure of the Matacão's material composition. The computer was completely straightforward in proclaiming the nature of the material: "NHCOO linkages indicate rigid, tightly bound polymer. Polyurethane family commonly known as plastic."

Another study was finally able to arrive at a method of penetrating or cutting through the Matacão's rigid plastic. It involved a complicated combination of laser cutting with amino acids and other chemical compounds. When the process was refined, a core sample was extricated from the Matacão. It was discovered that the Matacão was a solid piece of plastic. This agreed with sonar information, which revealed a continuous block of plastic five feet deep. Subsequent tests showed that this plastic material was virtually indestructible, a substance harder than stainless steel—or diamonds, for that matter. This news excited the NASA researchers who were naturally at the forefront of these studies, anxious to find new materials for their space vehicles. This was a breakthrough tantamount to Teflon. Some people even believed that the Matacão *was* Teflon.

AGHA SHAHID ALI

In Search of Evanescence

Agha Shahid Ali (1949–2001), born in New Delhi and raised in Kashmir, combines free verse with the rigors of the *ghazal*, cross-stitching Hindu and Muslim faiths and elements of Arabic, Urdu, and Persian poetic traditions. Though Ali spent most of his life in America, many of his poems continue to dwell on the turmoil of his homeland. Ali received wide acclaim, beginning with *A Walk Through the Yellow Pages* (1987) and continuing with *A Nostalgist's Map of America* (1991), a shimmering journey through superimposed American and Kashmiri landscapes. His next collection, *The Country Without a Post Office* (1997), was inspired by the 1990 Kashmir uprising against India, during which the post office was closed for seven months. *Rooms Are Never Finished* (2001) followed. Ali also translated the poetry of Urdu poet Faiz Ahmed Faiz and edited a collection of contemporary poetry, *Ravishing Discontinuities: Real Ghazals in English* (2000). The *ghazal* was also the chosen form in his posthumously published work, *Call Me Ishmael Tonight* (2001). This poem from *A Nostalgist's Map of America* imagines Kolkata (or Calcutta) as a highway exit in Ohio.

When on Route 80 in Ohio
I came across an exit
to Calcutta

the temptation to write a poem
led me to pass the exit
so I could say

India always exists
off the turnpikes
of America

so I could say
I did take the exit
and crossed Howrah

and even mention the Ganges
as it continued its sobbing
under the bridge

so when I paid my toll
I saw the trains rush by
one after one

on their roofs old passengers
each ready to surrender
his bones for tickets

so that I heard
the sun's percussion
on tamarind leaves

heard the empty cans of children
filling only with the shadows
of leaves

that behind the unloading trucks
were the voices of vendors
bargaining over women

so when the trees
let down their tresses
the monsoon oiled and braided them

and when the wind again parted them
this was the temptation
to end the poem this way:

The warm rains have left
many dead on the pavements

The signs to Route 80
all have disappeared

And now the road is a river
polished silver by cars

The cars are urns
carrying the ashes to the sea

HERMAN MELVILLE

"The Monkey Rope," from *Moby-Dick*

Herman Melville (1819–1891) wrote *Moby-Dick* as a fusion of many genres. Not simply an epic voyage centered on Ahab's obsessive quest for the white whale, it is also a comic look at the power dynamics at meal-time (as we have seen in the "Food" section of this volume) and, in this excerpt, "The Monkey-Rope," a meditation on the fate of being interconnected, sharing hazards and liabilities to the full.

In the tumultuous business of cutting-in and attending to a whale, there is much running backwards and forwards among the crew. Now hands are wanted here, and then again hands are wanted there. There is no staying in any one place; for at one and the same time everything has to be done everywhere. It is much the same with him who endeavors the description of the scene. We must now retrace our way a little. It was mentioned that upon first breaking ground in the whale's back, the blubber-hook was inserted into the original hole there cut by the spades of the mates. But how did so clumsy and weighty a mass as that same hook get fixed in that hole? It was inserted there by my particular friend Queequeg, whose duty it was, as harpooneer, to descend upon the monster's back for the special purpose referred to. But in very many cases, circumstances require that the harpooneer shall remain on the whale till the whole tensing or stripping operation is concluded. The whale, be it observed, lies almost entirely submerged, excepting the immediate parts operated upon. So down there, some ten feet below the level of the deck, the poor harpooneer flounders about, half on the whale and half in the water, as the vast mass revolves like a tread-mill beneath him. On the occasion in question, Queequeg figured in the Highland costume—a shirt and socks—in which to my eyes, at least, he appeared to uncommon advantage; and no one had a better chance to observe him, as will presently be seen.

Being the savage's bowsman, that is, the person who pulled the bow-oar in his boat (the second one from forward), it was my cheerful duty to attend upon him while taking that hard-scrabble scramble upon the dead whale's back. You have seen Italian organ-boys holding a dancing-ape by a long cord. Just so, from the ship's steep side, did I hold Queequeg down there in the sea, by what is technically called in the fishery a monkey-rope, attached to a strong strip of canvas belted round his waist.

It was a humorously perilous business for both of us. For, before we proceed further, it must be said that the monkey-rope was fast at both ends; fast to Queequeg's broad canvas belt, and fast to my narrow leather one. So that for better or for worse, we two, for the time, were wedded; and should poor Queequeg sink to rise no more, then both usage and honor demanded, that instead of cutting the cord, it should drag me down in his wake. So, then, an elongated Siamese ligature united us. Queequeg was my own inseparable twin brother; nor could I any way get rid of the dangerous liabilities which the hempen bond entailed.

So strongly and metaphysically did I conceive of my situation then, that while earnestly watching his motions, I seemed distinctly to perceive that my own individuality was now merged in a joint stock company of two; that my free will had received a mortal wound; and that another's mistake or misfortune might plunge innocent me into unmerited disaster and death. Therefore, I saw that here was a sort of interregnum in Providence; for its even-handed equity never could have so gross an injustice. And yet still further pondering—while I jerked him now and then from between the whale and ship, which would threaten to jam him—still further pondering,

I say, I saw that this situation of mine was the precise situation of every mortal that breathes; only, in most cases, he, one way or other, has this Siamese connexion with a plurality of other mortals. If your banker breaks, you snap; if your apothecary by mistake sends you poison in your pills, you die. True, you may say that, by exceeding caution, you may possibly escape these and the multitudinous other evil chances of life. But handle Queequeg's monkey-rope heedfully as I would, sometimes he jerked it so, that I came very near sliding overboard. Nor could I possibly forget that, do what I would, I only had the management of one end of it.

The monkey-rope is found in all whalers; but it was only in the Pequod that the monkey and his holder were ever tied together. This improvement upon the original usage was introduced by no less a man than Stubb, in order to afford to the imperilled harpooneer the strongest possible guarantee for the faithfulness and vigilance of his monkey-rope holder.

I have hinted that I would often jerk poor Queequeg from between the whale and the ship—where he would occasionally fall, from the incessant rolling and swaying of both. But this was not the only jamming jeopardy he was exposed to. Unappalled by the massacre made upon them during the night, the sharks now freshly and more keenly allured by the before pent blood which began to flow from the carcass—the rabid creatures swarmed round it like bees in a beehive.

And right in among those sharks was Queequeg; who often pushed them aside with his floundering feet. A thing altogether incredible were it not that attracted by such prey as a dead whale, the otherwise miscellaneously carnivorous shark will seldom touch a man.

Nevertheless, it may well be believed that since they have such a ravenous finger in the pie, it is deemed but wise to look sharp to them. Accordingly, besides the monkey-rope, with which I now and then jerked the poor fellow from too close a vicinity to the maw of what seemed a peculiarly ferocious shark—he was provided with still another protection. Suspended over the side in one of the stages, Tashtego and Daggoo continually flourished over his head a couple of keen whale-spades, wherewith they slaughtered as many sharks as they could reach. This procedure of theirs, to be sure, was very disinterested and benevolent of them. They meant Queequeg's best happiness, I admit; but in their hasty zeal to befriend him, and from the circumstance that both he and the sharks were at times half hidden by the blood-muddled water, those indiscreet spades of theirs would come nearer amputating a leg than a tail. But poor Queequeg, I suppose, straining and gasping there with that great iron hook—poor Queequeg, I suppose, only prayed to his Yojo, and gave up his life into the hands of his gods.

Well, well, my dear comrade and twin-brother, thought I, as I drew in and then slacked off the rope to every swell of the sea—what matters it, after all? Are you not the precious image of each and all of us men in this whaling world? That unsounded ocean you gasp in, is Life; those sharks, your foes; those spades, your friends; and what between sharks and spades you are in a sad pickle and peril, poor lad.

But courage! there is good cheer in store for you, Queequeg. For now, as with blue lips and blood-shot eyes the exhausted savage at last climbs up the chains and stands all dripping and involuntarily trembling over the side; the steward advances, and with a benevolent, consolatory glance hands him— what? Some hot Cognac? No! hands him, ye gods! hands him a cup of tepid ginger and water!

"Ginger? Do I smell ginger?" suspiciously asked Stubb, coming near. "Yes, this must be ginger," peering into the as yet untasted cup. Then standing as if incredulous for a while, he calmly walked towards the astonished steward slowly saying, "Ginger? ginger? and will you have the goodness to tell me, Mr. Dough-Boy, where lies the virtue of ginger? Ginger! is ginger the sort of fuel you use, Dough-boy, to kindle a fire in this shivering cannibal? Ginger!—what the devil is ginger?—sea-coal? firewood?—lucifer matches?—tinder?—gunpowder?—what the devil is ginger, I say, that you offer this cup to our poor Queequeg here."

"There is some sneaking Temperance Society movement about this business," he suddenly added, now approaching Starbuck, who had just come from forward. "Will you look at that kannakin, sir; smell of it, if you please." Then watching the mate's countenance, he added, "The steward, Mr. Starbuck, had the face to offer that calomel and jalap to Queequeg, there, this instant off the whale. Is the steward an apothecary, sir? and may I ask whether this is the sort of bitters by which he blows back the life into a half-drowned man?"

"I trust not," said Starbuck, "it is poor stuff enough."

"Aye, aye, steward," cried Stubb, "we'll teach you to drug it harpooneer; none of your apothecary's medicine here; you want to poison us, do ye? You have got out insurances on our lives and want to murder us all, and pocket the proceeds, do ye?"

"It was not me," cried Dough-Boy, "it was Aunt Charity that brought the ginger on board; and bade me never give the harpooneers any spirits, but only this ginger-jub—so she called it."

"Ginger-jub! you gingerly rascal! take that! and run along with ye to the lockers, and get something better. I hope I do no wrong, Mr. Starbuck. It is the captain's orders—grog for the harpooneer on a whale."

"Enough," replied Starbuck, "only don't hit him again, but—"

"Oh, I never hurt when I hit, except when I hit a whale or something of that sort; and this fellow's a weazel. What were you about saying, sir?"

"Only this: go down with him, and get what thou wantest thyself."

When Stubb reappeared, he came with a dark flask in one hand, and a sort of tea-caddy in the other. The first contained strong spirits, and was handed to Queequeg; the second was Aunt Charity's gift, and that was freely given to the waves.

HARRIET BEECHER STOWE

Uncle Tom's Cabin

Harriet Beecher Stowe (1811–1896) is best known for *Uncle Tom's Cabin*, one of the most influential political novels ever written. Born in Litchfield, Connecticut, she moved with her family to Cincinnati in 1832 when her father took a position at the Lane Theological Seminary. There she married Calvin Stowe, also on the faculty, and became active in the Underground Railroad. *Uncle Tom's Cabin* (1852), first published serially and then in book form, soon became a national best-seller, selling ten thousand copies in its first week, 300,000 copies by the end of the year, and more than two million copies by the end of the decade. President Lincoln, whom she met on November 25, 1862, reportedly greeted the small woman (Stowe was not quite five feet tall) with these words: "so this is the little lady who made this big war." *Uncle Tom's Cabin* was also a runaway success abroad, counting among its admirers Queen Victoria as well as Ivan Turgenev, Victor Hugo, Leo Tolstoy, and George Eliot. In the following excerpt, George Harris, an escaped slave, writes to a friend about his plans to move to Liberia to found a nation of his own.

"I feel somewhat at a loss, as to my future course. True, as you have said to me, I might mingle in the circles of the whites, in this country, my shade of color is so slight, and that of my wife and family scarce perceptible. Well, perhaps, on sufferance, I might. But, to tell you the truth, I have no wish to.

"My sympathies are not for my father's race, but for my mother's. To him I was no more than a fine dog or horse: to my poor heart-broken mother I was a *child*; and, though I never saw her, after the cruel sale that separated us, till she died, yet I *know* she always loved me dearly. I know it by my own heart. When I think of all she suffered, of my own early sufferings, of the distresses and struggles of my heroic wife, of my sister, sold in the New Orleans slave-market,—though I hope to have no unchristian sentiments, yet I may be excused for saying, I have no wish to pass for an American, or to identify myself with them.

"It is with the oppressed, enslaved African race that I cast in my lot; and, if I wished anything, I would wish myself two shades darker, rather than one lighter.

"The desire and yearning of my soul is for an African *nationality*. I want a people that shall have a tangible, separate existence of its own; and where am I to look for it? Not in Hayti; for in Hayti they had nothing to start with. A stream cannot rise above its fountain. The race that formed the character of the Haytiens was a worn-out, effeminate one; and, of course, the subject race will be centuries in rising to anything.

"Where, then, shall I look? On the shores of Africa I see a republic,—a republic formed of picked men, who, by energy and self-educating force, have, in many cases, individually, raised themselves above a condition of slavery. Having gone through a preparatory stage of feebleness, this republic has, at last, become an acknowledged nation on the face of the earth,— acknowledged by both France and England. There it is my wish to go, and find myself a people.

"I am aware, now, that I shall have you all against me; but, before you strike, hear me. During my stay in France, I have followed up, with intense interest, the history of my people in America. I have noted the struggle between abolitionist and colonizationist, and have received some impressions, as a distant spectator, which could never have occurred to me as a participator.

"I grant that this Liberia may have subserved all sorts of purposes, by being played off, in the hands of our oppressors, against us. Doubtless the scheme may have been used, in unjustifiable ways, as a means of retarding our emancipation. But the question to me is, Is there not a God above all man's schemes? May He not have over-ruled their designs, and founded for us a nation by them?

"In these days, a nation is born in a day. A nation starts, now, with all the great problems of republican life and civilization wrought out to its hand;— it has not to discover, but only to apply. Let us, then, all take hold together, with all our might, and see what we can do with this new enterprise, and the whole splendid continent of Africa opens before us and our children. *Our nation* shall roll the tide of civilization and Christianity along its shores, and plant there mighty republics, that, growing with the rapidity of tropical vegetation, shall be for all coming ages.

"Do you say that I am deserting my enslaved brethren? I think not. If I forget them one hour, one moment of my life, so may God forget me! But, what can I do for them, here? Can I break their chains? No, not as an individual; but, let me go and form part of a nation, which shall have a voice in the councils of nations, and then we can speak. A nation has a right to argue, remonstrate, implore, and present the cause of its race,—which an individual has not.

"If Europe ever becomes a grand council of free nations,—as I trust in God it will,—if, there, serfdom, and all unjust and oppressive social inequalities, are done away; and if they, as France and England have done, acknowledge our position,—then, in the great congress of nations, we will make our appeal, and present the cause of our enslaved and suffering race; and it cannot be that free, enlightened America will not then desire to wipe from her escutcheon that bar sinister which disgraces her among nations, and is as truly a curse to her as to the enslaved.

"But, you will tell me, our race have equal rights to mingle in the American republic as the Irishman, the German, the Swede. Granted, they have. We *ought* to be free to meet and mingle,—to rise by our individual worth, without any consideration of caste or color; and they who deny us this right are false to their own professed principles of human equality. We ought, in particular, to be allowed *here*. We have *more* than the rights of common men;—we have the claim of an injured race for reparation. But, then, *I do not want it*; I want a country, a nation, of my own. I think that the African race has peculiarities, yet to be unfolded in the light of civilization and Christianity, which, if not the same with those of the Anglo-Saxon, may prove to be, morally, of even a higher type.

"To the Anglo-Saxon race has been intrusted the destinies of the world, during its pioneer period of struggle and conflict. To that mission its stern, inflexible, energetic elements, were well adapted; but, as a Christian, I look for another era to arise. On its borders I trust we stand; and the throes that now convulse the nations are, to my hope, but the birth-pangs of an hour of universal peace and brotherhood.

"I trust that the development of Africa is to be essentially a Christian one. If not a dominant and commanding race, they are, at least, an affectionate, magnanimous, and forgiving one. Having been called in the furnace of injustice and oppression, they have need to bind closer to their hearts that sublime doctrine of love and forgiveness, through which alone they are to conquer, which it is to be their mission to spread over the continent of Africa.

"In myself, I confess, I am feeble for this,—full half the blood in my veins is the hot and hasty Saxon; but I have an eloquent preacher of the Gospel ever by my side, in the person of my beautiful wife. When I wander, her gentler spirit ever restores me, and keeps before my eyes the Christian calling and mission of our race. As a Christian patriot, as a teacher of Christianity, I go to *my country*,—my chosen, my glorious Africa!—and to her, in my heart, I sometimes apply those splendid words of prophecy: 'Whereas thou hast been forsaken and hated, so that no man went through thee; *I* will make thee an eternal excellence, a joy of many generations!'

"You will call me an enthusiast: you will tell me that I have not well considered what I am undertaking. But I have considered, and counted the cost. I go to *Liberia*, not as an Elysium of romance, but as to *a field of work*. I expect to work with both hands,—to work *hard*; to work against all sorts of difficulties and discouragements; and to work till I die. This is what I go for; and in this I am quite sure I shall not be disappointed.

"Whatever you may think of my determination, do not divorce me from your confidence; and think that, in whatever I do, I act with a heart wholly given to my people.

"GEORGE HARRIS."

W. E. B. DU BOIS

Dark Princess

W. E. B. [William Edward Burghardt] Du Bois (1868–1963), historian, philosopher, and civil rights leader, was one of the seminal figures of the twentieth century. Born in Great Barrington, Massachusetts, he studied at the historically black Fisk University as well as in Berlin and at Harvard, where he earned a PhD in history in 1895. Bringing all these intellectual traditions to bear on the burgeoning field of sociology, he served as an influential editor of *The Crisis*, the NAACP's monthly magazine that reached a circulation of 100,000 in 1920. In *The Souls of Black Folk* (1903), he made the now celebrated prediction that "the problem of the twentieth century is the problem of the color-line." Another equally well-known concept, "double consciousness," describes the structural and psychological conditions under which African Americans see themselves "as though through the eyes of others." Du Bois died in Accra, Ghana, his home for the last two years of his life. In this excerpt from *Dark Princess* (1928), he stages another kind of double consciousness, one brought about by a reversed color line in a Berlin drawing room.

Matthew sat in the dining-room of the Princess on Lützower Ufer. Looking about, his heart swelled. For the first time since he had left New York, he felt himself a man, one of those who could help build a world and guide it. He had no regrets. Medicine seemed a far-off, dry-as-dust thing.

The oak paneling of the room went to the ceiling and there broke softly with carven light against white flowers and into long lucent curves. The table below was sheer with lace and linen, sparkling with silver and crystal. The servants moved deftly, and all of them were white save one who stood behind the Princess' high and crimson chair. At her right sat Matthew himself, hardly realizing until long afterward the honor thus done an almost nameless guest.

Fortunately he had the dinner jacket of year before last with him. It was not new, but it fitted his form perfectly, and his was a form worth fitting.

He was a bit shocked to note that all the other men but two were in full evening dress. But he did not let this worry him much.

Ten of them sat at the table. On the Princess' left was a Japanese, faultless in dress and manner, evidently a man of importance, as the deference shown him and the orders on his breast indicated. He was quite yellow, short and stocky, with a face which was a delicately handled but perfect mask. There were two Indians, one a man grave, haughty, and old, dressed richly in turban and embroidered tunic, the other, in conventional dress and turban, a young man, handsome and alert, whose eyes were ever on the Princess. There were two Chinese, a young man and a young woman, he in a plain but becoming Chinese costume of heavy blue silk, she in a pretty dress, half Chinese, half European in effect. An Egyptian and his wife came next, he suave, talkative, and polite—just a shade too talkative and a bit too polite, Matthew thought; his wife a big, handsome, silent woman, elegantly jeweled and gowned, with much bare flesh. Beyond them was a cold and rather stiff Arab who spoke seldom, and then abruptly.

Of the food and wine of such dinners, Matthew had read often but never partaken; and the conversation, now floating, now half submerged, gave baffling glimpses of unknown lands, spiritual and physical. It was all something quite new in his experience, the room, the table, the service, the company.

He could not keep his eyes from continually straying sidewise to his hostess. Never had he seen color in human flesh so regally set: the rich and flowing grace of the dress out of which rose so darkly splendid the jeweled flesh. The black and purple hair was heaped up on her little head, and in its depths gleamed a tiny coronet of gold. Her voice and her poise, her self-possession and air of quiet command, kept Matthew staring almost unmannerly, despite the fact that he somehow sensed a shade of resentment in the young and handsome Indian opposite.

They had eaten some delicious tidbits of meat and vegetables and then were served with a delicate soup when the Princess, turning slightly to her right, said:

"You will note, Mr. Towns, that we represent here much of the Darker World. Indeed, when all our circle is present, we represent all of it, save your world of Black Folk."

"All the darker world except the darkest," said the Egyptian.

"A pretty large omission," said Matthew with a smile.

"I agree," said the Chinaman; but the Arab said something abruptly in French. Matthew had said that he knew "some" French. But his French was of the American variety which one excavates from dictionaries and cements with grammar, like bricks. He was astounded at the ease and the fluency with which most of this company used languages, so easily, without groping or hesitation and with light, sure shading. They talked art in French, literature in Italian, politics in German, and everything in clear English.

"M. Ben Ali suggests," said the Princess, "that even you are not black, Mr. Towns."

"My grandfather was, and my soul is. Black blood with us in America is a matter of spirit and not simply of flesh."

"Ah! mixed blood," said the Egyptian.

"Like all of us, especially me," laughed the Princess.

"But, your Royal Highness—not Negro," said the elder Indian in a tone that hinted a protest.

"Essentially," said the Princess lightly, "as our black and curly-haired Lord Buddha testifies in a hundred places. But"—a bit imperiously—"enough of that. Our point is that Pan-Africa belongs logically with Pan-Asia; and for that reason Mr. Towns is welcomed tonight by you, I am sure, and by me especially. He did me a service as I was returning from the New Palace."

They all looked interested, but the Egyptian broke out:

"Ah, Your Highness, the New Palace, and what is the fad today? What has followed expressionism, cubism, futurism, vorticism? I confess myself at sea. Picasso alarms me. Matisse sets me aflame. But I do not understand them. I prefer the classics."

"The Congo," said the Princess, "is flooding the Acropolis. There is a beautiful Kandinsky on exhibit, and some lovely and startling things by unknown newcomers."

"*Mais,*" replied the Egyptian, dropping into French—and they were all off to the discussion, save the silent Egyptian woman and the taciturn Arab.

Here again Matthew was puzzled. These persons easily penetrated worlds where he was a stranger. Frankly, but for the context he would not have known whether Picasso was a man, a city, or a vegetable. He had never heard of Matisse. Lightly, almost carelessly, as he thought, his companions leapt to unknown subjects. Yet they knew. They knew art, books, and literature, politics of all nations, and not newspaper politics merely, but inner currents and whisperings, unpublished facts.

"Ah, pardon," said the Egyptian, returning to English, "I forgot Monsieur Towns speaks only English and does not interest himself in art."

Perhaps Matthew was sensitive and imagined that the Egyptian and the Indian rather often, if not purposely, strayed to French and subjects beyond him.

"Mr. Towns is a scientist?" asked the Japanese.

"He studies medicine," answered the Princess.

"Ah—a high service," said the Japanese. "I was reading only today of the work on cancer by your Peyton Rous in Carrel's laboratory."

Towns was surprised. "What, has he discovered the etiological factor? I had not heard."

"No, not yet, but he's a step nearer."

For a few moments Matthew was talking eagerly, until a babble of unknown tongues interrupted him across the table.

"Proust is dead, that 'snob of humor'—yes, but his *Recherche du Temps Perdu* is finished and will be published in full. I have only glanced at parts of it. Do you know Gasquet's *Hymnes?*"

"Beraud gets the Prix Goncourt this year. Last year it was the Negro, Maran—"

"I have been reading Croce's *Aesthetic* lately—"

"Yes, I saw the Meyerhold theater in Moscow—gaunt realism—*Howl China* was tremendous."

Then easily, after the crisp brown fowl, the Princess tactfully steered them back to the subject which some seemed willing to avoid.

"And so," she said, "the darker peoples who are dissatisfied—"

She looked at the Japanese and paused as though inviting comment. He bowed courteously.

"If I may presume, your Royal Highness, to suggest," he said slowly, "the two categories are not synonymous. We ourselves know no line of color. Some of us are white, some yellow, some black. Rather, is it not, your Highness, that we have from time to time taken council with the oppressed peoples of the world, many of whom by chance are colored?"

"True, true," said the Princess.

"And yet," said the Chinese lady, "it is dominating Europe which has flung this challenge of the color line, and we cannot avoid it."

"And on either count," said Matthew, "whether we be bound by oppression or by color, surely we Negroes belong in the foremost ranks."

There was a slight pause, a sort of hesitation, and it seemed to Matthew as though all expected the Japanese to speak. He did, slowly and gravely:

"It would be unfair to our guest not to explain with some clarity and precision that the whole question of the Negro race both in Africa and in America is for us not simply a question of suffering and compassion. Need we say that for these peoples we have every human sympathy? But for us here and for the larger company we represent, there is a deeper question— that of the ability, qualifications, and real possibilities of the black race in Africa or elsewhere."

Matthew left the piquant salad and laid down his fork slowly. Up to this moment he had been quite happy. Despite the feeling of being out of it now and then, he had assumed that this was his world, his people, from the high and beautiful lady whom he worshiped more and more, even to the Egyptians, Indians, and Arab who seemed slightly, but very slightly, aloof or misunderstanding.

Suddenly now there loomed plain and clear the shadow of a color line within a color line, a prejudice within prejudice, and he and his again the sacrifice. His eyes became somber and did not lighten even when the Princess spoke.

JOHN STEINBECK

East of Eden

John Steinbeck (1902–1968), awarded the Nobel Prize in 1962, was born to a family of modest means in California, working his way through Stanford without graduating. Among his best-known work is his fiction set in Monterey, such as *Tortilla Flat* (1935) and *Cannery Row* (1945), and his novels about labor disputes and the aspirations of migrant farm workers, such as *In Dubious Battle* (1936), *Of Mice and Men* (1937), and the Pulitzer Prize–winning *The Grapes of Wrath* (1939). But Steinbeck was also at home in many other genres. *The Log from the Sea of Cortez* (1951) recounts a natural history expedition with Ed Ricketts to the Gulf of California, while *The Moon Is Down* (1942) imagines resistance to Nazi occupation in a village in northern Europe. The latter was immediately made into a film, as were *Tortilla Flat*, *Of Mice and Men*, and *The Grapes of Wrath*. In this excerpt from *East of Eden* (1952), a novel about the intertwined lives of two families in the Salinas Valley and probably Steinbeck's most ambitious work, a prosperous Irish American discusses pidgin English with a Chinese American cook.

"What's your name?" Samuel asked pleasantly.

"Lee. Got more name. Lee papa family name. Call Lee."

"I've read quite a lot about China. You born in China?"

"No. Born here."

Samuel was silent for quite a long time while the buggy lurched down the wheel track toward the dusty valley. "Lee," he said at last, "I mean no disrespect, but I've never been able to figure why you people still talk pidgin when an illiterate baboon from the black bogs of Ireland, with a head full of Gaelic and a tongue like a potato, learns to talk a poor grade of English in ten years."

Lee grinned. "Me talkee Chinese talk," he said.

"Well, I guess you have your reasons. And it's not my affair. I hope you'll forgive me if I don't believe it, Lee."

Lee looked at him and the brown eyes under their rounded upper lids seemed to open and deepen until they weren't foreign any more, but man's eyes, warm with understanding. Lee chuckled. "It's more than a convenience," he said. "It's even more than self-protection. Mostly we have to use it to be understood at all."

Samuel showed no sign of having observed any change. "I can understand the first two," he said thoughtfully, "but the third escapes me."

Lee said, "I know it's hard to believe, but it has happened so often to me and to my friends that we take it for granted. If I should go up to a lady or a gentleman, for instance, and speak as I am doing now, I wouldn't be understood."

"Why not?"

"Pidgin they expect, and pidgin they'll listen to. But English from me they don't listen to, and so they don't understand it."

"Can that be possible? How do I understand you?"

"That's why I'm talking to you. You are one of the rare people who can separate your observation from your preconception. You see what is, where most people see what they expect."

"I hadn't thought of it. And I've not been so tested as you, but what you say has a candle of truth. You know, I'm very glad to talk to you. I've wanted to ask so many questions."

"Happy to oblige."

"So many questions. For instance, you wear the queue. I've read that it is a badge of slavery imposed by conquest by the Manchus on the Southern Chinese."

"That is true."

"Then why in the name of God do you wear it here, where the Manchus can't get at you?"

"Talkee Chinese talk. Queue Chinese fashion—you savvy?"

Samuel laughed loudly. "That does have the green touch of convenience," he said. "I wish I had a hidey-hole like that."

"I'm wondering whether I can explain," said Lee. "Where there is no likeness of experience it's very difficult. I understand you were not born in America."

"No, in Ireland."

"And in a few years you can almost disappear; while I, who was born in Grass Valley, went to school and several years to the University of California, have no chance of mixing."

"If you cut your queue, dressed and talked like other people?"

"No. I tried it. To the so-called whites I was still a Chinese, but an untrustworthy one; and at the same time my Chinese friends steered clear of me. I had to give it up."

Lee pulled up under a tree, got out and unfastened the check rein. "Time for lunch," he said. "I made a package. Would you like some?"

"Sure I would. Let me get down in the shade there. I forget to eat sometimes, and that's strange because I'm always hungry. I'm interested in what you say. It has a sweet sound of authority. Now it peeks into my mind that you should go back to China."

Lee smiled satirically at him. "In a few minutes I don't think you'll find a loose bar I've missed in a lifetime of search. I did go back to China. My father was a fairly successful man. It didn't work. They said I looked like a foreign devil; they said I spoke like a foreign devil. I made mistakes in manners, and I didn't know delicacies that had grown up since my father left. They wouldn't have me. You can believe it or not—I'm less foreign here than I was in China."

"I'll have to believe you because it's reasonable. You've given me things to think about until at least February twenty-seventh. Do you mind my questions?"

"As a matter of fact, no. The trouble with pidgin is that you get to thinking in pidgin. I write a great deal to keep my English up. Hearing and reading aren't the same as speaking and writing."

"Don't you ever make a mistake? I mean, break into English?"

"No, I don't. I think it's a matter of what is expected. You look at a man's eyes, you see that he expects pidgin and a shuffle, so you speak pidgin and shuffle."

"I guess that's right," said Samuel. "In my own way I tell jokes because people come all the way to my place to laugh. I try to be funny for them even when the sadness is on me."

"But the Irish are said to be a happy people, full of jokes."

"There's your pidgin and your queue. They're not. They're a dark people with a gift for suffering way past their deserving. It's said that without whisky to soak and soften the world, they'd kill themselves. But they tell jokes because it's expected of them."

Lee unwrapped a little bottle. "Would you like some of this? Chinee drink ng-ka-py."

"What is it?"

"Chinee blandy. Stlong dlink—as a matter of fact it's a brandy with a dosage of wormwood. Very powerful. It softens the world."

Samuel sipped from the bottle. "Tastes a little like rotten apples," he said.

"Yes, but nice rotten apples. Taste it back along your tongue toward the roots."

Samuel took a big swallow and tilted his head back. "I see what you mean. That *is* good."

LANGSTON HUGHES

Something in Common

Langston Hughes (1902–1967), as noted in the "War" section of this anthology, was a key figure of the Harlem Renaissance. His "The Negro Artist and the Racial Mountain" (1926) is often taken as a manifesto of the Harlem Renaissance, one that celebrates the vernacular language and the street-wise, improvisatory cadences of jazz. Hughes collaborated with many musicians, including Kurt Weill in the Broadway opera *Street Scene* (1947) and Charles Mingus in the *Weary Blues* album (1959). In "Something in Common," he depicts a different kind of collaboration, the improvised solidarity of two Americans, one black and one white, and both down and out in the British colony of Hong Kong.

Hong Kong. A hot day. A teeming street. A mélange of races. A pub, over the door the Union Jack.

The two men were not together. They came in from the street, complete strangers, through different doors, but they both reached the bar at about the same time. The big British bartender looked at each of them with a wary, scornful eye. He knew that, more than likely, neither had the price of more than a couple of drinks. They were distinctly down at the heel, had been drinking elsewhere, and were not customers of the bar. He served them with a deliberation that was not even condescending—it was menacing.

"A beer," said the old Negro, rattling a handful of Chinese and English coins at the end of a frayed cuff.

"A scotch," said the old white man, reaching for a pretzel with thin fingers.

"That's the tariff," said the bartender, pointing to a sign.

"Too high for this lousy Hong Kong beer," said the old Negro. The barman did not deign to answer.

"But, reckon it's as good as some we got back home," the elderly colored man went on as he counted out the money.

"I'll bet you wouldn't mind bein' back there, George," spoke up the old white man from the other end of the bar, "in the good old U.S.A."

"Don't *George* me," said the Negro, "'cause I don't know you from Adam."

"Well, don't get sore," said the old white man, coming nearer, sliding his glass along the bar. "I'm from down home, too."

"Well, I ain't from no *down home*," answered the Negro wiping beer foam from his mouth. "I'm from the North."

"Where?"

"North of Mississippi," said the black man. "I mean Missouri."

"I'm from Kentucky," vouched the old white fellow swallowing his whisky. "Gimme another one," to the bartender.

"Half a dollar," said the bartender.

"Mex, you mean?"

"Yeah, mex," growled the bartender picking up the glass.

"All right, I'll pay you," said the white man testily. "Gimme another one."

"They're tough in this here bar," said the old Negro sarcastically. "Looks like they don't know a Kentucky colonel when they see one."

"No manners in these damned foreign joints," said the white man seriously. "How long you been in Hong Kong?"

"Too long," said the old Negro.

"Where'd you come from here?"

"Manila," said the Negro.

"What'd you do there?"

"Now what else do you want to know?" asked the Negro.

"I'm askin' you a civil question," said the old white man.

"Don't ask so many then," said the Negro, "and don't start out by callin' me *George*. My name ain't George."

"What is your name, might I ask?" taking another pretzel.

"Samuel Johnson. And your'n?"

"Colonel McBride."

"Of Kentucky?" grinned the Negro impudently toothless.

"Yes, sir, of Kentucky," said the white man seriously.

"Howdy, Colonel," said the Negro. "Have a pretzel."

"Have a drink, boy," said the white man, beckoning the bartender.

"Don't call me *boy*," said the Negro. "I'm as old as you, if not older."

"Don't care," said the white man, "have a drink."

"Gin," said the Negro.

"Make it two," said the white man. "Gin's somethin' we both got in common."

"I love gin," said the Negro.

"Me, too," said the white man.

"Gin's a sweet drink," mused the Negro, "especially when you're around women."

"Gimme one white woman," said the old white man, "and you can take all these Chinee gals over here."

"Gimme one yellow gal," said the old Negro, "and you can take all your white women anywhere."

"Hong Kong's full of yellow gals," said the white man.

"I mean *high-yellow* gals," said the Negro, "like we have in Missouri."

"Or in Kentucky," said the white man, "where half of 'em has white pappys."

"Here! Don't talk 'bout my women," said the old Negro. "I don't allow no white man to talk 'bout my women."

"Who's talkin' about your women? Have a drink, George."

"I told you, don't *George* me. My name is Samuel Johnson. White man, you ain't in Kentucky now. You in the Far East."

"I know it. If I was in Kentucky, I wouldn't be standin' at this bar with you. Have a drink."

"Gin."

"Make it two."

"Who's payin'?" said the bartender.

"Not me," said the Negro. "Not *me*."

"Don't worry," said the old white man grandly.

"Well, I am worryin'," growled the bartender. "Cough up."

"Here," said the white man, pulling out a few shillings. "Here, even if it is my last penny, here!"

The bartender took it without a word. He picked up the glasses and wiped the bar.

"I can't seem to get ahead in this damn town," said the old white man, "and I been here since Coolidge."

"Neither do I," said the Negro, "and I come before the War."

"Where is your home, George?" asked the white man.

"You must think it's Georgia," said the Negro. "Truth is I ain't got no home—no more home than a dog."

"Neither have I," said the white man, "but sometimes I wish I was back in the States."

"Well, I don't," said the Negro. "A black man ain't got a break in the States."

"What?" said the old white man, drawing up proudly.

"States is no good," said the Negro. "No damned good."

"Shut up," yelled the old white man waving a pretzel.

"What do you mean, shut up?" said the Negro.

"I won't listen to nobody runnin' down the United States," said the white man. "You better stop insultin' America, you big black ingrate."

"You better stop insultin' me, you poor-white trash," bristled the aged Negro. Both of them reeled indignantly.

"Why, you black bastard!" quavered the old white man.

"You white cracker!" trembled the elderly Negro.

These final insults caused the two old men to square off like roosters, rocking a little from age and gin, but glaring fiercely at one another, their gnarled fists doubled up, arms at boxing angles.

"Here! Here!" barked the bartender. "Hey! Stop it now!"

"I'll bat you one," said the white man to the Negro.

"I'll fix you so you can't leave, neither can you stay," said the Negro to the white.

"Yuh will, will yuh?" sneered the bartender to both of them. "I'll see about batting—and fixing, too."

He came around the end of the bar in three long strides. He grabbed the two old men unceremoniously by the scruff of their necks, cracked their heads together twice, and threw them both calmly into the street. Then he wiped his hands.

The white and yellow world of Hong Kong moved by, rickshaw runners pushed and panted, motor horns blared, pedestrians crowded the narrow sidewalks. The two old men picked themselves up from the dust and dangers of a careless traffic. They looked at one another, dazed for a moment and considerably shaken.

"Well, I'll be damned!" sputtered the old white man. "Are we gonna stand for this—from a Limey bartender?"

"Hell, no," said the old Negro. "Let's go back in there and clean up that joint."

"He's got no rights to put his Cockney hands on Americans," said the old white man.

"Sure ain't," agreed the old Negro.

Arm in arm, they staggered back into the bar, united to protect their honor against the British.

JAMES BALDWIN

Encounter on the Seine: Black Meets Brown

James Baldwin (1924–1987), raised in a Pentecostal home, began preaching at an early age and drawing large crowds. In his teens he drifted away from Christianity while attending the mostly Jewish DeWitt Clinton High School in the Bronx. In 1948 he left for Paris, spending many years in France and Turkey and producing a large and diverse corpus shaped by his experience of religion, racism, and homosexuality on both sides of the Atlantic. His first novel, *Go Tell it On the Mountain* (1953), is followed by *The Amen Corner* (1954), his first play, and the essay collections *Notes of a Native Son* (1955) and *The Fire Next Time* (1963). He returned to the United States in 1963 to take an active part in the Civil Rights Movement. In *No Name in the Street* (1972), he wrote about the assassinations of three personal friends: Medgar Evers, Malcolm X, and Martin Luther King, Jr. In the following essay from *Notes of a Native Son,* he affirms his hybrid identity as an African American from the United States, against the foil of Africans from Africa, whom he encountered in Paris.

In Paris nowadays it is rather more difficult for an American Negro to become a really successful entertainer than it is rumored to have been some thirty years ago. For one thing, champagne has ceased to be drunk out of slippers, and the frivolously colored thousand-franc note is neither as elastic nor as freely spent as it was in the 1920's. The musicians and singers who are here now must work very hard indeed to acquire the polish and style which will land them in the big time. Bearing witness to this eternally tantalizing possibility, performers whose eminence is unchallenged, like Duke Ellington or Louis Armstrong, occasionally pass through. Some of their ambitious followers are in or near the big time already; others are gaining reputations which have yet to be tested in the States. Gordon Heath, who will be remembered for his performances as the embattled soldier in Broadway's *Deep Are the Roots* some seasons back, sings ballads nightly in his own night club on the Rue L'Abbaye; and everyone who comes to Paris these days sooner or later discovers Chez Inez, a night club in the Latin Quarter run by a singer named Inez Cavanaugh, which specializes in fried chicken and jazz. It is at Chez Inez that many an unknown first performs in public, going on thereafter, if not always to greater triumphs, at least to other night clubs, and possibly landing a contract to tour the Riviera during the spring and summer.

In general, only the Negro entertainers are able to maintain a useful and unquestioning comradeship with other Negroes. Their nonperforming, colored countrymen are, nearly to a man, incomparably more isolated, and it must be conceded that this isolation is deliberate. It is estimated that there are five hundred American Negroes living in this city, the vast majority of them veterans studying on the G.I. Bill. They are studying everything from the Sorbonne's standard *Cours de Civilisation Française* to abnormal psychology, brain surgery, music, fine arts, and literature. Their isolation from each other is not difficult to understand if one bears in mind the axiom, unquestioned by American landlords, that Negroes are happy only when they are kept together. Those driven to break this pattern by leaving the U.S. ghettos not merely have effected a social and physical leave-taking but also have been precipitated into cruel psychological warfare. It is altogether inevitable that past humiliations should become associated not only with one's traditional oppressors but also with one's traditional kinfolk.

Thus the sight of a face from home is not invariably a source of joy, but can also quite easily become a source of embarrassment or rage. The American Negro in Paris is forced at last to exercise an undemocratic discrimination rarely practiced by Americans, that of judging his people, duck by duck, and distinguishing them one from another. Through this deliberate isolation, through lack of numbers, and above all through his own overwhelming need to be, as it were, forgotten, the American Negro in Paris is very nearly the invisible man.

The wariness with which he regards his colored kin is a natural extension of the wariness with which he regards all of his countrymen. At the beginning, certainly, he cherishes rather exaggerated hopes of the French. His white countrymen, by and large, fail to justify his fears, partly because the social climate does not encourage an outward display of racial bigotry, partly out of their awareness of being ambassadors, and finally, I should think, because they are themselves relieved at being no longer forced to think in terms of color. There remains, nevertheless, in the encounter of white Americans and Negro Americans the high potential of an awkward or an ugly situation.

The white American regards his darker brother through the distorting screen created by a lifetime of conditioning. He is accustomed to regard him either as a needy and deserving martyr or as the soul of rhythm, but he is more than a little intimidated to find this stranger so many miles from home. At first he tends instinctively, whatever his intelligence may belatedly clamor, to take it as a reflection on his personal honor and good-will; and at the same time, with that winning generosity, at once good-natured and uneasy, which characterizes Americans, he would like to establish communication, and sympathy, with his compatriot. "And how do *you* feel about it?" he would like to ask, "it" being anything—the Russians, Betty Grable, the Place de la Concorde. The trouble here is that any "it," so tentatively offered, may suddenly become loaded and vibrant with tension, creating in the air between the two thus met an intolerable atmosphere of danger.

The Negro, on the other hand, via the same conditioning which constricts the outward gesture of the whites, has learned to anticipate: as the mouth opens he divines what the tongue will utter. He has had time, too, long before he came to Paris, to reflect on the absolute and personally expensive futility of taking any one of his countrymen to task for his status in America, or of hoping to convey to them any of his experience. The American Negro and white do not, therefore, discuss the past, except in considerately guarded snatches. Both are quite willing, and indeed quite wise, to remark instead the considerably overrated impressiveness of the Eiffel Tower.

The Eiffel Tower has naturally long since ceased to divert the French, who consider that all Negroes arrive from America, trumpet-laden and twinkle-toed, bearing scars so unutterably painful that all of the glories of the French Republic may not suffice to heal them. This indignant generosity poses problems of its own, which, language and custom being what they are, are not so easily averted.

The European tends to avoid the really monumental confusion which might result from an attempt to apprehend the relationship of the forty-eight states to one another, clinging instead to such information as is afforded by radio, press, and film, to anecdotes considered to be illustrative of American life, and to the myth that we have ourselves perpetuated. The result, in conversation, is rather like seeing one's back yard reproduced with extreme fidelity, but in such a perspective that it becomes a place which one has never seen or visited, which never has existed, and which never can exist. The Negro is forced to say "Yes" to many a difficult question, and yet to deny the conclusion to which his answers seem to point. His past, he now realizes, has not been simply a series of ropes and bonfires and humiliations, but something vastly more complex, which, as he thinks painfully, "It was much worse than that," was also, he irrationally feels, something much better. As it is useless to excoriate his countrymen, it is galling now to be pitied as a victim, to accept this ready sympathy which is limited only by its failure to accept him as an American. He finds himself involved, in another language, in the same old battle: the battle for his own identity. To accept the reality of his being an American becomes a matter involving his integrity and his greatest hopes, for only by accepting this reality can he hope to make articulate to himself or to others the uniqueness of his experience, and to set free the spirit so long anonymous and caged.

The ambivalence of his status is thrown into relief by his encounters with the Negro students from France's colonies who live in Paris. The French African comes from a region and a way of life which—at least from the American point of view—is exceedingly primitive, and where exploitation takes more *naked* forms. In Paris, the *African Negro's* status, conspicuous and subtly inconvenient, is that of a colonial; and he leads here the intangibly precarious life of someone abruptly and recently uprooted. His bitterness is unlike that of his American kinsman in that it is not so treacherously likely to be turned against himself. He has, not so very many miles away, a homeland to which his relationship, no less than his responsibility, is overwhelmingly clear: His country must be given—or it must seize—its freedom. This bitter ambition is shared by his fellow colonials, with whom he has a common language, and whom he has no wish whatever to avoid; without whose sustenance, indeed, he would be almost altogether lost in Paris. They live in groups together, in the same neighborhoods, in student hotels and under conditions which cannot fail to impress the American as almost unendurable.

Yet what the American is seeing is not simply the poverty of the student but the enormous gap between the European and American standards of living. *All* of the students in the Latin Quarter live in ageless, sinister-looking hotels; they are all forced continually to choose between cigarettes and cheese at lunch.

It is true that the poverty and anger which the American Negro sees must be related to Europe and not to America. Yet, as he wishes for a moment that he were home again, where at least the terrain is familiar, there begins to race within him, like the despised beat of the tom-tom, echoes of a past which he has not yet been able to utilize, intimations of a responsibility which he has not yet been able to face. He begins to conjecture how much he has gained and lost during his long sojourn in the American republic. The African before him has endured privation, injustice, medieval cruelty; but the African has not yet endured the utter alienation of himself from his people and his past. His mother did not sing "Sometimes I Feel Like a Motherless Child," and he has not, all his life long, ached for acceptance in a culture which pronounced straight-hair and white skin the only acceptable beauty.

They face each other, the Negro and the African, over a gulf of three hundred years—an alienation too vast to be conquered in an evening's goodwill, too heavy and too double-edged ever to be trapped in speech. This alienation causes the Negro to recognize that he is a hybrid. Not a physical hybrid merely: in every aspect of his living he betrays the memory of the auction block and the impact of the happy ending. In white Americans he finds reflected—repeated, as it were, in a higher key—his tensions, his terrors, his tenderness. Dimly and for the first time, there begins to fall into perspective the nature of the roles they have played in the lives and history of each other. Now he is bone of their bone, flesh of their flesh; they have loved and hated and obsessed and feared each other and his blood is in their soil. Therefore he cannot deny them, nor can they ever be divorced.

The American Negro cannot explain to the African what surely seems in himself to be a want of manliness, of racial pride, a maudlin ability to forgive. It is difficult to make clear that he is not seeking to forfeit his birthright as a black man, but that, on the contrary, it is precisely this birthright which he is struggling to recognize and make articulate. Perhaps it now occurs to him that in this need to establish himself in relation to his past he is most American, that this depthless alienation from oneself and one's people is, in sum, the American experience.

Yet one day he will face his home again; nor can he realistically expect to find overwhelming changes. In America, it is true, the appearance is perpetually changing, each generation greeting with short-lived exultation yet more dazzling additions to our renowned façade. But the ghetto, anxiety, bitterness, and guilt continue to breed their indescribable complex of tensions. What time will bring Americans is at last their own identity. It is on this dangerous voyage and in the same boat that the American Negro will make peace with himself and with the voiceless many thousands gone before him.

MAYA ANGELOU

All God's Children Need Traveling Shoes

Maya Angelou (1928–2014) was the author of seven autobiographies, five books of essays, and several volumes of poetry, some of which have been made into plays, movies, and television shows. The child of a broken home, she lived haphazardly in St. Louis; Stamps, Arkansas; and Oakland, California before the age of seventeen, when she became a single mother. She made a living as a calypso singer and dancer during the 1950s. In the 1960s, she worked as a journalist in Egypt and Ghana, becoming close friends with Malcolm X while in the latter country. Her first autobiography, *I Know Why the Caged Bird Sings* (1969), brought her international acclaim. She was President Clinton's inaugural poet in 1993, reading "On the Pulse of Morning." In this excerpt from her fifth autobiography, *All God's Children Need Traveling Shoes* (1986), Angelou describes the mutual racism traded back and forth between black Americans and black Africans in Ghana.

The editor's office of the *Ghanaian Times* had all the excitement of a busy city intersection. People came, left, talked, shouted, laid down papers, picked up packages, spoke English, Fanti, Twi, Ga and Pidgin on the telephone or to each other.

T. D. Kwesi Bafoo perched behind his desk as if it was the starting mark for a one hundred yard sprint. At a signal he would leap up and hurl himself past me, through the crowded room and out of the door.

His cheeks, brows, eyes and hands moved even before he talked.

I said, "I am a journalist. I've brought some examples of my work. These are from the *Arab Observer* in Cairo." He waved away my folder and said, "We know who you are. A good writer, and that you are a Nkrumaist." I was certainly the latter and not yet the former.

As he stuffed papers into a briefcase he asked, "Can you write a piece on America today?"

"Today? Do you mean right now?"

He looked at me and grinned, "No. America today. America, capitalism and racial prejudice."

"In one article?" I didn't want him to know the request was implausible.

He said, "A sort of overview. You understand?"

I asked, seriously, "How many words, three thousand?"

He answered without looking at me, "Three hundred. Just the high points."

The seething energy would no longer be contained. Bafoo was on his feet and around the desk before I could rise.

"We'll pay you the standard fee. Have it here by Friday. I have another meeting. Pleasure meeting you. Good-bye."

He passed and disappeared through the door before I had gathered my purse and briefcase. I imagined him running up to the next appointment, arriving there in a heat, simmering during the meeting, then racing away to the next, and on and on. The picture of Mr. Bafoo so entertained me that I was outside on the street before the realization came to me that I had another job which paid "the standard fee." I was earning that at the university. In order to afford luxuries I had to look further.

The Ghana Broadcasting office was as to the *Times* newspaper office what a drawing room was to a dance hall. The lobby was large, well furnished and quiet. A receptionist, pretty and dressed in western clothes, looked at me so quizzically, I thought perhaps she knew something I needed to know.

She frowned, wrinkling her careful loveliness. "Yes? You want to talk to someone about writing?" Her voice was as crisp as a freshly starched and ironed doily.

I said, "Yes. I am a writer."

She shook her head, "But who? Who do you want to talk to?" She couldn't believe in my ignorance.

I said, "I don't know. I suppose the person who hires writers."

"But what is his name?" She had begun to smile, and I heard her sarcasm.

"I don't know his name. Don't you know it?" I knew that hostility would gain me nothing but the front door, so I tried to charm her. "I mean, surely you know who I should see." I gave her a little submissive smile and knew that if I got a job I'd never speak to her again.

She dismissed my attempt at flattery by saying curtly, "I am the receptionist. It is my job to know everyone in the building," and picked up the morning paper.

I persisted, "Well, who should I see?"

She looked up from the page and smiled patronizingly. "You should see who you want to see. Who do you want to see?" She knew herself to be a cat and I was a wounded bird. I decided to remove myself from her grasp. I leaned forward and imitating her accent. I said, "You silly ass, you can take a flying leap and go straight to hell."

Her smile never changed. "American Negroes are always crude."

ISHMAEL REED

Flight to Canada

Ishmael Reed (born 1938) is best known for his satirical works, including *Yellow Back Radio Broke-Down* (1969), *Mumbo Jumbo* (1972), and *Flight to Canada* (1976), taking shots at ethnic and political pieties of all stripes, and at traditional genres such as the slave narrative and the cowboy Western. Born in Chattanooga, Tennessee, and educated at the University at Buffalo, he spent his formative years in New York City as a member of the Umbra Writer's Workshop. Moving to Oakland, California, in the late sixties, he taught at UC Berkeley for thirty-five years, retiring in 2005. His corpus includes ten novels, six collections of poetry, ten collections of essays, a libretto, and six plays. He has also edited thirteen anthologies, championing the works of many contemporary writers. His lyrics have been set to music by Carla Bley, Taj Mahal, and Allen Toussaint, among others. Reed received a MacArthur Fellowship in 1998. *Flight to Canada,* excerpted below, mockingly stages a competition between an ex-slave and a Jewish immigrant over who was more victimized by history.

―――――――――――――――――――――――――――――――――――――――

The Slave Hole Café is where the "community" in Emancipation City hangs out. The wallpaper shows a map of the heavens. Prominent is the North Star. A slave with rucksack is pointing it out to his dog. The cafe is furnished with tables, chairs, sofas, from different periods. There are quite a few captain's chairs, deacon's benches. There are posters and paintings and framed programs: *Our American Cousin,* a play by Tom Tyler; a photo of Lincoln boarding a train on the way back to Washington from a trip to Emancipation. Sawdust on the floor. A barrel of dill pickles. Above the long bar is a sign: PABST BLUE RIBBON. Corn-row and nappy-haired field slaves are here as well as a quadroon or two. Carpetbaggers, Abolitionists, Secessionists, or "Seceshes," as they are called, even some Copperheads. The secret society known as the "Rattlesnake" order meets here. They advertise their meetings in the Emancipation newspaper: "Attention, Rattlesnakes, come out of your holes ... by order of President Grand Rattle. Poison Fang, Secretary."

Confederate sympathizers go to places named the Alabama Club, but some come here, too. They've been known to smash a bottle after a slave has drunk from it. Ducktail hairdos go here. Crossbars of the Confederate fly from pickup trucks.

Quickskill ran into the Slave Hole out of breath, went to a table where he saw Leechfield's Indentured Servant friend, the Immigrant, Mel Leer. Well, he wasn't indentured any more. He had served his contract and was now at liberty. He and Leechfield were inseparable. When he plopped into the chair the Immigrant rustled his newspaper in annoyance. His hair was wild, uncombed black curls, and he kept brushing some away from the left side of his forehead. He had an intense look, like Yul Brynner, wore long flowing ties and velvet suits and some kind of European shoes. Lace cuffs. Jewelry.

"Man, two guys just tried to confiscate me. Put a claim check on me just like I was somebody's will-call or something," panted Quickskill.

"Kvetch! Always kvetch!"

"What do you mean kvetch? If I hadn't run away, I'd be in a van on the way back to Virginia."

The waitress brought him a frosty mug of beer like the kind they feature at Sam's Chinese restaurant on Yonge Street in Toronto.

The Immigrant looked at him. "Your people think that you corner the market on the business of atrocity. My relatives were dragged through the streets of St. Petersburg, weren't permitted to go to school in Moscow, were pogrommed in Poland. There were taxes on our synagogues and even on our meat. We were forbidden to trade on Sundays and weren't allowed to participate in agriculture. They forced us into baptism against our wishes. Hooligans were allowed to attack us with weapons, and the police just stood there, laughing. Your people haven't suffered that much. I can prove it, statistically."

"Oh yeah? Nobody's stoning you in the streets here. You are doing quite well, hanging in cafes, going to parties with Leechfield. And you have a nice place to live. What are you bitchin about? All you and Leechfield seem to do is party and eat ice cream topped with creme de menthe."

"There are more types of slavery than merely material slavery. There's a cultural slavery. I have to wait as long as two weeks sometimes before I can get a *Review of Books* from New York. This America, it has no salvation. Did you see what happened in those battles? At Bull Run? They were like picnics attended by the rich. Cowboyland. Look at this filth …" It was a copy of *Life* magazine; a photo of the carnage at Gettysburg. "Filth! Obscene! Disgusting! Just as this country is. Why, during the whole time I've been in this town, I haven't seen one person reading Dostoevsky. Your people! Requesting wages and leaving their plantations. They should pay for themselves. Look at us. We were responsible. We paid for ourselves. Paid our way. I earned myself! We never sassed the master, and when we were punished we always admitted that we were in the wrong. The whole world, sometimes, seems to be against us. Always passing resolutions against us. Hissing us. Nobody has suffered as much as we have."

"Nobody has suffered as much as my people," says Quickskill calmly.

The Immigrant, Mel Leer, rises. "Don't tell me that lie."

The whole cafe turns to the scene.

"Our people have suffered the most."

"My people!"

"My people!"

"My people!"

"My people!"

"We suffered under the hateful Czar Nicholas!"

"We suffered under Swille and Legree, the most notorious Masters in the annals of slavery!"

AUDRE LORDE

Zami: A New Spelling of My Name

Audre Lorde (1934–1992), poet, essayist, and novelist, was born in New York City to parents from Grenada. Her mother spoke patois and told the children stories from Carriacou, an island of the Grenadines. Lorde (who dropped the "y" from "Audrey" so that the two halves of her name would be symmetrical) strongly identified with this mythic Grenada. While attending Hunter College she spent a crucial year, 1954, at the National University of Mexico. In her "biomythography," *Zami: A New Spelling of My Name* (1982), she wrote that her new identity as lesbian and poet was signaled by this "Carriacou word for women who work together as friends and lovers." Born near-sighted, indeed legally blind, Lorde also spent the last fourteen years of her life battling cancer, an ordeal she recounts in *Cancer Journals* (1980). Her last book of poetry, *The Marvelous Arithmetics of Distance* (1993), was published posthumously. In this selection from *Zami*, Lorde describes the exhilarating, interracial world of Mexico City and Cuernavaca.

From the Palace of Fine Arts to El Angel de la Reforma, along the broad Avenida Insurgentes, lay the central hub of the Districto Federal, Mexico City. It was a sea of strange sounds and smells and experiences that I swam into with delight daily. It took me two days to adjust to the high altitude of the city, and to the realization that I was in a foreign country, alone, with only rudimentary language skills.

The first day I explored tentatively. By the second day, alight with the bustle and easy warmth of the streets, I felt filled with the excitement of curiosity and more and more at home. I walked miles and miles through the city, past modern stores and old museums, and families eating beans and tortillas over a brazier between two buildings.

Moving through street after street filled with people with brown faces had a profound and exhilarating effect upon me, unlike any other experience I had ever known.

Friendly strangers, passing smiles, admiring and questioning glances, the sense of being somewhere I wanted to be and had chosen. Being noticed, and accepted without being known, gave me a social contour and surety as I moved through the city sightseeing, and I felt bold and adventurous and special. I reveled in the attention of the shopkeepers around the hotel, from whom I bought my modest provisions.

"¡Ah, la Señorita Moreña! [*moreña* means dark] buenas dias!" The woman from whom I bought my newspaper on the corner of Reforma reached up and patted my short natural hair. "¡Ay, que bonita! ¿Está la Cubana?"

I smiled in return. Because of my coloring and my haircut, I was frequently asked if I was Cuban. "Gracias, señora," I replied, settling the bright *rebozo* I had bought the day before around my shoulders. "No, yo estoy de Nueva York."

Her bright dark eyes widened in amazement and she patted the back of my hand with her dry wrinkled fingers, still holding the coin I had just given her. "Ay, con Dios, niña," she called after me, as I moved on up the street.

By noon, it amazed me that the streets of a city could be so busy and so friendly and the same time. Even with all the new building going on there was a feeling of color and light, made more festive by the colorful murals decorating the sides of high buildings, public and private. Even the university buildings were covered with mosaic murals in dazzling colors.

Lottery-sellers at every corner, and strolling through Chapultepec Park, with strings of gaily colored tickets pinned to their shirts. Children in uniforms coming home from school in groups, and other children, equally bright-eyed, too poor to go to school, sitting crosslegged with their parents on a blanket in the shadow of a building, cutting out soles for cheap sandals from the worn-out treads of discarded tires.

The National Pawn Shop across from the Seguro Social on Friday at noon, long lines of young government workers redeeming guitars and dancing shoes for the weekend ahead. Wide-eyed toddlers who took my hand and led me over to their mothers' wares, set out upon tables shielded by blankets from the sun. People in the street who smiled without knowing me, just because that was what you did with strangers.

There was a beautiful park called the Alameda which ran for blocks through the middle of the district, from Netzahuacoytl down behind the Palacio de Bellas Artes. Some mornings, I left my hotel as soon as it was light, taking a bus to the center of the city to walk in the Alameda. I would have loved to walk there in the astonishing moonlight, but I had heard that single women did not go out alone after dark in Mexico City, so I spent my evenings those early days in Mexico reading *War and Peace*, which I had never been able to get into before.

I got down from the bus in front of the Fine Arts Museum, breathing in the clean smells of wet bushes and morning blossoms and the beautiful delicate trees. Before I entered the park, I bought a *pan dulce* from a delivery boy pedaling past, his huge sombrero with the upturned brim carefully balanced upon his head and piled high with the tasty little buns, still warm from his mother's ovens.

Marble statues dotted the paths throughout the park, where later on in the day workers from the buildings across the street would take their lunchtime *paseo*. My favorite statue was one of a young naked girl in beige stone, kneeling, closely folded in upon herself, head bent, greeting the dawn. As I walked through the fragrant morning quiet in the Alameda, the nearby sounds of traffic increasing yet dimming, I felt myself unfolding like some large flower, as if the statue of the kneeling girl had come alive, raising her head to look full-faced into the sun. As I stepped out into the early morning flow of the *avenida* I felt the light and beauty of the park shining out of me, and the woman lighting her coals in a brazier on the corner smiled back at it in my face.

It was in Mexico City those first few weeks that I started to break my lifelong habit of looking down at my feet as I walked along the street. There was always so much to see, and so many interesting and open faces to read, that I practiced holding my head up as I walked, and the sun felt hot and good on my face. Wherever I went, there were brown faces of every hue meeting mine, and seeing my own color reflected upon the streets in such great numbers was an affirmation for me that was brand-new and very exciting. I had never felt visible before, nor even known I lacked it.

I had not made any friends in Mexico City, although I existed quite happily on part-English, part-Spanish conversations with the chambermaid about the weather, my clothes, and the bidet; with the señora from whom I bought my daily evening meal of two hot tamales wrapped in cornhusks and a bottle of blue-labeled milk; and with the day clerk of the small second-class hotel where I had my tiny room.

At the end of my first week, I went out to the newly bemuraled University City and registered for two courses in the history and ethnology of Mexico, and in folklore. I began to think of looking around for cheaper and more permanent living accommodations. Even with eating inexpensive foods bought from street vendors, not being able to cook was cutting into my small store of money. It also restricted my diet greatly, since I ate only those foods I could be sure would not give me the diarrhea which was the visitors' downfall in Mexico City.

One day, after two weeks in and around the District, I traveled south to Cuernavaca by bus to see Frieda Mathews and her young daughter Tammy. Frieda's name had been given to me by a friend of Rhea's who had been a nurse with Frieda in the Lincoln Brigade during the Spanish Civil War. I had been visiting museums and pyramids, wandering the streets of the city, and generally satisfying my hunger and curiosity for the feel of this new place. Although I was feeling more and more at home, I began to feel the need for someone to talk to in English. Classes a Ciudad Universitaria began the following week.

Cuernavaca was a garden spot south of the District and closer to sea level, in the Morelos Valley about forty-five miles from Mexico City.

When I telephoned, Frieda greeted me warmly and immediately invited me down to Cuernavaca to spend the day. She and Tammy met me at the bus. The weather was warmer and sunnier than in the District, and there was a much more relaxed air about the town square.

As soon as the bus pulled into the square, I recognized the tall blond American woman and the tanned smiling young girl beside her. Frieda looked like she sounded over the phone, a calm, intelligent, and forthright woman in her early forties. Frieda and Tammy had lived in Cuernavaca for nine years, and Frieda was always hungry for news from New York, her original home. "Is the Essex Street Market still open, and what are the writers doing?"

We spent the morning talking about mutual acquaintances and then wandered through the markets on Guerrero buying foodstuffs for diner, which Tammy brought back to their housekeeper to cook. Later, we sat drinking foamy *café con leche* at a table in the open-air café that occupied one whole corner of the town square. Strolling musicians were tuning their guitars in the afternoon suns, and the *chamaquitos*, street urchins, descended upon us begging for pennies, then ran away laughing as Tammy engaged them in rapid Spanish. In short order, other Americans, all of them white and most of them women, strolled over to our table to see who was this new face in town. Frieda introduced me to a host of cordial welcomes.

After the day spent in the easy beauty of Cuernavaca and easy-going company of Frieda and her friends, it took little urging on Frieda's part to persuade me to consider moving down to Cuernavaca. I was still anxious to find cheaper lodgings than the Hotel Fortin. I could commute to the District for classes, she assured me. Many people in Cuernavaca worked in Mexico City, and transportation by bus or group *taximetro* was very inexpensive.

"I think you'll be happier living here than in Mexico City," Frieda offered. It's a lot quieter. You can probably get one of the small houses in the compound over at Humboldt Number Twenty-four, which is a pretty place to live."

Tammy, who was twelve, was delighted to have somebody come to town who was closer to her age than Frieda and her friends.

"And Jesús can help you with your things from the District," Frieda added. With her divorce settlement, Frieda had bought a small farm in Tepotzlán, a tiny village further up the mountain. Jesús managed the farm, she explained. They had once been lovers. "But that's all quite different now," Frieda said brusquely, as Tammy called to us from the patio to come see her *patoganso*, a duck so big it could have been a goose.

I went to see about the little house in the compound that same afternoon.

RAYMOND CHANDLER

The Long Goodbye

Raymond Chandler (1888–1959), one of the great practitioners of hardboiled crime fiction, was born in Chicago, moved with his mother to England, and lived there from 1896 to 1912. He then returned to the United States, fought for Canada on the Western Front in World War I, and worked odd jobs before taking a position at the Dabney Oil Syndicate in 1922. Laid off in 1932 in the midst of the Depression, he finally turned to writing. Chandler published his first story, "Blackmailers Don't Shoot," in the crime fiction magazine *Black Mask* in 1933. His first novel, *The Big Sleep* (1939), introduced Philip Marlowe to the world and won instant acclaim. Terse, tough, and cool, Marlowe, like Dashiell Hammett's Sam Spade, is the quintessential "private eye," immortalized on screen by Humphrey Bogart, with William Faulkner as screenwriter. Marlowe appeared in all of Chandler's subsequent novels, including *Farewell, My Lovely* (1940), *The Little Sister* (1949), and *The Long Goodbye* (1953), from which this excerpt is taken. Here, Marlowe seems to have been outmatched by an elegant, smooth-talking Mexican.

He sat down in the customer's chair and crossed his knees. "You wish certain information about Señor Lennox, I am told."

"The last scene only."

"I was there at the time, señor. I had a position in the hotel." He shrugged. "Unimportant and of course temporary. I was the day clerk." He spoke perfect English but with a Spanish rhythm. Spanish—American Spanish that is—has a definite rise and fall which to an American ear seems to have nothing to do with the meaning. It's like the swell of the ocean.

"You don't look the type," I said.

"One has difficulties."

"Who mailed the letter to me?"

He held out a box of cigarettes. "Try one of these."

I shook my head. "Too strong for me. Colombian cigarettes I like. Cuban cigarettes are murder."

He smiled faintly, lit another pill himself, and blew smoke. The guy was so goddam elegant he was beginning to annoy me.

"I know about the letter, señor. The mozo was afraid to go up to the room of this Señor Lennox after the guarda was posted. The cop or dick, as you say. So I myself took the letter to the correo. After the shooting, you understand."

"You ought to have looked inside. It had a large piece of money in it."

"The letter was sealed," he said coldly. "El honor no se mueve de lado como los congrejos. That is, honor does not move sidewise like a crab, señor."

"My apologies. Please continue."

"Señor Lennox had a hundred-peso note in his left hand when I went into the room and shut the door in the face of the guarda. In his right hand was a pistol. On the table before him was the letter. Also another paper which I did not read. I refused the note."

"Too much money," I said, but he didn't react to the sarcasm.

"He insisted. So I took the note finally and gave it to the mozo later. I took the letter out under the napkin on the tray from the previous service of coffee. The dick looked hard at me. But he said nothing. I was halfway down the stairs when I heard the shot. Very quickly I hid the letter and ran back upstairs. The dick was trying to kick the door open. I used my key. Señor Lennox was dead."

He moved his fingertips gently along the edge of the desk and sighed. "The rest no doubt you know."

"Was the hotel full?"

"Not full, no. There were half a dozen guests."

"Americans?"

"Two Americanos del Norte. Hunters."

"Real Gringos or just transplanted Mexicans?"

He drew a fingertip slowly along the fawn-colored cloth above his knee. "I think one of them could well have been of Spanish origin. He spoke border Spanish. Very inelegant."

"They go near Lennox's room at all?"

He lifted his head sharply but the green cheaters didn't do a thing for me. "Why should they, señor?"

I nodded. "Well, it was damn nice of you to come in here and tell me about it, Señor Maioranos. Tell Randy I'm ever so grateful, will you?"

"No hay de que, señor. It is nothing."

"And later on, if he has time, he could send me somebody who knows what he is talking about."

"Señor?" His voice was soft, but icy. "You doubt my word?"

ROLANDO HINOJOSA

Partners in Crime

Rolando Hinojosa (born 1929) was born to a Texan family with strong south-of-the-border ties, his father having fought in the Mexican Revolution. He was raised speaking Spanish until junior high school, and continues to write in Spanish, though he has also translated his own works and written several in English. His career-spanning project is the ongoing fifteen-volume murder mystery, *Klail City Death Trip Series*, a generational narrative tracing 250 years of Anglo, Spanish, and Mexican life in the Lower Río Grande Valley. The independence and subsequent annexation of Texas into the United States is the background to much of the social conflict depicted in his works. Also a poet and English professor at the University of Texas at Austin, Hinojosa gives genre fiction a memorable Tex-Mex flavor, very much in evidence in this excerpt from *Partners in Crime* (1985), highlighting the complicated work partnerships between law enforcement officers from both sides of the border.

The four men at the Lone Star were in for a longish night. It was business, and it was visiting as well; a fine, old Valley custom, on both banks of the River. Newcomers chafed, but they either succumbed to the habit or they didn't succeed. Life *is* short and serious business can be, must be, conducted civilly. Civility also means taking one's time in eating or in listening or in the telling of a story; tonight's story (business) was deadly. But, all of them knew the rules. And, since they didn't meet as often as they would have liked, they did meet for these Sunday dinners when the Homicide Squad needed all the help it could get on matters where the northern and southern banks of the Rio Grande were concerned.

Lisandro Gómez Solís, too, did not, would not, hesitate to ask for help. A civil arrangement.

There had been several cases recently to serve as examples of cooperation, and the most recent of all had been during the Christmas season of 1971, the celebrated Peggy MacDougall case.

One week after she confessed—gloated, actually—how she had hacked up her husband, "My Norman," and with the evidence clearly against her, she dropped from sight and forfeited the full 10 percent of her $100,000 bond.

She was gone before the day was over. Her lawyers, Jesse Maldonado and Curtis McIlhenny, had promised Judge O. Loren Ewald that their client would abide by the terms of her release, and now they had to face Judge Ewald on the day of the trial.

No one won with Ewald: the State, the defense; no one. After a public reaming-out in front of colleagues, a *harrumph,* and an incoherent lecture on morality, responsibility, and law and order, Ewald led the procession to his chambers. It wasn't a pretty picture there, either.

But, Peggy Mack had been found. She had holed up at La Quinta Medrano, in the heart of Barrones' business district; who would look for her there, right?

One of Gómez Solís's agents did; a forty-one year old policewoman had received the tip, reported it to her boss, and within an hour or two, the policewoman was dressed as a maid and keeping an eye on Peggy Mack.

The policewoman also gave Gómez Solís and Donovan's Homicide Squad a headstart: Peggy Mack had booked a flight on American from Jonesville to Mexico City, and she was due to leave the next day, a Wednesday.

After this, it was a matter for the Belken County Homicide Squad to wait around the airport for Peggy Mack to show up; a simple affair, then. But it wasn't.

For one thing, the flight was delayed out of Jonesville by some creeping Gulf fog which refused to go away. For another, there was a fight at the bar: The reporters and photographers from the Jonesville Herald and the Klail City Enterprise-News had become irritable and somewhat drunk after the six-hour delay. (Harvey Bollinger had informed—if not exactly invited, he said later—the reporters to witness the arrest by "his homicide squad.")

When a waitress refused the reporters further service, one of them followed her to the bar; he then pushed her, she spilled some drinks on a customer, and the bar customer then punched out the reporter. The other members of the Fourth Estate wobbled over to the rescue of their fallen comrade; this brought out the airport security guards who had a hard time getting into the bar in the first place: the door was jammed with passengers and onlookers who wanted to see what *that* was all about.

This allowed Peggy MacDougall to sneak into the now empty waiting room, down the ramp leading to the aircraft, and to board it with no trouble whatsoever.

Rafe Buenrostro and Sam Dorson, however, had spotted her and saw her walk past the guards and into the ramp. They talked it over with Donovan, and the three of them waited five minutes for Peggy Mack to find a seat or whatever.

Rafe then talked with Harry Biggs of airport security who ordered the waiting room and the gate closed. A general announcement requested all waiting passengers in the lobby to please transfer to gate six; the flight would be taking off shortly, they were told. This appeased them somewhat, but the put-upon passengers had nothing to do but to follow orders, and so they went on to gate six.

This done, Rafe, followed by Sam Dorson and Culley Donovan, entered the aircraft in search of Peggy MacDougall. The aircraft commander had been in contact with Harry Biggs and continued to reassure the passengers that they'd be on the apron shortly and on into the strip in less than ten minutes; in the meantime, he said, why not enjoy a free drink on the house? This was followed by wild cheers from the crowd and by groans from the women working on the flight.

When questioned if she'd seen a six-foot blonde woman enter the plane five minutes before, a harried flying waitress motioned with her head and said, "Some big broad got in the john, just now."

With Donovan and Dorson standing in the galley, backs to the rear toilets, Rafe stood directly behind the toilets themselves. When the *Occupied* slot moved to *Vacant,* Rafe Buenrostro stepped backward and with his back to MacDougall's toilet, pretended to enter the one opposite. He turned around, nodded to the six-foot one-inch Peggy Mack, and she moved out to her seat. At this moment, with her back toward Rafe and walking away, Donovan and Dorson moved in and each one grabbed an arm as Rafe Buenrostro took her by the hair, yanked it backward and said: "You're under arrest. Move it!" Hoarsely.

How goddammed dramatic, he thought. Still, this was business, and they led her out of the aircraft. As they did so and through the ramp and on out the gate, some bystanders saw three men escorting a woman passenger who was apparently in need of help. "Must have fainted," someone said. Poor thing.

A Belken County Police emergency unit was waiting outside and two good-sized male nurses took Peggy Mack inside and strapped her to one of the cots. She had passed out, and it was later determined (The Lab Man) that Peggy Mack had taken six valium tablets shortly before boarding the plane. This explained the ease of the arrest, why she had gone along peacefully, dreamily almost, as she waved and smiled at a grim-faced child sitting in a crowded waiting room.

The Peggy Mack capture was one of the most recent examples of the tacit, informal, north-south bank cooperation. It could be that the mayor of Jonesville and the alcalde of Barrones would not have approved, but then, they didn't need to know, either.

SHERMAN ALEXIE

The Game Between the Jews and the Indians Is Tied Going Into the Bottom of the Ninth Inning

Sherman Alexie (born 1966), poet, novelist, and filmmaker, grew up on the Spokane Indian Reservation, enduring extreme poverty and the ridicule he received for an abnormally large head caused by hydrocephalus. He took refuge in reading and writing early on. His first book of stories and poems, *The Business of Fancydancing* (1992), won immediate acclaim. This was followed by a novel, *Reservation Blues* (1995), winning an American Book Award. Since then Alexie has published many other works, including a young-adult novel, *The Absolutely True Diary of a Part-Time Indian* (2007), which won the National Book Award; and a collection of stories and poems, *War Dances* (2010), recipient of the PEN/Faulkner Award. He also wrote the screenplay for *Smoke Signals* (1998), a film based on his book *The Lone Ranger and Tonto Fistfight in Heaven* (1993). The following poem, from *First Indian on the Moon* (1993), invokes Sand Creek and Wounded Knee, Auschwitz and Buchenwald only to set them aside, returning to the immediacy of a baseball game between Jews and Indians, survivors into the future.

So, now, when you touch me
my skin, will you think
of Sand Creek, Wounded Knee?
And what will you remember

when your skin is next to mine
Auschwitz, Buchenwald?
No, we will only think of the past
as one second before

where we are now, the future
just one second ahead

but every once in a while
we can remind each other

that we are both survivors and children
and grandchildren of survivors.

WALT WHITMAN

Proud Music of the Storm

Walt Whitman (1819–1892) grew up on Long Island and became a print-er's apprentice at the age of twelve, as well as a voracious reader, immers-ing himself in the works of Homer, Dante, and Shakespeare. In 1841 he turned to journalism, serving as editor of the *Brooklyn Eagle* (1846–1848), and the New Orleans *Crescent* (1848). It was in New Orleans that he saw slavery firsthand. Upon returning to Brooklyn, he founded a free soil newspaper, the *Brooklyn Freeman*. The first edition of *Leaves of Grass*—twelve untitled poems and a preface—was self-published in 1855, receiv-ing a strong endorsement from Ralph Waldo Emerson. For the rest of his life, Whitman continued to add to the volume, publishing six more edi-tions. With the outbreak of the Civil War, he traveled to Washington, D.C., staying there for eleven years to care for his wounded brother as well as soldiers in the area hospitals while working as a clerk for the Department of the Interior. He was fired when his identity as author of *Leaves of Grass* was discovered. Whitman settled in Camden, New Jersey, his last home, in the early 1870s. His lifelong love of music is very much in evidence in this poem about the auditory cultures of the world.

1

Proud music of the storm,
Blast that careers so free, whistling across the prairies,
Strong hum of forest tree-tops—wind of the mountains,
Personified dim shapes—you hidden orchestras,

You serenades of phantoms with instruments alert,
Blending with Nature's rhythmus all the tongues of nations;
You chords left as by vast composers—you choruses,
You formless, free, religious dances—you from the Orient,
You undertone of rivers, roar of pouring cataracts,
You sounds from distant guns with galloping cavalry,
Echoes of camps with all the different bugle-calls,
Trooping tumultuous, filling the midnight late, bending me powerless,
Entering my lonesome slumber-chamber, why have you seiz'd me?

2

Come forward O my soul, and let the rest retire,
Listen, lose not, it is toward thee they tend,
Parting the midnight, entering my slumber-chamber,
For thee they sing and dance O soul.

A festival song,
The duet of the bridegroom and the bride, a marriage-march,
With lips of love, and hearts of lovers fill'd to the brim with love,
The red-flush'd cheeks and perfumes, the cortege swarming full of
friendly faces young and old,
To flutes' clear notes and sounding harps' cantabile.
Now loud approaching drums,
Victoria! seest thou in powder-smoke the banners torn but flying?
the rout of the baffled?
Hearest those shouts of a conquering army?

(Ah soul, the sobs of women, the wounded groaning in agony,
The hiss and crackle of flames, the blacken'd ruins, the embers of cities,
The dirge and desolation of mankind.)
Now airs antique and mediaeval fill me,
I see and hear old harpers with their harps at Welsh festivals,
I hear the minnesingers singing their lays of love,
I hear the minstrels, gleemen, troubadours, of the middle ages.

Now the great organ sounds,
Tremulous, while underneath, (as the hid footholds of the earth,
On which arising rest, and leaping forth depend,

All shapes of beauty, grace and strength, all hues we know,
Green blades of grass and warbling birds, children that gambol and
play, the clouds of heaven above,)
The strong base stands, and its pulsations intermits not,
Bathing, supporting, merging all the rest, maternity of all the rest,
And with it every instrument in multitudes,
The players playing, all the world's musicians,
The solemn hymns and masses rousing adoration,
All passionate heart-chants, sorrowful appeals,
The measureless sweet vocalists of ages,
And for their solvent setting earth's own diapason,
Of winds and woods and mighty ocean waves,
A new composite orchestra, binder of years and climes, ten-fold renewer,
As of the far-back days the poets tell, the Paradiso,
The straying thence, the separation long, but now the wandering done,
The journey done, the journeyman come home,
And man and art with Nature fused again.

Tutti! for earth and heaven;
(The Almighty leader now for once has signal'd with his wand.)

The manly strophe of the husbands of the world,
And all the wives responding.

The tongues of violins,
(I think O tongues ye tell this heart, that cannot tell itself,
This brooding yearning heart, that cannot tell itself.)

3
Ah from a little child,
Thou knowest soul how to me all sounds became music,
My mother's voice in lullaby or hymn,
(The voice, O tender voices, memory's loving voices,
Last miracle of all, O dearest mother's, sister's, voices;)
The rain, the growing corn, the breeze among the long-leav'd corn,
The measur'd sea-surf beating on the sand,
The twittering bird, the hawk's sharp scream,

The wild-fowl's notes at night as flying low migrating north or south,
The psalm in the country church or mid the clustering trees, the
open air camp-meeting,
The fiddler in the tavern, the glee, the long-strung sailor-song,
The lowing cattle, bleating sheep, the crowing cock at dawn.

All songs of current lands come sounding round me,
The German airs of friendship, wine and love,
Irish ballads, merry jigs and dances, English warbles,
Chansons of France, Scotch tunes, and o'er the rest,
Italia's peerless compositions.

Across the stage with pallor on her face, yet lurid passion,
Stalks Norma brandishing the dagger in her hand.

I see poor crazed Lucia's eyes' unnatural gleam,
Her hair down her back falls loose and dishevel'd.

I see where Ernani walking the bridal garden,
Amid the scent of night-roses, radiant, holding his bride by the hand,
Hears the infernal call, the death-pledge of the horn.

To crossing swords and gray hairs bared to heaven,
The clear electric base and baritone of the world,
The trombone duo, Libertad forever!

From Spanish chestnut trees' dense shade,
By old and heavy convent walls a wailing song,
Song of lost love, the torch of youth and life quench'd in despair,
Song of the dying swan, Fernando's heart is breaking.

Awaking from her woes at last retriev'd Amina sings,
Copious as stars and glad as morning light the torrents of her joy.

(The teeming lady comes,
The lustrious orb, Venus contralto, the blooming mother,
Sister of loftiest gods, Alboni's self I hear.)

4

I hear those odes, symphonies, operas,
I hear in the William Tell the music of an arous'd and angry people,
I hear Meyerbeer's Huguenots, the Prophet, or Robert,
Gounod's Faust, or Mozart's Don Juan.

I hear the dance-music of all nations,
The waltz, some delicious measure, lapsing, bathing me in bliss,
The bolero to tinkling guitars and clattering castanets.

I see religious dances old and new,
I hear the sound of the Hebrew lyre,
I see the crusaders marching bearing the cross on high, to the
martial clang of cymbals,
I hear dervishes monotonously chanting, interspers'd with frantic
shouts, as they spin around turning always towards Mecca,
I see the rapt religious dances of the Persians and the Arabs,
Again, at Eleusis, home of Ceres, I see the modern Greeks dancing,
I hear them clapping their hands as they bend their bodies,
I hear the metrical shuffling of their feet.

I see again the wild old Corybantian dance, the performers wounding
each other,
I see the Roman youth to the shrill sound of flageolets throwing and
catching their weapons,
As they fall on their knees and rise again.

I hear from the Mussulman mosque the muezzin calling,
I see the worshippers within, nor form nor sermon, argument nor word,
But silent, strange, devout, rais'd, glowing heads, ecstatic faces.

I hear the Egyptian harp of many strings,
The primitive chants of the Nile boatmen,
The sacred imperial hymns of China,
To the delicate sounds of the king, (the stricken wood and stone,)
Or to Hindu flutes and the fretting twang of the vina,
A band of bayaderes.

5

Now Asia, Africa leave me, Europe seizing inflates me,
To organs huge and bands I hear as from vast concourses of voices,
Luther's strong hymn *Eine feste Burg ist unser Gott*,
Rossini's Stabat *Mater dolorosa*,
Or floating in some high cathedral dim with gorgeous color'd windows,
The passionate *Agnus Dei* or *Gloria in Excelsis*.

Composers! mighty maestros!
And you, sweet singers of old lands, soprani, tenori, bassi!
To you a new bard caroling in the West,
Obeisant sends his love.

(Such led to thee O soul,
All senses, shows and objects, lead to thee,
But now it seems to me sound leads o'er all the rest.)

I hear the annual singing of the children in St. Paul's cathedral,
Or, under the high roof of some colossal hall, the symphonies,
oratorios of Beethoven, Handel, or Haydn,
The Creation in billows of godhood laves me.

Give me to hold all sounds, (I madly struggling cry,)
Fill me with all the voices of the universe,
Endow me with their throbbings, Nature's also,
The tempests, waters, winds, operas and chants, marches and dances,
Utter, pour in, for I would take them all!

6

Then I woke softly,
And pausing, questioning awhile the music of my dream,
And questioning all those reminiscences, the tempest in its fury,
And all the songs of sopranos and tenors,
And those rapt oriental dances of religious fervor,
And the sweet varied instruments, and the diapason of organs,
And all the artless plaints of love and grief and death,

I said to my silent curious soul out of the bed of the slumber-chamber,
Come, for I have found the clew I sought so long,
Let us go forth refresh'd amid the day,
Cheerfully tallying life, walking the world, the real,
Nourish'd henceforth by our celestial dream.

And I said, moreover,
Haply what thou hast heard O soul was not the sound of winds,
Nor dream of raging storm, nor sea-hawk's flapping wings nor harsh scream,
Nor vocalism of sun-bright Italy,
Nor German organ majestic, nor vast concourse of voices, nor layers
of harmonies,
Nor strophes of husbands and wives, nor sound of marching soldiers,
Nor flutes, nor harps, nor the bugle-calls of camps,
But to a new rhythmus fitted for thee,
Poems bridging the way from Life to Death, vaguely wafted in night
air, uncaught, unwritten,
Which let us go forth in the bold day and write.

CLAUDE MCKAY

Banjo

Claude McKay (1889–1948), born in Jamaica, began writing poetry in both standard English and the Jamaican dialect, notably in *Songs of Jamaica* (1912) and *Constab Ballads* (1912). He arrived in the United States in 1912 to study at the Tuskegee Institute but stayed only a few months, shocked by the racism that he encountered in the segregated South. Moving to New York in 1914, he became a labor activist while his poetic career flourished, winning wide acclaim for poems such as "If We Must Die," subsequently published in his 1922 volume, *Harlem Shadows*. In that year he also traveled to Moscow, meeting key communist figures, including Leon Trotsky and Nikolai Bukharin. His first novel,

Home to Harlem (1928), with its vibrant depiction of street life, would have a major impact on black intellectuals in the Caribbean and Europe, as well as the United States. This excerpt from *Banjo* (1929) describes a parallel scene in Marseilles, France, bringing together sailors from five continents to dance to an ancient African instrument.

Shake That Thing. The opening of the Café African by a Senegalese had brought all the joy-lovers of darkest color together to shake that thing. Never was there such a big black-throated guzzling of red wine, white wine, and close, indiscriminate jazzing of all the Negroes of Marseilles.

For the Negro-Negroid population of the town divides sharply into groups. The Martiniquans and Guadeloupans, regarding themselves as constituting the dark flower of all Marianne's blacks, make a little aristocracy of themselves. The Madagascans with their cousins from the little dots of islands around their big island and the North African Negroes, whom the pure Arabs despise, fall somewhere between the Martiniquans and the Senegalese, who are the savages. Senegalese is the geographically inaccurate term generally used to designate all the Negroes from the different parts of French West Africa.

The magic thing had brought all shades and grades of Negroes together. Money. A Senegalese had emigrated to the United States, and after some years had returned with a few thousand dollars. And he had bought a café on the quay. It was a big café, the first that any Negro in the town ever owned.

The tiny group of handsomely-clothed Senegalese were politely proud of the bar, and all the blue overall boys of the docks and the ships were boisterously glad of a spacious place to spread joy in.

All shades of Negroes came together there. Even the mulattoes took a step down from their perch to mix in. For, as in the British West Indies and South Africa, the mulattoes of the French colonies do not usually intermingle with the blacks.

But the magic had brought them all together to shake that thing and drink red wine, white wine, sweet wine. All the British West African blacks, Portuguese blacks, American blacks, all who had drifted into this port that the world goes through.

A great event! And to Banjo it had brought a unique feeling of satisfaction. He did not miss it, as he never missed anything rich that came within his line of living. There was music at the bar and Banjo made much of it.

He got a little acquainted with the *patron,* who often chatted with him. The *patron* was proud of his English and liked to display it when there was any distinguished-appearing person at the café.

"Shake That Thing!" That was the version of the "Jelly-Roll Blues" that Banjo loved and always played. And the Senegalese boys loved to shake to it. Banjo was treated to plenty of red wine and white wine when he played that tune. And he would not think of collecting sous. Latnah had gone about once and collected sous in her tiny jade tray. But she never went again. She loved Banjo, but she could not enter into the spirit of that all-Negro-atmosphere of the bar. Banjo was glad she stayed away. He did not want to collect sous from a crowd of fellows just like himself. He preferred to play for them and be treated to wine. Sous! How could he respect sous? He who had burnt up dollars. Why should he care, with a free bed, free love, and wine?

His plan of an orchestra filled his imagination now. Maybe he could use the Café African as a base to get some fellows together. Malty could play the guitar right splendid, but he had no instrument. If that Senegalese *patron* had a little imagination, he might buy Malty a guitar and they would start a little orchestra that would make the bar unique and popular.

Many big things started in just such a little way. Only give him a chance and he would make this dump sit up and take notice—show it how to be sporty and game. How he would love to see a couple of brown chippies from Gawd's own show this Ditch some decent movement—turn themselves jazzing loose in a back-home, brownskin Harlem way. Oh, Banjo's skin was itching to make some romantic thing.

And one afternoon he walked straight into a dream—a cargo boat with a crew of four music-making colored boys, with banjo, ukelele, mandolin, guitar, and horn. That evening Banjo and Malty, mad with enthusiam, literally carried the little band to the Vieux Port. It was the biggest evening ever at the Senegalese bar. They played several lively popular tunes, but the Senegalese boys yelled for "Shake That Thing." Banjo picked it off and the boys from the boat quickly got it. Then Banjo keyed himself up and began playing in his own wonderful wild way.

"Old Uncle Jack, the jelly-roll king,
Just got back from shaking that thing!
  He can shake that thing, he can shake that thing
  For he's a jelly-roll king. Oh, shake that thing!"

It roused an Arab-black girl from Algeria into a shaking-mad mood. And she jazzed right out into the center of the floor and shook herself in a low-down African shimmying way. The mandolin player, a stocky, cocky lad of brown-paper complexion, the lightest-skinned of the playing boys, had his eyes glued on her. Her hair was cropped and stood up shiny, crinkly like a curiously-wrought bird's nest. She was big-boned and well-fleshed and her full lips were a savage challenge. Oh, shake that thing!

"*Cointreau!*" The Negroid girl called when, the music ceasing, the paper-brown boy asked her to take a drink.

"That yaller nigger's sure gone on her," Malty said to Banjo.

"And she knows he's got a roll can reach right up to her figure," said Banjo. "Looka them eyes she shines on him! Oh, boy! it was the same for you and I when we first landed—every kind of eyes in the chippies' world shining for us!"

"Yes, but you ain't got nothing to kick about. The goodest eyes in this burg ain't shining for anybody else but you."

"Hheh-hheh," Banjo giggled. "I'll be dawggone, Malty, ef I don't think sometimes youse getting soft. Takem as they come, easy and jolly, ole boh."

He poured out a glass of red wine, chinked his glass against Malty's, and toasted, "Oh, you Dixieland, here's praying for you' soul salvation."

"And here is joining you," said Malty.

"Dry land will nevah be my land,
Gimme a wet wide-open land for mine."

Handsome, happy brutes. The music is on again. The Senegalese boys crowd the floor, dancing with one another. They dance better male with male or individually, than with the girls, putting more power in their feet, dancing more wildly, more natively, more savagely. Senegalese in blue overalls, Madagascan soldiers in khaki, dancing together. A Martiniquan with his mulattress flashing her gold teeth. A Senegalese sergeant goes round with his fair blonde. A Congo boxer struts it with his Marguerite. And Banjo, grinning, singing, white teeth, great mouth, leads the band. . . . Shake that thing.

The banjo dominates the other instruments; the charming, pretty sound of the ukelele, the filigree notes of the mandolin, the sensuous color of the guitar. And Banjo's face shows that he feels that his instrument is first. The Negroes and Spanish Negroids of the evenly-warm, evergreen and ever-flowering Antilles may love the rich chords of the guitar, but the banjo is preëminently the musical instrument of the American Negro. The sharp, noisy notes of the banjo belong to the American Negro's loud music of life—an affirmation of his hardy existence in the midst of the biggest, the most tumultuous civilization of modern life.

Sing, Banjo! Play, Banjo! Here I is, Big Boss, keeping step, sure step, right long with you in some sort a ways. He-ho, Banjo! Play that thing! Shake that thing!

"Old Brother Mose is sick in bed.
Doctor says he is almost dead
   From shaking that thing, shaking that thing.
   He was a jelly-roll king. Oh, shake that thing!"

A little flock of pinks from the Ditch floated into the bar. Seamen from Senegal. Soldiers from Madagascar. Pimps from Martinique. Pimps from everywhere. Pimps from Africa. Seamen fed up with the sea. Young men weary of the work of the docks, scornful of the meager reward—doing that now. Black youth close to the bush and the roots of jungle trees, trying to live the precarious life of the poisonous orchids of civilization.

Shake That Thing! . . .

The slim, slate-colored Martiniquan dances with a gold-brown Arab girl in a purely sensual way. His dog's mouth shows a tiny, protruding bit of pink tongue. Oh, he jazzes like a lizard with his girl. A dark-brown lizard and a gold-brown lizard. . . .

"Oh, shake that thing,
He's a jelly-roll king."

A coffee-black boy from Cameroon and a chocolate-brown from Dakar stand up to each other to dance a native sex-symbol dance. Bending knee and nodding head, they dance up to each other. As they almost touch, the smaller boy spins suddenly round and dances away. Oh, exquisite movement! Like a ram goat and a ram kid. Hands and feet! Shake that thing!

Black skin itching, black flesh warm with the wine of life, the music of life, the love and deep meaning of life. Strong smell of healthy black bodies in a close atmosphere, generating sweat and waves of heat. Oh, shake that thing!

Suddenly in the thick joy of it there was a roar and a rush and sheering apart as a Senegalese leaped like a leopard bounding through the jazzers, and, gripping an antagonist, butted him clean on the forehead once, twice, and again, and turned him loose to fall heavily on the floor like a felled tree.

The *patron* dashed from behind the bar. A babel of different dialects broke forth. Policemen appeared and the musicians slipped outside, followed by most of the Martiniquans.

"Hheh-hheh," Banjo laughed. "The music so good it put them French fellahs in a fighting mood."

AMIRI BARAKA

Blues People

Amiri Baraka (1934–2014) was born Everett LeRoi Jones in Newark and served in the United States Air Force after attending Rutgers and Howard universities. Moving to Greenwich Village in 1957, he founded the Totem Press and began publishing the works of Allen Ginsberg and Jack Kerouac. *Blues People* (1963), on the persistence of African music, remains a classic. In 1964, his play *Dutchman* opened in New York and subsequently won an Obie award (for the best Off-Broadway play); later it was also made into a film. Following the assassination of Malcolm X in 1965, Jones repudiated his former life, moved to Harlem and then back to Newark, became a Muslim in 1968, and changed his name to Imamu Amiri Baraka. He founded the Congress of African People in 1970. Beyond his plays and essays, Baraka also wrote poetry as well as fiction such as *The System of Dante's Hell* (1965). He was honored with the PEN/Faulkner Award, the Rockefeller Foundation Award for Drama, the Langston Hughes Award, and a Lifetime Achievement Award from the Before Columbus Foundation. In this excerpt from *Blues People*, he discusses the complex genesis of the slaves' work song.

The work song took on its own peculiar qualities in America for a number of reasons. First, although singing to accompany one's labor was quite common in West Africa, it is obvious that working one's own field in one's own land is quite different from forced labor in a foreign land. And while the physical insistence necessary to suggest a work song was still present, the references accompanying the work changed radically. Most West Africans were farmers and, I am certain, these agricultural farm songs could have been used in the fields of the New World in the same manner as the Old. But the lyrics of a song that said, "After the planting, if the gods bring rain,/ My family, my ancestors, be rich as they are beautiful," could not apply in the dreadful circumstance of slavery. Secondly, references to the gods or religions of Africa were suppressed by the white masters as soon as they realized what these were—not only because they naturally thought of any African religious customs as "barbarous" but because the whites soon learned that too constant evocation of the African gods could mean that those particular Africans were planning on leaving that plantation as soon as they could! The use of African drums was soon prevented too, as the white man learned that drums could be used to incite revolt as well as to accompany dancers.

So the work song, as it began to take shape in America, first had to be stripped of any purely African ritual and some cultural reference found for it in the New World. But this was difficult to do within the African-language songs themselves. The diverse labors of the African, which were the sources of this kind of song, had been funneled quite suddenly into one labor, the cultivation of the white man's fields. The fishing songs, the weaving songs, the hunting songs, all had lost their pertinence. But these changes were not immediate. They became the realized circumstances of a man's life after he had been exposed sufficiently to their source and catalyst—his enslavement.

And this is the basic difference between the first slaves and their offspring. The African slave continued to chant his native chants, sing his native songs, at work, even though the singing of them might be forbidden or completely out of context. But being forbidden, the songs were after a time changed into other forms that weren't forbidden in contexts that were contemporary. The African slave might have realized he was losing something, that his customs and the memory of his land were being each day drained from his life. Still there was a certain amount of forbearance. No one can simply decree that a man change the way he thinks. But the first black Americans had no native cultural references other than the slave culture. A work song about fishing when one has never fished seems meaningless, especially when one works each day in a cotton field. The context of the Africans' life had changed, but the American-born slaves never knew what the change had been.

It is impossible to find out exactly how long the slaves were in America before the African work song actually did begin to have extra-African references. First, of course, there were mere additions of the foreign words—French, Spanish or English, for the most part, after the British colonists gained power in the United States. Krehbiel lists a Creole song transcribed by Lafcadio Hearn, which contains both French (or patois) and African words (the italicized words are African):

Ouendé, ouendé, macaya!
  Mo pas barrasse, *macaya!*
Ouendé, ouendé, macaya!
  Mo bois bon divin, *macaya!*
Ouendé, ouendé, macaya!
  Mo mange bon poulet, *macaya!*
Ouendé, ouendé, macaya!
  Mo pas barrasse, *macaya!*
Ouendé, ouendé, macaya!
    Macaya!

Hearn's translation was:

Go on! go on! eat enormously!
  I ain't one bit ashamed—*eat outrageously!*
Go on! go on! eat prodigiously!
  I drink good wine!—*eat ferociously!*
Go on! go on! eat unceasingly!
  I eat good chicken—*gorging myself!*
Go on! go on! etc.

It is interesting to note, and perhaps more than coincidence, that the portions of the song emphasizing excess are in African, which most of the white men could not understand, and the portions of the song elaborating some kind of genteel, if fanciful, existence are in the tongue of the masters. But there was to come a time when there was no black man who understood the African either, and those allusions to excess, or whatever the black man wished to keep to himself, were either in the master's tongue or meaningless, albeit rhythmical, sounds to the slave also.

Aside from the actual transfer or survival of African words in the songs and speech of the early slaves, there was also some kind of syntactical as well as rhythmical transfer since Africans and their descendants tended to speak their new languages in the same manner as they spoke their West African dialects. What is called now a "Southern accent" or "Negro speech" was once simply the accent of a foreigner trying to speak a new and unfamiliar language, although it was characteristic of the white masters to attribute the slave's "inability" to speak perfect English to the same kind of "childishness" that was used to explain the African's belief in the supernatural.

TONI MORRISON

Song of Solomon

Toni Morrison (born 1931), Nobel laureate, was born Chloe Anthony Wofford to a working class family in Lorain, Ohio. She began as a college teacher and editor at Random House, publishing her first two novels, *The Bluest Eye* (1970) and *Sula* (1973), while working full-time and raising two children. Her next novel, *Song of Solomon* (1977), won her wide acclaim as well as the National Book Critics Circle Award. She followed with *Tar Baby* (1981) and the Pulitzer Prize–winning *Beloved* (1987). Subsequent works include *Jazz* (1992), *Paradise* (1997), *Love* (2003), *A Mercy* (2008), *Home* (2012), and *God Help the Child* (2015), complex works with multiple narrators, split time frames, and a variety of settings. Morrison has also written children's books with her son Slade, along with plays such as *Dreaming Emmet* (1986) and essay collections such as *Playing in the Dark* (1992). She delivered the Jefferson Lecture in 1996, and in 2006 curated a month-long series of museum events, "The Foreigner's Home," at the Louvre in Paris. From 1989 until her retirement in 2006, she taught at Princeton University. In this excerpt from *Song of Solomon*, children sing a song about intertwined African and Native American ancestry.

O Solomon don't leave me here.

The children were starting the round again. Milkman rubbed the back of his neck. Suddenly he was tired, although the morning was still new. He pushed himself away from the cedar and sank to his haunches.

Jay the only son of Solomon
Come booba yalle, come . . .

Everybody in this town is named Solomon, he thought wearily. Solomon's General Store, Luther Solomon (no relation), Solomon's Leap, and now the children were singing "*Solomon* don't leave me" instead of "*Sugarman.*" Even the name of the town sounded like Solomon: Shalimar, which Mr. Solomon and everybody else pronounced *Shalleemone.*

Milkman's scalp began to tingle. Jay the only son of Solomon? Was that *Jake* the only son of Solomon? Jake. He strained to hear the children. That was one of the people he was looking for. A man named Jake who lived in Shalimar, as did his wife, Sing.

He sat up and waited for the children to begin the verse again. "Come booba yalle, come booba tambee," it sounded like, and didn't make sense. But another line—"Black lady fell down on the ground"—was clear enough. There was another string of nonsense words, then "Threw her body all around." Now the child in the center began whirling, spinning to lyrics sung in a different, faster tempo: "Solomon 'n' Reiner Belali Shalut . . ."

Solomon again, and Reiner? Ryna? Why did the second name sound so familiar? Solomon and Ryna. The woods. The hunt. Solomon's Leap and Ryna's Gulch, places they went to or passed by that night they shot the bobcat. The gulch was where he heard that noise that sounded like a woman crying, which Calvin said came from Ryna's Gulch, that there was an echo there that folks said was "a woman name Ryna" crying. You could hear her when the wind was right.

But what was the rest: Belali . . . Shalut . . . Yaruba? If Solomon and Ryna were names of people, the others might be also. The verse ended in another clear line. "Twenty-one children, the last one *Jake!*" And it was at the shout of *Jake* (who was also, apparently, "the only son of Solomon") that the twirling boy stopped. Now Milkman understood that if the child's finger pointed at nobody, missed, they started up again. But if it pointed directly to another child, that was when they fell to their knees and sang Pilate's song.

Milkman took out his wallet and pulled from it his airplane ticket stub, but he had no pencil to write with, and his pen was in his suit. He would just have to listen and memorize it. He closed his eyes and concentrated while the children, inexhaustible in their willingness to repeat a rhythmic, rhyming action game, performed the round over and over again. And Milkman memorized all of what they sang.

Jake the only son of Solomon
Come booba yalle, come booba tambee
Whirled about and touched the sun
Come konka yalle, come konka tambee

Left that baby in a white man's house
Come booba yalle, come booba tambee
Heddy took him to a red man's house
Come konka yalle, come konka tambee

Black lady fell down on the ground
Come booba yalle, come booba tambee
Threw her body all around
Come konka yalle, come konka tambee

Solomon and Ryna Belali Shalut
Yaruba Medina Muhammet too.
Nestor Kalina Saraka cake.
Twenty-one children, the last one Jake!

O Solomon don't leave me here
Cotton balls to choke me

O Solomon don't leave me here
Buckra's arms to yoke me

Solomon done fly, Solomon done gone
Solomon cut across the sky, Solomon gone home.

He almost shouted when he heard "Heddy took him to a red man's house." Heddy was Susan Byrd's grandmother on her father's side, and therefore Sing's mother too. And "red man's house" must be a reference to the Byrds as Indians. Of course! Sing was an Indian or part Indian and her name was Sing Byrd or, more likely, Sing Bird. No—Singing Bird! That must have been her name originally—Singing Bird. And her brother, Crowell Byrd, was probably Crow Bird, or just Crow. They had mixed their Indian names with American-sounding names. Milkman had four people now that he could recognize in the song: Solomon, Jake, Ryna and Heddy, and a veiled reference to Heddy's Indianness. All of which seemed to put Jake and Sing together in Shalimar, just as Circe had said they were. He couldn't be mistaken. These children were singing a story about his own people! He hummed and chuckled as he did his best to put it all together.

ROBERT PINSKY

Ginza Samba

Robert Pinsky (born 1940), a former saxophonist as noted earlier, has always seen jazz as an inspiration and template. In the poem below, he celebrates this musical form as a perennial hybrid, with input from every part of the world.

A monosyllabic European called Sax
Invents a horn, walla whirledy wah, a kind of twisted
Brazen clarinet, but with its column of vibrating

Air shaped not in a cylinder but in a cone
Widening ever outward and bawaah spouting
Infinitely upward through an upturned
Swollen golden bell rimmed
Like a gloxinia flowering
In Sax's Belgian imagination

And in the unfathomable matrix
Of mothers and fathers as a genius graven
Humming into the cells of the body
Or cupped in the resonating grail
Of memory changed and exchanged
As in the trading of brasses,
Pearls and ivory, calicos and slaves,
Laborers and girls, two

Cousins in a royal family
Of Niger known as the Birds or Hawks.
In Christendom one cousin's child
Becomes a "favorite negro" ennobled
By decree of the Czar and founds
A great family, a line of generals,
Dandies and courtiers including the poet
Pushkin, killed in a duel concerning
His wife's honor, while the other cousin sails

In the belly of a slaveship to the port
Of Baltimore where she is raped
And dies in childbirth, but the infant
Will marry a Seminole and in the next
Chorus of time their child fathers
A great Hawk or Bird, with many followers
Among them this great-grandchild of the Jewish
Manager of a Pushkin estate, blowing

His American breath out into the wiggly
Tune uncurling its triplets and sixteenths—the Ginza

Samba of breath and brass, the reed
Vibrating as a valve, the aether, the unimaginable
Wires and circuits of an ingenious box
Here in my room in this house built
A hundred years ago while I was elsewhere:

It is like falling in love, the atavistic
Imperative of some one
Voice or face—the skill, the copper filament,
The golden bellful of notes twirling through
Their invisible element from
Rio to Tokyo and back again gathering
Speed in the variations as they tunnel
The twin haunted labyrinths of stirrup
And anvil echoing here in the hearkening
Instrument of my skull.

IV. Religions

I n a 1790 letter to the synagogue of Newport, Rhode Island, George Washington congratulated the United States "for having given to the world examples of an enlightened and liberal policy," granting to each and all "liberty of conscience and immunities of citizenship." He predicted that every son "of the stock of Abraham" would "sit in safety under his own vine and fig tree and there shall be none to make him afraid."

Washington was not the only Founding Father to wax eloquent on religious toleration as a guiding principle for the nation, an example to the rest of the world. Benjamin Franklin, in "A Parable against Persecution" (1755), went further, using his literary talent to add a new chapter to the King James Bible to make his point. In this hitherto unknown parable, Abraham drives away from his house a weary traveler who refuses to share his worship even while seeking shelter. This does not win favor with the Lord, who chides him, and Abraham soon sees the error of his ways and welcomes back the dissident guest with open arms.

In the early nineteenth century, Washington Irving also took an emphatic stand on religious toleration, but taking it in a different direction. The seven years that he spent in Spain, including five years (1842–46) as U.S. minister, gave him a unique insight into its Islamic heritage. In a series of works, including *Chronicle of the Conquest of Granada* (1829), *Tales of the Alhambra* (1832), and *Lives of Mahomet and His Successors* (1850), Irving detailed three-hundred-year war waged by Christian monarchs against the Islamic cities of Toledo, Seville, and Granada. He also wrote about the founding of

Islam and the early hardships and eventual triumph of the prophet Moham-med, portraying this religion through its own aspirations. In the story fea-tured in our anthology, "Legend of the Arabian Astrologer," he takes a more humorous approach, poking fun at both Islam and Christianity, putting both on the same footing as Egyptian magic, all three driven less by reli-gious piety than national security.

From this whimsical legend, it is a long and dramatic journey to Malcolm X's *Autobiography* (1965) and its thoroughgoing—and rhapsodic—embrace of Islam. Born Malcolm Little, Malcolm X converted to the Nation of Islam while in jail for burglary, but broke with that group in 1964 over disagree-ment with Elijah Mohammed, its founder. Shortly afterward he converted to Sunni Islam and made the pilgrimage to Mecca, an epiphany for him, inspiring a vision of multiracial harmony that he set forth in a letter to his congregation, included in full here. Other selections—excerpts from John Updike's *Terrorist* (2006) and Mohsin Hamid's *The Reluctant Fundamen-talist* (2007), as well as The Grateful Dead's "Blues for Allah" (1975)—will qualify that rhapsodic vision, but it is important to have this on record, perhaps never more urgently than now.

It is worth noting that there is no denouncing of Christianity in Malcolm X's autobiography. For a more upfront critique, we need to look else-where—surprisingly, to none other than Ralph Waldo Emerson. Starting out as a Unitarian pastor at Boston's Second Church, Emerson resigned from the ministry in 1832 over the sacrament of the Lord's Supper. In 1838 he gave the commencement speech at the Harvard Divinity School (one that would make him *persona non grata* for almost three decades), saying in no uncertain terms that Christianity was founded on a literal-minded mistake, the attribution of divinity to a mere human being, Jesus Christ, who was speaking only metaphorically—using poetic license—when he referred to himself as the "Son of God." Building an entire religion on this metaphor, Christian worship was a misguided, "petrified" form of worship, no more true than the worship of "Osiris or Apollo" by the "Orientals or the Greeks."

Emerson had been emboldened to make statements such as these by the "Higher Criticism" he had been reading, German biblical scholarship that cast doubt on the authority of the Bible. He was not alone. The Bible—the cornerstone of Christianity as a revealed religion, but a document writ-ten by fallible human beings, and susceptible to errors of composition and transcription—was becoming suspect for a variety of reasons in the nineteenth century. Emily Dickinson, from the relative seclusion of Amherst, Massachusetts, and without the benefit of such cosmopolitan reading, also came to be skeptical on her own. For her, the Bible was an "antique volume" written by "faded men," featuring stock figures such as Satan and Judas, the stuff melodrama was made of. Dickinson's irreverence, reverberating from poem to poem, serves as an interesting prelude to "Why I am a Pagan" (1902), Zitkala-Ša's pointed rejection of the faith of her cousin, the "native preacher," who urges her to embrace Christianity to "avoid the after-doom of hell fire!" For this modern pagan, such vehemence only bespeaks a "new superstition," infinitely less compelling than the traditional Native belief in the "voice of the Great Spirit," speaking without anger and without threat through the cherished sounds of His creation.

One would not expect Zitkala-Ša to be in the company of Malcolm X, Emerson, and Dickinson, let alone Washington and Franklin. But such adjacencies will happen again and again. The cross-referencing field of religions is a field of surprises.

OLAUDAH EQUIANO

The Interesting Narrative of Olaudah Equiano

Olaudah Equiano (c. 1745–1797) is best known for his autobiography, *The Interesting Narrative of Olaudah Equiano, or Gustavus Vassa, the African* (1789), quickly translated into French, Spanish, Dutch, and Russian, which became a significant force behind the passage of the 1807 Slave Trade Act. This act of legislation by the British Parliament abolished slave trade within the British Empire. According to his own account, Equiano was born and initially enslaved in Africa, brought in a slave ship first to the West Indies, then to Virginia. Some scholars, notably Vincent Carretta, have disputed this claim. While Equiano's African birth cannot be fully verified, the *Interesting Narrative* is nonetheless crucial as the first slave autobiography to be widely read, featuring the business savvy and combat excitement of a protagonist serving the British navy as well as commercial vessels, crisscrossing the Atlantic, with forays also to the Mediterranean, the Arctic, and South America. In the excerpt below, from Chapter One, Equiano offers an intriguing account of the affinities between the indigenous religion of Africa and the Jewish faith.

We practised circumcision like the Jews, and made offerings and feasts on that occasion in the same manner as they did. Like them also, our children were named from some event, some circumstance, or fancied foreboding at the time of their birth. I was named *Olaudah*, which, in our language, signifies vicissitude or fortune also, one favoured, and having a loud voice and well spoken. I remember we never polluted the name of the object of our adoration; on the contrary, it was always mentioned with the greatest reverence; and we were totally unacquainted with swearing, and all those terms of abuse and reproach which find their way so readily and copiously into the languages of more civilized people. The only expressions of that kind I remember were "May you rot, or may you swell, or may a beast take you."

I have before remarked that the natives of this part of Africa are extremely cleanly. This necessary habit of decency was with us a part of religion, and therefore we had many purifications and washings; indeed almost as many, and used on the same occasions, if my recollection does not fail me, as the Jews. Those that touched the dead at any time were obliged to wash and purify themselves before they could enter a dwelling-house. Every woman too, at certain times, was forbidden to come into a dwelling-house, or touch any person, or any thing we ate. I was so fond of my mother I could not keep from her, or avoid touching her at some of those periods, in consequence of which I was obliged to be kept out with her, in a little house made for that purpose, till offering was made, and then we were purified.

Though we had no places of public worship, we had priests and magicians, or wise men. I do not remember whether they had different offices, or whether they were united in the same persons, but they were held in great reverence by the people. They calculated our time, and foretold events, as their name imported, for we called them Ah-affoe-way-cah, which signifies calculators or yearly men, our year being called Ah-affoe. They wore their beards, and when they died they were succeeded by their sons. Most of their implements and things of value were interred along with them. Pipes and tobacco were also put into the grave with the corpse, which was always perfumed and ornamented, and animals were offered in sacrifice to them. None accompanied their funerals but those of the same profession or tribe. These buried them after sunset, and always returned from the grave by a different way from that which they went.

These magicians were also our doctors or physicians. They practised bleeding by cupping; and were very successful in healing wounds and expelling poisons. They had likewise some extraordinary method of discovering jealousy, theft, and poisoning; the success of which no doubt they derived from their unbounded influence over the credulity and superstition of the people. I do not remember what those methods were, except that as to poisoning: I recollect an instance or two, which I hope it will not be deemed impertinent here to insert, as it may serve as a kind of specimen of the rest, and is still used by the negroes in the West Indies. A virgin had been poisoned, but it was not known by whom: the doctors ordered the corpse to be taken up by some persons, and carried to the grave. As soon as the bearers had raised it on their shoulders, they seemed seized with some sudden impulse, and ran to and fro unable to stop themselves. At last, after having passed through a number of thorns and prickly bushes unhurt, the corpse fell from them close to a house, and defaced it in the fall; and, the owner being taken up, he immediately confessed the poisoning.

The natives are extremely cautious about poison. When they buy any eatable the seller kisses it all round before the buyer, to shew him it is not poisoned; and the same is done when any meat or drink is presented, particularly to a stranger. We have serpents of different kinds, some of which are esteemed ominous when they appear in our houses, and these we never molest. I remember two of those ominous snakes, each of which was as thick as the calf of a man's leg, and in colour resembling a dolphin in the water, crept at different times into my mother's night-house, where I always lay with her, and coiled themselves into folds, and each time they crowed like a cock. I was desired by some of our wise men to touch these, that I might be interested in the good omens, which I did, for they were quite harmless, and would tamely suffer themselves to be handled; and then they were put into a large open earthen pan, and set on one side of the highway. Some of our snakes, however, were poisonous: one of them crossed the road one day when I was standing on it, and passed between my feet without offering to touch me, to the great surprise of many who saw it; and these incidents were accounted by the wise men, and therefore by my mother and the rest of the people, as remarkable omens in my favour.

Such is the imperfect sketch my memory has furnished me with of the manners and customs of a people among whom I first drew my breath. And here I cannot forbear suggesting what has long struck me very forcibly, namely, the strong analogy which even by this sketch, imperfect as it is, appears to prevail in the manners and customs of my countrymen and those of the Jews, before they reached the Land of Promise, and particularly the patriarchs while they were yet in that pastoral state which is described in Genesis—an analogy, which alone would induce me to think that the one people had sprung from the other. Indeed this is the opinion of Dr. Gill, who, in his commentary on Genesis, very ably deduces the pedigree of the Africans from Afer and Afra, the descendants of Abraham by Keturah his wife and concubine (for both these titles are applied to her).

It is also conformable to the sentiments of Dr. John Clarke, formerly Dean of Sarum, in his *Truth of the Christian Religion*: both these authors concur in ascribing to us this original. The reasonings of these gentlemen are still further confirmed by the scripture chronology; and if any further corroboration were required, this resemblance in so many respects is a strong evidence in support of the opinion. Like the Israelites in their primitive state, our government was conducted by our chiefs or judges, our wise men and elders; and the head of a family with us enjoyed a similar authority over his household with that which is ascribed to Abraham and the other patriarchs. The law of retaliation obtained almost universally with us as with them: and even their religion appeared to have shed upon us a ray of its glory, though broken and spent in its passage, or eclipsed by the cloud with which time, tradition, and ignorance might have enveloped it; for we had our circumcision (a rule I believe peculiar to that people:) we had also our sacrifices and burnt-offerings, our washings and purifications, on the same occasions as they had.

GEORGE WASHINGTON

Letter to the Hebrew Congregation of Newport, August 21, 1790

George Washington (1732–1799), first president of the United States, served as commander-in-chief of the Continental Army (1775–1783) during the Revolutionary War, forcing the British out of Boston in 1776 while also suffering many setbacks. The loss of New York City later that year necessitated the crossing of the Delaware River in the dead of winter, a defeat subsequently reversed by the decisive victory of Yorktown (1781). Washington was unanimously elected president in 1789, and later set a precedent for a two-term limit. Dedicated to the preservation of liberty and the building of infrastructure, he created a federal government bound by the U.S. Constitution and the rule of law, and was able to remain neutral during the French revolutionary wars. His Farewell Address was a warning against partisanship and ill-considered foreign interventions. Washington died two years after his retirement from the presidency in his home in Mount Vernon. Though a slave owner his entire adult life, he freed all his slaves in his final will. In the letter below, Washington takes an emphatic stand on religious sectarianism.

Gentlemen:

While I received with much satisfaction your address replete with expressions of esteem, I rejoice in the opportunity of assuring you that I shall always retain grateful remembrance of the cordial welcome I experienced on my visit to Newport from all classes of citizens.

The reflection on the days of difficulty and danger which are past is rendered the more sweet from a consciousness that they are succeeded by days of uncommon prosperity and security.

If we have wisdom to make the best use of the advantages with which we are now favored, we cannot fail, under the just administration of a good government, to become a great and happy people.

The citizens of the United States of America have a right to applaud themselves for having given to mankind examples of an enlarged and liberal policy—a policy worthy of imitation. All possess alike liberty of conscience and immunities of citizenship.

It is now no more that toleration is spoken of as if it were the indulgence of one class of people that another enjoyed the exercise of their inherent natural rights, for, happily, the Government of the United States, which gives to bigotry no sanction, to persecution no assistance, requires only that they who live under its protection should demean themselves as good citizens in giving it on all occasions their effectual support.

It would be inconsistent with the frankness of my character not to avow that I am pleased with your favorable opinion of my administration and fervent wishes for my felicity.

May the children of the stock of Abraham who dwell in this land continue to merit and enjoy the good will of the other inhabitants—while every one shall sit in safety under his own vine and fig tree and there shall be none to make him afraid.

May the father of all mercies scatter light, and not darkness, upon our paths, and make us all in our several vocations useful here, and in His own due time and way everlastingly happy.

G. Washington

BENJAMIN FRANKLIN

A Parable against Persecution

Benjamin Franklin (1706–1790) received only two years of schooling at the Boston Latin School before going to work, first for his father and then for his brother, a printer, while writing under the name of "Mrs. Silence Dogood." At seventeen he ran away to Philadelphia, quickly making his name as the publisher of the *Philadelphia Gazette* and *Poor Richard's Almanack*. His lifelong pursuit of knowledge led to countless discoveries and inventions, from lightning rods to bifocals. As a civic leader, Franklin founded the Library Company of Philadelphia (1731), organized the Union Fire Company (1736), and helped establish the University of Pennsylvania (1743). He was made the first postmaster general of the fledgling United States in 1775. Franklin served on the "Committee of Five" at the Second Continental Congress in 1776, tasked with composing the first draft of the Declaration of Independence. As the first ambassador to France (1776–1785), he helped negotiate the Treaty of Alliance with that country (1778), as well as the Treaty of Paris (1783), which formally ended the American Revolutionary War. Franklin freed all his slaves toward the end of his life. In his final speech at the Constitutional Convention (1787), he noted that "most Men indeed as well as most Sects in Religion think themselves in Possession of all Truth," a belief he found altogether questionable. In the essay below, he channeled the King James Bible to deliver a lesson in religious tolerance.

1. And it came to pass after these Things, that Abraham sat in the Door of his Tent, about the going down of the Sun.

2. And behold a Man, bowed with Age, came from the Way of the Wilderness, leaning on a Staff.

3. And Abraham arose and met him, and said unto him, Turn in, I pray thee, and wash thy Feet, and tarry all Night, and thou shalt arise early on the Morrow, and go on thy Way.

4. And the Man said, Nay, for I will abide under this Tree.

5. But Abraham pressed him greatly; so he turned, and they went into the Tent; and Abraham baked unleavened Bread, and they did eat.

6. And when Abraham saw that the Man blessed not God, he said unto him, Wherefore dost thou not worship the most high God, Creator of Heaven and Earth?

7. And the Man answered and said, I do not worship the God thou speakest of; neither do I call upon his Name; for I have made to myself a God, which abideth always in mine House, and provideth me with all Things.

8. And Abraham's Zeal was kindled against the Man; and he arose, and fell upon him, and drove him forth with Blows into the Wilderness.

9. And at Midnight God called unto Abraham, saying, Abraham, where is the Stranger?

10. And Abraham answered and said, Lord, he would not worship thee, neither would he call upon thy Name; therefore have I driven him out from before my Face into the Wilderness.

11. And God said, Have I born with him these hundred ninety and eight Years, and nourished him, and cloathed him, notwithstanding his Rebellion against me, and couldst not thou, that art thyself a Sinner, bear with him one Night?

12. And Abraham said, Let not the Anger of my Lord wax hot against his Servant. Lo, I have sinned; forgive me, I pray Thee:

13. And Abraham arose and went forth into the Wilderness, and sought diligently for the Man, and found him, and returned with him to his Tent; and when he had entreated him kindly, he sent him away on the Morrow with Gifts.

14. And God spake again unto Abraham, saying, For this thy Sin shall thy Seed be afflicted four Hundred Years in a strange Land:

15. But for thy Repentance will I deliver them; and they shall come forth with Power, and with Gladness of Heart, and with much Substance.

THOMAS PAINE

Profession of Faith

Thomas Paine (1737–1809), born in Thetford, England, arrived in the American colonies in 1774 and shortly thereafter published *Common Sense* (1776), the fiery pamphlet that prompted John Adams to say, "Without the pen of the author of *Common Sense*, the sword of Washington would have been raised in vain." The power of Paine's pamphlets in fact went further: he also took it upon himself to defend the French Revolution in *Rights of Man* (1791) against Edmund Burke's attack. In December 1792 he was convicted for sedition by an English court for Part 2 of *Rights of Man* and fled to France. Deemed too moderate by the French Jacobins, he was in turn arrested and imprisoned in Paris in 1793 and barely escaped execution. He made still more enemies with *The Age of Reason*, a series of pamphlets published in three parts in 1794, 1795, and 1807, reading the Bible as "an ordinary piece of literature rather than as a divinely inspired text." Even though his return to the United States was at the invitation of President Jefferson, his unpopularity was such that, upon his death in 1809, only six mourners attended his funeral. In the following excerpt from *The Age of Reason*, Paine argues that a "pure, unmixed, and unadulterated belief" in God is possible only when there is a strict separation between church and state.

It has been my intention, for several years past, to publish my thoughts upon religion; I am well aware of the difficulties that attend the subject, and from that consideration, had reserved it to a more advanced period of life. I intended it to be the last offering I should make to my fellow-citizens of all nations, and that at a time when the purity of the motive that induced me to it could not admit of a question, even by those who might disapprove the work.

The circumstance that has now taken place in France, of the total abolition of the whole national order of priesthood, and of everything appertaining to compulsive systems of religion, and compulsive articles of faith, has not only precipitated my intention, but rendered a work of this kind exceedingly necessary, lest, in the general wreck of superstition, of false systems of government, and false theology, we lose sight of morality, of humanity, and of the theology that is true.

As several of my colleagues, and others of my fellow-citizens of France, have given me the example of making their voluntary and individual profession of faith, I also will make mine; and I do this with all that sincerity and frankness with which the mind of man communicates with itself.

I believe in one God, and no more; and I hope for happiness beyond this life.

I believe the equality of man, and I believe that religious duties consist in doing justice, loving mercy, and endeavoring to make our fellow-creatures happy.

But, lest it should be supposed that I believe many other things in addition to these, I shall, in the progress of this work, declare the things I do not believe, and my reasons for not believing them.

I do not believe in the creed professed by the Jewish church, by the Roman church, by the Greek church, by the Turkish church, by the Protestant church, nor by any church that I know of. My own mind is my own church.

All national institutions of churches, whether Jewish, Christian, or Turkish, appear to me no other than human inventions set up to terrify and enslave mankind, and monopolize power and profit.

I do not mean by this declaration to condemn those who believe otherwise; they have the same right to their belief as I have to mine. But it is necessary to the happiness of man, that he be mentally faithful to himself. Infidelity does not consist in believing, or in disbelieving; it consists in professing to believe what he does not believe.

It is impossible to calculate the moral mischief, if I may so express it, that mental lying has produced in society. When a man has so far corrupted and prostituted the chastity of his mind, as to subscribe his professional belief to things he does not believe, he has prepared himself for the commission of every other crime. He takes up the trade of a priest for the sake of gain, and, in order to qualify himself for that trade, he begins with a perjury. Can we conceive anything more destructive to morality than this?

Soon after I had published the pamphlet COMMON SENSE, in America, I saw the exceeding probability that a revolution in the system of government would be followed by a revolution in the system of religion.

The adulterous connection of church and state, wherever it had taken place, whether Jewish, Christian, or Turkish, had so effectually prohibited, by pains and penalties, every discussion upon established creeds, and upon first principles of religion, that until the system of government should be changed, those subjects could not be brought fairly and openly before the world; but that whenever this should be done, a revolution in the system of religion would follow. Human inventions and priest-craft would be detected; and man would return to the pure, unmixed, and unadulterated belief of one God, and no more.

RALPH WALDO EMERSON

The Divinity School Address

Ralph Waldo Emerson (1803–1882), born in Boston, joined the Unitarian ministry in 1829 as junior pastor of Boston's Second Church. The death of his nineteen-year-old wife, Ellen, in 1831 had a profound effect on him—in a journal entry dated March 29, 1832, he wrote: "I visited Ellen's tomb and opened the coffin." With his faith in the Bible undermined by German "Higher Criticism," he found himself no longer able to administer the sacrament of the Lord's Supper, and left the ministry in 1832. Traveling in Europe, he met John Stuart Mill, William Wordsworth, Thomas Carlyle, and Samuel Taylor Coleridge, all of whom would help shape his Transcendentalist philosophy, founded on the power of the individual and the interconnectedness of the universe. Emerson's first book, *Nature* (1836), and his celebrated essays, "The American Scholar" (1837) and "Self-Reliance" (1841), distilled these ideas in oracular and highly quotable prose. His career was not without controversies, however. On July 15, 1838, he was invited to give the graduation address at the Harvard Divinity School, a speech that would come to be known as "The Divinity School Address." It created an instant uproar; Emerson was roundly denounced and not invited to speak at Harvard for another thirty years. In the following excerpt, he insists that Jesus was speaking only metaphorically, using poetic license when he referred to himself as the "Son of God," and that the Christian faith was founded on a literal-minded mistake, turning a human being into a "demigod, as the Orientals or the Greeks would describe Osiris or Apollo."

Jesus Christ belonged to the true race of prophets. He saw with open eye the mystery of the soul. Drawn by its severe harmony, ravished with its beauty, he lived in it, and had his being there. Alone in all history, he estimated the greatness of man. One man was true to what is in you and me. He saw that God incarnates himself in man, and evermore goes forth anew to take possession of his world. He said, in this jubilee of sublime emotion, 'I am divine. Through me, God acts; through me, speaks. Would you see God, see me; or, see thee, when thou also thinkest as I now think.' But what a distortion did his doctrine and memory suffer in the same, in the next, and the following ages! There is no doctrine of the Reason which will bear to be taught by the Understanding. The understanding caught this high chant from the poet's lips, and said, in the next age, 'This was Jehovah come down out of heaven. I will kill you, if you say he was a man.' The idioms of his language, and the figures of his rhetoric, have usurped the place of his truth; and churches are not built on his principles, but on his tropes. Christianity became a Mythus, as the poetic teaching of Greece and of Egypt, before. He spoke of miracles; for he felt that man's life was a miracle, and all that man doth, and he knew that this daily miracle shines, as the character ascends. But the word Miracle, as pronounced by Christian churches, gives a false impression; it is Monster. It is not one with the blowing clover and the falling rain.

He felt respect for Moses and the prophets; but no unfit tenderness at postponing their initial revelations, to the hour and the man that now is; to the eternal revelation in the heart. Thus was he a true man. Having seen that the law in us is commanding, he would not suffer it to be commanded. Boldly, with hand, and heart, and life, he declared it was God. Thus is he, as I think, the only soul in history who has appreciated the worth of a man.

1. In this point of view we become very sensible of the first defect of historical Christianity. Historical Christianity has fallen into the error that corrupts all attempts to communicate religion. As it appears to us, and as it has appeared for ages, it is not the doctrine of the soul, but an exaggeration

of the personal, the positive, the ritual. It has dwelt, it dwells, with noxious exaggeration about the person of Jesus. The soul knows no persons. It invites every man to expand to the full circle of the universe, and will have no preferences but those of spontaneous love. But by this eastern monarchy of a Christianity, which indolence and fear have built, the friend of man is made the injurer of man. The manner in which his name is surrounded with expressions, which were once sallies of admiration and love, but are now petrified into official titles, kills all generous sympathy and liking. All who hear me, feel, that the language that describes Christ to Europe and America, is not the style of friendship and enthusiasm to a good and noble heart, but is appropriated and formal,—paints a demigod, as the Orientals or the Greeks would describe Osiris or Apollo.

HERMAN MELVILLE

"A Bosom Friend," from *Moby-Dick*

Herman Melville (1819–1891), as we have seen in earlier sections, was a multifaceted, multitasking author. In Chapter 10 of *Moby-Dick*, "A Bosom Friend," he offers a comic account of Ishmael joining Queequeg in his idol worship, explaining to himself that this is his way of obeying God.

Returning to the Spouter-Inn from the Chapel, I found Queequeg there quite alone; he having left the Chapel before the benediction some time. He was sitting on a bench before the fire, with his feet on the stove hearth, and in one hand was holding close up to his face that little negro idol of his; peering hard into its face, and with a jack-knife gently whittling away at its nose, meanwhile humming to himself in his heathenish way.

But being now interrupted, he put up the image; and pretty soon, going to the table, took up a large book there, and placing it on his lap began counting the pages with deliberate regularity; at every fiftieth page—as I fancied—stopping for a moment, looking vacantly around him, and giving utterance to a long-drawn gurgling whistle of astonishment. He would then begin again at the next fifty; seeming to commence at number one each time, as though he could not count more than fifty, and it was only by such a large number of fifties being found together, that his astonishment at the multitude of pages was excited.

With much interest I sat watching him. Savage though he was, and hideously marred about the face—at least to my taste—his countenance yet had a something in it which was by no means disagreeable. You cannot hide the soul. Through all his unearthly tattooings, I thought I saw the traces of a simple honest heart; and in his large, deep eyes, fiery black and bold, there seemed tokens of a spirit that would dare a thousand devils. And besides all this, there was a certain lofty bearing about the Pagan, which even his uncouthness could not altogether maim. He looked like a man who had never cringed and never had had a creditor. Whether it was, too, that his head being shaved, his forehead was drawn out in freer and brighter relief, and looked more expansive than it otherwise would, this I will not venture to decide; but certain it was his head was phrenologically an excellent one. It may seem ridiculous, but it reminded me of General Washington's head, as seen in the popular busts of him. It had the same long regularly graded retreating slope from above the brows, which were likewise very projecting, like two long promontories thickly wooded on top. Queequeg was George Washington cannibalistically developed.

Whilst I was thus closely scanning him, half-pretending meanwhile to be looking out at the storm from the casement, he never heeded my presence, never troubled himself with so much as a single glance; but appeared wholly occupied with counting the pages of the marvellous book. Considering how sociably we had been sleeping together the night previous, and especially considering the affectionate arm I had found thrown over me upon waking in the morning, I thought this indifference of his very strange. But savages are strange beings; at times you do not know exactly how to take them. At first they are overawing; their calm self-collectedness of simplicity seems as Socratic wisdom. I had noticed also that Queequeg never consorted at all, or but very little, with the other seamen in the inn. He made no advances whatever; appeared to have no desire to enlarge the circle of his acquaintances. All this struck me as mighty singular; yet, upon second thoughts, there was something almost sublime in it. Here was a man some twenty thousand miles from home, by the way of Cape Horn, that is—which was the only way he could get there—thrown among people as strange to him as though he were in the planet Jupiter; and yet he seemed entirely at his ease; preserving the utmost serenity; content with his own companionship; always equal to himself. Surely this was a touch of fine philosophy; though no doubt he had never heard there was such a thing as that. But, perhaps, to be true philosophers, we mortals should not be conscious of so living or so striving. So soon as I hear that such or such a man gives himself out for a philosopher, I conclude that, like the dyspeptic old woman, he must have "broken his digester."

As I sat there in that now lonely room; the fire burning low, in that mild stage when, after its first intensity has warmed the air, it then only glows to be looked at; the evening shades and phantoms gathering round the casements, and peering in upon us silent, solitary twain; the storm booming without in solemn swells; I began to be sensible of strange feelings. I felt a melting in me. No more my splintered heart and maddened hand were turned against the wolfish world. This soothing savage had redeemed it. There he sat, his very indifference speaking a nature in which there lurked no civilized hypocrisies and bland deceits. he was; a very sight of sights to see; yet I began to feel myself mysteriously drawn towards him. And those same things that would have repelled most others, they were the very magnets that thus drew me. I'll try a pagan friend, thought I, since Christian kindness has proved but hollow courtesy. I drew my bench near him, and made some friendly signs and hints, doing my best to talk with him meanwhile. At first he little noticed these advances; but presently, upon my referring to his last night's hospitalities, he made out to ask me whether we were again to be bedfellows. I told him yes; whereat I thought he looked pleased, perhaps a little complimented.

We then turned over the book together, and I endeavored to explain to him the purpose of the printing, and the meaning of the few pictures that were in it. Thus I soon engaged his interest; and from that we went to jabbering the best we could about the various outer sights to be seen in this famous town. Soon I proposed a social smoke; and, producing his pouch and tomahawk, he quietly offered me a puff. And then we sat exchanging puffs from that wild pipe of his, and keeping it regularly passing between us.

If there yet lurked any ice of indifference towards me in the Pagan's breast, this pleasant, genial smoke we had, soon thawed it out, and left us cronies. He seemed to take to me quite as naturally and unbiddenly as I to him; and when our smoke was over, he pressed his forehead against mine, clasped me round the waist, and said that henceforth we were married; meaning, in his country's phrase, that we were bosom friends; he would gladly die for me, if need should be. In a countryman, this sudden flame of friendship would have seemed far too premature, a thing to be much distrusted; but in this simple savage those old rules would not apply.

After supper, and another social chat and smoke, we went to our room together. He made me a present of his embalmed head; took out his enormous tobacco wallet, and groping under the tobacco, drew out some thirty dollars in silver; then spreading them on the table, and mechanically dividing them into two equal portions, pushed one of them towards me, and said it was mine. I was going to remonstrate; but he silenced me by pouring them into my trowsers' pockets. I let them stay. He then went about his evening prayers, took out his idol, and removed the paper firebrand. By certain signs and symptoms, I thought he seemed anxious for me to join him; but well knowing what was to follow, I deliberated a moment whether, in case he invited me, I would comply or otherwise.

I was a good Christian; born and bred in the bosom of the infallible Presbyterian Church. How then could I unite with this wild idolator in worshipping his piece of wood? But what is worship? thought I. Do you suppose now, Ishmael, that the magnanimous God of heaven and earth—pagans and all included—can possibly be jealous of an insignificant bit of black wood? Impossible! But what is worship?—to do the will of God? that is worship. And what is the will of God?—to do to my fellow man what I would have my fellow man to do to me—that is the will of God. Now, Queequeg is my fellow man. And what do I wish that this Queequeg would do to me? Why, unite with me in my particular Presbyterian form of worship. Consequently, I must then unite with him in his; ergo, I must turn idolator. So I kindled the shavings; helped prop up the innocent little idol; offered him burnt biscuit with Queequeg; salamed before him twice or thrice; kissed his nose; and that done, we undressed and went to bed, at peace with our own consciences and all the world. But we did not go to sleep without some little chat.

How it is I know not; but there is no place like a bed for confidential disclosures between friends. Man and wife, they say, there open the very bottom of their souls to each other; and some old couples often lie and chat over old times till nearly morning. Thus, then, in our hearts' honeymoon, lay I and Queequeg—a cosy, loving pair.

EMILY DICKINSON

The Bible is an Antique Volume —

and

Apparently with No Surprise —

Emily Dickinson (1830–1886), now celebrated as one of the greatest nineteenth-century poets, published only ten poems during her lifetime. After a life of seemingly self-chosen seclusion in Amherst, Massachusetts, forty hand-sewn bundles of poems (called "fascicles") were found after her death, containing a total of roughly 1,800 poems. Published posthumously in 1890, the idiosyncratic punctuation (especially the infamous dashes) and uncertain compositional sequence have given rise to countless scholarly speculations and controversies.

Born to a prominent family of lawyers and legislators, Dickinson was educated at the Amherst Academy and enrolled for one year at Mount Holyoke. She was well acquainted with the cutting-edge natural sciences of the day, especially astronomy and geology, casting doubt on the 6,000-year chronology of Earth derived from the Christian Bible. Unlike the rest of her family, Dickinson never joined the church during the Amherst religious revival in the 1850s. She also played fast and loose with the cadence and rhythm of the hymn genre, disrupting its customary structure with the force of enigmatic and unexpected words. We have included two of her poems here. The first, like Emerson's "The Divinity School Address," sees Christianity as a questionable religion founded on an "antique volume" written by "faded men." The second, "Apparently with no surprise," dramatizes the randomness and indifference that preside over the universe.

THE BIBLE IS AN ANTIQUE VOLUME —

The Bible is an antique Volume —
Written by faded men

At the suggestion of Holy Spectres —
Subjects — Bethlehem —
Eden — the ancient Homestead —
Satan — the Brigadier —
Judas — the Great Defaulter —
David — the Troubadour —
Sin — a distinguished Precipice
Others must resist —
Boys that "believe" are very lonesome —
Other Boys are "lost" —
Had but the Tale a warbling Teller —
All the Boys would come —
Orpheus' Sermon captivated —
It did not condemn —

APPARENTLY WITH NO SURPRISE —

Apparently with no surprise —
To any happy Flower
The Frost beheads it at its play —
In accidental power —
The blonde Assassin passes on —
The Sun proceeds unmoved
To measure off another Day
For an approving God.

ZITKALA-ŠA

Why I Am a Pagan

Zitkala-Ša (1876–1938), also known by the birth name "Gertrude Simmons Bonnin," grew up on the Yankton Indian Reservation in South Dakota until she was eight, when she was taken to the White's Manual Labor School in Indiana. The essays that she later published in the

Atlantic and *Harper's Monthly*—including "Impressions of an Indian Childhood" and "School Days of an Indian Girl," later collected in her *American Indian Stories* (1921)—dwell on the loss of her Sioux culture but also the excitement of learning to read, write, and play the violin. From 1897 to 1899 Zitkala-Ša played with the New England Conservatory of Music in Boston. In 1899 she started teaching at the Carlisle Indian Industrial School, playing with that school's band at the 1900 Paris Exposition. She later co-wrote the first Native American opera, *The Sun Dance Opera* (1913). An activist all her life, Zitkala-Ša co-founded the National Council for American Indians in 1926 and served as its president and publicist until her death, lobbying tirelessly for Native American citizenship and civil rights. In the following essay, "Why I Am a Pagan" (1902), another kind of advocacy comes to the foreground: religious non-sectarianism.

When the spirit swells my breast I love to roam leisurely among the green hills; or sometimes, sitting on the brink of the murmuring Missouri, I marvel at the great blue overhead. With half closed eyes I watch the huge cloud shadows in their noiseless play upon the high bluffs opposite me, while into my ear ripple the sweet, soft cadences of the river's song. Folded hands lie in my lap, for the time forgot. My heart and I lie small upon the earth like a grain of throbbing sand. Drifting clouds and tinkling waters, together with the warmth of a genial summer day, bespeak with eloquence the loving Mystery round about us. During the idle while I sat upon the sunny river brink, I grew somewhat, though my response be not so clearly manifest as in the green grass fringing the edge of the high bluff back of me.

At length retracing the uncertain footpath scaling the precipitous embankment, I seek the level lands where grow the wild prairie flowers. And they, the lovely little folk, soothe my soul with their perfumed breath.

Their quaint round faces of varied hue convince the heart which leaps with glad surprise that they, too, are living symbols of omnipotent thought. With a child's eager eye I drink in the myriad star shapes wrought in luxuriant color upon the green. Beautiful is the spiritual essence they embody.

I leave them nodding in the breeze, but take along with me their impress upon my heart. I pause to rest me upon a rock embedded on the side of a foothill facing the low river bottom. Here the Stone-Boy, of whom the

American aborigine tells, frolics about, shooting his baby arrows and shouting aloud with glee at the tiny shafts of lightning that flash from the flying arrow-beaks. What an ideal warrior he became, baffling the siege of the pests of all the land till he triumphed over their united attack. And here he lay,—Inyan our great-great-grandfather, older than the hill he rested on, older than the race of men who love to tell of his wonderful career.

Interwoven with the thread of this Indian legend of the rock, I fain would trace a subtle knowledge of the native folk which enabled them to recognize a kinship to any and all parts of this vast universe. By the leading of an ancient trail I move toward the Indian village.

With the strong, happy sense that both great and small are so surely enfolded in His magnitude that, without a miss, each has his allotted individual ground of opportunities, I am buoyant with good nature.

Yellow Breast, swaying upon the slender stem of a wild sunflower, warbles a sweet assurance of this as I pass near by. Breaking off the clear crystal song, he turns his wee head from side to side eyeing me wisely as slowly I plod with moccasined feet. Then again he yields himself to his song of joy. Flit, flit hither and yon, he fills the summer sky with his swift, sweet melody. And truly does it seem his vigorous freedom lies more in his little spirit than in his wing.

With these thoughts I reach the log cabin whither I am strongly drawn by the tie of a child to an aged mother. Out bounds my four-footed friend to meet me, frisking about my path with unmistakable delight. Chän is a black shaggy dog, "a thorough bred little mongrel" of whom I am very fond. Chän seems to understand many words in Sioux, and will go to her mat even when I whisper the word, though generally I think she is guided by the tone of the voice. Often she tries to imitate the sliding inflection and long drawn out voice to the amusement of our guests, but her articulation is quite beyond my ear. In both my hands I hold her shaggy head and gaze into her large brown eyes. At once the dilated pupils contract into tiny black dots, as if the roguish spirit within would evade my questioning.

Finally resuming the chair at my desk I feel in keen sympathy with my fellow creatures, for I seem to see clearly again that all are akin.

The racial lines, which once were bitterly real, now serve nothing more than marking out a living mosaic of human beings. And even here men of the same color are like the ivory keys of one instrument where each resembles all the rest, yet varies from them in pitch and quality of voice. And those creatures who are for a time mere echoes of another's note are not unlike the fable of the thin sick man whose distorted shadow, dressed like a real creature, came to the old master to make him follow as a shadow. Thus with a compassion for all echoes in human guise, I greet the solemn-faced "native preacher" whom I find awaiting me. I listen with respect for God's creature, though he mouth most strangely the jangling phrases of a bigoted creed.

As our tribe is one large family, where every person is related to all the others, he addressed me:—

"Cousin, I came from the morning church service to talk with you."

"Yes?" I said interrogatively, as he paused for some word from me.

Shifting uneasily about in the straight-backed chair he sat upon, he began: "Every holy day (Sunday) I look about our little God's house, and not seeing you there, I am disappointed. This is why I come to-day. Cousin, as I watch you from afar, I see no unbecoming behavior and hear only good reports of you, which all the more burns me with the wish that you were a church member. Cousin, I was taught long years ago by kind missionaries to read the holy book. These godly men taught me also the folly of our old beliefs.

"There is one God who gives reward or punishment to the race of dead men. In the upper region the Christian dead are gathered in unceasing song and prayer. In the deep pit below, the sinful ones dance in torturing flames.

"Think upon these things, my cousin, and choose now to avoid the after-doom of hell fire!" Then followed a long silence in which he clasped tighter and unclasped again his interlocked fingers.

Like instantaneous lightning flashes came pictures of my own mother's making, for she, too, is now a follower of the new superstition.

"Knocking out the chinking of our log cabin, some evil hand thrust in a burning taper of braided dry grass, but failed of his intent, for the fire died out and the half burned brand fell inward to the floor. Directly above it, on a shelf, lay the holy book. This is what we found after our return from a several days' visit. Surely some great power is hid in the sacred book!"

Brushing away from my eyes many like pictures, I offered midday meal to the converted Indian sitting wordless and with downcast face. No sooner had he risen from the table with "Cousin, I have relished it," than the church bell rang.

Thither he hurried forth with his afternoon sermon. I watched him as he hastened along, his eyes bent fast upon the dusty road till he disappeared at the end of a quarter of a mile.

The little incident recalled to mind the copy of a missionary paper brought to my notice a few days ago, in which a "Christian" pugilist commented upon a recent article of mine, grossly perverting the spirit of my pen. Still I would not forget that the pale-faced missionary and the hoodooed aborigine are both God's creatures, though small indeed their own conceptions of Infinite Love. A wee child toddling in a wonder world, I prefer to their dogma my excursions into the natural gardens where the voice of the Great Spirit is heard in the twittering of birds, the rippling of mighty waters, and the sweet breathing of flowers. If this is Paganism, then at present, at least, I am a Pagan.

ZORA NEALE HURSTON

Moses, Man of the Mountain

Zora Neale Hurston (1891–1960), a key figure of the Harlem Renaissance, was born in Notasulga, Alabama, and grew up in Eatonville, Florida, an all-black community whose storytelling culture would be featured in her 1928 essay, "How it Feels to be Colored Me," and in her best-known novel, *Their Eyes Were Watching God* (1937). Hurston made her debut with her short story "Spunk," which was included in Alain Locke's seminal anthology, *The New Negro* (1925). After initial studies at Howard University, Hurston received her BA in 1928 from Barnard College, Columbia University, the first African American woman to do so, working with the eminent anthropologist Franz Boaz and fellow student Margaret Mead. Her extensive fieldwork in Alabama, Florida, and Louisiana, and then Jamaica, Haiti, and Honduras, inspired works both fictional and nonfictional: *Jonah's Gourd Vine* (1934), *Mules and Men* (1935), and *Tell My Horse* (1938). Hurston also wrote an autobiography, *Dust Tracks on a Road* (1942). In *Moses, Man of the Mountain* (1939), she blends the Old Testament version with the Moses of Asia, Africa, and the Caribbean. The author's introduction to this work follows here.

Moses was an old man with a beard. He was the great law-giver. He had some trouble with Pharaoh about some plagues and led the Children of Israel out of Egypt and on to the Promised Land. He died on Mount Nebo and the angels buried him there. That is the common concept of Moses in the Christian world.

But there are other concepts of Moses abroad in the world. Asia and all the Near East are sown with legends of this character. They are so numerous and so varied that some students have come to doubt if the Moses of the Christian concept is real. Then Africa has her mouth on Moses. All across the continent there are the legends of the greatness of Moses, but not because of his beard nor because he brought the laws down from Sinai. No, he is revered because he had the power to go up the mountain and to bring them down. Many men could climb mountains. Anyone could bring down laws that had been handed to them. But who can talk with God face to face? Who had the power to command God to go to a peak of a mountain and there demand of Him laws with which to govern a nation? What other man has ever seen with his eyes even the back part of God's glory? Who else has ever commanded the wind and the hail? The light and darkness? That calls for power, and that is what Africa sees in Moses to worship. For he is worshipped as a god.

In Haiti, the highest god in the Haitian pantheon is Damballa Ouedo Ouedo Tocan Freda Dahomey and he is identified as Moses, the serpent god. But this deity did not originate in Haiti. His home is in Dahomey and is worshipped there extensively. Moses had his rod of power, which was a living serpent. So that in every temple of Damballa there is a living snake, or the symbol.

And this worship of Moses as the greatest one of magic is not confined to Africa. Wherever the children of Africa have been scattered by slavery, there is the acceptance of Moses as the fountain of mystic powers. This is not confined to Negroes. In America there are countless people of other races depending upon mystic symbols and seals and syllables said to have been used by Moses to work his wonders. There are millions of copies of a certain book, *The Sixth and Seventh Books of Moses,* being read and consulted in secret because the readers believe in Moses. Some even maintain that the stories of the miracles of Jesus are but Mosaic legends told again. Nobody can tell how many tales and legends of Moses are alive in the world nor how far they have travelled, so many have collected around his name.

So all across Africa, America, the West Indies, there are tales of the powers of Moses and great worship of him and his powers. But it does not flow

from the Ten Commandments. It is his rod of power, the terror he showed before all Israel and to Pharaoh, and THAT MIGHTY HAND.
THE AUTHOR.

GLORIA ANZALDÚA

Borderlands/La Frontera

Gloria Anzaldúa (1942–2004), Chicana queer theorist and feminist, grew up in the Rio Grande Valley of south Texas, of mixed indigenous and Spanish descent. The name Anzaldúa is of Basque origin. Best known for *Borderlands/La Frontera* (1987), Anzaldúa weaves Spanish and English into a lyrical prose, challenging the linguistic competence of mainstream readers while fashioning a manifesto for a "new Mestiza," an aesthetic that blurs the physical borders between Texas and Mexico as well as the less tangible borders that divide one sexual identity from another, and the human world from the nonhuman. Her autobiographical essay "La Prieta" was published in two forms: mostly in English in *This Bridge Called My Back* (1981), coedited with Cherrie Moraga, and mostly in Spanish in *Esta puente, mi espalda* (1989). Anzaldúa has also written children's books including *Friends from the Other Side/Amigos del Otro Lado* (1993) and *Prietita and the Ghost Woman/Prietita y la Llorona* (1995). In the following excerpt from *Borderlands/La Frontera*, she describes a Mesoamerican Virgin Mary.

COATLALOPEUH, SHE WHO HAS DOMINION OVER SERPENTS

Mi mamagrande Ramona toda su vida mantuvo un altar pequeño en la esquina del comedor. Siempre tenia las velas prendidas. Alli hacia promesas a la Virgen de Guadalupe. [My grandmother Ramona all her life maintained a small altar in the corner of the dining room. She always had candles lit. There she made vows to the Virgin of Guadalupe.] My family, like most Chicanos, did not practice Roman Catholicism but a folk Catholicism with many pagan elements. *La Virgen de Guadalupe*'s Indian name is *Coatlalopeuh*. She is the central deity connecting us to our Indian ancestry.

Coatlalopeuh is descended from, or is an aspect of, earlier Mesoamerican fertility and Earth Goddesses. The earliest is *Coatlicue*, or "Serpent Skirt." She had a human skull or serpent for a head, a necklace of human hearts, a skirt of twisted serpents and taloned feet. As creator goddess, she was mother of the celestial deities, and of *Huitzilopochtli* and his sister, *Coyolxauhqui*, She With Golden Bells, Goddess of the Moon, who was decapitated by her brother. Another aspect of *Coatlicue* is *Tonantsi*. (In some Nahuatl dialects *Tonantsi* is called *Tonatzin*, literally, "Our Holy Mother.") The Totonacs, tired of the Aztec human sacrifices to the male god, *Huitzilopochtli*, renewed their reverence for *Tonantsi* who preferred the sacrifice of birds and small animals.

The male-dominated Azteca-Mexica culture drove the powerful female deities underground by giving them monstrous attributes and by substituting male deities in their place, thus splitting the female Self and the female deities. They divided her who had been complete, who possessed both upper (light) and underworld (dark) aspects. *Coatlicue*, the Serpent goddess, and her more sinister aspects, *Tlazolteotl* and *Cihuacoatl*, were "darkened" and disempowered much in the same manner as the Indian *Kali*.

Tonantsi—split from her dark guises, *Coatlicue*, *Tlazolteotl*, and *Cihuacoatl*—became the good mother. The Nahuas, through ritual and prayer, sought to oblige *Tonantsi* to ensure their health and the growth of their crops. It was she who gave México the cactus plant to provide her people with milk and pulque. It was she who defended her children against the wrath of the Christian God by challenging God, her son, to produce mother's milk (as she had done) to prove that his benevolence equaled his disciplinary harshness.

After the Conquest, the Spaniards and their church continued to split *Tonantsi/Guadalupe*. They desexed *Guadalupe*, taking *Coatlalopeuh*, the serpent/sexuality, out of her. They completed the split begun by the Nahuas by making *la Virgen de Guadalupe / Virgin María* into chaste virgins and *Tlazolteotle/Coatlicuella Chingada* into *putas* [whores]; into the Beauties and the Beasts. They went even further; they made all Indian deities and religious practices the work of the devil.

Thus *Tonantsi* became *Guadalupe*, the chaste protective mother, the defender of the Mexican people . . .

Guadalupe appeared on December 9, 1531, on the spot where the Aztec goddess, *Tonantsi* ("Our Lady Mother"), had been worshipped by the Nahuas and where a temple to her had stood. Speaking Nahua, she told Juan Diego, a poor Indian crossing Tepeyac Hill, whose Indian name was *Cuautlaohuac* and who belonged to the *mazehual* class, the humblest within the Chichimeca tribe, that her name was *María Coatlalopeuh*. *Coatl* is the Nahuatl word for serpent. *Lopeuh* means "the one who has dominion over serpents." I interpret this as "the one who is at one with the beasts." Some spell her name *Coatlaxopeuh* (pronounced "*Cuatlashupe*" in Nahuatl) and say that "*xopeuh*" means "crushed or stepped on with distain." Some say it means "she who crushed the serpent," with the serpent as the symbol of the indigenous religion, meaning that her religion was to take the place of the Aztec religion. Because *Coatlalopeuh* was homophonous to the Spanish *Guadalupe*, the Spanish identified her with the dark virgin, *Guadalupe*, patroness of West Central Spain.

From that meeting, Juan Diego walked away with the image of *la Virgen* painted on his cloak. Soon after, Mexico ceased to belong to Spain, and *la Virgen de Guadalupe* began to eclipse all the other male and female religious figures in Mexico, Central America, and parts of the U.S. Southwest. "*Desde entonces para el mexicano ser Guadalupano es algo esencial/* Since then for the Mexican, to be a *Guadalupano* is something essential . . ."

Mi Virgen Morena	My brown virgin
Mi Virgen Ranchera	my country virgin
Eres nuestra Reina	you are our queen
México es tu tierra	Mexico is your land
Y tú su bandera.	and you its flag.

—"LA VIRGEN RANCHERA"

In 1660 the Roman Catholic Church named her Mother of God, considering her synonymous with *la Virgen María*; she became *la Santa Patrona de los mexicanos* [the patron saint of Mexicans]. The role of defender (or patron) has traditionally been assigned to male gods. During the Mexican Revolution, Emiliano Zapata and Miguel Hidalgo used her image to move *el pueblo mexicano* [the Mexican people] toward freedom. During the 1965 grape strike in Delano, California, and in subsequent Chicano farmworkers' marches in Texas and other parts of the Southwest, her image on banners heralded and united the farmworkers. *Pachucos* (zoot suiters) tattoo her image on their bodies. Today, in Texas and Mexico she is more venerated than Jesus or God the Father. In the Lower Rio Grande Valley of south Texas it is *la Virgen de San Juan de los Lagos* (an aspect of *Guadalupe*) that is worshipped by thousands every day at her shrine in San Juan. In Texas she is considered the patron saint of Chicanos. *Cuando Carito, mi hermanito* [when Carito, my brother], was missing in action and, later, wounded in Viet Nam, *mi mama got on her knees y le prometió a Ella que si su hijito volvía vivo* [and promised Her that if her son returned alive] she would crawl on her knees and light novenas in her honor.

Today, *la Virgen de Guadalupe* is the single most potent religious, political, and cultural image of the Chicano/*mexicano*. She, like my race, is a synthesis of the old world and the new, of the religion and culture of the two races in our psyche, the conquerors and the conquered. She is the symbol of the mestizo true to his or her Indian values. *La cultura chicana* identifies with the mother (Indian) rather than with the father (Spanish). Our faith is rooted in indigenous attributes, images, symbols, magic, and myth. Because *Guadalupe* took upon herself the psychological and physical devastation of the conquered and oppressed *indio*, she is our spiritual, political, and psychological symbol. As a symbol of hope and faith, she sustains and insures our survival. The Indian, despite extreme despair, suffering, and near genocide, has survived. To Mexicans on both sides of the border, *Guadalupe* is the symbol of our rebellion against the rich, upper and middle class; against their subjugation of the poor and the *indio*.

Guadalupe unites people of different races, religions, languages: Chicano protestants, American Indians, and whites. "*Nuestra abogada siempre serás/* Our mediatrix you will always be." She mediates between the Spanish and the Indian cultures (or three cultures as in the case of *mexicanos* of African or other ancestry) and between Chicanos and the white world. She mediates between humans and the divine, between this reality and the reality of spirit entities. *La Virgen de Guadalupe* is the symbol of ethnic identity and of the tolerance for ambiguity that Chicanos-*mexicanos*, people of mixed race, people who have Indian blood, people who cross cultures, by necessity possess. . . .

N. SCOTT MOMADAY

House Made of Dawn

N. Scott Momaday (born 1934) is best known for *House Made of Dawn* (1968), the first Native American novel to be awarded the Pulitzer Prize. Eighteen other books followed, poetry as well as prose, including *The Way to Rainy Mountain* (1969), *The Names* (1976), *The Ancient Child* (1989), and *Again the Far Morning: New and Selected Poems* (2011). Born in Lawton, Oklahoma, to a painter and a writer, Momaday inherited from his parents their Kiowa culture as well as their love of image and word. His father, Al Momaday, provided the illustrations for *The Way to Rainy Mountain*. Momaday has taught at Stanford, where he received his PhD, and the University of California, Berkeley, where he designed the graduate program for Indian Studies. He was the first American writer to be invited to teach at the University of Moscow. The recipient of twenty honorary degrees as well as the 2007 National Medal of Arts, Momaday also received the *Premio Letterario Internazionale Mondello*, Italy's highest literary award. In this excerpt from *House Made of Dawn*, he dramatizes the ritualized violence in the folk religion of the Southwest, a Christianity transformed by Native practices.

This, according to Father Olguin: Santiago rode southward into Mexico. Although his horse was sleek and well bred, he himself was dressed in the guise of a peon. When he had journeyed a long way, he stopped to rest at the house of an old man and his wife. They were poor and miserable people, but they were kind and gracious, too, and they bade Santiago welcome. They gave him cold water to slake his thirst and cheerful words to comfort him. There was nothing in the house to eat; but a single, aged rooster strutted back and forth in the yard. The rooster was their only possession of value, but the old man and woman killed and cooked it for their guest. That night they gave him their bed while they slept on the cold ground. When morning came, Santiago told them who he was. He gave them his blessing and continued on his way.

He rode on for many days, and at last he came to the royal city. That day the king proclaimed that there should be a great celebration and many games, dangerous contests of skill and strength. Santiago entered the games. He was derided at first, for everyone supposed him to be a peon and a fool. But he was victorious, and as a prize he was allowed to choose and marry one of the king's daughters. He chose a girl with almond-shaped eyes and long black hair, and he made ready to return with her to the north. The king was filled with resentment to think that a peon should carry his daughter away, and he conceived a plan to kill the saint. Publicly he ordered a company of soldiers to escort the travelers safely on their journey home. But under cover he directed that Santiago should be put to death as soon as the train was away from the city gates.

Now by a miracle Santiago brought forth from his mouth the rooster, whole and alive, which the old man and woman had given him to eat. The rooster warned him at once of what the soldiers meant to do and gave him the spur from its right leg. When the soldiers turned upon him, Santiago slew them with a magic sword.

At the end of the journey Santiago had no longer any need of his horse, and the horse spoke to him and said: "Now you must sacrifice me for the good of the people." Accordingly, Santiago stabbed the horse to death, and from its blood there issued a great herd of horses, enough for all the Pueblo people. After that, the rooster spoke to Santiago and said: "Now you must sacrifice me for the good of the people." And accordingly Santiago tore the bird apart with his bare hands and scattered the remains all about on the ground. The blood and feathers of the bird became cultivated plants and domestic animals, enough for all the Pueblo people.

The late afternoon of the feast of Santiago was still and hot, and there were no clouds in the sky. The river was low, and the grape leaves had begun to curl in the fire of the sun. The pale yellow grass on the river plain was tall, for the cattle and sheep had been taken to graze in the high meadows, and alkali lay like frost in the cracked beds of the irrigation ditches. It was a pale midsummer day, two or three hours before sundown.

Father Olguin went with Angela St. John out of the rectory. They walked slowly, talking together, along the street which ran uphill toward the Middle. There were houses along the north side of the street, patches of grapes and corn and melons on the south. There had been no rain in the valley for a long time, and the dust was deep in the street. By one of the houses a thin old man tended his long hair, careless of their passing. He was bent forward, and his hair reached nearly to the ground. His head was cocked, so that the hair hung all together on one side of his face and in front of the shoulder. He brushed slowly the inside of it, downward from the ear, with a bunch of quills. His hands worked easily, intimately, with the coarse, shining hair, in which there was no appearance of softness, except that light moved upon it as on a pouring of oil.

They saw faces in the dark windows and doorways of the houses, half in hiding, watching with wide, solemn eyes. The priest paused among them, and Angela drew away from him a little. She was among the houses of the town, and there was an excitement all around, a ceaseless murmur under the sound of the drum, lost in back of the walls, apart from the dead silent light of the afternoon. When she had got too far ahead, she waited beside a windmill and a trough, around which there was a muddy black ring filled with the tracks of animals. In the end of July the town smelled of animals, and smoke, and sawed lumber, and the sweet, moist smell of bread that has been cut open and left to stand.

When they came to the Middle, there was a lot of sound going on. The people of the town had begun to gather along the walls of the houses, and a group of small boys ran about, tumbling on the ground and shouting. The Middle was an ancient place, nearly a hundred yards long by forty wide. The smooth, packed earth was not level, as it appeared at first to be, but rolling and concave, rising slightly to the walls around it so that there were no edges or angles in the dry clay of the ground and the houses; there were only the soft contours and depressions of things worn down and away in time. From within, the space appeared to be enclosed, but there were narrow passages at the four corners and a wide opening midway along the south side, where once there had been a house; there was now a low, uneven ruin of earthen bricks, nearly indistinguishable from the floor and the back wall of the recess. There Angela and the priest entered and turned, waiting, conscious of themselves, to be absorbed in the sound and motion of the town.

The oldest houses, those at the west end and on the north side, were tiered, two and three stories high, and clusters of men and women stood about on the roofs. The drummer was there, on a rooftop, still beating on the drum, slowly, exactly in time, with only a quick, nearly imperceptible motion of the hand, standing perfectly still and even-eyed, old and imperturbable. Just there, in sight of him, the deep vibration of the drum seemed to Angela scarcely louder, deeper, than it had an hour before and a half mile away, when she was in a room of the rectory, momentarily alone with it and borne upon it. And it should not have seemed less had she been beyond the river and among the hills; the drum held sway in the valley, like the breaking of thunder far away, echoing on and on in a region out of time. One has only to take it for granted, she thought, like a storm coming up, and the certain, rare downfall of rain. She pulled away from it and caught sight of window frames, blue and white, earthen ovens like the hives of bees, vigas, dogs and flies. Equidistant from all the walls of the Middle there was a fresh hole in the ground, about eight inches in diameter, and a small mound of sandy earth.

In a little while the riders came into the west end in groups of three and four, on their best animals. There were seven or eight men and as many boys. They crossed the width of the Middle and doubled back in single file along the wall. Abel rode one of his grandfather's roan black-maned mares and sat too rigid in the saddle, too careful of the gentle mare. For the first time since coming home he had done away with his uniform. He had put on his old clothes: Levi's and a wide black belt, a gray work shirt, and a straw hat with a low crown and a wide, rolled brim. His sleeves were rolled high, and his arms and hands were newly sunburned. The appearance of one of the men was striking. He was large, lithe, and white-skinned; he wore little round colored glasses and rode a fine black horse of good blood. The black horse was high-spirited, and the white man held its head high on the reins and kept the stirrups free of it. He was the last in line, and when he had taken his place with the others in the shade of the wall, an official of the town brought a large white rooster from one of the houses. He placed it in the hole and moved the dirt in upon it until it was buried to the neck. Its white head jerked from side to side, so that its comb and wattles shook and its hackles were spread out on the sand. The townspeople laughed to see it so, buried and fearful, its round, unblinking eyes yellow and bright in the dying day. The official moved away, and the first horse and rider bolted from the shade. Then, one at a time, the others rode down upon the rooster and reached for it, holding to the horns of their saddles and leaning sharply down against the shoulders of their mounts. Most of the animals were untrained, and they drew up when their riders leaned. One and then another of the boys fell to the ground, and the townspeople jeered in delight. When it came Abel's turn, he made a poor showing, full of caution and gesture. Angela despised him a little; she would remember that, but for the moment her attention was spread over the whole fantastic scene, and she felt herself going limp. With the rush of the first horse and rider all her senses were struck at once. The sun, low and growing orange, burned on her face and arms. She closed her eyes, but it was there still, the brilliant disorder of motion: the dark and darker gold of the earth and earthen walls and the deep incisions of shade and the vague, violent procession of centaurs. So unintelligible the sharp sound of voices and hoofs, the odor of animals and sweat, so empty of meaning it all was, and yet so full of appearance. When he passed in front of her at a walk, on his way back, she was ready again to deceive. She smiled at him and looked away.

The white man was large and thickset, powerful and deliberate in his movements. The black horse started fast and ran easily, even as the white man leaned down from it. He got hold of the rooster and took it from the ground. Then he was upright in the saddle, suddenly, without once having shifted the center of his weight from the spine of the running horse. He reined in hard, so that the animal tucked in its haunches and its hoofs plowed in the ground. Angela thrilled to see it handled so, as if the white man were its will and all its shivering force were drawn to his bow. A perfect commotion, full of symmetry and sound. And yet there was something out of place, some flaw in proportion or design, some unnatural thing. She keened to it, whatever it was, and an old fascination returned upon her. The black horse whirled. The white man looked down the Middle toward the other riders and held the rooster up and away in his left hand while its great wings beat the air. He started back on the dancing horse, slowly, along the south wall, and the townspeople gave him room. Then he faced her, and Angela saw that under his hat the pale yellow hair was thin and cut close to the scalp; the tight skin of the head was visible and pale and pink. The face was huge and mottled white and pink, and the thick, open lips were blue and violet. The flesh of the jowls was loose, and it rode on the bone of the jaws. There were no brows, and the small, round black glasses lay like pennies close together and flat against the enormous face. The albino was directly above her for one instant, huge and hideous at the extremity of the terrified bird. It was then her eyes were drawn to the heavy, bloodless hand at the throat of the bird. It was like marble or chert, equal in the composure of stone to the awful frenzy of the bird, and the bright red wattles of the bird lay still among the long blue nails, and the comb on the swollen heel of the hand. And then he was past. He rode in among the riders, and they, too, parted for him, watching to see whom he would choose, respectful, wary, and on edge. After a long time of playing the game, he rode beside Abel, turned suddenly upon him, and began to flail him with the rooster. Their horses wheeled, and the others drew off. Again and again the white man struck him, heavily, brutally, upon the chest and shoulders and head, and Abel threw up his hands, but the great bird fell upon them and beat them down. Abel was not used to the game, and the white man was too strong and quick for him. The roan mare lunged, but it was hemmed in against the wall; the black horse lay close against it, keeping it off balance, coiled and wild in its eyes. The white man leaned and struck, back and forth, with only the mute malice of the act itself, careless, undetermined, almost composed in some final, preeminent sense. Then the bird was dead, and still he swung it down and across, and the neck of the bird was broken and the flesh torn open and the blood splashed everywhere about. The mare hopped and squatted and reared, and Abel hung on. The black horse stood its ground, cutting off every line of retreat, pressing upon the terrified mare. It was all a dream, a tumultuous shadow, and before it the fading red glare of the sun shone on bits of silver and panes of glass and softer on the glowing, absorbent walls of the town. The feathers and flesh and entrails of the bird were scattered about on the ground, and the dogs crept near and crouched, and it was finished. Here and there the townswomen threw water to finish it in sacrifice.

.

DENISE LEVERTOV

The Altars in the Street

Denise Levertov (1923–1997), born in England to a Welsh mother and a Hasidic Russian father who became an Anglican priest, would continue to ponder the mutability of faith throughout her life. Moving to the United States in 1948 after her marriage, Levertov became loosely affiliated with the Black Mountain poets during the 1950s. As poetry editor of *The Nation* during the '60s and '70s, she was an important influence

on other poets as well as a capable ally. Her own poetry, highly political and energized by her opposition to the Vietnam War, grew into a
substantial corpus: *The Sorrow Dance* (1967); *Relearning the Alphabet*
(1970); *To Stay Alive* (1971); and *The Freeing of the Dust* (1975), based
on her trip to North Vietnam in the fall of 1972. Levertov taught at many
universities, including MIT, Brandeis, and for eleven years at Stanford
(1982–1993). She converted to Christianity in 1984, becoming a Roman
Catholic in 1989. In this poem from *The Sorrow Dance*, the Buddhist
altars of the Vietnamese children are at once fragile and vital, greeting
the onslaught of tanks with anguish and exultation.

Children begin at green dawn to nimbly build
topheavy altars, overweighted with prayers
thronged each instant more densely
with almost-visible ancestors.
Where tanks have cracked the roadway
the frail altars shake; here a boy
with red stumps for hands steadies a corner,
here one adjusts with his crutch the holy base.
The vast silence of Buddha overtakes
and overrules the oncoming roar
of tragic life that fills alleys and avenues
it blocks the way of pedicabs, police, convoys.
The hale and maimed together
hurry to construct for the Buddha
a dwelling at each intersection. Each altar
made from whatever stones, sticks, dreams, are at hand,
is a facet of one altar; by noon
the whole city in all its corruption,
all its shed blood the monsoon cannot wash away,
has become a temple,
fragile, insolent, absolute.

GARY SNYDER

Grace

Gary Snyder (born 1930), as noted in the "Food" section of this volume, brings together nature writing, indigenous religions, and Zen Buddhism to create a Pacific Rim aesthetic: spare, concrete, occasionally riddling, with a deep ecological awareness. In the following selection, he brings all of these to bear on the concept of "grace," a word with resonances in more than one religion.

There is a verse chanted by Zen Buddhists called the "Four Great Vows." The first line goes: "Sentient beings are numberless, I vow to save them." Shujo muhen seigando. It's a bit daunting to announce this intention—aloud—to the universe daily. This vow stalked me for several years and finally pounced: I realized that I had vowed to let the sentient beings save me. In a similar way, the precept against taking life, against causing harm, doesn't stop at the negative. It is urging us to give life, to undo harm.

Those who attain some ultimate understanding of these things are called "Buddhas," which means "awakened ones." The word is connected to the English verb "to bud." I once wrote a little parable:

WHO THE BUDDHAS ARE

All the beings of the universe are already realized. That is, with the exception of one or two beings. In those rare cases the cities, villages, meadows, and forests, with their birds, flowers, animals, rivers, trees, and humans, that surround such a person, all collaborate to educate, serve, challenge, and instruct such a one, until that person also becomes a New Beginner Enlightened Being. Recently realized beings are enthusiastic to teach and train and start schools and practices. Being able to do this develops their confidence and insight up to the point that they are fully ready to join the seamless world of interdependent play. Such new enlightened beginners are called "Buddhas" and they like to say things like "I am enlightened, together with the whole universe" and so forth.

Good luck! One might say. The test of the pudding is in the eating. It narrows down to a look at the conduct that is entwined with food. At mealtime (seated on the floor in lines) the Zen monks chant:

Porridge is effective in ten ways
To aid the student of Zen
No limit to the good result
Consummating eternal happiness

and

Oh, all you demons and spirits
We now offer this food to you
May all of you everywhere
Share it with us together

and

We wash our bowls in this water
It has the flavor of ambrosial dew
We offer it to all demons and spirits
May all be filled and satisfied
om makula sai svaha

And several other verses. These superstitious-sounding old ritual formulas are never mentioned in lectures, but they are at the heart of the teaching. Their import is older than Buddhism or any of the world religions. They are part of the first and last practice of the wild: Grace.

Everyone who ever lived took the lives of other animals, pulled plants, plucked fruit, and ate. Primary people have their own ways of trying to understand the precept of nonharming. They knew that taking life required gratitude and care. There is no death that is not somebody's food, no life that is not somebody's death. Some would take this as a sign that the universe is fundamentally flawed. This leads to a disgust with self, with humanity, and with nature. Otherworldly philosophies end up doing more damage to the planet (and human psyches) than the pain and suffering that is in the existential conditions they seek to transcend.

The archaic religion is to kill god and eat him. Or her. The shimmering food-chain, the food-web, is the scary, beautiful condition of the biosphere. Subsistence people live without excuses. The blood is on your own hands as you divide the liver from the gallbladder. You have watched the color fade on the glimmer of the trout. A subsistence economy is a sacramental economy because it has faced up to one of the critical problems of life and death: the taking of life for food. Contemporary people do not need to hunt, many cannot even afford meat, and in the developed world the variety of foods available to us makes the avoidance of meat an easy choice. Forests in the tropics are cut to make pasture to raise beef for the American market. Our distance from the source of our food enables us to be superficially more comfortable, and distinctly more ignorant.

Eating is a sacrament. The grace we say clears our hearts and guides the children and welcomes the guest, all at the same time. We look at eggs, apples, and stew. They are evidence of plentitude, excess, a great reproductive exuberance. Millions of grains of grass-seed that will become rice or flour, millions of codfish fry that will never, and must never, grow to maturity. Innumerable little seeds are sacrifices to the food-chain. A parsnip in the ground is a marvel of living chemistry, making sugars and flavors from earth, air, water. And if we do eat meat it is the life, the bounce, the swish, of a great alert being with keen ears and lovely eyes, with foursquare feet and a huge beating heart that we eat, let us not deceive ourselves.

We too will be offerings—we are all edible. And if we are not devoured quickly, we are big enough (like old down trees) to provide a long slow meal to the smaller critters. Whale carcasses that sink several miles deep in the ocean feed organisms in the dark for fifteen years. (It seems to take about two thousand to exhaust the nutrients in a high civilization.)

At our house we say a Buddhist grace—

We venerate the Three Treasures (teachers, the wild, and friends)
And are thankful for this meal
The work of many people
And the sharing of other forms of life.

Anyone can use a grace from their own tradition (and really give it meaning)—or make up their own. Saying some form of grace is never inappropriate, and speeches and announcements can be tacked onto it. It is a plain, ordinary, old-fashioned little thing to do that connects us with all our ancestors.

> A monk asked Dong-shan: "Is there a practice for people to follow?"
> Dong-shan answered: "When you become a real person, there is such a practice."

Sarvamangalam. Good luck to all.

JACK KEROUAC

The Dharma Bums

Jack [Jean-Louis] Kerouac (1922–69), born in Lowell, Massachusetts, to Québécois parents, spoke Joual, a dialect of the French-Canadian working class, untill age six. An early draft of *On the Road* (1957) was also in that language. Athletic prowess won him a football scholarship to Columbia, but he dropped out after one year, joining the United States Merchant Marine and then the U.S. Navy. *On the Road,* the Beat classic featuring road trips with Neal Cassady, was completed around April 1951, though it was not immediately accepted by publishers. Kerouac took various jobs— as railroad brakeman and fire lookout—as he proceeded with his jazz-and-Buddhism-inspired autobiographical works, including *The Dharma Bums* (1958), *The Subterraneans* (1958), *Visions of Cody* (1960), *Big Sur* (1962), and *Desolation Angels* (1965)—tributes in various ways to his friends Gary Snyder, Allen Ginsberg, and William Burroughs. Kerouac's poetry, especially *Mexico City Blues* (1959), is also eclectic and improvisational. This excerpt from *The Dharma Bums* features Chinatown Buddhism with a heady mix of African American Christianity.

And that's what I said to myself, "I am now on the road to Heaven." Suddenly it became clear to me that there was a lot of teaching for me to do in my lifetime. As I say, I saw Japhy before I left, we wandered sadly to the Chinatown park, had a dinner in Nam Yuen's, came out, sat in the Sunday morning grass and suddenly here was this group of Negro preachers standing in the grass preaching to desultory groups of uninterested Chinese families letting their kiddies romp in the grass and to bums who cared just a little bit more. A big fat woman like Ma Rainey was standing there with her legs outspread howling out a tremendous sermon in a booming voice that kept breaking from speech to blues-singing music, beautiful, and the reason why this woman, who was such a great preacher, was not preaching in a church was because every now and then she just simply had to go sploosh and spit as hard as she could off to the side in the grass, "And I'm tellin you, the Lawd will take care of you if you recognize that you have a new field . . . Yes!"—and sploosh, she turns and spits about ten feet away a great sploosh of spit. "See," I told Japhy, "she couldn't do that in a church, that's her flaw as a preacher as far as the churches are concerned but boy have you ever heard a greater preacher?"

"Yeah," says Japhy. "But I don't like all that Jesus stuff she's talking about."

"What's wrong with Jesus? Didn't Jesus speak of Heaven? Isn't Heaven Buddha's nirvana?"

"According to your own interpretation, Smith."

"Japhy, there were things I wanted to tell Rosie and I felt suppressed by this schism we have about separating Buddhism from Christianity, East from West, what the hell difference does it make? We're all in Heaven now, ain't we?"

"Who said so?"

"Is this nirvana we're in now or ain't it?"

"It's both nirvana and samsara we're in now."

"Words, words, what's in a word? Nirvana by any other name. Besides don't you hear that big old gal calling you and telling you you've got a new field, a new Buddha-field boy?" Japhy was so pleased he wrinkled his eyes and smiled. "Whole Buddha-fields in every direction for each one of us, and Rosie was a flower we let wither."

"Never spoke more truly, Ray."

The big old gal came up to us, too, noticing us, especially me. She called me darling, in fact. "I kin see from your eyes that you understand ever word I'm sayin, darling. I want you to know that I want you to go to Heaven and be happy. I want you to understand ever word I'm sayin."

"I hear and understand."

Across the street was the new Buddhist temple some young Chamber of Commerce Chinatown Chinese were trying to build, by themselves, one night I'd come by there and, drunk, pitched in with them with a wheelbarrow hauling sand from outside in, they were young Sinclair Lewis idealistic forwardlooking kids who lived in nice homes but put on jeans to come down and work on the church, like you might expect in some midwest town some midwest lads with a bright-faced Richard Nixon leader, the prairie all around. Here in the heart of the tremendously sophisticated little city called San Francisco Chinatown they were doing the same thing but their church was the church of Buddha. Strangely Japhy wasn't interested in the Buddhism of San Francisco Chinatown because it was traditional Buddhism, not the Zen intellectual artistic Buddhism he loved—but I was trying to make him see that everything was the same. In the restaurant we'd eaten with chopsticks and enjoyed it. Now he was saying goodbye to me and I didn't know when I'd see him again.

Behind the colored woman was a man preacher who kept rocking with his eyes closed saying "That's right." She said to us "Bless both you boys for listenin to what I have to say. Remember that we know that all things work together for good to them that loves God, to them who are the called accordin to His purpose. Romans eight eighteen, younguns. And there's a new field a-waitin for ya, and be sure you live up to every one of your obligations. Hear now?"

"Yes, ma'am, be seein ya." I said goodbye to Japhy.

JOANNE KYGER

Here in Oaxaca It's the Night of the Radishes

Joanne Kyger (born 1934), poet and Zen Buddhist, became part of the San Francisco poetry scene in 1957, moving in the circles of Jack Spicer and Robert Duncan as well as those of the Beat Poets. In 1960 she joined Gary Snyder in Japan, marrying him upon her arrival. Together they traveled with Allen Ginsberg and Peter Orlovsky to India, meeting with the Dalai

Lama. Her first book of poetry, *The Tapestry and the Web* (1965), published after her return to the United States, was widely read and praised. Her prose from those years, *Strange Big Moon: Japan and India Journals, 1960–1964*, republished in 2000, remains one of the most interesting experiments in journal writing since Thoreau. Kyger later also traveled widely throughout Mexico. This selection from *God Never Dies* (2004) describes the "Night of the Radishes," December 23, when the residents of Oaxaca carve votive figures out of radishes, here featuring a catholic Buddha.

Here in Oaxaca it's the Night of the Radishes
    Now I wave from the green
       balcony above the gardenia
         in my shoes without socks the sun
  is frankly generous
   today when everyone needs
room at the inn   Time to put
  the buddha back in place
He doesn't mind being 'catholic'
  in Mexico
    Part of the long preliminaries of the days
     preparation
       for carving through the red skin

DECEMBER 23 TUESDAY

WASHINGTON IRVING

Legend of the Arabian Astrologer

Washington Irving (1783–1859), short story writer, essayist, and historian, is best known for "Rip Van Winkle" and "The Legend of Sleepy Hollow," both collected in *The Sketch Book of Geoffrey Crayon, Gent.* (1819–1820). His historical work includes a spoof, *A History of New*

*York from the Beginning of the World to the End of the Dutch Dynasty,
by Dietrich Knickerbocker* (1809); a serious biography, *Mahomet and His
Successors* (1850); and a five-volume life of George Washington. Irving
lived in Europe for seventeen years, beginning in 1815; *The Sketch Book*
was written in England. In 1826 he paid his first visit to Spain. An outpouring of works on that country soon followed: *A History of the Life
and Voyages of Christopher Columbus* (1828), *Chronicles of the Conquest
of Granada* (1829), and *Tales of the Alhambra* (1832). Irving also served
as the United States minister to Spain from 1842 to 1846. The following
excerpt from *Tales of the Alhambra* (1832) is as much about national
security as about Islamic faith and Egyptian magic.

In old times, many hundred years ago, there was a Moorish king named
Aben Habuz, who reigned over the kingdom of Granada. He was a retired
conqueror, that is to say, one who having in his more youthful days led a
life of constant foray and depredation, now that he was grown feeble and
superannuated, "languished for repose," and desired nothing more than to
live at peace with all the world, to husband his laurels, and to enjoy in quiet
the possessions he had wrested from his neighbors.

It so happened, however, that this most reasonable and pacific old monarch had young rivals to deal with; princes full of his early passion for fame
and fighting, and who were disposed to call him to account for the scores he
had run up with their fathers. Certain distant districts of his own territories,
also, which during the days of his vigor he had treated with a high hand, were
prone, now that he languished for repose, to rise in rebellion and threaten to
invest him in his capital. Thus he had foes on every side; and as Granada is
surrounded by wild and craggy mountains, which hide the approach of an
enemy, the unfortunate Aben Habuz was kept in a constant state of vigilance
and alarm, not knowing in what quarter hostilities might break out.

It was in vain that he built watchtowers on the mountains, and stationed
guards at every pass with orders to make fires by night and smoke by day,
on the approach of an enemy. His alert foes, baffling every precaution,
would break out of some unthought-of defile, ravage his lands beneath
his very nose, and then make off with prisoners and booty to the mountains. Was ever peaceable and retired conqueror in a more uncomfortable
predicament?

While Aben Habuz was harassed by these perplexities and molestations, an ancient Arabian physician arrived at his court. His gray beard descended to his girdle, and he had every mark of extreme age, yet he had travelled almost the whole way from Egypt on foot, with no other aid than a staff, marked with hieroglyphics. His fame had preceded him. His name was Ibrahim Ebn Abu Ayub, he was said to have lived ever since the days of Mahomet, and to be son of Abu Ayub, the last of the companions of the Prophet. He had, when a child, followed the conquering army of Amru into Egypt, where he had remained many years studying the dark sciences, and particularly magic, among the Egyptian priests.

It was, moreover, said that he had found out the secret of prolonging life, by means of which he had arrived to the great age of upwards of two centuries, though, as he did not discover the secret until well stricken in years, he could only perpetuate his gray hairs and wrinkles.

This wonderful old man was honorably entertained by the king, who, like most superannuated monarchs, began to take physicians into great favor. He would have assigned him an apartment in his palace, but the astrologer preferred a cave in the side of the hill which rises above the city of Granada, being the same on which the Alhambra has since been built. He caused the cave to be enlarged so as to form a spacious and lofty hall, with a circular hole at the top, through which, as through a well, he could see the heavens and behold the stars even at mid-day. The walls of this hall were covered with Egyptian hieroglyphics, with cabalistic symbols, and with the figures of the stars in their signs. This hall he furnished with many implements, fabricated under his directions by cunning artificers of Granada, but the occult properties of which were known only to himself.

In a little while the sage Ibrahim became the bosom counsellor of the king, who applied to him for advice in every emergency. Aben Habuz was once inveighing against the injustice of his neighbors, and bewailing the restless vigilance he had to observe to guard himself against their invasions; when he had finished, the astrologer remained silent for a moment, and then replied, "Know, O King, that when I was in Egypt I beheld a great marvel devised by a pagan priestess of old. On a mountain, above the city of Borsa, and overlooking the great valley of the Nile, was a figure of a ram, and above it a figure of a cock, both of molten brass, and turning upon a pivot. Whenever the country was threatened with invasion, the ram would turn in the direction of the enemy, and the cock would crow; upon this the inhabitants of the city knew of the danger, and of the quarter from which it was approaching, and could take timely means to guard against it."

"God is great!" exclaimed the pacific Aben Habuz, "what a treasure would be such a ram to keep an eye upon these mountains around me; and then such a cock, to crow in time of danger! Allah Akbar! how securely I might sleep in my palace with such sentinels on the top!"

The astrologer waited until the ecstasies of the king had subsided, and then proceeded:

"After the victorious Amru (may he rest in peace!) had finished his conquest of Egypt, I remained among the priests of the land, studying the rites and ceremonies of their idolatrous faith, and seeking to make myself master of the hidden knowledge for which they are renowned. I was one day seated on the banks of the Nile, conversing with an ancient priest, when he pointed to the mighty pyramids which rose like mountains out of the neighboring desert. 'All that we can teach thee,' said he, 'is nothing to the knowledge locked up in those mighty piles. In the centre of the central pyramid is a sepulchral chamber, in which is inclosed the mummy of the high-priest, who aided in rearing that stupendous pile; and with him is buried a wondrous book of knowledge containing all the secrets of magic and art. This book was given to Adam after his fall, and was handed down from generation to generation to King Solomon the wise, and by its aid he built the temple of Jerusalem. How it came into the possession of the builder of the pyramids, is known to him alone who knows all things.'

"When I heard these words of the Egyptian priest, my heart burned to get possession of that book. I could command the services of many of the soldiers of our conquering army, and of a number of the native Egyptians: with these I set to work, and pierced the solid mass of the pyramid, until, after great toil, I came upon one of its interior and hidden passages. Following this up, and threading a fearful labyrinth, I penetrated into the very heart of the pyramid, even to the sepulchral chamber, where the mummy of the high-priest had lain for ages. I broke through the outer cases of the mummy, unfolded its many wrappers and bandages, and at length found the precious volume on its bosom. I seized it with a trembling hand, and groped my way out of the pyramid, leaving the mummy in its dark and silent sepulchre, there to await the final day of resurrection and judgment."

"Son of Abu Ayub," exclaimed Aben Habuz, "thou hast been a great traveller, and seen marvellous things; but of what avail to me is the secret of the pyramid, and the volume of knowledge of the wise Solomon?"

"This it is, O king! By the study of that book I am instructed in all magic arts, and can command the assistance of genii to accomplish my plans. The mystery of the Talisman of Borsa is therefore familiar to me, and such a talisman can I make; nay, one of greater virtues."

"O wise son of Abu Ayub," cried Aben Habuz, "better were such a talisman, than all the watchtowers on the hills, and sentinels upon the borders. Give me a safeguard, and the riches of my treasury are at thy command."

The astrologer immediately set to work to gratify the wishes of the monarch. He caused a great tower to be erected upon the top of the royal palace, which stood on the brow of the hill of the Albaycin. The tower was built of stones brought from Egypt, and taken, it is said, from one of the pyramids. In the upper part of the tower was a circular hall, with windows looking towards every point of the compass, and before each window was a table, on which was arranged, as on a chess-board, a mimic army of horse and foot, with the effigy of the potentate that ruled in that direction, all carved of wood. To each of these tables there was a small lance, no bigger than a bodkin, on which were engraved certain Chaldaic characters. This hall was kept constantly closed, by a gate of brass, with a great lock of steel, the key of which was in possession of the king.

On the top of the tower was a bronze figure of a Moorish horseman, fixed on a pivot, with a shield on one arm, and his lance elevated perpendicularly. The face of this horseman was towards the city, as if keeping guard over it; but if any foe were at hand, the figure would turn in that direction, and would level the lance as if for action.

When this talisman was finished, Aben Habuz was all impatient to try its virtues; and longed as ardently for an invasion as he had ever sighed after repose. His desire was soon gratified. Tidings were brought, early one morning, by the sentinel appointed to watch the tower, that the face of the bronze horseman was turned towards the mountains of Elvira, and that his lance pointed directly against the Pass of Lope.

"Let the drums and trumpets sound to arms, and all Granada be put on the alert," said Aben Habuz.

"O king," said the astrologer, "Let not your city be disquieted, nor your warriors called to arms; we need no aid of force to deliver you from your enemies. Dismiss your attendants, and let us proceed alone to the secret hall of the tower."

The ancient Aben Habuz mounted the staircase of the tower, leaning on the arm of the still more ancient Ibrahim Ebn Abu Ayub. They unlocked the brazen door and entered. The window that looked towards the Pass of Lope was open. "In this direction," said the astrologer, "lies the danger; approach, O king, and behold the mystery of the table."

King Aben Habuz approached the seeming chess-board, on which were arranged the small wooden effigies, when, to his surprise, he perceived that they were all in motion. The horses pranced and curveted, the warriors brandished their weapons, and there was a faint sound of drums and trumpets, and the clang of arms, and neighing of steeds; but all no louder, nor more distinct, than the hum of the bee, or the summer-fly, in the drowsy ear of him who lies at noontide in the shade.

"Behold, O king," said the astrologer, "a proof that thy enemies are even now in the field. They must be advancing through yonder mountains, by the Pass of Lope. Would you produce a panic and confusion amongst them, and cause them to retreat without loss of life, strike these effigies with the butt-end of this magic lance; would you cause bloody feud and carnage, strike with the point."

A livid streak passed across the countenance of Aben Habuz; he seized the lance with trembling eagerness; his gray beard wagged with exultation as he tottered toward the table: "Son of Abu Ayub," exclaimed he, in chuckling tone, "I think we will have a little blood!"

So saying, he thrust the magic lance into some of the pigmy effigies, and belabored others with the but-end, upon which the former fell as dead upon the board, and the rest turning upon each other began, pell-mell, a chance-medley fight.

It was with difficulty the astrologer could stay the hand of the most pacific of monarchs, and prevent him from absolutely exterminating his foes; at length he prevailed upon him to leave the tower, and to send out scouts to the mountains by the Pass of Lope.

They returned with the intelligence, that a Christian army had advanced through the heart of the Sierra, almost within sight of Granada, where a dissension had broken out among them; they had turned their weapons against each other, and after much slaughter had retreated over the border.

Aben Habuz was transported with joy on thus proving the efficacy of the talisman. "At length," said he, "I shall lead a life of tranquillity, and have all my enemies in my power. O wise son of Abu Ayub, what can I bestow on thee in reward for such a blessing?"

"The wants of an old man and a philosopher, O king, are few and simple; grant me but the means of fitting up my cave as a suitable hermitage, and I am content."

"How noble is the moderation of the truly wise!" exclaimed Aben Habuz, secretly pleased at the cheapness of the recompense. He summoned his treasurer, and bade him dispense whatever sums might be required by Ibrahim to complete and furnish his hermitage.

The astrologer now gave orders to have various chambers hewn out of the solid rock, so as to form ranges of apartments connected with his astrological hall; these he caused to be furnished with luxurious ottomans and divans, and the walls to be hung with the richest silks of Damascus. "I am an old man," said he, "and can no longer rest my bones on stone couches, and these damp walls require covering."

He had baths too constructed, and provided with all kinds of perfumes and aromatic oils: "For a bath," said he, "is necessary to counteract the rigidity of age, and to restore freshness and suppleness to the frame withered by study."

He caused the apartments to be hung with innumerable silver and crystal lamps, which he filled with a fragrant oil, prepared according to a receipt discovered by him in the tombs of Egypt. This oil was perpetual in its nature, and diffused a soft radiance like the tempered light of day. "The light of the sun," said he, "is too garish and violent for the eyes of an old man, and the light of the lamp is more congenial to the studies of a philosopher."

The treasurer of King Aben Habuz groaned at the sums daily demanded to fit up this hermitage, and he carried his complaints to the king. The royal word, however, had been given; Aben Habuz shrugged his shoulders: "We must have patience," said he, "this old man has taken his idea of a philosophic retreat from the interior of the pyramids, and of the vast ruins of Egypt; but all things have an end, and so will the furnishing of his cavern."

The king was in the right; the hermitage was at length complete, and formed a sumptuous subterranean palace. The astrologer expressed himself perfectly content, and, shutting himself up, remained for three whole days buried in study. At the end of that time he appeared again before the treasurer. "One thing more is necessary," said he, "one trifling solace for the intervals of mental labor."

"O wise Ibrahim, I am bound to furnish every thing necessary for thy solitude; what more dost thou require?"

"I would fain have a few dancing women."

"Dancing women!" echoed the treasurer, with surprise.

"Dancing women," replied the sage, gravely; "and let them be young and fair to look upon; for the sight of youth and beauty is refreshing. A few will suffice, for I am a philosopher of simple habits and easily satisfied."

While the philosophic Ibrahim Ebn Abu Ayub passed his time thus sagely in his hermitage, the pacific Aben Habuz carried on furious campaigns in effigy in his tower. It was a glorious thing for an old man, like himself, of quiet habits, to have war made easy, and to be enabled to amuse himself in his chamber by brushing away whole armies like so many swarms of flies.

For a time he rioted in the indulgence of his humors, and even taunted and insulted his neighbors, to induce them to make incursions; but by degrees they grew wary from repeated disasters, until no one ventured to invade his territories. For many months the bronze horseman remained on the peace establishment with his lance elevated in the air, and the worthy old monarch began to repine at the want of his accustomed sport, and to grow peevish at his monotonous tranquillity.

At length, one day, the talismanic horseman veered suddenly round, and lowering his lance, made a dead point towards the mountains of Guadix. Aben Habuz hastened to his tower, but the magic table in that direction remained quiet; not a single warrior was in motion. Perplexed at the circumstance, he sent forth a troop of horse to scour the mountains and reconnoitre. They returned after three days' absence.

"We have searched every mountain pass," said they, "but not a helm nor spear was stirring. All that we have found in the course of our foray, was a Christian damsel of surpassing beauty, sleeping at noontide beside a fountain, whom we have brought away captive."

"A damsel of surpassing beauty!" exclaimed Aben Habuz, his eyes gleaming with animation; "let her be conducted into my presence."

PAUL BOWLES

The Spider's House

Paul Bowles (1910–1999), author, translator, and composer, spent almost his entire working life in Europe and North Africa, beginning with his trip to Paris in 1930 to study music with Aaron Copland. He visited Morocco for the first time with Copland in the summer of 1931. Back in his native New York, Bowles collaborated with Orson Welles, Tennessee Williams, Merce Cunningham, and Leonard Bernstein in musical and stage productions. He moved permanently to Morocco in 1947, spending the next 52 years in the city of Tangier. *The Sheltering Sky* (1950), his first novel, won wide acclaim, and was followed almost immediately by a short story collection, *The Delicate Prey and Other Stories* (1950), and another novel, *The Spider's House* (1955), the first to tackle Morocco's factious politics under French rule. In the 1960s he started collecting and translating the works of oral Moroccan storytellers as well as French, Spanish, and Portuguese authors, including Jean-Paul Sartre, Jorge Luis Borges, and Giorgio de Chirico. In this excerpt from *The Spider's House,* Bowles shows the city of Fez unable to celebrate the religious holiday of Eid, caught between the exile of Sultan Mohammed V by the French colonial administration and the ruthless intrigue of the Istiqlal, the secular force of Moroccan independence.

The young spring grew, wheeled along toward summer, bringing drier nights, a higher sun and longer days. And along with the numberless infinitesimal natural things that announced the slow seasonal change, there was another thing, quite as impalpable and just as perceptible. Perhaps if Amar had not been made aware of it by the potter, he could have continued for a while not suspecting its presence, but now he wondered how it had been possible for him to go on as long as he had without noticing It. One might have said that It hung in the air with the particles of dust, and settled with them into the pores of the walls, so completely was it a part of the light and atmosphere of the great town lying sprawled there between its hills. But It expressed itself in the startled look over the shoulder that followed the tap on the back, in the silence that fell over a café when an unfamiliar figure appeared and sat down, in the anguished glances that darted from one pair of eyes to another when the family, squatting around the evening *tajine*, ceased chewing at the sound of a knock on the door. People went out less; at night the twisting lanes of the Medina were empty, and Friday afternoons, when there should have been many thousands of people, all in their best clothing, in the Djenane es Sebir—the men walking hand in hand or in noisy groups among the fountains and across the bridges between the islands, the women sitting in tiers on the steps or on the benches in their own reserved bamboo grove—there were only a few unkempt kif-smokers who sat staring vacantly in front of them while urchins scuffed up the dust as they kicked around an improvised football made of rags and string.

It was strange to see the city slowly withering, like some doomed plant. Each day it seemed that the process could go no further, that the point of extreme withdrawal from normal life had been reached, that an opening-up would now begin; but each new day people realized with a kind of awe that no such point was in sight.

They wanted their own Sultan back—that went without saying—and in general they had faith in the political party that had pledged to bring about his return. Also, a certain amount of intrigue and secrecy had never frightened them; the people of Fez were well known to be the most devious and clever Moslems in Morocco. But scheming in their own traditional fashion was one thing, and being caught between the diabolical French colonial secret police and the pitiless Istiqlal was another. They were not used to living in an *ambiance* of suspicion and fear quite so intense as the state of affairs their politicians were now asking them to accept as an everyday condition.

Slowly life was assuming a monstrous texture. Nothing was necessarily what it seemed; everything had become suspect—particularly that which was pleasant. If a man smiled, beware of him because he was surely a *chkam*, an informer for the French. If he plucked on an *oud* as he walked through the street he was being disrespectful to the memory of the exiled Sultan. If he smoked a cigarette in public he was contributing to French revenue, and he risked a beating or a knifing later in some dark alley. The thousands of students from the Medersa Karouine and the College of Moulay Idriss went so far as to declare an unlimited period of national mourning, and took to walking morosely by themselves, muttering a few inaudible syllables to each other when they met.

For Amar it was difficult to accept this sudden transition. Why should there be no more drums beaten, no flutes played, in the market at Sidi Ali bou Ralem, through which he liked to pass on his way home from work? He knew it was necessary to drive the French out, but he had always imagined that this would be done gloriously, with thousands of men on horseback flashing their swords and calling upon Allah to aid them in their holy mission as they rode down the Boulevard Moulay Youssef toward the Ville Nouvelle. And the Sultan would get an army from the Germans or the Americans and return victorious to his throne in Rabat. It was hard to see any connection between the splendid war of liberation and all this whispering and frowning. For a long time he debated with himself whether to discuss his doubts with the potter. He was earning good wages now and was on excellent terms with his master. Since the night several weeks ago when they had gone to the café, he had attempted no further consolidation of intimate friendship, because he was not sure that he really liked Saïd. It seemed to him partly the man's fault that everything was going wrong in the town, and he could not help feeling that had he never known him, somehow his own life would be different now.

He decided finally to take the risk of speaking with him, but at the same time to make sure that his real question was masked with another.

One afternoon he and Saïd had locked themselves into the upper shed to have a cigarette together. (No one smoked any more save in the strictest secrecy, because the Istiqlal's decision to destroy the French government's tobacco monopoly provided not only for the burning of the warehouses and all shops that sold tobacco, but also for the enforcement by violence of the party's anti-smoking campaign. The commonest punishment for being caught smoking was to have your cheek slashed with a razor.) Being shut into this small space with his master, and sharing with him the delightful sensation of danger which their forbidden activity occasioned, gave Amar the impetus to speak. He turned to the older man and said nonchalantly: "What do you think of the story that the Istiqlal may sell out to the French?"

The potter almost choked on his smoke. "What?" he cried.

Amar invented swiftly. "I heard that the Resident, the *civil* they have there now, offered the big ones a hundred million francs to forget the whole thing. But I don't think they'll take it, do you?"

"What?" the man roared, again. Amar felt a thrill of excitement as he watched his reaction. It was as if until this moment he had never seen him save asleep, and now were seeing him awake for the first time.

"Who told you that?" he yelled. The intensity of his expression was so great that Amar, a little alarmed, decided to make the report easily discreditable.

"A boy I know."

"But who?" the man insisted.

"Ah, a crazy *derri,* a kid who goes to the College of Moulay Idriss. Moto, we call him. I don't even know his real name."

"Have you repeated this story to anyone else?" The potter was glaring at him with a frightening fixity. Amar felt uncomfortable.

"No," he said.

"It's lucky for you. That's a story invented by the French. Your friend was paid by them to spread it. He'll probably be killed soon."

MALCOLM X

The Autobiography of Malcolm X

Malcolm X (1925–1965), born Malcolm Little, grew up in foster homes. He changed his name after his conversion to the Nation of Islam while in prison for burglary. Upon his release, he became a minister and spokesperson for the movement, significantly enlarging its membership in the 1950s and 1960s. During that time, he began to use the name Malik el-Shabazz, though he was still known as Malcolm X to the general public. His success pitted him against Elijah Muhammad, the leader of the Nation of Islam; he broke with that group in 1964. Shortly thereafter he converted to Sunni Islam and made the pilgrimage to Mecca, claiming the honorific title El-Hajj. This succession of names reflects the evolution of Malcolm X's identity—from hustler to Nation of Islam minister to Muslim pilgrim—a progress highlighted in his *Autobiography,* written with Alex Haley. Malcolm X traveled extensively in Africa and Europe in 1964–1965, advocating harmony between blacks and whites through spiritual renewal, a vision urged with great eloquence in the following letter, sent to his congregation after his return from Mecca and just before his assassination in 1965.

Here is what I wrote . . . from my heart:

"Never have I witnessed such sincere hospitality and the overwhelming spirit of true brotherhood as is practiced by people of all colors and races here in this Ancient Holy Land, the home of Abraham, Muhammad, and all the other prophets of the Holy Scriptures. For the past week, I have been utterly speechless and spellbound by the graciousness I see displayed all around me by people *of all colors.*

"I have been blessed to visit the Holy City of Mecca. I have made my seven circuits around the Ka'ba, led by a young *Mutawaf* named Muhammad. I drank water from the well of Zem Zem. I ran seven times back and forth between the hills of Mt. Al-Safa and Al-Marwah. I have prayed in the ancient city of Mina, and I have prayed on Mt. Arafat.

"There were tens of thousands of pilgrims, from all over the world. They were all colors, from blue-eyed blonds to black-skinned Africans. But we were all participating in the same ritual, displaying a spirit of unity and brotherhood that my experiences in America had led me to believe never could exist between the white and the non-white.

"America needs to understand Islam, because this is the one religion that erases from its society the race problem. Throughout my travels in the Muslim world, I have met, talked to, and even eaten with people who in America would have been considered 'white'—but the 'white' attitude was removed from their minds by the religion of Islam. I have never before seen *sincere* and *true* brotherhood practiced by all colors together, irrespective of their color.

"You may be shocked by these words coming from me. But on this pilgrimage, what I have seen, and experienced, has forced me to *re-arrange* much of my thought-patterns previously held, and to *toss aside* some of my previous conclusions. This was not too difficult for me. Despite my firm convictions, I have been always a man who tries to face facts, and to accept the reality of life as new experience and new knowledge unfolds it. I have always kept an open mind, which is necessary to the flexibility that must go hand in hand with every form of intelligent search for truth.

"During the past eleven days here in the Muslim world, I have eaten from the same plate, drunk from the same glass, and slept in the same bed (or on the same rug)—while praying to the *same* God—with fellow Muslims, whose eyes were the bluest of blue, whose hair was the blondest of blond, and whose skin was the whitest of white. And in the *words* and in the *actions* and in the *deeds* of the 'white' Muslims, I felt the same sincerity that I felt among the black African Muslims of Nigeria, Sudan, and Ghana.

"We were *truly* all the same (brothers)—because their belief in one God had removed the 'white' from their *minds,* the 'white' from their *behavior,* and the 'white' from their *attitude.*

"I could see from this, that perhaps if white Americans could accept the Oneness of God, then perhaps, too, they could accept *in reality* the One-ness of Man—and cease to measure, and hinder, and harm others in terms of their 'differences' in color.

"With racism plaguing America like an incurable cancer, the so-called 'Christian' white American heart should be more receptive to a proven so-lution to such a destructive problem. Perhaps it could be in time to save America from imminent disaster—the same destruction brought upon Germany by racism that eventually destroyed the Germans themselves.

"Each hour here in the Holy Land enables me to have greater spiritual insights into what is happening in America between black and white. The American Negro never can be blamed for his racial animosities—he is only reacting to four hundred years of the conscious racism of the Ameri-can whites. But as racism leads America up the suicide path, I do believe, from the experiences that I have had with them, that the whites of the younger generation, in the colleges and universities, will see the hand-writing on the wall and many of them will turn to the *spiritual* path of *truth*—the *only* way left to America to ward off the disaster that racism inevitably must lead to."

JOHN UPDIKE

Terrorist

John Updike (1932–2009), one of only three authors to win the Pulit-zer Prize for Fiction more than once, wrote more than twenty novels, as well as a dozen short-story collections, poetry, art criticism, chil-dren's books, and columns for the *New Yorker.* Raised in Berks County,

Pennsylvania, he made the middle-class, Protestant, suburban world his lifelong subject, beginning with the Rabbit Angstrom novels and ending with *The Widows of Eastwick* (2008), his last published novel and a sequel to *The Witches of Eastwick* (1984). His *Scarlet Letter* trilogy—*A Month of Sundays* (1975), *Roger's Version* (1986), and *S* (1988)—were rewritings of Hawthorne. Updike also experimented with other genres, including light verse in *The Carpentered Hen* (1958); magical realism in *Brazil* (1994); science fiction in *Towards the End of Time* (1997); and sports writing in *Hub Fans Bid Kid Farewell,* originally published in the *New Yorker* in 1960, Ted Williams's last year at bat. This excerpt from *Terrorist* (2006) features the conflicted mental universe of a young Islamic fundamentalist.

―――――――――――――――――――――――――――――――――――――――

Devils, Ahmad thinks. *These devils seek to take away my God.* All day long, at Central High School, girls sway and sneer and expose their soft bodies and alluring hair. Their bare bellies, adorned with shining navel studs and low-down purple tattoos, ask, *What else is there to see?* Boys strut and saunter along and look dead-eyed, indicating with their edgy killer gestures and careless scornful laughs that this world is all there is—a noisy varnished hall lined with metal lockers and having at its end a blank wall desecrated by graffiti and roller-painted over so often it feels to be coming closer by millimeters.

The teachers, weak Christians and nonobservant Jews, make a show of teaching virtue and righteous self-restraint, but their shifty eyes and hollow voices betray their lack of belief. They are paid to say these things, by the city of New Prospect and the state of New Jersey. They lack true faith; they are not on the Straight Path; they are unclean. Ahmad and the two thousand other students can see them scuttling after school into their cars on the crackling, trash-speckled parking lot like pale crabs or dark ones restored to their shells, and they are men and women like any others, full of lust and fear and infatuation with things that can be bought. Infidels, they think safety lies in accumulation of the things of this world, and in the corrupting diversions of the television set. They are slaves to images, false ones of happiness and affluence. But even true images are sinful imitations of God, who can alone create. Relief at escaping their students unscathed for another day makes the teachers' chatter of farewell in the halls and on the parking lot too loud, like the rising excitement of drunks. The teachers revel when they are away from the school. Some have the pink lids and bad breaths and puffy bodies of those who habitually drink too much. Some get divorces; some live with others unmarried. Their lives away from the school are disorderly and wanton and self-indulgent. They are paid to instill virtue and democratic values by the state government down in Trenton, and that Satanic government farther down, in Washington, but the values they believe in are Godless: biology and chemistry and physics. On the facts and formulas of these their false voices firmly rest, ringing out into the classroom. They say that all comes out of merciless blind atoms, which cause the cold weight of iron, the transparency of glass, the stillness of clay, the agitation of flesh. Electrons pour through copper threads and computer gates and the air itself when stirred to lightning by the interaction of water droplets. Only what we can measure and deduce from measurement is true. The rest is the passing dream that we call our selves.

Ahmad is eighteen. This is early April; again green sneaks, seed by seed, into the drab city's earthy crevices. He looks down from his new height and thinks that to the insects unseen in the grass he would be, if they had a consciousness like his, God. In the year past he has grown three inches, to six feet—more unseen materialist forces, working their will upon him. He will not grow any taller, he thinks, in this life or the next. *If there is a next,* an inner devil murmurs. What evidence beyond the Prophet's blazing and divinely inspired words proves that there is a next? Where would it be hidden? Who would forever stoke Hell's boilers? What infinite source of energy would maintain opulent Eden, feeding its dark-eyed houris, swelling its heavy-hanging fruits, renewing the streams and splashing fountains in which God, as described in the ninth sura of the Qur'an, takes eternal good pleasure? What of the second law of thermodynamics?

MOHSIN HAMID

The Reluctant Fundamentalist

Mohsin Hamid (born 1971) was born in Lahore, Pakistan, and did his undergraduate work at Princeton, where he studied with Toni Morrison and Joyce Carol Oates, self-consciously playing with the form of the novel from the outset. *Moth Smoke* (2000), the first draft of which was written for a fiction workshop taught by Morrison, reaches back to the seventeenth-century Mughal emperor Aurangzeb while telling the story of a fast-paced, drug-dealing, Lahore ex-banker. *The Reluctant Fundamentalist* (2007), chosen by the *Guardian* as one of the novels that defined the decade, features a Pakistani man's dramatic monologue about his high-powered job in the United States and his decision to leave after 9/11, with the American listener, presumably a CIA agent, remaining inaudible throughout. *How to Get Filthy Rich in Rising Asia* (2013) uses the form of the self-help book to address a second-person "you" on his way to becoming a tycoon. In the following excerpt from *The Reluctant Fundamentalist*, the protagonist sees his native Lahore and his U.S. employer, a McKinsey-like consulting firm, through a reciprocally disorienting lens.

There are adjustments one must make if one comes here from America; a different way of *observing* is required. I recall the Americanness of my own gaze when I returned to Lahore that winter when war was in the offing. I was struck at first by how shabby our house appeared, with cracks running through its ceilings and dry bubbles of paint flaking off where dampness had entered its walls. The electricity had gone that afternoon, giving the place a gloomy air, but even in the dim light of the hissing gas heaters our furniture appeared dated and in urgent need of reupholstery and repair. I was saddened to find it in such a state—no, more than saddened, I was shamed. *This* was where I came from, this was my provenance, and it smacked of lowliness.

But as I reacclimatized and my surroundings once again became familiar, it occurred to me that the house had not changed in my absence. *I* had changed; I was looking about me with the eyes of a foreigner, and not just any foreigner, but that particular type of entitled and unsympathetic American who so annoyed me when I encountered him in the classrooms and workplaces of your country's elite. This realization angered me; staring at my reflection in the speckled glass of my bathroom mirror I resolved to exorcise the unwelcome sensibility by which I had become possessed.

It was only after so doing that I saw my house properly again, appreciating its enduring grandeur, its unmistakable personality and idiosyncratic charm. Mughal miniatures and ancient carpets graced its reception rooms; an excellent library abutted its veranda. It was far from impoverished; indeed, it was rich with history. I wondered how I could ever have been so ungenerous—and so blind—to have thought otherwise, and I was disturbed by what this implied about myself: that I was a man lacking in substance and hence easily influenced by even a short sojourn in the company of others.

But far more significant than these inward-oriented musings of mine was the external reality of the threat facing my home. My brother had come to collect me from the airport; he embraced me with sufficient force to cause my rib cage to flex. As he drove he ruffled my hair with his hand. I felt suddenly very young—or perhaps I felt my age: an almost childlike twenty-two, rather than that permanent middle-age that attaches itself to the man who lives alone and supports himself by wearing a suit in a city not of his birth. It had been some time since I had been touched so easily, so familiarly, and I smiled. "How are things?" I asked him. He shrugged. "There is an artillery battery dug in at the country house of a friend of mine, half an hour from here, and a colonel billeted in his spare bedroom," he replied, "so things are not good."

My parents seemed well; they were more frail than when I had seen them last, but at their age that was to be expected with the passage of a year. My mother twirled a hundred-rupee note around my head to bless my return; later it would be given to charity. My father's eyes glistened, moist and brown. "Contact lenses," he said, dabbing them with a handkerchief, "quite smart, eh?" I said they suited him, and they did; his glasses had come late in life, and they had concealed the strength of his face. Neither he nor my mother wanted to discuss the possibility of war; they insisted on feeding me and hearing in detail about my life in New York and my progress at my new job. It was odd to speak of that world here, as it would be odd to sing in a mosque; what is natural in one place can seem unnatural in another, and some concepts travel rather poorly, if at all. I censored any mention of Erica, for example, and indeed of anything that I thought might disturb them.

But that night a family banquet was held in my honor, and there the conflict with India dominated conversation. Opinion was divided as to whether the men who had attacked the Indian parliament had anything to do with Pakistan, but there was unanimity in the belief that India would do all it could to harm us, and that despite the assistance we had given America in Afghanistan, America would not fight at our side. Already, the Indian army was mobilizing, and Pakistan had begun to respond: convoys of trucks, I was told, were passing through the city, bearing supplies to our troops on the border; as we ate, we could hear the sounds of military helicopters flying low overhead; a rumor circulated that soon traffic would be halted on the motorway so that our fighter planes could practice landing on it, in case all of our airfields were destroyed in a nuclear exchange.

It will perhaps be odd for you—coming, as you do, from a country that has not fought a war on its own soil in living memory, the rare sneak attack or terrorist outrage excepted—to imagine residing within commuting distance of a million or so hostile troops who could, at any moment, attempt a full-scale invasion. My brother cleaned his shotgun. One of my uncles stocked up on bottled water and canned food. Our part-time gardener was deployed with the reserves. But for the most part, people seemed to go about their lives normally; Lahore was the last major city in a contiguous swath of Muslim lands stretching west as far as Morocco and had therefore that quality of understated bravado characteristic of frontier towns.

But I worried. I felt powerless; I was angry at our weakness, at our vulnerability to intimidation of this sort from our—admittedly much larger—neighbor to the east. Yes, we had nuclear weapons, and yes, our soldiers would not back down, but we were being threatened nonetheless, and there was nothing I could do about it but lie in my bed, unable to sleep. Indeed, I would soon be gone, leaving my family and my home behind, and this made me a kind of coward in my own eyes, a traitor. What sort of man abandons his people in such circumstances? And what was I abandoning them for? A well-paying job and a woman whom I longed for but who refused even to see me? I grappled with these questions again and again.

When the time came for me to return to New York I told my parents I wanted to stay longer, but they would not hear of it. Perhaps they sensed that I was myself divided, that something called me back to America; perhaps they were simply protecting their son. "Do not forget to shave before you go," my mother said to me. "Why?" I asked, indicating my father and brother. "They have beards." "They," she replied, "have them only because they wish to hide the fact that they are bald. Besides, you are still a boy." She stroked my stubble with her fingers and added, "It makes you look like a mouse."

On the flight I noticed how many of my fellow passengers were similar to me in age: college students and young professionals, heading back after the holidays. I found it ironic; children and the elderly were meant to be sent away from impending battles, but in our case it was the fittest and brightest who were leaving, those who in the past would have been most expected to remain. I was filled with contempt for myself, such contempt that I could not bring myself to converse or to eat. I shut my eyes and waited, and the hours took from me the responsibility even to flee.

You are not unfamiliar with the anxieties that precede armed conflict, you say? Aha! Then you have been in the service, sir, just as I suspected! Would you not agree that waiting for what is to come is the most difficult part? Yes, quite so, not as difficult as the time of carnage itself—said, sir, like a true soldier. But I see that you have paused in your eating; perhaps you are waiting for fresh bread. Here, have half of mine. No, I insist; our waiter will bring us more momentarily.

Given your background, you will doubtless have experienced the peculiar phenomenon that is the return to an environment more or less at peace from one where the prospect of large-scale bloodshed is a distinct possibility. It is an odd transition. My colleagues greeted with considerable—although often partially suppressed—consternation my reappearance in our offices. For despite my mother's request, and my knowledge of the difficulties it could well present me at immigration, I had not shaved my two-week-old beard. It was, perhaps, a form of protest on my part, a symbol of my identity, or perhaps I sought to remind myself of the reality I had just left behind; I do not now recall my precise motivations. I know only that I did not wish to blend in with the army of clean-shaven youngsters who were my coworkers, and that inside me, for multiple reasons, I was deeply angry.

It is remarkable, given its physical insignificance—it is only a hairstyle, after all—the impact a beard worn by a man of my complexion has on your fellow countrymen. More than once, traveling on the subway—where I had always had the feeling of seamlessly blending in—I was subjected to verbal abuse by complete strangers, and at Underwood Samson I seemed to become overnight a subject of whispers and stares. Wainwright tried to offer me some friendly advice. "Look, man," he said, "I don't know what's up with the beard, but I don't think it's making you Mister Popular around here." "They are common where I come from," I told him. "Jerk chicken is common where I come from," he replied, "but I don't smear it all over my face. You need to be careful. This whole corporate collegiality veneer only goes so deep. Believe me."

THE GRATEFUL DEAD

Blues for Allah

The Grateful Dead, a rock band initially made up of Jerry Garcia, Bob Weir, Ron "Pigpen" McKernan, Phil Lesh, and Bill Kreutzmann, began in Palo Alto, California, in 1965 and flourished until 1995, when Garcia died. Emblematic of the hippie culture of Haight-Ashbury and best known for their long improvisations, the band fused elements of folk, rock, blues, reggae, country, jazz, and psychedelic music. They participated at many seminal events, including Ken Kesey's Acid Tests and the Mantra-Rock Dance at the Avalon Theatre, performing with Allen Ginsberg. They also had some famously disastrous appearances: Woodstock (1969) and Altamont (1969). Later joined by drummer Mickey Hart, and keyboardists replacing Pigpen, they crisscrossed the United States, accompanied by "Deadheads" who would follow them for months or years at a time, religiously taping their live performances and never hearing the same music twice. The song below, from their album *Blues for Allah* (1975), was written after the assassination of King Faisal of Saudi Arabia. Invoking the blues of the American South, lyricist Robert Hunter wonders why so many are killed in the name of the god of Abraham, a prophet shared by Judaism, Christianity, and Islam.

Arabian wind
the needle's eye is thin
The ships of state sail on mirage

and drown in sand
Out in no man's land
where Allah does command

What good is spilling
blood? It will not
grow a thing
"Taste eternity"
the sword sings Blues for Allah
Insh' Allah

They lie where they fall
there's nothing more to say
The desert stars are bright tonight,
let's meet as friends
The flower of Islam
the fruit of Abraham

The thousand stories have
come round to one again
Arabian night
our gods pursue their flight
What fatal flowers of
darkness spring from
seeds of light

Bird of Paradise—Fly
in the white sky
Blues for Allah
Insh' Allah

Let's see with our heart
these things our eyes have seen
and know the truth must still lie
somewhere in between
Under eternity
Under eternity

Under eternity
Blue
Bird of Paradise
Fly
In white sky
Under eternity
Blues
for Allah
Insh' Allah

V. Human
& Nonhuman
Interfaces

I n this final section of the anthology, we revisit many of the threads
in the preceding sections, connecting them anew, weaving them
into a different pattern through a new lens, the longstanding and
ongoing interaction between humans and nonhumans, a phenomenon of
great interest to many authors and now increasingly global in scope, and
with practical consequences felt both in the texture of everyday life and in
the future of the planet as a whole.

We begin on a micro scale, with a lowly insect that has left an indelible
footprint on American literature. Whether singly or collectively, the ant has
always been there: an integral, versatile, and often conspicuous part of stories, poems, essays, novels. We might expect it to show up when the subject
happens to be regimented combat or mass society (as is indeed the case
with Thoreau and Lowell), but the ant has also made its appearance in settings as varied as the cloistered halls of Oxford; the U.S. army's disciplinary
facilities in Pisa, Italy; the first-class comfort of a 707 fight to Paris; and the
Belgium Congo on the eve of Independence. The sheer range of locations
and the drama of the encounters suggest that humans and nonhumans have
always met on fertile ground, with unpredictable and nontrivial outcomes.
As the fraught settings make clear, these are not chance meetings, casually
reported. On the contrary, each is carefully staged, and often staged at just
those moments when much is hanging in the balance—when the political

passions of the revolution are at their peak, when the hardships and vulner-abilities of incarceration are at their most unbearable. Ants might be tiny, but the stories told through them are urgent and ample.

From drama at this micro level, we move on to the next plane, the world of commodities and markets, beginning with the transatlantic slave trade and the specter of mutiny—the "skin to skin in the hold and the picked handcuff locks"—as Elizabeth Alexander writes in "Amistad" (2005). The enchained human body has been the oldest commodity on earth. The ship, the handcuffs, the whip, the invisible hand of the market, and the Atlantic itself, "with no land in sight"—these make up the landscape through which that commodified body travels. In her austere tally of the inanimate forces that rule the world, Alexander casts human speech as the occasional "stan-zas" punctuating the "whack of the lashes," heard briefly against the "silence and silence and silence" of enforced slavery, a "last quatrain" likely to be futile. This grim understanding of humanity as a fragile sound existing only in the interstices of a vast sea of nonhumanity sets the terms for the selec-tions that follow, from the triumphant expansion of the railroad and the global marketing of wheat in Frank Norris's *Octopus* (1901), to John Dos Passos's biting portrait in *U.S.A.* (1937) of Henry Ford and the automobile that conquers the world, to the crucial role played by oil in Sudan's civil war in Dave Eggers's *What is the What* (2006).

Indeed, violence in all its forms—all-out world wars as well as one-on-one encounters mediated by the whip—could be understood as forms of human and nonhuman interaction. This is not just a fanciful way of put-ting things. It is a mental reset button of sorts, reversing the customary relation between background and foreground, between subject and object, bringing into relief the claim of the nonhuman, long taken for granted and seen only as an inert canvas behind human action. Against this increas-ingly untenable anthropocentrism, our selections highlight the primacy and agency of the nonhuman world, a world of micro as well as macro cau-sation, with consequences so far beyond the human calculus that our spe-cies might be seen, in this reversed perspective, as no more than an aside. From the pandemic that kills off much of the earth's population in Jack Lon-don's "The Scarlet Plague" (1912), to the nuclear holocaust that, in George Oppen's "The Crowded Countries of the Bomb" (1962), awaits humanity as a whole, the survival of our species has so far rested only on "chance, which has spared us," and "Choice, which has shielded us." How long can these two protect us from large-scale catastrophes? And how long can they protect us, for that matter, from small and efficient killers, such as the bullet, addressed as a "you" in Iraq veteran Brian Turner's poem dedicated to it? "If a body is what you want, / then here is bone and gristle and flesh. / Here is the clavicle-snapped wish, / the aorta's opened valves," Turner writes. In a bullet-centered world, the human body becomes only a receptacle, the last leg of a trajectory inscribed by the aim and precision of this lethal agent, "finish[ing] what you've started," "complet[ing] the word you bring hissing through the air."

With agency increasingly redistributed from the human to the nonhuman end of the spectrum, we come to a momentary resting place in this section and in the anthology as a whole, wrapping up with six selections that explore the scope, efficacy, and vulnerability of the nonhuman in its liveliest and most provocative form: nonhuman intelligence. From the androids in Philip K. Dick's *Do Androids Dream of Electric Sheep?* (1968), to Helen, the computer-based neural network who signs off and terminates her own life in Richard Powers's *Galatea 2.2* (1995), to the gene-trading Oankali who have rescued and colonized the few surviving humans from an uninhabitable earth in Octavia Butler's *Dawn* (1987), speculative fiction is showing us a world in which humans are not the only ones who matter. As we collectively face a world radically altered by climate change, this new orientation might be just what we need to have a shot at the future.

HENRY DAVID THOREAU

Walden

Henry David Thoreau (1817–1862), as noted in the "War" section of this anthology, is the author of *Walden* (1854), an experiment in "simple living"; and of "Resistance to Civil Government" (or "Civil Disobedience"), written after he was jailed for one night in 1846 for refusing to pay the poll tax as a protest against slavery and the Mexican-American War. The doctrine of nonviolent resistance has since inspired countless followers from Tolstoy to Gandhi to Martin Luther King, Jr. In this excerpt from Chapter 12 of *Walden*, Thoreau observes the phenomenon of war as enacted by ants.

One day when I went out to my wood-pile, or rather my pile of stumps, I observed two large ants, the one red, the other much larger, nearly half an inch long, and black, fiercely contending with one another. Having once got hold they never let go, but struggled and wrestled and rolled on the chips incessantly. Looking farther, I was surprised to find that the chips were covered with such combatants, that it was not a *duellum*, but a *bellum*, a war between two races of ants, the red always pitted against the black, and frequently two red ones to one black. The legions of these Myrmidons covered all the hills and vales in my wood-yard, and the ground was already strewn with the dead and dying, both red and black. It was the only battle which I have ever witnessed, the only battle-field I ever trod while the battle was raging; internecine war; the red republicans on the one hand, and the black imperialists on the other. On every side they were engaged in deadly combat, yet without any noise that I could hear, and human soldiers never fought so resolutely. I watched a couple that were fast locked in each other's embraces, in a little sunny valley amid the chips, now at noonday prepared to fight till the sun went down, or life went out. The smaller red champion had fastened himself like a vice to his adversary's front, and through all the tumblings on that field never for an instant ceased to gnaw at one of his feelers near the root, having already caused the other to go by the board; while the stronger black one dashed him from side to side, and, as I saw on looking nearer, had already divested him of several of his members. They fought with more pertinacity than bulldogs. Neither manifested the least disposition to retreat. It was evident that their battle-cry was "Conquer or die." In the meanwhile there came along a single red ant on the hillside of this valley, evidently full of excitement, who either had dispatched his foe, or had not yet taken part in the battle; probably the latter, for he had lost none of his limbs; whose mother had charged him to return with his shield or upon it. Or perchance he was some Achilles, who had nourished his wrath apart, and had now come to avenge or rescue his Patroclus. He saw this unequal combat from afar,—for the blacks were nearly twice the size of the red,—he drew near with rapid pace till he stood on his guard within half an inch of the combatants; then, watching his opportunity, he sprang upon the black warrior, and commenced his operations near the root of his right fore leg, leaving the foe to select among his own members; and so there were three united for life, as if a new kind of attraction had been invented which put all other locks and cements to shame. I should not have wondered by this time to find that they had their respective musical bands stationed on some eminent chip, and playing their national airs the while to excite the slow and cheer the dying combatants. I was myself excited somewhat even as if they had been men. The more you think of it, the less the difference. And certainly there is not the fight recorded in Concord history, at least, in the history of America, that will bear a moment's comparison with this, whether for the numbers engaged in it, or for the patriotism and heroism displayed. For numbers and for carnage it was an Austerlitz or Dresden. Concord Fight! Two killed on the patriots' side, and Luther Blanchard wounded! Why every ant was a Buttrick,—"Fire! For God's sake fire!"—and thousands shared the fate of Davis and Hosmer. There was not one hireling there. I have no doubt that it was a principle they fought for, as much as our ancestors, and not to avoid a three-penny tax on their tea; and the results of this battle will be as important and memorable to those whom it concerns as those of the battle of Bunker Hill, at least.

I took up the chip on which the three I have particularly described were struggling, carried it into my house, and placed it under a tumbler on my windowsill, in order to see the issue. Holding a microscope to the first-mentioned red ant, I saw that, though he was assiduously gnawing at the near fore leg of his enemy, having severed his remaining feeler, his own breast was all torn away, exposing what vitals he had there to the jaws of the black warrior, whose breastplate was apparently too thick for him to pierce; and the dark carbuncles of the sufferer's eyes shone with ferocity such as war only could excite. They struggled half an hour longer under the tumbler, and when I looked again the black soldier had severed the heads of his foes from their bodies, and the still living heads were hanging on either side of him like ghastly trophies at his saddlebow, still apparently as firmly fastened as ever, and he was endeavoring with feeble struggles, being without feelers and with only the remnant of a leg, and I know not how many other wounds, to divest himself of them; which at length, after half an hour more, he accomplished. I raised the glass, and he went off over the window-sill in that crippled state. Whether he finally survived that combat, and spent the remainder of his days in some Hotel des Invalides, I do not know; but I thought that his industry would not be worth much thereafter. I never learned which party was victorious, nor the cause of the war; but I felt for the rest of the day as if I had my feelings excited and harrowed by witnessing the struggle, the ferocity and carnage, of a human battle before my door.

Kirby and Spence tell us that the battles of ants have long been celebrated and the date of them recorded, though they say that Huber is the only modern author who appears to have witnessed them. "Aeneas Sylvius," say they, "after giving a very circumstantial account of one contested with great obstinacy by a great and small species on the trunk of a pear tree," adds that "this action was fought in the pontificate of Eugenius the Fourth, in the presence of Nicholas Pistoriensis, an eminent lawyer, who related the whole history of the battle with the greatest fidelity." A similar engagement between great and small ants is recorded by Olaus Magnus, in which the small ones, being victorious, are said to have buried the bodies of their own soldiers, but left those of their giant enemies a prey to the birds. This event happened previous to the expulsion of the tyrant Christiern the Second from Sweden." The battle which I witnessed took place in the Presidency of Polk, five years before the passage of Webster's Fugitive-Slave Bill.

MARIANNE MOORE

Critics and Connoisseurs

Marianne Moore (1887–1972), as noted in the "Food" section of this volume, was a key figure in transatlantic Modernism, both in her own allusive, encyclopedic poetry and in her editorship of the influential literary magazine, the *Dial*, from 1925–1929, publishing works as diverse as the poetry of Rilke and Valery; the philosophy of Benedetto Croce and Bertrand Russell; and the fiction of D. H. Lawrence, Maxim Gorky, and Jean Toomer. In this poem, she uses the academic setting of Oxford University and the appearance there of a battleship-like swan and a "fastidious ant carrying a stick" to meditate on the "ambition without understanding" of critics and connoisseurs.

There is a great amount of poetry in unconscious
    fastidiousness. Certain Ming
       products, imperial floor coverings of coach-
wheel yellow, are well enough in their way but I have seen something
that I like better—a
       mere childish attempt to make an imperfectly ballasted animal
stand up,
          similar determination to make a pup
             eat his meat from the plate.

I remember a swan under the willows in Oxford,
    with flamingo-colored, maple-
       leaflike feet. It reconnoitered like a battle-
ship. Disbelief and conscious fastidiousness were
    ingredients in its
       disinclination to move. Finally its hardihood was
          not proof against its
       proclivity to more fully appraise such bits
          of food as the stream

bore counter to it; it made away with what I gave it
   to eat. I have seen this swan and
      I have seen you; I have seen ambition without
   understanding in a variety of forms. Happening to stand
      by an ant-hill, I have
         seen a fastidious ant carrying a stick north, south,
            east, west, till it turned on
         itself, struck out from the flower bed into the lawn,
         and returned to the point

from which it had started. Then abandoning the stick as
  useless and overtaxing its
     jaws with a particle of whitewash—pill-like but
  heavy—it again went through the same course of procedure.
        What is
     there in being able
       to say that one has dominated the stream in an attitude of
         self-defense;
        in proving that one has had the experience
           of carrying a stick?

EZRA POUND

Canto LXXXI

Ezra Pound (1885–1972) embraced the classical traditions of Europe, Asia, and Africa to make Modernist poetry "new." Moving to Europe in 1908, he spent twelve years in London, then settled in Paris and eventually Rapallo, Italy. His love of Chinese poetry and philosophy, and of the Japanese Noh play—both of which he translated—along with his immersion in the works of Homer, Dante, and the Provençal poets, and the ethnographic work of Leo Frobenius, made for a heady brew, already evident in *Cathay* (1915) and running through the *Cantos*, an epic to which he devoted almost fifty years. His fascist politics, meanwhile, led to his arrest for treason by United States forces in April 1945. He was kept for 25 days in an iron cage at Pisa, the setting for the poetic sequence that would come to be known as *The Pisan Cantos* (1948), for which he received a much-disputed Bollingen Prize. In this work, solace seems to come from the nonhuman world: "When the mind swings by a glass-blade / an ant's forefoot shall save you," Pound says in Canto LXXXIII. He learns another lesson from the ant in the following excerpt, from Canto LXXXI.

The ant's a centaur in his dragon world.
Pull down thy vanity, it is not man
Made courage, or made order, or made grace,
Pull down thy vanity, I say pull down.
Learn of the green world what can be thy place
In scaled invention or true artistry . . .

ROBERT LOWELL

Ants

Robert Lowell (1917–1977) wrote *Life Studies* (1959), poems about his prominent Boston family and mental breakdowns, often taken as a landmark in "confessional" poetry. He began as a formalist, however, in *Lord Weary's Castle* (1946), which won his first Pulitzer Prize. As he departed from his family traditions—attending Harvard but receiving his BA from Kenyon College, and converting from Episcopalism to Catholicism in 1941—he also became increasingly public and political. Lowell was a conscientious objector during World War II, and was jailed for several months (recounted in the poem "Memories of West Street and Lepke"). In the 1960s he actively opposed the Vietnam War, turning down an invitation to the White House Festival of the Arts from President Lyndon Johnson and taking part in the 1967 March on the Pentagon, an event colorfully reported by Norman Mailer in *Armies of the Night* (1968). The 1960s was a productive decade for Lowell. *Imitations* (1961)—translations of Baudelaire, Montale, Pasternak, Rilke, and Rimbaud—received the Bollingen Prize. *For the Union Dead* (1964) and *Near the Ocean* (1967) were also widely praised. Lowell's one-act play, *Old Glory* (1964), meanwhile won five Obie awards, including one for best play. He received his second Pulitzer Prize for *The Dolphin* (1973). In "Ants," from *Day by Day* (1977), he considers Plato, the nation-state, and Socialism before circling back to Thoreau's ant-war.

Ants
are not under anathema to make it new—
they are too small and penny-proud
to harm us much or hold the human eye
looking downward on them,
like a Goth watching a game of chess.

On this tenth hot day,
the best of a drought summer,
the unthinking insects
leave their heated hills:
warrior, honey-cow and slave.
The earth is rock;
the ants waver
with thread antennae
emptily . . . as if one tactic
did for feeding or seeking
barren fields for drill.

Ants are amazing but not exemplary;
their beehive hurry excludes romance.

Once in time out of mind,
on such a warm day as this,
the ant-heads must have swarmed beyond
the illusive shimmer of the ant-hill,

and crowned slavery with socialism.
They invented the state before and after
Plato's grim arithmetic—a state
unchanging, limited, beyond our reach,
decadence, or denial . . .
their *semper eadem* of good fortune.
Yet not always the same;
the ants repair it yearly,
like the Chinese traditional painter
renewing his repertory flowers—
each touch a stroke for tradition.

They are the lost case of the mind.

I lie staring under an old oak,
stubby, homely, catacombed by ants,
more of a mop than a tree.
I fear the clumsy boughs will fall.
Is its weak, wooden heart strong enough
to bear my weight if I should climb
from knob to knob to the top?
How uneasily I am myself,
as a child I found the sky too close.
Why am I childish now and ask
for daffy days when I tried to read
Walden's ant-war aloud to you for love?

TONI MORRISON

Tar Baby

Toni Morrison (born 1931), as noted in the "Work, Play, Travel" section
of this anthology, experiments with multiple narrators, split time frames,

and a variety of settings. In this selection from *Tar Baby* (1981), she maps her social identities onto a nonhuman world, as her protagonist, Jadine, settling into her first-class seat on a flight to Paris, thinks about the "four-million-year-old" work ethic of the Amazon queen ant, and the dreams she might or might not have allowed herself to have.

Aboard the 707 Jadine had free use of the seat next to her. Not many passengers in first class. She checked her five luggage claim tickets stapled to the envelope that held a copy of her one-way ticket to Orly. Everything was in order. As soon as the plane was airborne, she reached above her head to adjust the air flow. Bringing her hand down she noticed a tiny irregularity in the nail of her forefinger. She opened her purse and took out an emery board. Two swift strokes and it was gone. Her nail was perfect again. She turned her sealskin coat lining side out and folded it carefully into the empty seat beside her. Then she adjusted the headrest. The same sixteen answers to the question What went wrong? kicked like a chorus line. Having sixteen answers meant having none. So none it was. Zero. She would go back to Paris and begin at Go. Let loose the dogs, tangle with the woman in yellow—with her and with all the night women who had *looked* at her. No more shoulders and limitless chests. No more dreams of safety. No more. Perhaps that was the thing—the thing Ondine was saying. A grown woman did not need safety or its dreams. She *was* the safety she longed for.

The plane lifted itself gracefully over the island; its tail of smoke widened, then dispersed. It was evening and the stars were already brilliant. The hills below crouched on all fours under the weight of the rain forest where liana grew and soldier ants marched in formation. Straight ahead they marched, shamelessly single-minded, for soldier ants have no time for dreaming. Almost all of them are women and there is so much to do—the work is literally endless. So many to be born and fed, then found and buried. There is no time for dreaming. The life of their world requires organization so tight and sacrifice so complete there is little need for males and they are seldom produced. When they are needed, it is deliberately done by the queen who surmises, by some four-million-year-old magic she is heiress to, that it is time. So she urges a sperm from the private womb where they were placed when she had her one, first and last copulation. Once in life, this little Amazon trembled in the air waiting for a male to mount her. And when he did, when he joined a cloud of others one evening just before a summer storm, joined colonies from all over the world gathered for the marriage flight, he knew at last what his wings were for. Frenzied, he flies into the humming cloud to fight gravity and time in order to do, just once, the single thing he was born for. Then he drops dead, having emptied his sperm into his lady-love. Sperm which she keeps in a special place to use at her own discretion when there is need for another dark and singing cloud of ant folk mating in the air. Once the lady has collected the sperm, she too falls to the ground, but unless she breaks her back or neck or is eaten by one of a thousand things, she staggers to her legs and looks for a stone to rub on, cracking and shredding the wings she will never need again. Then she begins her journey searching for a suitable place to build her kingdom. She crawls into the hollow of a tree, examines its walls and corners. She seals herself off from all society and eats her own wing muscles until she bears her eggs. When the first larvae appear, there is nothing to feed them so she gives them their unhatched sisters until they are old enough and strong enough to hunt and bring their prey back to the kingdom. That is all. Bearing, hunting, eating, fighting, burying. No time for dreaming, although sometimes, late in life, somewhere between the thirtieth and fortieth generation she might get wind of a summer storm one day. The scent of it will invade her palace and she will recall the rush of wind on her belly—the stretch of fresh wings, the blinding anticipation and herself, there, airborne, suspended, open, trusting, frightened, determined, vulnerable—girlish, even, for an entire second and then another and another. She may lift her head then, and point her wands toward the place where the summer storm is entering her palace and in the weariness that ruling queens alone know, she may wonder whether his death was sudden. Or did he languish? And if so, if there was a bit of time left, did he think how mean the world was, or did he fill that space of time thinking of her? But soldier ants do not have time for dreaming. They are women and have much to do. Still it would be hard. So very hard to forget the man who fucked like a star.

BARBARA KINGSOLVER

The Poisonwood Bible

Barbara Kingsolver (born 1955) is the author of numerous books, including *The Poisonwood Bible* (1998), about a missionary family in the Congo. Shortlisted for both the Pulitzer Prize and the PEN/Faulkner Award, the novel also won the National Book Prize of South Africa. Kingsolver grew up in rural Kentucky and lived in the Congo as a child, returning to the United States to study biology. Human and nonhuman ecologies have been a persistent theme in her novels, essays, and poetry, beginning with *Animal Dreams* (1990) and *Pigs in Heaven* (1993). She is an advocate for predator species in *Prodigal Summer* (2000), and celebrates eating locally in *Animal, Vegetable, and Miracle* (2007). Her recent work, *Flight Behavior* (2012), takes on global warming and its many ramifications. Each of her books since 1993 has been on the *New York Times* best-seller list. Kingsolver was awarded the National Humanities Award by President Clinton in 2000. In this excerpt from *The Poisonwood Bible*, the *nsongonya* (driver ant) in the Congo reminds us that humans can be challenged and undone on scales both minuscule and vast.

This awful night is the worst we've ever known: the *nsongonya*. They came on us like a nightmare. Nelson bang-bang-banging on the back door got tangled up with my sleep, so that, even after I was awake, the next hours had the unsteady presence of a dream. Before I even knew where I was, I found myself pulled along by somebody's hand in the dark and a horrible fiery sting sloshing up my calves. We were wading through very hot water, I thought, but it couldn't be water, so I tried to ask the name of the burning liquid that had flooded our house—no, for we were already outside—that had flooded the whole world?

"*Nsongonya*," they kept shouting, "*Les fourmis! Un corps d'armée!*" Ants. We were walking on, surrounded, enclosed, enveloped, being eaten by ants. Every surface was covered and boiling, and the path like black flowing lava in the moonlight. Dark, bulbous tree trunks seethed and bulged. The grass had become a field of dark daggers standing upright, churning and crumpling in on themselves. We walked on ants and ran on them, releasing their vinegary smell to the weird, quiet night. Hardly anyone spoke. We just ran as fast as we could alongside our neighbors. Adults carried babies and goats; children carried pots of food and dogs and younger brothers and sisters, the whole village of Kilanga. I thought of Mama Mwanza: would her sluggish sons carry her? Crowded together we moved down the road like a rushing stream, ran till we reached the river, and there we stopped. All of us shifting from foot to foot, slapping, some people moaning in pain but only the babies shrieking and wailing out loud. Strong men sloshed in slow motion through waist-deep water, dragging their boats, while the rest of us waited our turn to get in someone's canoe.

"Béene, where is your family?"

I jumped. The person beside me was Anatole.

"I don't know. I don't really know where anybody is, I just ran." I was still waking up and it struck me now with force that I should have been looking out for my family. I'd thought to worry about Mama Mwanza but not my own crippled twin. A moan rose out of me: "Oh, God!"

"What is it?"

"I don't know where they are. Oh, dear God. Adah will get eaten alive. Adah and Ruth May."

His hand touched mine in the dark. "I'll find them. Stay here until I come back for you."

He spoke softly to someone next to me, then disappeared. It seemed impossible to stand still where the ground was black with ants, but there was nowhere else to go. *How could I leave Adah behind again?* Once in the womb, once to the lion, and now like Simon Peter I had denied her for the third time. I looked for her, or Mother or anyone, but only saw other mothers running into the water with small, sobbing children, trying to splash and rub their arms and legs and faces clean of ants. A few old people had waded out neck-deep. Far out in the river I could see the half-white, half-black head of balding old Mama Lalaba, who must have decided crocodiles were preferable to death by *nsongonya*. The rest of us waited in the shallows, where the water's slick shine was veiled with a dark lace of floating ants. *Father forgive me according unto the multitude of thy mercies. I have done everything so wrong, and now there will be no escape for any of us.* An enormous moon trembled on the dark face of the Kwilu River. I stared hard at the ballooning pink reflection, believing this might be the last thing I would look upon before my eyes were chewed out of my skull. Though I didn't deserve it, I wanted to rise to heaven remembering something of beauty from the Congo.

ELIZABETH ALEXANDER

Amistad

Elizabeth Alexander (born 1962) read "Praise Song for the Day" at the 2009 presidential inauguration of Barack Obama. This celebration of ordinary lives, and of commonplace work done incrementally, runs through her entire corpus, from *Venus Hottentot* (1991) to *Antebellum Dream Book* (2001) to *American Sublime* (2005). Even though her poetry engages some of the most sensational characters in African American history—Sarah Baartman, the nineteenth-century African woman exhibited as a freak throughout Europe; and Joseph Cinqué, the leader of the rebellious slaves on the *Amistad*—she chooses to dwell on the steadfast rhythms and threads of continuity woven into such high drama. In this poem from *American Sublime*, Alexander depicts the transatlantic slave trade as a market force that tries to silence the enslaved but fails to, confronted instead by mutiny and insubordinate words, even if transitory.

After the tunnel of no return
After the roiling Atlantic, the black Atlantic, black and mucilaginous
After skin to skin in the hold and the picked handcuff locks
After the mutiny
After the fight to the death on the ship
After picked handcuff locks and the jump overboard
After the sight of no land and the zigzag course
After the Babel which settles like silt into silence
and silence and silence, and the whack
of lashes and waves on the side of the boat

After the half cup of rice, the half cup of sea-water
the dry swallow and silence
After the sight of no land
After two daughters sold to pay off a father's debt
After Cinque himself a settled debt

After, white gulf between stanzas
the space at the end
the last quatrain

HERMAN MELVILLE

"The Advocate," from *Moby-Dick*

Herman Melville (1819–1891), as noted in earlier sections of this anthology, was encyclopedic both in his subject and in his choice of genres. In Chapter 24 of *Moby-Dick*, "The Advocate," he offers a tour de force—a polemic combining economic analysis, political philosophy, and secular catechism—calling attention to the business of whaling as the unsung foundation of the world, at once a powerful market force and a wellspring of enlightenment.

As Queequeg and I are now fairly embarked in this business of whaling; and as this business of whaling has somehow come to be regarded among landsmen as a rather unpoetical and disreputable pursuit; therefore, I am all anxiety to convince ye, ye landsmen, of the injustice hereby done to us hunters of whales.

In the first place, it may be deemed almost superfluous to establish the fact, that among people at large, the business of whaling is not accounted on a level with what are called the liberal professions. If a stranger were introduced into any miscellaneous metropolitan society, it would but slightly advance the general opinion of his merits, were he presented to the company as a harpooneer, say; and if in emulation of the naval officers he should append the initials S.W.F. (Sperm Whale Fishery) to his visiting card, such a procedure would be deemed preeminently presuming and ridiculous.

Doubtless one leading reason why the world declines honoring us whalemen, is this: they think that, at best, our vocation amounts to a butchering sort of business; and that when actively engaged therein, we are surrounded by all manner of defilements. Butchers we are, that is true. But butchers, also, and butchers of the bloodiest badge have been all Martial Commanders whom the world invariably delights to honor. And as for the matter of the alleged uncleanliness of our business, ye shall soon be initiated into certain facts hitherto pretty generally unknown, and which, upon the whole, will triumphantly plant the sperm whale-ship at least among the cleanliest things of this tidy earth. But even granting the charge in question to be true; what disordered slippery decks of a whale-ship are comparable to the unspeakable carrion of those battle-fields from which so many soldiers return to drink in all ladies' plaudits? And if the idea of peril so much enhances the popular conceit of the soldier's profession; let me assure ye that many a veteran who has freely marched up to a battery, would quickly recoil at the apparition of the sperm whale's vast tail, fanning into eddies the air over his head. For what are the comprehensible terrors of man compared with the interlinked terrors and wonders of God!

But, though the world scouts at us whale hunters, yet does it unwittingly pay us the profoundest homage; yea, an all-abounding adoration! for almost all the tapers, lamps, and candles that burn round the globe, burn, as before so many shrines, to our glory!

But look at this matter in other lights; weigh it in all sorts of scales; see what we whalemen are, and have been.

Why did the Dutch in De Witt's time have admirals of their whaling fleets? Why did Louis XVI of France, at his own personal expense, fit out whaling ships from Dunkirk, and politely invite to that town some score or two of families from our own island of Nantucket? Why did Britain between the years 1750 and 1788 pay to her whalemen in bounties upwards of £1,000,000? And lastly, how comes it that we whalemen of America now outnumber all the rest of the banded whalemen in the world; sail a navy of upwards of seven hundred vessels; manned by eighteen thousand men; yearly consuming 4,000,000 of dollars; the ships worth, at the time of sailing, $20,000,000! and every year importing into our harbors a well reaped harvest of $7,000,000. How comes all this, if there be not something puissant in whaling?

But this is not the half; look again.

I freely assert, that the cosmopolite philosopher cannot, for his life, point out one single peaceful influence, which within the last sixty years has operated more potentially upon the whole broad world, taken in one aggregate, than the high and mighty business of whaling. One way and another, it has begotten events so remarkable in themselves, and so continuously momentous in their sequential issues, that whaling may well be regarded as that Egyptian mother, who bore offspring themselves pregnant from her womb. It would be a hopeless, endless task to catalogue all these things. Let a handful suffice. For many years past the whale-ship has been the pioneer in ferreting out the remotest and least known parts of the earth. She has explored seas and archipelagoes which had no chart, where no Cooke or Vancouver had ever sailed. If American and European men-of-war now peacefully ride in once savage harbors, let them fire salutes to the honor and glory of the whale-ship, which originally showed them the way, and first interpreted between them and the savages. They may celebrate as they will the heroes of Exploring Expeditions, your Cookes, your Krusensterns; but I say that scores of anonymous Captains have sailed out of Nantucket, that were as great, and greater, than your Cooke and your Krusenstern. For in their succorless empty-handedness, they, in the heathenish sharked waters, and by the beaches of unrecorded, javelin islands, battled with virgin wonders and terrors that Cooke with all his marines and muskets would not have willingly dared. All that is made such a flourish of in the old South Sea Voyages, those things were but the life-time commonplaces of our heroic Nantucketers. Often, adventures which Vancouver dedicates three chapters to, these men accounted unworthy of being set down in the ship's common log. Ah, the world! Oh, the world!

Until the whale fishery rounded Cape Horn, no commerce but colonial, scarcely any intercourse but colonial, was carried on between Europe and the long line of the opulent Spanish provinces on the Pacific coast. It was the whalemen who first broke through the jealous policy of the Spanish crown, touching those colonies; and, if space permitted, it might be distinctly shown how from those whalemen at last eventuated the liberation of Peru, Chili, and Bolivia from the yoke of Old Spain, and the establishment of the eternal democracy in those parts.

That great America on the other side of the sphere, Australia, was given to the enlightened world by the whaleman. After its first blunder-born discovery by a Dutchman, all other ships, long shunned those shores as pestiferously barbarous; but the whale-ship touched there. The whale-ship is the true mother of that now mighty colony. Moreover, in the infancy of the first Australian settlement, the emigrants were several times saved from starvation by the benevolent biscuit of the whale-ship luckily dropping an anchor in their waters. The uncounted isles of all Polynesia confess the same truth, and do commercial homage to the whale-ship, that cleared the way for the missionary and the merchant, and in many cases carried the primitive missionaries to their first destinations. If that double-bolted land, Japan, is ever to become hospitable, it is the whale-ship alone to whom the credit will be due; for already she is on the threshold.

But if, in the face of all this, you still declare that whaling has no aesthetically noble associations connected with it, then am I ready to shiver fifty lances with you there, and unhorse you with a split helmet every time.

The whale has no famous author, and whaling no famous chronicler, you will say.

The whale no famous author, and whaling no famous chronicler? Who wrote the first account of our Leviathan? Who but mighty Job? And who composed the first narrative of a whaling-voyage? Who, but no less a prince than Alfred the Great, who, with his own royal pen, took down the words from Other, the Norwegian whale-hunter of those times! And who pronounced our glowing eulogy in Parliament? Who, but Edmund Burke!

True enough, but then whalemen themselves are poor devils; they have no good blood in their veins.

No good blood in their veins? They have something better than royal blood there. The grandmother of Benjamin Franklin was Mary Morrel; afterwards, by marriage, Mary Folger, one of the old settlers of Nantucket, and the ancestress to a long line of Folgers and harpooneers—all kith and kin to noble Benjamin—this day darting the barbed iron from one side of the world to the other.

Good again; but then all confess that somehow whaling is not respectable.

Whaling not respectable? Whaling is imperial! By old English statutory law, the whale is declared "a royal fish."

Oh, that's only nominal! The whale himself has never figured in any grand imposing way.

The whale never figured in any grand imposing way? In one of the mighty triumphs given to a Roman general upon his entering the world's capital, the bones of a whale, brought all the way from the Syrian coast, were the most conspicuous object in the cymballed procession.

Grant it, since you cite it; but say what you will, there is no real dignity in whaling.

No dignity in whaling? The dignity of our calling the very heavens attest. Cetus is a constellation in the south! No more! Drive down your hat in presence of the Czar, and take it off to Queequeg! No more! I know a man that, in his lifetime has taken three hundred and fifty whales. I account that man more honorable than that great captain of antiquity who boasted of taking as many walled towns.

And, as for me, if, by any possibility, there be any as yet undiscovered prime thing in me; if I shall ever deserve any real repute in that small but high hushed world which I might not be unreasonably ambitious of; if hereafter I shall do anything upon the whole, a man might rather have done than to have left undone; if, at my death, my executors, or more properly my creditors, find any precious MSS. in my desk, then here I prospectively ascribe all the honor and the glory to whaling; for a whale-ship was my Yale College and my Harvard.

FRANK NORRIS

The Octopus

Frank Norris (1870–1902) established his reputation with *McTeague* (1899) and *The Octopus* (1901), "naturalist" novels inspired by the work of Émile Zola that chronicled the irresistible march of large-scale forces. Like several other naturalists—Stephen Crane, Theodore Dreiser, and Jack London—Norris began as a journalist, initially reporting from South Africa before he was expelled by the Boer government. He then traveled to Cuba to cover the 1898 Spanish-American War for *McClure's Magazine. The Octopus*, meant to be the first of a "wheat trilogy," depicts a fierce battle over freight rates and land rights between the Californian ranchers and the Pacific and Southwest Railroad, ending with a fatal shootout. In spite of this bloodbath, the novel offers an upbeat (though possibly also ironic) concluding vision, with the triumphant wheat carried by the railroad and shipped all over the world. This excerpt shows it descending "like a flood from the Sierras to the Himalayas to feed thousands of starving scarecrows on the barren plains of India."

The "Swanhilda" cast off from the docks at Port Costa two days after Presley had left Bonneville and the ranches and made her way up to San Francisco, anchoring in the stream off the City front. A few hours after her arrival, Presley, waiting at his club, received a despatch from Cedarquist to the effect that she would clear early the next morning and that he must be aboard of her before midnight.

He sent his trunks aboard and at once hurried to Cedarquist's office to say good-bye. He found the manufacturer in excellent spirits.

"What do you think of Lyman Derrick now, Presley?" he said, when Presley had sat down. "He's in the new politics with a vengeance, isn't he? And our own dear Railroad openly acknowledges him as their candidate. You've heard of his canvass."

"Yes, yes," answered Presley. "Well, he knows his business best."

But Cedarquist was full of another idea: his new venture—the organizing of a line of clipper wheat ships for Pacific and Oriental trade—was prospering.

"The 'Swanhilda' is the mother of the fleet, Pres. I had to buy *her*, but the keel of her sister ship will be laid by the time she discharges at Calcutta. We'll carry our wheat into Asia yet. The Anglo-Saxon started from there at the beginning of everything and it's manifest destiny that he must circle the globe and fetch up where he began his march. You are up with procession, Pres, going to India this way in a wheat ship that flies American colours. By the way, do you know where the money is to come from to build the sister ship of the 'Swanhilda'? From the sale of the plant and scrap iron of the Atlas Works. Yes, I've given it up definitely, that business. The people here would not back me up. But I'm working off on this new line now. It may break me, but we'll try it on. You know the 'Million Dollar Fair' was formally opened yesterday. There is," he added with a wink, "a Midway

Pleasance in connection with the thing. Mrs. Cedarquist and our friend Hartrath 'got up a subscription' to construct a figure of California—heroic size—out of dried apricots. I assure you," he remarked with prodigious gravity, "it is a real work of art and quite a 'feature' of the Fair. Well, good luck to you, Pres. Write to me from Honolulu, and bon voyage. My respects to the hungry Hindoo. Tell him 'we're coming, Father Abraham, a hundred thousand more.' Tell the men of the East to look out for the men of the West. The irrepressible Yank is knocking at the doors of their temples and he will want to sell 'em carpet-sweepers for their harems and electric light plants for their temple shrines. Good-bye to you."

"Good-bye, sir."

"Get fat yourself while you're about it, Presley," he observed, as the two stood up and shook hands.

"There shouldn't be any lack of food on a wheat ship. Bread enough, surely."

"Little monotonous, though. 'Man cannot live by bread alone.' Well, you're really off. Good-bye."

"Good-bye, sir."

And as Presley issued from the building and stepped out into the street, he was abruptly aware of a great wagon shrouded in white cloth, inside of which a bass drum was being furiously beaten. On the cloth, in great letters, were the words:

"Vote for Lyman Derrick, Regular Republican Nominee for Governor of California."

The "Swanhilda" lifted and rolled slowly, majestically on the ground swell of the Pacific, the water hissing and boiling under her forefoot, her cordage vibrating and droning in the steady rush of the trade winds. It was drawing towards evening and her lights had just been set. The master passed Presley, who was leaning over the rail smoking a cigarette, and paused long enough to remark:

"The land yonder, if you can make it out, is Point Gordo, and if you were to draw a line from our position now through that point and carry it on about a hundred miles further, it would just about cross Tulare County not very far from where you used to live."

"I see," answered Presley, "I see. Thanks. I am glad to know that."

The master passed on, and Presley, going up to the quarter deck, looked long and earnestly at the faint line of mountains that showed vague and bluish above the waste of tumbling water.

Those were the mountains of the Coast range and beyond them was what once had been his home. Bonneville was there, and Guadalajara and Los Muertos and Quien Sabe, the Mission of San Juan, the Seed ranch, Annixter's desolated home and Dyke's ruined hop-fields.

Well, it was all over now, that terrible drama through which he had lived. Already it was far distant from him; but once again it rose in his memory, portentous, sombre, ineffaceable. He passed it all in review from the day of his first meeting with Vanamee to the day of his parting with Hilma. He saw it all—the great sweep of country opening to view from the summit of the hills at the head waters of Broderson's Creek; the barn dance at Annixter's, the harness room with its jam of furious men; the quiet garden of the Mission; Dyke's house, his flight upon the engine, his brave fight in the chaparral; Lyman Derrick at bay in the dining-room of the ranch house; the rabbit drive; the fight at the irrigating ditch, the shouting mob in the Bonneville Opera House.

The drama was over. The fight of Ranch and Railroad had been wrought out to its dreadful close. It was true, as Shelgrim had said, that forces rather than men had locked horns in that struggle, but for all that the men of the Ranch and not the men of the Railroad had suffered. Into the prosperous valley, into the quiet community of farmers, that galloping monster, that terror of steel and steam had burst, shooting athwart the horizons, flinging the echo of its thunder over all the ranches of the valley, leaving blood and destruction in its path.

Yes, the Railroad had prevailed. The ranches had been seized in the tentacles of the octopus; the iniquitous burden of extortionate freight rates had been imposed like a yoke of iron. The monster had killed Harran, had killed Osterman, had killed Broderson, had killed Hooven. It had beggared Magnus and had driven him to a state of semi-insanity after he had wrecked his honour in the vain attempt to do evil that good might come. It had enticed Lyman into its toils to pluck from him his manhood and his honesty, corrupting him and poisoning him beyond redemption; it had hounded Dyke from his legitimate employment and had made of him a highwayman and criminal. It had cast forth Mrs. Hooven to starve to death upon the City streets. It had driven Minna to prostitution. It had slain Annixter at the very moment when painfully and manfully he had at last achieved his own salvation and stood forth resolved to do right, to act unselfishly and to live for others. It had widowed Hilma in the very dawn of her happiness. It had killed the very babe within the mother's womb, strangling life ere yet it had been born, stamping out the spark ordained by God to burn through all eternity.

What then was left? Was there no hope, no outlook for the future, no rift in the black curtain, no glimmer through the night? Was good to be thus overthrown? Was evil thus to be strong and to prevail? Was nothing left?

Then suddenly Vanamee's words came back to his mind. What was the larger view, what contributed the greatest good to the greatest numbers? What was the full round of the circle whose segment only he beheld? In the end, the ultimate, final end of all, what was left? Yes, good issued from this crisis, untouched, unassailable, undefiled.

Men—motes in the sunshine—perished, were shot down in the very noon of life, hearts were broken, little children started in life lamentably handicapped; young girls were brought to a life of shame; old women died in the heart of life for lack of food. In that little, isolated group of human insects, misery, death, and anguish spun like a wheel of fire.

But the wheat remained. Untouched, unassailable, undefiled, that mighty world-force, that nourisher of nations, wrapped in Nirvanic calm, indifferent to the human swarm, gigantic, resistless, moved onward in its appointed grooves. Through the welter of blood at the irrigation ditch, through the sham charity and shallow philanthropy of famine relief committees, the great harvest of Los Muertos rolled like a flood from the Sierras to the Himalayas to feed thousands of starving scarecrows on the barren plains of India.

JOHN DOS PASSOS

The Big Money

John Dos Passos (1896–1970) wrote many novels, including *The U.S.A. Trilogy*, featuring *The Forty-Second Parallel* (1930), *1919* (1932), and *The Big Money* (1936). A seasoned traveler, he was in France and Italy during World War I, initially with the American Volunteer Motor Ambulance Corps, then with the U.S. Army Medical Corps. He was in Spain in 1937 during the Spanish Civil War, a key member of the left-leaning League of American Writers, but broke with the group—and ended his friendship with Hemingway—over the murder of José Robles, his good friend and translator. In later years his politics would shift and he campaigned actively for presidential candidates Barry Goldwater and Richard M. Nixon. The following excerpt from *The Big Money* portrays the Ford Motor Company, the world's largest automobile manufacturer, producing the Model-T and inventing the assembly-line system of management, eventually spearheading an anti-Semitic military-industrial complex.

For twenty years or more,

ever since he'd left his father's farm when he was sixteen to get a job in a Detroit machine shop, Henry Ford had been nuts about machinery. First it was watches, then he designed a steam tractor, then he built a horseless carriage with an engine adapted from the Otto gas engine he'd read about in The World of Science, then a mechanical buggy with a one cylinder four cycle motor, that would run forward but not back;

at last, in ninety eight, he felt he was far enough along to risk throwing up his job with the Detroit Edison Company, where he'd worked his way up from night fireman to chief engineer, to put all his time into working on a new gasoline engine, (in the late eighties he'd met Edison at a meeting of electric light employees in Atlantic City. He'd gone up to Edison after Edison had delivered an address and asked him if he thought gasoline was practical as a motor fuel. Edison had said yes. If Edison said it, it was true. Edison was the great admiration of Henry Ford's life);

and in driving his mechanical buggy, sitting there at the lever jauntily dressed in a tight buttoned jacket and a high collar and a derby hat, back and forth over the level ill paved streets of Detroit,

scaring the big brewery horses and the skinny trotting horses and the sleek rumped pacers with the motor's loud explosions,

looking for men scatterbrained enough to invest money in a factory for building automobiles.

He was the eldest son of an Irish immigrant who during the Civil War had married the daughter of a prosperous Pennsylvania Dutch farmer and settled down to farming near Dearborn in Wayne County, Michigan;

like plenty of other Americans, young Henry grew up hating the endless sogging through the mud about the chores, the hauling and pitching manure, the kerosene lamps to clean, the irk and sweat and solitude of the farm.

He was a slender, active youngster, a good skater, clever with his hands; what he liked was to tend the machinery and let the others do the heavy work. His mother had told him not to drink, smoke, gamble or go into debt, and he never did.

When he was in his early twenties his father tried to get him back from Detroit, where he was working as mechanic and repairman for the Drydock Engine Company that built engines for steamboats, by giving him forty acres of land.

Young Henry built himself an up to date square white dwelling house with a false mansard roof and married and settled down on the farm,

but he let the hired men do the farming;

he bought himself a buzzsaw and rented a stationary engine and cut the timber off the woodlots.

He was a thrifty young man who never drank or smoked or gambled or coveted his neighbor's wife, but he couldn't stand living on the farm.

He moved to Detroit, and in the brick barn behind his house tinkered for years in his spare time with a mechanical buggy that would be light enough to run over the clayey wagon roads of Wayne County, Michigan.

By 1900 he had a practicable car to promote.

He was forty years old before the Ford Motor Company was started and production began to move.

Speed was the first thing the early automobile manufacturers went after. Races advertised the makes of cars.

Henry Ford himself hung up several records at the track at Grosse Pointe and on the ice on Lake St. Clair. In his 999 he did the mile in thirty nine and four fifths seconds.

But it had always been his custom to hire others to do the heavy work. The speed he was busy with was speed in production, the records in efficient output. He hired Barney Oldfield, a stunt bicycle rider from Salt Lake City, to do the racing for him.

Henry Ford had ideas about other things than the designing of motors, carburetors, magnetos, jigs and fixtures, punches and dies; he had ideas about sales,

that the big money was in economical quantity production, quick turnover, cheap interchangeable, easily replaced standardized parts;

it wasn't until 1909, after years of arguing with his partners, that Ford put out the first Model T.

Henry Ford was right.

That season he sold more than ten thousand tin lizzies, ten years later he was selling almost a million a year.

In these years the Taylor Plan was stirring up plant managers and manufacturers all over the country. Efficiency was the word. The same ingenuity that went into improving the performance of a machine could go into improving the performance of the workmen producing the machine.

In 1913 they established the assembly line at Ford's. That season the profits were something like twenty five million dollars, but they had trouble in keeping the men on the job, machinists didn't seem to like it at Ford's.

Henry Ford had ideas about other things than production.

He was the largest automobile manufacturer in the world; he paid high wages; maybe if the steady workers thought they were getting a cut (a very small cut) in the profits, it would give trained men an inducement to stick to their jobs,

wellpaid workers might save enough money to buy a tin lizzie; the first day Ford's announced that clean cut properly married American workers who wanted jobs had a chance to make five bucks a day (of course it turned out that there were strings to it; always there were strings to it)

such an enormous crowd waited outside the Highland Park plant all through the zero January night

that there was a riot when the gates were opened; cops broke heads, job hunters threw bricks; property, Henry Ford's own property, was destroyed. The company dicks had to turn on the firehose to beat back the crowd.

The American Plan; automotive prosperity seeping down from above; it turned out there were strings to it.

But that five dollars a day

paid to good, clean American workmen

who didn't drink or smoke cigarettes or read or think,

and who didn't commit adultery

and whose wives didn't take in boarders,

made America once more the Yukon of the sweated workers of the world;

made all the tin lizzies and the automotive age, and incidentally,

made Henry Ford the automobileer, the admirer of Edison, the birdlover,

the great American of his time.

DAVE EGGERS AND VALENTINO ACHAK DENG

What Is the What

Dave Eggers (born 1970) is known for his wide corpus; for McSweeney's, his independent publishing house; and for 826 Valencia, a literacy project tutoring underprivileged students. His memoir, *A Heartbreaking Work of Staggering Genius* (2000), was a finalist for the Pulitzer Prize. This was followed by a novel, *You Shall Know Our Velocity* (2002); a collection of short stories, *How We Are Hungry* (2004); a book of interviews with prisoners sentenced to death and later exonerated, *Surviving Justice* (2005); and a fictionalized autobiography, *What Is the What* (2006), co-authored with Valentino Achak Deng, a Sudanese "lost boy." Eggers received the Courage in Media award from the Council on American-Islamic

Relations for *Zeitoun* (2009), his story about a Syrian immigrant arrested and imprisoned while helping neighbors during Hurricane Katrina. More recently, *A Hologram for the King* (2012) deals with the financial crisis of the late 2000s, while *The Circle* (2013) depicts life inside a San Francisco high-tech company. This excerpt, a history lesson for a hospital receptionist in Atlanta from *What Is the What*, discusses oil as a key player in the Sudanese Civil War.

Achor Achor is rifling through the magazines on the end table. He finds something of interest and shows me a newsmagazine with a cover story about Sudan. A Darfurian woman, with cracked lips and yellow eyes, looks into the camera, at once despairing and defiant. Do you know what she wants, Julian? She is a woman who had a camera pushed into her face and she stared into the lens. I have no doubt that she wanted to tell her story, or some version of it. But now that it has been told, now that the countless murders and rapes have been documented, or extrapolated from those few reported, the world can wonder how to approach Sudan's violence against Darfur. There are a few thousand African Union troops there, but Darfur is the size of France, and the Darfurians would much prefer Western troops; they are presumed to be better trained and better armed and less susceptible to bribes.

Does this interest you, Julian? You seem to be well informed and of empathetic nature, though your compassion surely has a limit. You hear my story of being attacked in my own home, and you shake my hand and look into my eyes and promise treatment to me, but then I wait. We wait for someone, perhaps doctors behind curtains or doors, perhaps bureaucrats in unseen offices, to decide when and how I will receive attention. You wear a uniform and have worked at a hospital for some time; I would accept treatment from you, even if you were unsure. But you sit and think you can do nothing.

Achor Achor and I glance through the Darfur article and see some passing mention of oil, the role oil has played in the conflict in Sudan. Admittedly, oil is not at the center of what has happened in Darfur, but Lino can tell you, Julian, about the role oil played in his own displacement. Do you know these things, Julian? Do you know that it was George Bush, the father, who found the major oil deposits under the soil of Sudan? Yes, this is what is said. This was 1974, and at the time, Bush Sr. was the U.S. ambassador to the United Nations. Mr. Bush was an oil person, of course, and he was looking at some satellite maps of Sudan that he had access to, or that his oil friends had made, and these maps indicated that there was oil in the region. He told the government of Sudan about this, and this was the beginning of the first significant exploration, the beginning of U.S. oil involvement in Sudan, and, to some extent, the beginning of the middle of the war. Would it have lasted so long without oil? There is no chance.

Julian, the discovery of oil occurred shortly after the Addis Ababa agreement, the pact that ended the first civil war, that first one lasting almost seventeen years. In 1972, the north and south of Sudan met in Ethiopia, and the peace agreement was signed, including, among other things, provisions to share any of the natural resources of the south, fifty-fifty. Khartoum had agreed to this, but at the time, they believed the primary natural resource in the south was uranium. But at Addis Ababa, no one know about oil, so when the oil was found, Khartoum was concerned. They had signed this agreement, and the agreement insisted that all resources be split evenly . . . But not with oil! To share oil with blacks? This would not do! It was terrible for them, I think, and that is when much of the hard-liners in Khartoum began thinking about canceling Addis Ababa and keeping the oil for themselves.

Lino's family lived in the Muglad Basin, a Nuer area near the border between north and south. Unhappily for them, in 1978 Chevron found a large oil field here, and Khartoum, which had authorized the exploration, renamed this area using the Arabic word for unity. Do you like that name, Julian? Unity means the coming together of people, many peoples coming together as one. Is it too obviously ironic? Extending the joke, in 1980 Khartoum tried to redraw the border between the north and south, so the oil fields would be in the north! They didn't get away with that, thank the lord. But still, something needed to be done to cut the Nuer who lived there out of the process, to separate them from the oil, and to ensure that there would be no interference in the future.

It was 1982 when the government got serious about dealing with those, like Lino's family, living above the oil. The murahaleen began to show up with automatic weapons, precisely as they later did in Marial Bai. The idea was that they would force the Nuer out and the oil fields would be protected by Baggara or private security forces, and thus would be inoculated against any kind of rebel tampering. So the horsemen came, as they always come, with their guns and with their random looting and violence. But it was mild this first time; it was a message sent to the Nuer living atop the oil; leave the area and do not come back.

Lino's family did not leave their village. They didn't get the message, or chose to ignore it. Six months later, Sudanese army soldiers visited the village to clarify their suggestion. The Nuer were told to leave at once, to cross the river and move to the south. They were told that their names would be registered, and they would later receive compensation for their land, homes, crops, and whatever possessions they needed to abandon. So that day, Lino's family, and all those in the village, gave their names to the soldiers, and the soldiers left. But even then, Lino's family didn't leave. They were stubborn, Julian, as so many Sudanese are stubborn. You have no doubt heard of the thousand Sudanese in Cairo, those who were trampled? This was not long ago. A thousand Sudanese, squatting in a small park in Cairo, demanding citizenship or safe passage to other nations. Months pass, they will not leave, they cannot be appeased until their demands are met. The Egyptians don't see it as their problem, and the park where the Sudanese are squatting has become an eyesore, and unsanitary. Finally Egyptian troops move in to destroy the shantytown, killing twenty-seven Sudanese in the process, including eleven children. A stubborn people, the Sudanese.

So Lino's family remained. They and hundreds more decided to simply stay where they were. One month later, as might have been expected, a regiment of militiamen and army soldiers rolled onto the village. They very calmly strolled into the town, as they had when they took the names. They said nothing to anyone; once positioned, they began to shoot. They shot nineteen people in the first minute. They nailed one man to a tree, and dropped an infant into a well. They killed thirty-two in all, and then climbed back onto their trucks and left. That day, the survivors of the village packed and fled, traveling south. By 1984, Lino's village and the villages near it, all of those sitting atop the oil, were all cleared of Nuer, and Chevron was free to drill.

"Hey, sick man!"

Lino has arrived, wearing a blue pinstriped zoot suit, and three gold chains around his neck. There is a store in Atlanta, God help us, where too many Sudanese are buying their clothes. Julian looks up from his reading, amused by Lino's outfit, interested in the three of us speaking quickly in Dinka. I catch his eye and he returns to his book.

JACK LONDON

The Scarlet Plague

Jack London (1876–1916), as noted in the "Work, Play, Travel" section of this anthology, wrote about germs and pandemics as well as *The Call of the Wild* (1903) and *White Fang* (1906). In "The Scarlet Plague" (1912), excerpted below, a few survivors discuss (some without comprehension) the "invisible micro-organic" bacteria that wiped out much of the world's population.

"You was telling about germs, the things you can't see but which make men sick," Edwin prompted.

"Yes, that's where I was. A man did not notice at first when only a few of these germs got into his body. But each germ broke in half and became two germs, and they kept doing this very rapidly so that in a short time there were many millions of them in the body. Then the man was sick. He had a disease, and the disease was named after the kind of a germ that was in him. It might be measles, it might be influenza, it might be yellow fever; it might be any of thousands and thousands of kinds of diseases.

"Now this is the strange thing about these germs. There were always new ones coming to live in men's bodies. Long and long and long ago, when there were only a few men in the world, there were few diseases. But as men increased and lived closely together in great cities and civilizations, new diseases arose, new kinds of germs entered their bodies. Thus were countless of millions and billions of human beings killed. And the more thickly men packed together, the more terrible were the new diseases that came to be. Long before my time, in the middle ages, there was the Black Plague that swept across Europe. It swept across Europe many times. There was tuberculosis, that entered into men wherever they were thickly packed. A hundred years before my time there was the bubonic plague. And in Africa was the sleeping sickness. The bacteriologists fought all those sicknesses and destroyed them, just as you boys fight the wolves away from your goats, or squash the mosquitoes that light on you. The bacteriologists—"

"But, Granser, what is a what-you-call-it?" Edwin interrupted.

"You, Edwin, are a goatherd. Your task is to watch the goats. You know a great deal about goats. A bacteriologist watches germs. That's his task, and he knows a great deal about them. So, as I was saying, the bacteriologists fought with the germs and destroyed them—sometimes. There was leprosy, a horrible disease. A hundred years before I was born, the bacteriologists discovered the germ of leprosy. They knew all about it. They made pictures. But they never found a way to kill it. But in 1984 [sic], there was the Pantoblast Plague, a disease that broke out in a country called Brazil and that killed millions of people. But the bacteriologists found it out, and found the way to kill it, so that the Pantoblast Plague went no farther. They made what they called a serum, which they put into a man's body and which killed the pantoblast germs without killing the man. And in 1910, there was Pellagra, and also the hookworm. These were easily killed by the bacteriologists. But in 1947 there arose a new disease that had never been seen before. It got into the bodies of babies of only ten months old or less, and it made them unable to move their hands and feet, or to eat, or anything; and the bacteriologists were eleven years in discovering how to kill that particular germ and save the babies.

"In spite of all these diseases, and of all the new ones that continued to arise, there were more and more men in the world. This was because it was easy to get food. The easier it was to get food, the more men there were; the more men there were, the more thickly were they packed together on the earth; and the more thickly they were packed, the more new kinds of germs became diseases. There were warnings. Soldervetzsky, as early as 1929, told the bacteriologists that they had no guaranty against some new disease, a thousand times more deadly than any they knew, arising and killing by the hundreds of millions and even by the billion. You see, the micro-organic world remained a mystery to the end. They knew there was such a world, and that from time to time armies of new germs emerged from it to kill men. And that was all they knew about it. For all they knew, in that invisible micro-organic world there might be as many different kinds of germs as there are grains of sand on this beach. And also, in that same invisible world it might well be that new kinds of germs came to be. It might be there that life originated—the 'abysmal fecundity,' Soldervetzsky called it, applying the words of other men who had written before him . . ."

It was at this point that Hare-Lip rose to his feet, an expression of huge contempt on his face.

"Granser," he announced, "you make me sick with your gabble. Why don't you tell about the Red Death? If you ain't going to, say so, an' we'll start back for camp."

SAUL BELLOW

Henderson the Rain King

Saul Bellow (1915–2005), Nobel laureate, is known for many iconic works: *The Adventures of Augie March* (1953), *Seize the Day* (1956), *Herzog* (1964), *Mr. Sammler's Planet* (1970), *Humboldt's Gift* (1975), and *Ravelstein* (2000). Born in Quebec, he moved with his family to Chicago when he was nine, the beginning of his long association with that city. His first novel, *Dangling Man* (1944), was completed while he served in the merchant marine. *The Adventures of Augie March* followed, written in France, Austria, and Italy, a picaresque novel about a protagonist traveling by land and by sea, from Chicago to Mexico to Paris. Eugene Henderson, the protagonist of *Henderson the Rain King* (1959), also embarks on a journey. In the following excerpt, he brings death and destruction to frogs and to the Arnewi tribe in Africa.

In the dead of the heat we reached the cistern and I went forward alone into the weeds on the edge. All the rest remained behind, and not even Romilayu came up with me. That was all right, too. In a crisis a man must be prepared to stand alone, and actually standing alone is the kind of thing I'm good at. I was thinking, "By Judas, I should be good, considering how experienced I am in going it by myself." And with the bomb in my left hand and the lighter with the slender white wick in the other—this patriarchal-looking wick—I looked into the water. There in their home medium were creatures, the polliwogs with fat heads and skinny tails and their budding little scratchers, and the mature animals with eyes like ripe gooseberries, submerged in their slums of ooze. While I myself, Henderson, like a great pine whose roots have crossed and choked one another—but never mind about me now. The figure of their doom, I stood over them and the frogs didn't—of course they couldn't—know what I augured. And meanwhile, all the chemistry of anxious fear, which I know so well and hate so much, was taking place in me—the light wavering before my eyes, the saliva drying, my parts retracting, and the cables of my neck hardening. I heard the chatter of the expectant Arnewi, who held their cattle on ornamented tethers, as a drowning man will hear the bathers on the beach, and I saw Mtalba, who stood between them and me in her red baize like a poppy, the black at the center of the blazing red. Then I blew on the wick of my device, to free it from dust (or for good luck), and spun the wheel of the lighter, and when it responded with a flame, I lit the fuse, formerly my shoelace. It started to burn and first the metal tip dropped off. The spark sank pretty steadily toward the case. There was nothing for me to do but clutch the thing, and fix my eyes upon it; my legs, bare to the heat, were numb. The burning took quite a space of time and even when the point of the spark descended through the hole in the wood, I held on because I couldn't risk quenching it. After this I had to call on intuition plus luck, and as there now was nothing I especially wanted to see in the external world I closed my eyes and waited for the spirit to move me. It was not yet time, and still not time, and I pressed the case and thought I heard the spark as it ate the lace and fussed toward the powder. At the last moment I took a Band-Aid which I had prepared for this moment and fastened it over the hole. Then I lobbed the bomb, giving it an underhand toss. It touched the thatch and turned on itself only once before it fell into the yellow water. The frogs fled from it and the surface closed again; the ripples traveled outward and that was all. But then a new motion began; the water swelled at the middle and I realized that the thing was working. Damned if my soul didn't rise with the water even before it began to spout, following the same motion, and I cried to myself, "Hallelujah! Henderson, you dumb brute, this time you've done it!" Then the water came shooting upward. It might not have been Hiroshima, but it was enough of a gush for me, and it started raining frogs' bodies upward. They leaped for the roof with the blast, and globs of mud and stones and polliwogs struck the thatch. I wouldn't have thought a dozen or so shells from the .375 had such a charge in them, and from the periphery of my intelligence the most irrelevant thoughts, which are fastest and lightest, rushed to the middle as I congratulated myself, the first thought being,

"They'd be proud of old Henderson at school." (The infantry school. I didn't get high marks when I was there.) The long legs and white bellies and the thicker shapes of the infant frogs filled the column of water. I myself was spattered with the mud, but I started to yell, "Hey, Itelo—Romilayu! How do you like that? Boom! You wouldn't believe me!"

I had gotten more of a result than I could have known in the first instants, and instead of an answering cry I heard shrieks from the natives, and looking to see what was the matter I found that the dead frogs were pouring out of the cistern together with the water.

The explosion had blasted out the retaining wall at the front end. The big stone blocks had fallen and the yellow reservoir was emptying fast. "Oh! Hell!" I grabbed my head, immediately dizzy with the nausea of disaster, seeing the water spill like a regular mill race with the remains of those frogs. "Hurry, hurry!" I started to yell. "Romilayu! Itelo! Oh, Judas priest, what's happening! Give a hand. Help, you guys, help!" I threw myself down against the escaping water and tried to breast it back and lift the stones into place. The frogs charged into me like so many prunes and fell into my pants and into the open shoe, the lace gone. The cattle started to riot, pulling at their tethers and straining toward the water. But it was polluted and nobody would allow them to drink. It was a moment of horror, with the cows of course obeying nature and the natives begging them and weeping, and the whole reservoir going into the ground. The sand got it all. Romilayu waded up beside me and did his best, but these blocks of stone were beyond our strength and because of the cistern's being also a dam we were downstream, or however the hell it was. Anyway, the water was lost—lost! In a matter of minutes I saw (sickening!) the yellow mud of the bottom and the dead frogs settling there. For them death was instantaneous by shock and it was all over. But the natives, the cows leaving under protest, moaning for the water! Soon everyone was gone except for Itelo and Mtalba.

"Oh, God, what's happened?" I said to them. "This is ruination. I have made a disaster." And I pulled up my wet and stained T-shirt and hid my face in it. Thus exposed, I said through the cloth, "Itelo, kill me! All I've got to offer is my life. So take it. Go ahead, I'm waiting."

I listened for his approach but all I could hear, instead of footsteps, were the sounds of heartbreak that escaped from Mtalba. My belly hung forth and I was braced for the blow of the knife.

"Mistah Henderson. Sir! What has happened?"

"Stab me," I said, "don't ask me. Stab, I say. Use my knife if you haven't got your own. It's all the same," I said, "and don't forgive me. I couldn't stand it. I'd rather be dead."

This was nothing but God's own truth, as with the cistern I had blown up everything else, it seemed. And so I held my face in the bagging, sopping shirt with the unbearable complications at heart. I waited for Itelo to cut me open, my naked middle with all its fevers and its suffering prepared for execution. Under me the water of the cistern was turning to hot vapor and the sun was already beginning to corrupt the bodies of the frog dead.

ROBERT FROST

Fire and Ice

Robert Frost (1874–1963), a poet of everyday life and colloquial speech in rural New England, was born in San Francisco, attending Dartmouth and Harvard without graduating from either. He took odd jobs, including working as a bobbin boy in a cotton mill, and struggled as a farmer in New Hampshire. His poetic career took off only after he moved to England in 1912, where he published his first two books of poetry, *A Boy's Will* (1913) and *North of Boston* (1914). Many other volumes followed after his return to the United States, including *New Hampshire* (1924), *West-Running Brook* (1928), *A Further Range* (1937), and *A Witness Tree* (1943). Many awards followed as well, including four Pulitzer Prizes and more than forty honorary degrees. For forty-two years, from 1921–1963, he taught every summer and fall at the Bread Loaf School in Vermont. He was awarded the Congressional Medal in 1960 and read "The Gift Outright" at the inauguration of President John F. Kennedy. Though Frost is often associated with a warm folksiness, poems such as "Home Burial," "Death of the Hired Man," "Out, Out—," and "The Witch of Coos" point to something stark and elemental. The short poem here proceeds in that vein.

Some say the world will end in fire,
Some say in ice.
From what I've tasted of desire
I hold with those who favor fire.
But if it had to perish twice,
I think I know enough of hate
To say that for destruction ice
Is also great
And would suffice.

CARL SANDBURG

Buttons

Carl Sandburg (1878–1967) became famous as the poet of Chicago, celebrating the vitality of its workforce in *Chicago Poems* (1916), *Corn Huskers* (1918), and *Smoke and Steel* (1920). Beginning as a journalist for the *Chicago Daily News,* he would go on to win three Pulitzer Prizes, including one for his 1939 biography, *Abraham Lincoln: The War Years*. He also wrote children's books such as *Rootabaga Stories* (1922), set in a fictionalized Midwest with corn fairies as well farms and trains and narrated by an old minstrel, a Potato Face Blind Man. Sandburg was also one of the earliest urban folk singers, accompanying himself on the guitar at lectures and poetry readings. His 1927 anthology, *The American Songbag,* went through several editions and was hailed by Pete Seeger as a "landmark." Sandburg was very much an institution by the time he died. In tribute, President Lyndon B. Johnson simply said: "He was America." Rarely a cheerleader, there is often a hard edge to his poetry, as demonstrated here.

I have been watching the war map slammed up for
    advertising in front of the newspaper office.

Buttons—red and yellow buttons—blue and black buttons—
   are shoved back and forth across the map.

A laughing young man, sunny with freckles,
Climbs a ladder, yells a joke to somebody in the crowd,
And then fixes a yellow button one inch west
And follows the yellow button with a black button one inch west.

(Ten thousand men and boys twist on their bodies in
   a red soak along a river edge,
Gasping of wounds, calling for water, some rattling
  death in their throats.)
Who would guess what it cost to move two buttons one
   inch on the war map here in front of the newspaper
   office where the freckle-faced young man is laughing
   to us?

RANDALL JARRELL

The Death of the Ball Turret Gunner

Randall Jarrell (1914–1965) wrote terse, often emotionally tumultuous poetry; his prose as a literary critic was equally fierce. He published his first work, *Blood for a Stranger* (1942), in the same year that he entered the United States Air Force. In *Little Friend, Little Friend* (1945), *Losses* (1948), and *The Seven-League Crutches* (1951), he drew on his experience in World War II, often creating poetic monologues out of stories heard from other soldiers. Jarrell served as poet laureate of the United States from 1956 to 1958. He also wrote a satirical novel, *Pictures from an Institution* (1954), translated a play by Chekhov and several Grimm fairy tales, and wrote children's books including *The Bat-Poet* (1964) and *The Animal Family* (1965), with illustrations by Maurice Sendak. In the following poem, Jarrell shows that fairy tales can sometimes be nightmarish.

From my mother's sleep I fell into the State,
And I hunched in its belly till my wet fur froze.
Six miles from earth, loosed from its dream of life,
I woke to black flak and the nightmare fighters.
When I died they washed me out of the turret with a hose.

ADRIENNE RICH

The School among the Ruins

Adrienne Rich (1929–2012), one of the most celebrated poets of the twentieth century, was also one of the most politically engaged. Her first book, *Change of World* (1951), published while she was a senior at Radcliffe College, was selected by W. H. Auden for the Yale Series of Younger Poets. Rich's activism in the Civil Rights Movement and the Vietnam War protests informed much of her poetry. Awarded the 1974 National Book Award for *Diving into the Wreck,* she expressed her solidarity with two other nominated poets, Audre Lorde and Alice Walker, by appearing with them at the award ceremony. In 1997 she declined the National Medal of Arts to protest a vote by Congress to stop funding the National Endowment for the Arts. Rich began a lifelong partnership with Jamaica-born novelist Michelle Cliff in 1976, a partnership reflected in her poetry from *Dream of a Common Language* (1978) to *A Wild Patience Has Taken Me This Far* (1981) to *The Fact of a Doorframe* (2001), and in critical essays such as "Compulsory Heterosexuality and Lesbian Existence" (1980). In this poem from a 2004 collection of the same title, she describes the onsite reality of war.

Beirut. Baghdad. Sarajevo. Bethlehem. Kabul. Not of course here.

1
Teaching the first lesson and the last
—great falling light of summer will you last
longer than schooltime?

When children flow
in columns at the doors
BOYS GIRLS and the busy teachers

open or close high windows
with hooked poles   drawing darkgreen shades

closets unlocked, locked
questions unasked, asked, when

love of the fresh impeccable
sharp-pencilled   yes
order without cruelty

a street on earth   neither heaven nor hell
busy with commerce and worship
young teachers walking to school

fresh bread and early-open foodstalls

2
When the offensive rocks the sky when nightglare
misconstrues day and night when lived-in
rooms from the upper city
tumble cratering lower streets

cornices of olden ornament   human debris
when fear vacuums out the streets

When the whole town flinches
blood on the undersole thickening to glass

Whoever crosses   hunched   knees bent   a contested zone
knows why she does this suicidal thing

School's now in session day and night
children sleep
in the classrooms   teachers rolled close

3

How the good teacher loved
his school   the students
the lunchroom with fresh sandwiches
lemonade and milk
the classroom   glass cages
of moss and turtles
teaching responsibility

A morning breaks without bread or fresh-poured milk
parents or lesson plans

diarrhea first question of the day
children shivering   it's September
Second question: where is my mother?

4

One: I don't know where your mother
is   Two: I don't know
why they are trying to hurt us
Three: or the latitude and longitude
of their hatred   Four: I don't know if we
hate them as much   I think there's more toilet paper
in the supply closet   I'm going to break it open

Today this is your lesson:
write as clearly as you can
your name   home street   and number
down on this page
No you can't go home yet
but you aren't lost
this is our school

I'm not sure what we'll eat
we'll look for healthy roots and greens
searching for water though the pipes are broken

5

There's a young cat sticking
her head through window bars
she's hungry like us
but can feed on mice
her bronze erupting fur
speaks of a life already wild

her golden eyes
don't give quarter   She'll teach us   Let's call her
Sister
when we get milk we'll give her some

6

I've told you, let's try to sleep in this funny camp
All night pitiless pilotless things go shrieking
above us to somewhere

Don't let your faces turn to stone
Don't stop asking me why
Let's pay attention to our cat   she needs us

Maybe tomorrow the bakers can fix their ovens

7

"We sang them to naps   told stories   made
shadow-animals with our hands

wiped human debris off boots and coats
sat learning by heart the names
some were too young to write
some had forgotten how"

BRIAN TURNER

Here, Bullet

Brian Turner (born 1967) represents a new generation of literary voices shaped by war. After earning an MFA from the University of Oregon and briefly living in South Korea, he joined the United States Army, serving first in Bosnia-Herzegovina (1990–2000) and later in Iraq (2003–2004). His first book, *Here, Bullet* (2005), a stark but affirmative volume, is among the best poetry written about the Iraq War. His second book, *Phantom Noise* (2010), focusing more on the haunted lives of veterans back home, was shortlisted for the T. S. Eliot Prize. His most recent work, *My Life as a Foreign Country*, a memoir, was published in 2014. In this poem from *Here, Bullet*, he addresses the bullet as a "you," turning the human body into its nonhuman operating theater.

If a body is what you want,
then here is bone and gristle and flesh.
Here is the clavicle-snapped wish,
the aorta's opened valves, the leap
thought makes at the synaptic gap.
Here is the adrenaline rush you crave,
that inexorable flight, that insane puncture
into heat and blood. And I dare you to finish
what you've started. Because here, Bullet,
here is where I complete the word you bring
hissing through the air, here is where I moan
the barrel's cold esophagus, triggering
my tongue's explosives for the rifling I have
inside of me, each twist of the round
spun deeper, because here, Bullet,
here is where the world ends, every time.

GEORGE OPPEN

The Crowded Countries of the Bomb

George Oppen (1908–1984) is most often associated with "Objectivism," a school of poetry valuing clarity and precision over formal metrics. In 1932 he helped found the Objectivist Press, which published his first book of poems, *Discrete Series* (1934). Almost immediately, however, he abandoned poetry for politics, making a living as a factory worker while serving as an organizer for the Communist Party. He was in the Armed Forces in World War II. In 1950 Oppen was summoned by Senator McCarthy's Un-American Activities Committee. Rather than serving as an informer or serving a jail term, he and his wife moved to Mexico for the next eight years. Only in 1958, after the death of Senator McCarthy, did he return to the United States, an event that also marked his return to poetry. *The Materials* (1962) and *This in Which* (1965) followed. Oppen won the Pulitzer Prize for *Of Being Numerous* (1968), a meditation on the city as an artifact that affirmed humanity as a social collectivity, with the capacity for large-scale actions. The following poem, from *The Materials*, considers that possibility in the form of a nuclear holocaust.

What man could do,
And could not
And chance which has spared us
Choice, which has shielded us

As if a god. What is the name of that place
We have entered:
Despair? Ourselves?

That we can destroy ourselves
Now

Walking in the shelter,
The young and the old,
of each other's backs and shoulders

Entering the country that is
Impenetrably ours.

DENISE LEVERTOV

Dom Helder Camara at the Nuclear Test Site

Denise Levertov (1923–1997), as noted in the "Religions" section of this anthology, was born to a Welsh mother and a Russian Hasidic father who later became an Anglican priest. For the rest of her life she continued to wrestle with the mutability of faith, with catastrophe and redemption pivoted at a "turning core," as we can see in the following poem.

Dom Helder, octogenarian wisp
of human substance arrived from Brazil,
raises his arms and gazes toward a sky pallid with heat, to implore
"Peace!"
—then waves a "goodbye for now"
to God, as to a *compadre*.
"The Mass is over, go in peace
to love and serve the Lord": he walks
down with the rest of us to cross
the cattle-grid, entering forbidden ground
where marshals wait, with their handcuffs.
After hours of waiting,
penned into two wire-fenced enclosures, sun
climbing to cloudless zenith, till everyone
has been processed, booked, released to trudge

one by one up the slope to the boundary line
back to a freedom that's not so free,
we are all reassembled. We form
two circles, one contained in the other, to dance,
clockwise and counterclockwise
like children in Duncan's vision.
But not to the song of ashes, of falling:
we dance in the unity that brought us here,
instinct pulls us into the ancient
rotation, symbol of continuance.
Light and persistent as tumbleweed,
but not adrift, Dom Helder, too,
faithful pilgrim, dances,
dances at the turning core.

ISAAC ASIMOV

I, Robot

Isaac Asimov (1920–1992), born Isaak Yudovich Ozimov in Russia, moved with his family to Brooklyn when he was three. He grew up speaking Yiddish and English and traced his love of the written word to the newspapers and pulp magazines that he read while working in his parents' candy store. He wrote more than 500 works, from the three-volume *Understanding Physics* (1966) to essays on Shakespeare and Sherlock Holmes, but he will probably best be remembered for his science fiction. Asimov began publishing in 1939 and gained wide recognition for "Nightfall" (1941), a story spearheading the trend in "social science fiction," reorienting the genre toward speculations on the human consequences of advanced technology. Among his most popular works are the *Foundation* trilogy (1951–1953), the *Galactic Empire* series (1950–1952), and the *Robot* series (1950–1985). This selection from *I, Robot* (1950) imagines a "planetary region" run entirely by robotics.

And yet Ching Hso-lin was a Regional Vice-Co-ordinator, with the economic welfare of half the people of Earth in his care.

Perhaps it was with the thought of all that in mind, that Ching had two maps as the only ornaments on the wall of his office. One was an old hand-drawn affair tracing out an acre or two of land, and marked with the now outmoded pictographs of old China. A little creek trickled aslant the faded markings and there were the delicate pictorial indications of lowly huts, in one of which Ching's grandfather had been born.

The other map was a huge one, sharply delineated, with all markings in neat Cyrillic characters. The red boundary that marked the Eastern Region swept within its grand confines all that had once been China, India, Burma, Indo-China, and Indonesia. On it, within the old province of Szechuan, so light and gentle that none could see it, was the little mark placed there by Ching which indicated the location of his ancestral farm.

Ching stood before these maps as he spoke to Stephen Byerley in precise English, "No one knows better than you, Mr. Co-ordinator, that my job, to a large extent, is a sinecure. It carries with it a certain social standing, and I represent a convenient focal point for administration, but otherwise it is the Machine!—The Machine does all the work. What did you think, for instance, of the Tientsin Hydroponics works?"

"Tremendous!" said Byerley.

"It is but one of dozens and not the largest. Shanghai, Calcutta, Batavia, Bangkok—They are widely spread and they are the answer to feeding the billion and three quarters of the East."

"And yet," said Byerley, "you have an unemployment problem there at Tientsin. Can you be over-producing? It is incongruous to think of Asia as suffering from too much food."

Ching's dark eyes crinkled at the edges. "No. It has not come to that yet. It is true that over the last few months, several vats at Tientsin have been shut down, but it is nothing serious. The men have been released only temporarily and those who do not care to work in the fields have been shipped to Colombo in Ceylon, where a new plant is being put into operation."

"But why should the vats be closed down?"

Ching smiled gently, "You do not know how much of hydroponics, I see. Well, that is not surprising. You are a Northerner, and there soil farming is still profitable. It is fashionable in the North to think of hydroponics, when it is thought of at all, as a device for growing turnips in a chemical solution, and so it is—in an infinitely complicated way.

"In the first place, by far the largest crop we deal with (and the percentage is growing) is yeast. We have upward of two thousand strains of yeast in production and new strains are added monthly. The basic food-chemicals of the various yeasts are nitrates and phosphates among the inorganics together with proper amounts of the trace metals needed, down to the fractional parts per million of boron and molybdenum which are required. The organic matter is mostly sugar mixtures derived from the hydrolysis of cellulose, but, in addition, there are various food factors which must be added.

"For a successful hydroponics industry—one which can feed seventeen hundred million people—we must engage in an immense reforestation program throughout the East; we must have huge wood-conversion plants to deal with our southern jungles; we must have power, and steel, and chemical synthetics above all."

"Why the last, sir?"

"Because, Mr. Byerley, these strains of yeast have each their peculiar properties. We have developed, as I said, two thousand strains. The beef steak you thought you ate today was yeast. The frozen fruit confection you had for dessert was iced yeast. We have filtered yeast juice with the taste, appearance, and all the food value of milk.

"It is flavor, more than anything else, you see, that makes yeast feeding popular and for the sake of flavor we have developed artificial, domesticated strains that can no longer support themselves on a basic diet of salts and sugar. One needs biotin; another needs pteroyl-glutamic acid; still others need seventeen different amino acids supplied them as well as all the Vitamins B, but one (and yet it is popular and we cannot, with economic sense, abandon it)—"

Byerley stirred in his seat, "To what purpose do you tell me all this?"

"You asked me, sir, why men are out of work in Tientsin. I have a little more to explain. It is not only that we must have these various and varying foods for our yeast; but there remains the complicating factor of popular fads with passing time; and of the possibility of the development of new strains with the new requirements and new popularity. All this must be foreseen, and the Machine does the job—"

"But not perfectly."

"Not very *im*perfectly, in view of the complications I have mentioned. Well, then, a few thousand workers in Tientsin are temporarily out of a job. But, consider this, the amount of waste in this past year (waste that is, in terms of either defective supply or defective demand) amounts to not one-tenth of one percent of our total productive turnover. I consider that—"

RICHARD POWERS

Galatea 2.2

Richard Powers (born 1957) grapples with the consequences of artificial intelligence, molecular genetics, and music in many of his works. He spent his adolescence in Bangkok before returning to the United States to major in physics and then literature. His experiments with parallel and nested stories were developed in his first novel, *Three Farmers on Their Way to a Dance* (1985), and continued through many of his other works, including the next three, written in the Netherlands: *Prisoner's Dilemma* (1988), *The Gold Bug Variations* (1991), and *Operation Wandering Soul* (1993). His ninth novel, *The Echo Maker* (2006), winner of the National Book Award, interweaves a story about brain injury with the sandhill cranes of Nebraska and the land and water disputes along the Platte River. Powers was named a MacArthur Fellow in 1989. This excerpt from *Galatea 2.2* (1995) catalogs the dizzying amount of information that must be fed to a computer, Helen, to give her the overflowing contents of a human brain.

We fed her an eidetic image of the Bible. The complete Shakespeare. We gave her a small library on CD-ROM, six hundred scanned volumes she might curl up with. This constituted a form of cheating, I suppose. An open-book exam, where the human, in contrast, had to rely on memory alone. And yet we meant to test just this: whether silicon was such stuff as dreams might be made on.

Besides: Helen didn't *know* these texts. She just had a linear, digital array where she might go look them up. A kid with her own computer. A front-end index hasher helped her locate what she looked for. She could then place the complete text on her own input layers for mulling over.

This way she could read at night, while no one was around. And she didn't even need a flashlight. The one thing missing from her education was a sense of danger. The forbidden. The risk factor. Someone to come tell her to knock it off and get to bed.

In a wonderful twist, Helen acquired Chen and Keluga's physical-symbol rule base twice. At the low-level, we deep-wired many of the relationships into actual data structures. These we affixed at junctures in the net of nets, where they in effect applied semantic filters to her thought. But Helen also learned our colleagues' work by appending their culled knowledges herself, inefficiently, so her own weighted and qualified, high-level Platonic reflection.

Worldliness was massive, and deeper than any sea-dingle. It came, in the end, only in the form of a catalog.

We told her about parking tickets and two-for-one sales. About tuning forks and pitchforks and forked tongues and the road not taken. We told her about resistors and capacitors, baiters-and-switchers, alternating current, alternate lifestyles, very-large-scale integration and the failure of education to save society from itself.

We told her about wool and linen and damask. We told her about finches and feeders, bats and banyans, sonar and semaphores and trail markers made of anything the living body might shed. About mites and motes, insect galls and insecticides, about mating for life or for a fraction of a minute.

We taught her about the Securities and Exchange Commission. We told her about collectors who specialize in Depression-era glass. About the triple jump and the two-man luge. About how people used to teach their children about the big hand and the little hand. About defecation and respiration and circulation. About Post-it notes. Registered trademarks and draft resistance. The Oscar and Grammy and Emmy. Dying of heart disease. Divining with a fresh-cut alder rod.

We told her how the keys on a piano were laid out. About letterhead. Debutantes' balls. Talk radio and docudrama television. Colds and flus, and a brief five-century tour of their treatments. The Great Wall and the Burma Road and the Iron Curtain and the Light at the End of the Tunnel. About how the earth looked from space. About a fire that has raged underground beneath a Pennsylvania town for the last thirty years.

We showed her the difference between triforium and clerestory. We traced the famous pilgrims' routes through time and space. We told her about spoilage and refrigeration. How salt was once worth its weight in gold. How spice fueled the whole tragic engine of human expansion. How plastic wrap solved one of civilization's nightmares and started another.

We showed her Detroit, savaged by short-term economics. We showed her Sarajevo in 1911. Dresden and London in 1937. Atlanta in 1860. Baghdad, Tokyo, Cairo, Johannesburg, Calcutta, Los Angeles. Just before, and just after.

We told her East African in-law jokes. Java highland jokes about stupid Sumastrans. Aussie put-downs of Pommy bastards. Catskills jokes about unlicensed operation of knishes. City folk and country folk. Pat and Mike. Elephant riddles. Inuit jokes where fish and bears scoff at the mere idea of human existence.

We told her about revenge and forgiveness and contrition. We told her about retail outlets and sales tax, about ennui, about a world where you hear about everything yet where nothing happens to you. We told her how history always took place elsewhere.

We taught her never to draw to an inside straight and never to send a boy to do a man's job. We laid out the Queen's Necklace affair and the Cuban trade embargo. The rape of continent-sized forests and the South Sea bubble of cold fusion. Bar codes and baldness. Lint, lintels, lentils, Lent. The hope, blame, perversion, and crippled persistence of liberal humanism. Grace and disgrace and second chances. Suicide. Euthanasia. First love. Love at first sight.

WILLIAM GIBSON

Neuromancer

William Gibson (born 1948) is most often associated with a subgenre of speculative fiction, cyberpunk. His first novel, still his best known, *Neuromancer* (1984), popularized the concept of "cyberspace" as a computer-generated virtual environment, before the Internet of the 1990s gave it ubiquitous expression. Gibson grew up in Arizona, moved to Canada during the Vietnam War to elude the draft, and maintains dual U.S.-Canadian citizenship to this day. His work has evolved since *Neuromancer* but continues to dwell on multinational information systems and the kinship between technology and paranoia. *The Difference Machine* (1990), an alternative history written with Bruce Sterling, introduced the "steampunk" genre. Gibson saw the September 11, 2001, attack on the World Trade Center as the "true beginning of the 21st Century," marking a resurgent tribalism. *Pattern Recognition* (2003) was extensively revised to highlight the persistence of the infantilized under a high-tech regime. This excerpt from the opening of *Neuromancer* features the phantasmagoria of the human mind integrated into a virtual landscape.

The sky above the port was the color of television, tuned to a dead channel.

"It's not like I'm using," Case heard someone say, as he shouldered his way through the crowd around the door of the Chat. "It's like my body's developed this massive drug deficiency." It was a Sprawl voice and a Sprawl joke. The Chatsubo was a bar for professional expatriates; you could drink there for a week and never hear two words in Japanese.

Ratz was tending bar, his prosthetic arm jerking monotonously as he filled a tray of glasses with draft Kirin. He saw Case and smiled, his teeth a webwork of East European steel and brown decay. Case found a place at the bar, between the unlikely tan on one of Lonny Zone's whores and the crisp naval uniform of a tall African whose cheekbones were ridged with precise rows of tribal scars. "Wage was in here early, with two joeboys," Ratz said, shoving a draft across the bar with his good hand. "Maybe some business with you, Case?"

Case shrugged. The girl to his right giggled and nudged him.

The bartender's smile widened. His ugliness was the stuff of legend. In an age of affordable beauty, there was something heraldic about his lack of it. The antique arm whined as he reached for another mug. It was a Russian military prosthesis, a seven-function force-feedback manipulator, cased in grubby pink plastic. "You are too much the artiste, Herr Case." Ratz grunted; the sound served him as laughter. He scratched his overhang of white-shirted belly with the pink claw. "You are the artiste of the slightly funny deal."

"Sure," Case said, and sipped his beer. "Somebody's gotta be funny around here. Sure the fuck isn't you."

The whore's giggle went up an octave.

"Isn't you either, sister. So you vanish, okay? Zone, he's a close personal friend of mine."

She looked Case in the eye and made the softest possible spitting sound, her lips barely moving. But she left.

"Jesus," Case said, "what kinda creepjoint you running here? Man can't have a drink?"

"Ha," Ratz said, swabbing the scarred wood with a rag, "Zone shows a percentage. You I let work here for entertainment value."

As Case was picking up his beer, one of those strange instants of silence descended, as though a hundred unrelated conversations had simultaneously arrived at the same pause. Then the whore's giggle rang out, tinged with certain hysteria.

Ratz grunted. "An angel has passed."

"The Chinese," bellowed a drunken Australian, "Chinese bloody invented nerve-splicing. Give me the mainland for a nerve job any day. Fix you right, mate . . ."

"Now that," Case said to his glass, all his bitterness suddenly rising in him like bile, "that is so much bullshit."

The Japanese had already forgotten more neurosurgery than the Chinese had ever known. The black clinics of Chiba were the cutting edge, whole bodies of technique supplanted monthly, and still they couldn't repair the damage he'd suffered in that Memphis hotel.

A year here and he still dreamed of cyberspace, hope fading nightly. All the speed he took, all the turns he'd taken and the corners he'd cut in Night City, and still he'd see the matrix in his sleep, bright lattices of logic unfolding across that colorless void . . . The Sprawl was a long strange way home over the Pacific now, and he was no console man, no cyberspace cowboy. Just another hustler, trying to make it through. But the dreams came on in the Japanese night like livewire voodoo, and he'd cry for it, cry in his sleep, and wake alone in the dark, curled in his capsule in some coffin hotel, his hands clawed into the bedslab, temperfoam bunched between his fingers, trying to reach the console that wasn't there.

"I saw your girl last night," Ratz said, passing Case his second Kirin.

"I don't have one," he said, and drank.

"Miss Linda Lee."

Case shook his head.

"No girl? Nothing? Only biz, friend artiste? Dedication to commerce?" The bartender's small brown eyes were nested deep in wrinkled flesh. "I think I liked you better, with her. You laughed more. Now, some night, you get maybe too artistic; you wind up in the clinic tanks, spare parts."

"You're breaking my heart, Ratz." He finished his beer, paid and left, high narrow shoulders hunched beneath the rain-stained khaki nylon of his windbreaker. Threading his way through the Ninsei crowds, he could smell his own stale sweat.

Case was twenty-four. At twenty-two, he'd been a cowboy, a rustler, one of the best in the Sprawl. He'd been trained by the best, by McCoy Pauley and Bobby Quine, legends in the biz. He'd operated on an almost permanent adrenaline high, a byproduct of youth and proficiency, jacked into a custom cyberspace deck hat projected his disembodied consciousness into the consensual hallucination that was the matrix. A thief, he'd worked for other, wealthier thieves, employers who provided the exotic software required to penetrate the bright walls of corporate systems, opening windows into rich fields of data.

He's made the classic mistake, the one he's sworn he'd never make. He stole from his employers. He kept something for himself and tried to move it through a fence in Amsterdam. He still wasn't sure how he'd been discovered, not that it mattered now. He'd expected to die, then, but they only smiled. Of course he was welcome, they told him, welcome to the money. And he was going to need it. Because—still smiling—they were going to make sure he never worked again.

They damaged his nervous system with a wartime Russian mycotoxin.

Strapped to a bed in a Memphis hotel, his talent burning out micron by micron, he hallucinated for thirty hours.

The damage was minute, subtle, and utterly effective.

For Case, who'd lived for the bodiless exultation of cyberspace, it was the Fall. In the bars he'd frequented as a cowboy hotshot, the elite stance involved a certain relaxed contempt for the flesh. The body was meat. Case fell into the prison of his own flesh.

RAY BRADBURY

The Martian Chronicles

Ray Bradbury (1920–2012) is best known for such classic works as *Fahrenheit 451* (1953), *The Martian Chronicles* (1950), *The Illustrated Man* (1951), as well as a semi-autobiographical novel, *Dandelion Wine* (1957). Growing up in Waukegan, Illinois, he immersed himself in the works of H. G.Wells, Jules Verne, and Edgar Rice Burroughs. Later, when asked about his lyrical prose, he mentioned the habit of reading poetry every day, citing Robert Frost and Shakespeare as influences. Moving with his family to Los Angeles in 1934, he graduated from high school during the Depression and did not attend college, instead reading in libraries three days a week for ten years. It was in UCLA's Powell Library that he wrote a story about a book-burning future, "The Fireman," later to become *Fahrenheit 451*. In 2007 Bradbury received a special citation from the Pulitzer Prize jury for his "unmatched" contribution to science fiction and fantasy. His stories have been widely adapted throughout the world; the film version of *Fahrenheit 451* (1966) was directed by François Truffaut. In this excerpt from *The Martian Chronicles,* he pokes fun at American provincialism in space.

Whoever was knocking at the door didn't want to stop. Mrs. Ttt threw the door open. "Well?"

"You speak *English?*" The man standing there was astounded.

"I speak what I speak," she said.

"It's wonderful *English*!" The man was in uniform. There were three men with him, in a great hurry, all smiling, all dirty.

"What do you want?" demanded Mrs. Ttt.

"You are a *Martian!*" The man smiled. "The word is not familiar to you, certainly. It's an Earth expression." He nodded at his men. "We are from Earth. I'm Captain Williams. We've landed on Mars within the hour. Here we are, the *Second* Expedition! There was a First Expedition, but we don't know what happened to it. But here we are, anyway. And you are the first Martian we've met!"

"Martian?" Her eyebrows went up.

"What I mean to say is, you live on the fourth planet from the sun. Correct?"

"Elementary," she snapped, eyeing them.

"And we"—he pressed his chubby pink hand to his chest—"we are from Earth. Right, men?"

"Right, sir!" A chorus.

"This is the planet Tyrr," she said, "if you want to use the proper name."

"Tyrr, Tyrr." The captain laughed exhaustedly. "What a *fine* name! But, my good woman, how is it you speak such perfect English?"

"I'm not speaking, I'm thinking," she said. "Telepathy! Good day!" And she slammed the door.

A moment later there was that dreadful man knocking again.

She whipped the door open. "What now?" she wondered.

The man was still there, trying to smile, looking bewildered. He put out his hands. "I don't think you *understand*—"

"What?" she snapped.

The man gazed at her in surprise. "We're from *Earth!*"

"I haven't time," she said. "I've a lot of cooking today and there's cleaning and sewing and all. You evidently wish to see Mr. Ttt; he's upstairs in his study."

"Yes," said the Earth Man confusedly, blinking. "By all means, let us see Mr. Ttt."

"He's busy." She slammed the door again.

This time the knock on the door was most impertinently loud.

"See here!" cried the man when the door was thrust open again. He jumped in as if to surprise her. "This is no way to treat visitors!"

"All over my clean floor!" she cried. "Mud! Get out! If you come in my house, wash your boots first."

The man looked in dismay at his muddy boots. "This," he said, "is no time for trivialities. I think," he said, "we should be celebrating." He looked at her for a long time, as if looking might make her understand.

"If you've made my crystal buns fall in the oven," she exclaimed, "I'll hit you with a piece of wood!" She peered into a little hot oven. She came back, red, steamy-faced. Her eyes were sharp yellow, her skin was soft brown, she was thin and quick as an insect. Her voice was metallic and sharp. "Wait here. I'll see if I can let you have a moment with Mr. Ttt. What was your business?"

The man swore luridly, as if she'd hit his hand with a hammer. "Tell him we're from Earth and it's never been done before!"

"What hasn't?" She put her brown hand up. "Never mind. I'll be back."

The sound of her feet fluttered through the stone house.

Outside, the immense blue Martian sky was hot and still as a warm deep sea water. The Martian desert lay broiling like a prehistoric mud pot, waves of heat rising and shimmering. There was a small rocket ship reclining upon a hilltop nearby. Large footprints came from the rocket to the door of this stone house.

Now there was a sound of quarreling voices upstairs. The men within the door stared at one another, shifting on their boots, twiddling their fingers, and holding onto their hip belts. A man's voice shouted upstairs. The woman's voice replied. After fifteen minutes the Earth men began walking in and out the kitchen door, with nothing to do.

"Cigarette?" said one of the men.

Somebody got out a pack and they lit up. They puffed slow streams of pale white smoke. They adjusted their uniforms, fixed their collars. The voices upstairs continued to mutter and chant. The leader of the men looked at his watch.

"Twenty-five minutes," he said. "I wonder what they're up to up there." He went to a window and looked out.

"Hot day," said one of the men.

"Yeah," said someone else in the slow warm time of early afternoon. The voices had faded to a murmur and were now silent. There was not a sound in the house. All the men could hear was their own breathing.

An hour of silence passed. "I hope we didn't cause any trouble," said the captain. He went and peered into the living room.

Mrs. Ttt was there, watering some flowers that grew in the center of the room.

"I knew I had forgotten something," she said when she saw the captain. She walked out to the kitchen. "I'm sorry." She handed him a slip of paper. "Mr. Ttt is much too busy." She turned to her cooking. "Anyway, it's not Mr. Ttt you want to see; it's Mr. Aaa. Take that paper over to the next farm, by the blue canal, and Mr. Aaa'll advise you about whatever it is you want to know."

"We don't want to know anything," objected the captain, pouting out his thick lips. "We already *know* it."

"You have the paper, what more do you want?" she asked him straight off. And she would say no more.

"Well," said the captain, reluctant to go. He stood as if waiting for something. He looked like a child staring at an empty Christmas tree. "Well," he said again. "Come on, men."

The four men stepped out into the hot silent day.

PHILIP K. DICK

Do Androids Dream of Electric Sheep?

Philip K. Dick (1928–1982), as noted in the "War" section of this anthology, wrote about parallel universes and alternate histories radically different from our own and yet surprisingly recognizable. *Do Androids Dream of Electric Sheep?* (1968), made into the iconic film *Blade Runner* (1982), features a post-apocalyptic world of fake humans and animals that are impossible to tell apart from "real" ones. These artificial life-forms pose a tough challenge to the latter, as we can see in this conversation between bounty hunter Rick Deckard and a Nexus-6 android, Rachael Rosen.

Afterward they enjoyed a great luxury: Rick had room service bring up coffee. He sat for a long time within the arms of a green, black, and gold leaf lounge chair, sipping coffee and meditating about the next few hours. Rachael, in the bathroom, squeaked and hummed and splashed in the midst of a hot shower.

"You made a good deal when you made that deal," she called when she had shut off the water; dripping, her hair tied up with a rubber band, she appeared bare and pink at the bathroom door. "We androids can't control our physical, sensual passions. You probably knew that; in my opinion you took advantage of me." She did not, however, appear genuinely angry. If anything she had become cheerful and certainly as human as any girl he had known. "Do we really have to go track down those three andys tonight?"

"Yes," he said. Two for me to retire, he thought; one for you. As Rachael put it, the deal had been made.

Gathering a giant white bath towel about her, Rachael said, "Did you enjoy that?"

"Yes."

"Would you ever go to bed with an android again?"

"If it was a girl. If she resembled you."

Rachael said, "Do you know what the lifespan of a humanoid robot such as myself is? I've been in existence two years. How long do you calculate I have?"

After a hesitation he said, "About two more years."

"They never could solve that problem. I mean cell replacement. Perpetual or anyhow semi-perpetual renewal. Well, so it goes." Vigorously she began drying herself. Her face had become expressionless.

"I'm sorry," Rick said.

"Hell," Rachael said, "I'm sorry I mentioned it. Anyhow it keeps humans from running off and living with an android."

"And this is true with you Nexus-6 types too?"

"It's the metabolism. Not the brain unit." She trotted out, swept up her underpants, and began to dress.

He, too, dressed. Then together, saying little, the two of them journeyed to the roof field, where his hovercar had been parked by the pleasant white-clad human attendant.

As they headed toward the suburbs of San Francisco, Rachael said, "It's a nice night."

"My goat is probably asleep by now," he said. "Or maybe goats are nocturnal. Some animals never sleep. Sheep never do, not that I could detect; whenever you look at them they're looking back. Expecting to be fed."

"What sort of wife do you have?"

He did not answer.

"Do you—"

"If you weren't an android," Rick interrupted, "if I could legally marry you, I would."

Rachael said, "Or we could live in sin, except that I'm not alive."

"Legally you're not. But really you are. Biologically. You're not made out of transistorized circuits like a false animal; you're an organic entity." And in two years, he thought, you'll wear out and die. Because we never solved the problem of cell replacement, as you pointed out. So I guess it doesn't matter anyhow.

This is my end, he said to himself. As a bounty hunter. After the Batys there won't be any more. Not after this, tonight.

"You look so sad," Rachael said.

Putting his hand out he touched her cheek.

"You're not going to be able to hunt androids any longer," she said calmly. "So don't look sad. Please."

He stared at her.

"No bounty hunter ever has gone on," Rachael said. "After being with me. Except one. A very cynical man. Phil Resch. And he's nutty; he works out in left field on his own."

"I see," Rick said. He felt numb. Completely. Throughout his entire body.

OCTAVIA BUTLER

Dawn

Octavia Butler (1947–2006), a lifelong science fiction fan, was honored as a MacArthur Fellow in 1995. Born dyslexic and raised by a single mother and grandmother, she began writing seriously at age twelve after watching a bad science fiction movie, *Devil Girl from Mars*, and knowing she could do better. Among her best-known works are the five *Patternist* novels (1976–1984); *Kindred* (1979), about an African American woman transported from 1970s Los Angeles to nineteenth-century, slave-owning Maryland; and the *Lilith's Brood* trilogy (1987–1989), about human survivors from a nuclear war co-producing genetically altered offspring with the Oankali, gene-trading extraterrestrials. Though not primarily a short-story writer, Butler published an acclaimed collection, *Bloodchild and Other Stories* (1996). At her death, the *Parable* trilogy, featuring *Parable of the Sower* (1993) and *Parable of the Talents* (1998), was left unfinished. In this excerpt from *Dawn* (1987), the first of the *Lilith's Brood* trilogy, we are introduced to the Oankali, at once transparent and enigmatic.

"Yes. We trade the essence of ourselves. Our genetic material for yours."

Lilith frowned, then shook her head. "How? I mean, you couldn't be talking about interbreeding."

"Of course not." His tentacles smoothed. "We do what you would call genetic engineering. We know you had begun to do it yourselves a little, but it's foreign to you. We do it naturally. We *must* do it. It renews us, enables us to survive as an evolving species instead of specializing ourselves into extinction or stagnation."

"We all do it naturally to some degree," she said warily. "Sexual reproduction—"

"The ooloi do it for us. They have special organs for it. They can do it for you too—make sure of a good, viable gene mix. It is part of our reproduction, but it's much more deliberate than what any mated pair of humans have managed so far.

"We're not hierarchical, you see. We never were. But we are powerfully acquisitive. We acquire new life—seek it, investigate it, manipulate it, sort it, use it. We carry the drive to do this in a minuscule cell within a cell—a tiny organelle within every cell of our bodies. Do you understand me?"

"I understand your words. Your meaning, though . . . it's as alien to me as you are."

"That's the way we perceived your hierarchical drives at first." He paused. "One of the meanings of Oankali is gene trader. Another is that organelle—the essence of ourselves, the origin of ourselves. Because of that organelle, the ooloi can perceive DNA and manipulate it precisely."

"And they do this . . . inside their bodies?"

"Yes."

"And now they're doing something with cancer cells inside their bodies?"

"Experimenting, yes."

"That sounds . . . a long way from safe."

"They're like children now, talking and talking about possibilities."

"What possibilities?"

"Regeneration of lost limbs. Controlled malleability. Future Oankali may be much less frightening to potential trade partners if they're able to reshape themselves and look more like the partners before the trade. Even increased longevity, though compared to what you're used to, we're very long-lived now."

"All that from cancer."

"Perhaps. We listen to the ooloi when they stop talking so much. That's when we find out what our next generations will be like."

"You leave all that to them? They decide?"

"They show us the tested possibilities. We all decide."

He tried to lead her into his family's woods, but she held back. "There's something I need to understand now," she said. "You call it a trade. You've taken something you value from us and you're giving us back our world. Is that it? Do you have all you want from us?"

"You know it isn't," he said softly. "You've guessed that much."

She waited, staring at him.

"Your people will change. Your young will be more like us and ours more like you. Your hierarchical tendencies will be modified and if we learn to regenerate limbs and reshape our bodies, we'll share those abilities with you. That's a part of the trade. We're overdue for it."

"It is crossbreeding, then, no matter what you call it."

"It's what I said it was. A trade. The ooloi will make changes in your reproductive cells before conception and they'll control conception."

"How?"

"The ooloi will explain that when the time comes."

She spoke quickly, trying to blot out thoughts of more surgery or some sort of sex with the damned ooloi. "What will you make of us? What will our children be?"

"Different, as I said. Not quite like you. A little like us."

She thought of her son—how like her he had been, how like his father. "No!" she said. "No. I don't care what you do with what you've already learned—how you apply it to yourselves—but leave us out of it. Just let us go. If we have the problem you think we do, let us work it out as human beings."

"We are committed to the trade," he said, softly implacable.

"No! You'll finish what the war began. In a few generations—"

"One generation."

"No!"

He wrapped the many fingers of one hand around her arm. "Can you hold your breath, Lilith? Can you hold it by an act of will until you die?"

"Hold my—?"

"We are as committed to the trade as your body is to breathing. We were overdue for it when we found you. Now it will be done—to the rebirth of your people and mine."

"No!" she shouted. "A rebirth for us can only happen if you let us alone! Let us begin on our own."

Silence.

She pulled at her arm, and after a moment he let her go. She got the impression he was watching her very closely.

"I think I wish your people had left me on Earth," she whispered. "If this is what they found me for, I wish they'd left me." Medusa children. Snakes for hair. Nests of night crawlers for eyes and ears.

He sat down on the bare ground, and after a minute of surprise, she sat opposite him, not knowing why, simply following his movement.

"I can't *unfind* you," he said. "You're here. But there is . . . a thing I *can* do. It is . . . deeply wrong of me to offer it. I will never offer it again."

"What?" she asked barely caring. She was tired from the walk, overwhelmed by what he had told her. It made no sense. Good god, no wonder he couldn't go home—even if his home still existed. Whatever his people had been like when they left it, they must be very different now—as the children of the last surviving human beings would be different.

"Lilith?" he said.

She raised her head, stared at him.

"Touch me here now," he said, gesturing toward his head tentacles, "and I'll sting you. You'll die—very quickly and without pain."

She swallowed.

"If you want it," he said.

It was a gift he was offering. Not a threat.

"Why?" she whispered.

He would not answer.

She stared at his head tentacles. She raised her hand, let it reach toward him almost as though it had its own will, its own intent. No more Awakenings. No more questions. No more impossible answers. Nothing.

Nothing.

He never moved. Even his tentacles were utterly still. Her hand hovered, wanting to fall amid the tough, flexible, lethal organs. It hovered, almost brushing one by accident.

She jerked her hand away, clutched it to her. "Oh god," she whispered. "Why didn't I do it? Why can't I do it?"

He stood up and waited uncomplaining for several minutes until she dragged herself to her feet.

"You'll meet my mates and one of my children now," he said. "Then rest and food, Lilith."

She looked at him, longing for a human expression.

"Would you have done it?" she asked.

"Yes," he said.

"Why?"

"For you."

NOTES

* We have not enforced a uniform style in punctuation and spelling across the anthology, but have reproduced the selections as they appear in authorized editions.

1. Hemingway to Edmund Wilson, October 18, 1924, in *Ernest Hemingway: Selected Letters, 1917–1961*, ed. Carlos Baker (New York: Scribner's, 1981), 128–29.
2. Ursula Le Guin, Introduction to *The Left Hand of Darkness.* New York: Ace, 1969, ii.
3. F. Scott Fitzgerald, *The Great Gatsby.* New York: Scribner's, 1925, 47.
4. Fitzgerald, *The Great Gatsby,* 2.
5. Ibid. 66.
6. Ernest Hemingway, *A Farewell to Arms* (New York: Scribner, 1929), 184–85.
7. For Hemingway's work as a journalist, see *By-Line Ernest Hemingway: Selected Articles and Dispatches,* ed. William White. New York: Scribner, 1998.
8. For a list of dispatches, see William Braasch Watson, "Hemingway's Spanish Civil War Dispatches." *Hemingway Review* 7, no. 2 (1988): 4.
9. Bryan Bender, "With Cuban Help, Kennedy Library Gets Hemingway Trove," *Boston Globe*, May 4, 2013. Accessed April 8, 2016, at http://www.bostonglobe .com/2013/05/03/rare-partnership-provides-new-glimpse-into-hemingway-cuba /jczvfTSqilowGaDTW8W3KO/story.html.
10. Jay David Bolter and Richard Grusin, *Remediation: Understanding New Media.* Cambridge: MIT Press, 1999.
11. El Pariser refers to this hierarchical customizing (and filtering out of what Google thinks we might not like), as the "filter bubble." See Eli Pariser, *The Filter Bubble.* New York: Penguin, 2011.

12. Mark Sweney, "Facebook Quarterly Report Reveals 83m Profiles Are Fake," *Guardian*, August 2, 2012. Accessed April 8, 2016, at http://www.guardian.co.uk/technology/2012/aug/02/facebook-83m-profiles-bogus-fake.

13. The "Arab Spring" in Egypt famously began on Facebook. See, for instance, Jose Antonio Vargas, "Spring Awakening: How an Egyptian Revolution Began on Facebook," at http://www.nytimes.com/2012/02/19/books/review/how-an-egyptian-revolution-began-on-facebook.html?pagewanted=all&_r=0. Vargas is reviewing *Revolution 2.0: The Power of the People Is Greater Than the People in Power: A Memoir* (New York: Houghton Mifflin, 2012), by Wael Ghonim, a Google executive who spurred the Tahrir Square rallies by posting on Facebook the picture of Khaled Mohamed Said, a 28-year-old beaten to death by the Egyptian police.

14. Company Information. Accessed April 8, 2016, at http://newsroom.fb.com/company-info/ and http://www.statista.com/statistics/268136/top-15-countries-based-on-number-of-facebook-users/.

PERMISSIONS

AUTHOR INDEX

GENERAL INDEX